Microsoft®
Office 2010:
Brief

ALEC FEHL
A-B Tech

JUDY MARDAR
PC Source

SANDRA RITTMAN
Long Beach City College

RUSSEL STOLINS
Santa Fe Community College

PAMELA R. TOLIVER
Soft-Spec

LABYRINTH
LEARNING™

El Sobrante, CA

Microsoft Office 2010: Brief
by Alec Fehl, Judy Mardar, Sandra Rittman,
Russel Stolins, Pamela R. Toliver

Copyright © 2011 by Labyrinth Learning

Labyrinth Learning
P.O. Box 20818
El Sobrante, California 24820
800.522.9746
On the web at lablearning.com

President:
Brian Favro

Product Development Manager:
Jason Favro

Managing Editor:
Laura Popelka

Production Manager:
Rad Proctor

eLearning Production Manager:
Arl S. Nadel

Editorial/Production Team:
Donna Bacidore, John Barlow, Scott
Benjamin, Leona Benten, Teresa Bollinger,
Belinda Breyer, Eddie Bryant, Everett Mike
Cowan, Kay Gerken, Alona Harris, Nick
Keefe, Dan Marshall-Campbell, Sheryl
Trittin, Sandy Jones, PMG Media

Indexing: Joanne Sprott

Interior Design:
Mark Ong, Side-by-Side Studios

Cover Design:
Words At Work

ITEM: 1-59136-353-5
ISBN-13: 978-1-59136-353-8

Manufactured in the United States of America.

10 9 8 7 6 5 4 3

Contents in Brief

Table of Contents

UNIT 5
ACCESS 2010

List of Quick Reference Tables

List of Keyboard Shortcuts

DOCUMENT COMMANDS (ALL APPLICATIONS)

Help	`F1`
Open document	`Ctrl` + `O`
Print document	`Ctrl` + `P`
Save document	`Ctrl` + `S`
Select all	`Ctrl` + `A`

EDITING COMMANDS (ALL APPLICATIONS)

Bold	`Ctrl` + `B`
Copy	`Ctrl` + `C`
Cut	`Ctrl` + `X`
Find	`Ctrl` + `F`
Italic	`Ctrl` + `I`
Paste	`Ctrl` + `V`
Redo/Repeat	`Ctrl` + `Y`
Replace	`Ctrl` + `H`
Show/Hide Ribbon	`Ctrl` + `F1`
Underline	`Ctrl` + `U`
Undo	`Ctrl` + `Z`

EXCEL COMMANDS

AutoSum	`Alt` + `=`
Clear cell contents	`Delete`
Select a column	`Ctrl` + `Spacebar`
Select a row	`Shift` + `Spacebar`
Show formulas	`Ctrl` + `` ` ``

POWERPOINT COMMANDS

Advance a slide	`Spacebar` or `→`
Back up a slide	`Backspace` or `←`

WORD COMMANDS

Change the font case	`Shift` + `F3`
Insert date	`Alt` + `Shift` + `D`
Insert page break	`Ctrl` + `Enter`
New document	`Ctrl` + `N`
Spelling & Grammar check	`F7`
Thesaurus	`Alt` + (desired word)

Preface

Microsoft® Office 2010: Brief is an introduction to the Microsoft Office 2010 Suite. In Unit 1, students are introduced to basic computer concepts and file management skills. In Unit 2, students learn about Word 2010 as they create and enhance business letters, memoranda, and press releases. In Unit 3, students work with Excel 2010 to create and edit worksheets. In Unit 4, students create their own presentations in PowerPoint 2010. And finally, in Unit 5, students use Access 2010 to build a database.

This textbook follows the *Labyrinth Instruction Design,* our unique and proven approach that makes learning easy and effective for every learner. Our books begin with fundamental concepts and build through a systematic progression of exercises. Quick Reference Tables, precise callouts on screen captures, carefully selected illustrations, and minimal distraction combine to create a learning solution that is highly efficient and effective for both students and instructors.

NEW to this version: Our Critical Thinking and Work-Readiness Skills exercises have been completely rewritten to encourage students to show deep skill mastery. We've included tables identifying the work-readiness ("soft") skills needed to succeed in the workplace, and we've added optional coaching tips in our instructor support material to help educators discuss work-readiness topics with their students. These new features promote richer discussion and deeper thinking about applying Office skills in the workplace.

Our *eLab assessment and learning management tool* is available to supplement this course. eLab is an intuitive, affordable, web-based learning system that helps educators spend less time on course management and more time teaching. eLab integrates seamlessly with your Labyrinth textbook.

Visual Conventions

This book uses many visual and typographic cues to guide students through the lessons. This page provides examples and describes the function of each cue.

`Type this text`	Anything you should type at the keyboard is printed in this typeface.
	Tips, Notes, and Warnings are used throughout the text to draw attention to certain topics.
Command→ Command→ Command, etc.	This convention indicates how to give a command from the Ribbon. The commands are written: Ribbon Tab→Command Group→Command→ Subcommand.
FROM THE KEYBOARD Ctrl+S to save	These margin notes indicate shortcut keys for executing a task described in the text.
Video Lesson	This convention indicates a special video tutorial for the associated concept topic. You must purchase an eLab Video Library license key in order to view the videos.

Exercise Progression

The exercises in this book build in complexity as students work through a lesson toward mastery of the skills taught.

- **Develop Your Skills** exercises are introduced immediately after concept discussions. They provide detailed, step-by-step tutorials.
- **Reinforce Your Skills** exercises provide additional hands-on practice with moderate assistance.
- **Apply Your Skills** exercises test students' skills by describing the correct results without providing specific instructions on how to achieve them.
- **Critical Thinking and Work-Readiness Skills** exercises are the most challenging. They provide generic instructions, allowing students to use their skills and creativity to achieve the results they envision.

Acknowledgements

We are grateful to the many instructors who have used Labyrinth titles and suggested improvements to us over the many years we have been writing and publishing books. This book has benefited greatly from the reviews and suggestions of the following instructors.

Bev Amonson, *SIAST Woodland Campus*

Judith Andrews, *Feather River College*

Sandra Bailey, *Pikes Peak Community College*

Letty Barnes, *Lake Washington Technical College*

Illaina Baylor-Johnson, *College of Lake County*

David Beetham, *Whatcom Community College*

Pamela Beveridge, *Alamance Community College*

Edward Beyer, *Antelope Valley College*

Jeff Brabant, *Miles Community College*

Cheryl Braug-Doebrick, *Front Range Community College*

Steven Brennan, *Jackson Community College*

Rebecca Brown, *Pearl River Community College*

Pauline Camara, *Bristol Community College*

Denise Carrier, *Pathfinder Regional Vocational-Technical High School*

Carolyn Carvalho, *Kent State University (Ashtabula Campus)*

Kathleen Chatfield, *Clark College*

Earline Cocke, *Northwest Mississippi Community College*

Judith Cosgrave, *Adult Center at Mid-East Career & Technology Center*

Georgie D'Alessandro, *Glendale College*

Teresa Donat, *Las Positas College*

Kathie Doole, *A-B Tech*

Veronica Dooly, *A-B Tech*

David Easton, *Waubonsee Community College*

Janis Engwer, *North Idaho College*

Cathy Evans, *Tri-County Career Center*

Jean Evans, *Brevard Community College*

Cassandra Fine, *Colusa County of Education – Community Learning Classroom*

Jean Finley, *A-B Tech*

Wallace Fisher, *Walla Walla Community College*

Kay Gerken, *College of DuPage*

Diane Granger, *Lamar State College Port Arthur*

Vernita Harris, *Columbus Technical College*

Ira Hogan, *Ivy Tech Community College*

Jay Hopper, *Highline Community College*

Ron Houle, *Central Lakes College*

John Humphrey, *A-B Tech*

Constance Humphries, *A-B Tech*

Elailne Hutchings, *College of the North Atlantic (Prince Philip Drive Campus)*

Eduardo Jaramillo, *Peninsula College*

Ricky Keeling, *Arizona Western College*

David Kernazitskas, *Humphreys College*

Jeanne Lake, *Saline Country Career Center*

Jeanne Lanzer, *First Coast Technical College*

Ric Kube, *St. Martin's University*

Karen LaPlant, *Hennepin Technical College*

Gabriele Lenga, *Truckee Meadows Community College (TMCC)*

Teresa Loftis, *San Bernardino Adult School*

Carlos Lopez, *Hartnell Community College*

Peggy McCarthy, *College of DuPage*

Patricia Meier, *Alameda Adult School*

Sara Mercill, *Scottsdale Community College*

Janet Montgomery, *CVTC*

David Moore, *Sutter County Office of Education*

Judith Morris, *Northwest Community*

Sita Motipara, *Skyline College*

Sam Mryyan, *Friends University*

Vickie Murphy, *Craven Community College*

Stephanie Murre Wolf, *Moraine Park Technical College*

Kay Nelson, *The Lifelong Learning Center*

Arlene Orland, *College of the Canyons*

Felipe Payan, *Los Angeles Southwest Community College*

Carrie Pedersen, *Lower Columbia College*

Joanne Perez-Arreola, *Maricopa Skill Center*

Dan Petrosko, *College of Lake County*

Kari Phillips, *Davis Applied Technology College*

Ted Pobst, *Tennessee Rehabilitation Center*

Robin Pugh, *City College of San Francisco*

Cora Newcomb, *Technical College of the Lowcountry*

Rama Rasmussen, *Davis Applied Technology College*

Billy Richardson, *Rogue Community College*

Patricia Rise, *Brookdale Community College*

David Rosi, *Lower Columbia College*

Joann Santillo, *Mahoning County Career and Technical Center*

Judith Scheeren, *Westmoreland County Community College*

Raquel Segovia, *Midland College*

Junaid (Jay) Siddiqui, *El Camino College*

Susanne Silk, *Western Technology Center (Sayre Campus)*

Pamela Silvers, *A-B Tech*

Laurie Simon, *WITC*

Mary Sina, *Fox Valley Technical College*

Nancy Stewart, *Odessa College*

Sue Tannahill, *Central Georgia Technical College*

Robin Tartow, *Seattle Central Community College*

Julie Tyler, *Great Plains Technology Center*

June Uharriet, *Los Angeles Harbor College*

Angela Unruh, *Central Washington University*

Lilly R. Vigil, *Colorado Mountain College (Timberline Campus)*

Kimberly Walsh-Betthauser, *Western Technical College*

Sandra Weber, *Gateway Technical College*

Grace Windsheimer, *Columbia Gorge Community College*

Alane Wooster, *Western Colorado Community College*

Marjory Wooten, *Lanier Technical College*

U N I T

1

Computer Concepts and Windows

I n this unit, you will begin by learning how computers work. You will get an overview of basic hardware and software concepts that can help transform a computer from a mysterious box to a familiar tool. You will also get a view of the major components of a computer system and how they interact to help you work and play. Next, you will learn how to launch Windows programs, arrange program windows on the screen, save your work in files, and browse through the files you have on your computer.

Computer Concepts

LEARNING OBJECTIVES

After studying this lesson, you will be able to:

- Identify the basic parts of a computer system
- Describe the difference between random access memory and storage memory
- Identify whether a component of the computer system is hardware or software
- Describe the role of an operating system in a computer
- Describe the difference between application program files and user data files

A personal computer system is a complex machine with millions of circuits and millions of lines of software code. Fortunately, we don't have to understand how all of these components work in synch to help us get things done. But if you know some basic facts about how computer systems work, you are in a better position to purchase just the computer you need. In this lesson, you will learn what you need to know to intelligently compare computer models and interpret ads to figure out what a particular feature means in terms of computer performance.

CASE STUDY

Comparing Computers

Donna wants to replace her notebook computer. She got it about four years ago and notices that it's running her newest programs more slowly than she's used to. When she bought it, the notebook computer was a bargain-priced model at a discount store. It was her first computer, and Donna was pretty thrilled to have it. But she's since learned that sometimes a less expensive computer is not going to meet her needs.

Looking through inserts in her Sunday newspaper, Donna sees all sorts of ads for new computers. They describe things like a processor, RAM, and screen size. But is a bigger number always better or important? Donna's not sure, but there's definitely a price difference for some features. She wants a computer that will meet her needs for the next few years, but she doesn't want to buy more computer than she needs.

Core i5 Processor
4 GB RAM
500 GB Hard Drive
15.4" Screen

- Windows 7 Home Premium
- 4 USB 2.0, 2 USB 3.0, ports
- Wireless-N built-in

Free Ink Jet Printer

A Sunday paper insert lists basic details on a new notebook computer.

1.1 Categorizing Computer Systems

A computer system is an integrated set of hardware and software. Computer systems come in all shapes and sizes these days. However, there are a number of components common to all computer systems. These can be grouped into two basic categories: hardware and software.

■ **Hardware:** This is the physical component. If you can pick up and hold it, it is hardware. This includes devices that store software, such as USB flash drives.

■ **Software:** This is the logical component of the system. You can't actually see software, but you can see its workings on the screen.

Computer System Categories

Computer systems come in several basic categories. Each is optimized for particular types of activities and levels of mobility.

Category	Description	Optimized For
Desktop	The traditional computer type used in most office and academic settings; desktop computers are usually quite easy to customize and to add new hardware to	Running sophisticated programs on large screens
All-in-One	A variation of the desktop computer; contains all the components, including the screen, in a single package	General computing in a compact space
Notebook	Also called a "laptop" computer; a highly portable computer that is easy to carry and travel with	General computing on the go
Netbook	A notebook computer that is lighter and smaller than a traditional notebook	Basic web browsing, email, and word processing on the go

Units of Measure

We use various units of measure that indicate the performance and capacity of computer systems. When you shop for a computer, the following terms are often featured in advertising. These terms are broken down into three categories in the following tables.

VOLUME/CAPACITY

These terms help you determine the size of a file and the capacity of a disk drive or flash drive to hold those files.

Term	Meaning	Examples
Bit	A single on-off switch (transistor) in a byte	0, 1
Byte	Eight bits strung together in a specific order to represent a single character of data	A, B, C, &, @
Kilobyte (KB)	One thousand bytes (characters) of data	Approximately two paragraphs of single-spaced text
Megabyte (MB)	One million bytes of data	About 900 pages of single-spaced text or three medium-length novels
Gigabyte (GB)	One billion bytes of data	Approximately 200 typical 5 MB digital photos or 250 four-minute songs in high-quality MP3 format
Terabyte (TB)	One trillion bytes of data	About 250,000 four-minute songs in MP3 format, 380 hours of DVD-quality video, or about 120 hours of HD-quality video

RESOLUTION

These terms indicate the size and sharpness of the computer screen.

Term	Meaning	Examples
Resolution	The number of pixels (dots of light) arrayed horizontally and vertically on the screen	1360 × 768 (notebook screen) 1280 × 1024 (19" monitor) 1920 × 1080 (HD monitor)
Screen Size	A diagonal measurement of the screen's physical dimensions	20" monitor 16" screen (notebook)

SPEED

These terms indicate the speed of a computer's processor or of an Internet connection.

Term	Meaning	Examples
Gigahertz (GHz)	One billion cycles per second	1.8 GHz 2.2 GHz
Bits per second (bps)	The number of bits (not bytes) that a network connection can transmit or receive	6 Mbps (cable modem)

Computer Hardware Categories

Computer hardware comprises the physical components of the computer system. Regardless of the basic type of computer you are using, all computers have hardware components in common. The following table displays the basic categories of hardware and what they contribute to the computer system. All of these categories are explained in detail on the following pages.

Hardware Category	Role	Examples
Processing	Processes data and interprets your commands	Processor, RAM, motherboard
Storage	Stores programs you run and your own user data files	Hard drives, flash drives, DVD and Blu-ray drives
Viewing/Printing	Displays and prints your work	Monitor, printer, video adapter
Networking	Connects you to the Internet and to other computers	Modem, router, wireless connection
Human Interface	Lets you issue commands, type, and interact with the computer system	Mouse, keyboard, touch screen, pen tablet

1.2 Processing Hardware

The logical hardware of the computer contains its processing capabilities. This is the hardware that receives and interprets your commands, runs software, and supports the most basic controls over other hardware in the system. The processing hardware components most critical to computer performance are:

■ **Processor:** The "brain" of the computer
■ **RAM:** The "workbench" that passes code back and forth to the processor

Processor

This is the most important single component of a computer system. It contains all of the basic circuitry of a computer with millions of transistors. These are etched onto chips of silicon via incredibly precise microscopic techniques. New-and-improved processors are introduced every few months.

Photos courtesy of Intel Corporation

The inside of Intel's Core i5 processor (Do not try this at home!)

Multi-core Processors

Many new processors actually contain the circuitry for two to four computers inside the single chip. These are called *multi-core* processors. The advantage of multi-core processors is that different processors can simultaneously control or process different programs and hardware on the computer. For example, one processor might be controlling storing files on the hard drive while another processor might be sending a print request to a printer. Since a single processor core can focus on each task, the tasks get done more quickly and efficiently.

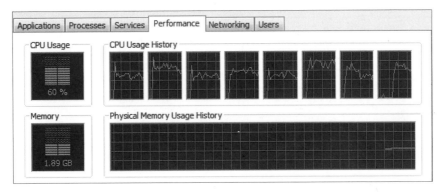

An Intel Core i7 processor actually appears to Windows as if it were eight individual processors. All of these processors are contained in the single multi-core chip.

Processor Performance

In addition to the number of cores, other features have a significant impact on processor performance. For example, processors are designed to run at specific speeds (measured in gigahertz, GHz). Higher-speed processors can often perform tasks more rapidly than slower processors. However, this is not a hard-and-fast rule. Many details of the computer system as a whole bear on its performance.

Random Access Memory (RAM)

Random access memory (RAM) is best thought of as the computer's "workbench." RAM is installed on the computer's motherboard in the form of slim modules. It's the place where the processor sends and receives software code for processing. Everything you see on the computer screen is taking place in RAM.

This RAM module fits into a slot on the bottom of a notebook computer.

One of the best ways to improve the performance of an older computer is to install more RAM.

RAM as a Workbench

RAM is the place where the work you see on the screen actually resides. The work isn't on your hard drive or USB flash drive until you save it. RAM allows the processor to work as quickly as possible, since RAM can shuttle data back and forth for processing hundreds of times faster than any storage drive. The following figure displays this process.

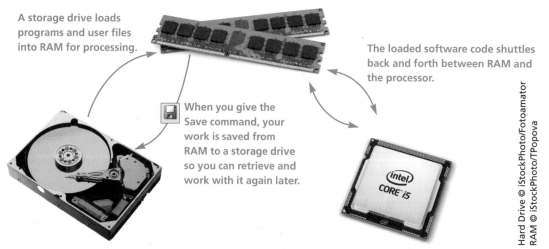

A storage drive loads programs and user files into RAM for processing.

The loaded software code shuttles back and forth between RAM and the processor.

When you give the Save command, your work is saved from RAM to a storage drive so you can retrieve and work with it again later.

Hard Drive © iStockPhoto/Fotoamator
RAM © iStockPhoto/TPopova

This figure demonstrates how storage drives, RAM, and the processor work together.

Don't confuse RAM with the storage memory provided by disk drives. While both are often called memory, their functions are quite different.

RAM and Performance

The amount of RAM available to the computer makes a significant difference in its performance. Most computer systems allow you to add more RAM if you need it. In particular, having plenty of RAM helps a computer run more efficiently in two situations:

- **Running sophisticated programs:** A very powerful program, such as one used to edit photographs or produce video, requires a large amount of RAM to hold all of its software components.

- **Running more than one program (multitasking):** Every program you run requires some space in RAM. When you run more programs than your available RAM can handle, the whole computer system slows down.

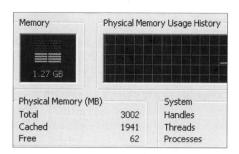

Windows displays current RAM usage.

Surge Protection

All of the delicate circuitry of the processor and RAM require protection from electrical power surges. A spike in the electrical grid from a nearby lightning strike could actually melt the circuits in the computer. Therefore, you should always power the computer and other components via a good surge protector. Even the cable for a cable or DSL modem should have surge protection.

Computer systems usually store most of the software you run and the work files that you save. Computer systems always have at least one storage drive, and sometimes several. The capacity of these drives is usually measured in gigabytes (GB), but many hard drives can hold one or more terabytes (TB) of data.

Types of Storage Drives

There are three primary types of storage drives that you should know about.

- **Hard disk drive:** This complex machine stores software on rapidly spinning platters. Read/write heads sweep back and forth across the platters to store and read data. The speed at which the platters spin can indicate the speed of the drive, anywhere from 5,400 to 10,000 rpm. Hard drive storage capacity is typically measured in *gigabytes* and *terabytes*.

- **Optical disc drive:** This drive reads (and often is able to write) data to optical discs such as CDs, DVDs, and Blu-ray Discs. Software is usually sold on discs read by optical drives. Some small computers don't have an optical disc drive built in, but most computers do. Their storage capacity is typically measured in *gigabytes*.

- **USB flash drive:** This is a small, solid-state storage device. Often called a "thumb drive" or a "pen drive," it can typically store anywhere from one to several gigabytes of data. You plug this drive into any USB port on the computer. Their storage capacity is typically measured in *gigabytes*.

Photo courtesy of SanDisk Corporation.

This 16 GB flash drive can hold more data than three DVDs.

- **Solid-state drive (SSD):** These are drives based on the same technology used for USB flash drives, but they hold far more data. At present, they are very expensive and can't hold as much data as a good hard disk drive. However, these drives are many times faster than traditional hard drives, use less electricity, and are bound to become very popular as prices go down. Their storage capacity is typically measured in *gigabytes*.

External Drives

You can purchase and connect external drives to supplement any drives built into your computer. For example, you can connect an external hard drive and use it to create backup copies of data on your internal hard disk drive. There are also external optical drives. USB flash drives are another example of external (sometimes called "removable") storage hardware.

Card Readers

Many computers have a device called a card reader. You use a card reader to conveniently plug in storage cards used with digital cameras, camcorders, mobile phones, and other devices. Many notebook computers also have built-in card reader slots.

1.4 Viewing and Printing Hardware

In order to display what you are doing, computers come with a built-in screen or a separate display called a *monitor*. These screens require hardware that sends the image from the computer system to the screen.

Computer Screens

A computer's screen (called a *monitor* on a desktop computer) is typically a liquid crystal display (LCD) that creates an image out of small dots of light called *pixels*. A backlight lets the pixel colors display brightly. Screens differ in their physical size (measured diagonally from corner to corner) and *resolution* (the number of pixels in the display). The higher the resolution, the sharper the image displayed on the screen. Most screens sold now have a *widescreen* proportion (aspect ratio) of 16:9. This aspect ratio is the same used for high-definition televisions (HDTVs). (Previously, most computer screens used a 4:3 aspect ratio.)

Measuring Resolution

The resolution of a screen is expressed in the pixels it can display horizontally and vertically. For example, most 19" screens have a native resolution (see below) of 1,280 pixels across by 1,024 pixels up and down, written 1280x1024. A typical 15.4" notebook screen might have a resolution of 1360x768. The higher these numbers, the higher the screen's resolution and the more it can display.

1600 pixels horizontally

20" measured diagonally

900 pixels vertically

This 20" screen has a resolution of 1600x900 pixels.

Native Resolution

All LCD screens have what's called a *native resolution* setting. This is the highest resolution the screen is physically capable of displaying. It is possible to reduce the resolution of the screen, but the resulting display is always either less sharp or the screen area used is smaller than what you see at the native resolution. Therefore, an LCD screen's native resolution setting always provides the best results for viewing.

Printers

A printer is a common feature of most personal computer setups. In most office settings, one printer may serve several computers via a network or even by wireless connections.

There are three types of printers that are most popular today.

- **Ink jet:** These printers are quite affordable and can print beautiful color prints from digital photos. The printing cost per page can be high, however, due to the cost of ink cartridges.

- **Laser:** These printers are excellent for busy offices that need to print many pages rapidly. Color laser printers are available, but they generally cannot print colors as vividly as ink jet printers can. Laser printers generally have a lower printing cost per page compared to ink jets.

- **All-in-one:** These are printers with built-in scanners and fax machines. The scanner allows you to create digital files from pages and also allows the printer to serve as a conventional copy machine.

1.5 Networking Hardware

Networking has become a necessity for getting the most out of a computer. Network connections give you access to the Internet. In a business environment, networks give access to printers and servers holding critical data, and also provide your Internet connection. Virtually all computers sold for the past decade contain a port to plug in a network cable. Notebook computers also feature built-in wireless connectivity. Three critical components of network hardware are modems, routers, and wireless access points.

Modems

A modem (*mo*dulator-*dem*odulator) is a device that takes digital data from the computer (bits and bytes) and converts it to sound (waves) that can travel along wires and cables. A modem and the receiving end of the transmission then converts the sound waves back into digital data bytes. All modems require a subscription with an Internet service provider (ISP) that provides the actual Internet connection.

There are three types of modem in common residential use today.

- **Cable modem:** This allows you to receive an Internet connection via a television cable system. Compared to other types of modems, cable modems typically permit the fastest Internet connection speeds.

- **DSL (digital subscriber line) modem:** This allows you to make an Internet connection via the wiring of a common telephone jack. However, in order for DSL to work, your local telephone company must install special hardware within a limited range of your home (often not available in rural areas).

- **Dial-up modem:** This older technology allows you to connect to the Internet via almost any telephone jack (no special hardware required on the telephone company's end). However, the speeds possible via a dial-up modem are much slower than cable or DSL.

Routers and Wireless Access Points

A *router* is a device that lets you connect multiple computers to a network. Most routers for home use contain four network cable ports, plus a port to connect the router to your Internet connection. This makes Internet connection sharing quite easy. A router also allows you to share files with other computers on your network.

Many routers are also a *wireless access point*. These can send data wirelessly to compatible wireless adapters on any computers that are within its range. This network connection includes any available Internet connection active on the router/wireless access point.

Types of Wireless Access

As with many other computing standards, wireless access standards have evolved over the years to allow ever-faster connections over an ever-increasing range. Most wireless access points can connect via multiple wireless connection standards.

- **Wireless-B:** This is the oldest standard still in common use. It is also the slowest and shortest ranged of the three most popular standards.
- **Wireless-G:** This standard emerged in 2003 and is still quite commonly used. Compared to wireless-B, G has similar range and can attain higher transfer speeds.
- **Wireless-N:** This is the latest standard, coming into common use around 2007. It, theoretically, has twice the range and greater speeds compared to the wireless-G standard.

Security/Encryption

Most wireless access points require the use of some sort of security measure such as encryption (encoding and decoding data transmissions). This prevents others from tapping into your wireless bandwidth without your permission. It also prevents someone from potentially monitoring your wireless transmissions and stealing private data (such as credit card numbers and online banking login information). Virtually all wireless access points support one or more encryption types.

1.6 Human Interface Hardware

Interface devices help you control the computer: giving commands, starting programs, and typing text. There are a wide variety of interface devices available to satisfy most any preference or physical limitation. Most interface (and many other) devices connect to the computer via a USB port.

Common Interface Devices

Twenty-five years ago, personal computers pretty much had just one interface device available, the keyboard. Now a variety of specialized devices allow you to control the computer.

- **Mouse:** First invented in the late 1960s, the mouse got its name from the tail-like wire connecting it to the computer. An optical mouse uses a light or laser to track its movement across a desk or other flat surface. In addition to buttons, most mice now feature a scroll wheel to help you smoothly scroll through web pages. Many mice are wireless and don't need a cord to connect them to the computer.
- **Touchpad:** This is the small pad at the base of the keyboard on notebook computers. Anything you can do with a mouse you can also do on a touchpad. Most touchpads let you tap the pad to make a click.
- **Keyboard:** Most keyboards have a conventional rectangular shape. Curved *ergonomic* keyboards allow typing with a more natural alignment of your forearms and hands. Like mice, many keyboards are available with a wireless connection to the computer, eliminating the clutter of cables.
- **Touch screen:** Some computers are equipped with a touch screen that functions much like a mouse. You point and tap on the screen to give various commands, including starting programs, scrolling through web pages, and controlling program windows.

- **Pen tablet:** This device lets you write and draw on a pad with a pen-like stylus. Pen tablets are especially useful for fine graphic arts work such as photo editing.
- **Trackball:** A trackball works like a stationery mouse. You move the mouse pointer by rolling a small ball.

USB Ports

Most interface devices connect to the computer via a rectangular connection called a *USB* (universal serial bus) *port*. USB ports allow you to connect all manner of hardware to the computer. Most computers have two to six USB ports built in. You can add even more USB ports by installing a *USB hub*. Another advantage to USB is the ability to supply electrical power to many USB devices. This helps avoid the need for yet another AC converter hanging off your surge protector.

This typical notebook computer features USB ports along its side.

USB Versions

Over the years, USB ports have evolved into three versions capable of ever-increasing data transfer speeds. All later USB ports are always compatible with previous versions.

- **USB 1.0:** This was the earliest version of USB port. It first became available in 1996.
- **USB 2.0:** First available in 2000, this version could theoretically support data transfer speeds up to four hundred times faster than USB 1.0.
- **USB 3.0:** The first computers to support USB 3.0 went on sale in early 2010. This version can theoretically attain speeds up to twenty times faster than USB 2.0. USB 3.0 can also provide more electrical power to USB devices that need it.

Webcams

A webcam is a small video camera that allows you to capture and transmit video and photos from your computer. Webcams are standard equipment on most notebook and netbook computers sold today. It is also very easy to purchase and connect a webcam for a desktop computer via a USB connection. Many webcams are compatible with Internet voice and conferencing systems. With compatible webcams and software at both ends, you can make video telephone calls from your computer. There are also some cool video email services available with which you can use your webcam.

1.7 Computer Software

The logical, non-physical component of a computer system is its software. Software is the key to making modern computers so incredibly flexible, able to perform a wide variety of tasks without any changes to their hardware. Without the right software, a computer system is just a very expensive doorstop. There are three basic categories of software you should be aware of:

- Operating system
- Application programs
- User data

Software comes in the form of files. So let's define this term before looking at these three categories in detail.

Software Files

A *file* is a group of data with a common purpose. No matter which type of drive it's stored on, all software is contained in the form of files. Sophisticated programs may be installed in the form of dozens or even hundreds of individual files stored on your hard drive. User data files are typically a single file. As you will learn later in this lesson, all software files have a *file format* (also called a *file type*).

Software Versions

Aside from the files you create and store yourself (user data), all software programs (including the operating system) typically come in the form of specific versions. Version identifications can come in the form of version numbers, such as 1.0, 2.0, etc. Years are another popular way to identify versions, such as Office 2010. Windows uses various names to indicate successive versions; examples follow.

The Operating System

An operating system (OS) is the most basic software your computer needs to function. When you first switch on the computer, it does a basic check of its hardware. The next thing the computer does is search for and load an operating system into RAM so it can begin doing work for you. Until the operating system loads, a computer can recognize only the most rudimentary of keyboard commands. After the operating system loads, the computer is ready to interact with you via all of your interface devices.

Examples of Operating Systems

There are many operating systems available to run personal computers. This book is based on Microsoft Windows, the most widely-used operating system in the world. Other computers run different operating systems. For example, Apple® Macintosh® computers run their own operating system, usually Mac OS X. *Linux* is an example of an *open source* operating system. The source code for the operating system is widely available and any programmer can contribute improvements to it. This book supports the three latest versions of Windows:

- **Windows XP,** released in 2001
- **Windows Vista,** released in 2006
- **Windows 7,** released in 2009

Throughout the rest of this book, Windows 7, Windows Vista, and Windows XP will be referred to as Win 7, Win Vista, and Win XP, respectively.

Roles of an Operating System

An operating system performs a wide variety of roles. These roles include the following.

- **Interpreting commands:** The operating system serves as the interface between you and all of the computer's hardware and software. When you point and click with the mouse or type on the keyboard, it is the operating system that receives this input and decides what to do with it.

- **Controlling hardware:** The operating system controls all hardware in the computer system. When you need to load a program or a user data file from a hard drive, the operating system locates it and sends it to RAM for processing. When you give a print command, the operating system takes care of telling the printer how to print the desired document.

- **Keeping track of all files:** All of the computer's software resides on one (or more) storage drive in the form of files. The operating system sets the rules for naming and storing these files. A hard drive can only think in terms of bits and bytes stored on various tracks and sectors of its storage system. Fortunately, the operating system allows you to give files easy-to-recall names and keeps track of how and where each file is stored. When you need a file or program, you tell the operating system what you want and the operating system in turn tells the hard drive how to get it.

- **Running application programs:** Application programs are the types of software that actually let you get work done. Most software is written and coded to run on a specific operating system. The operating system controls parts of the software being loaded into RAM and thence being shuttled back and forth to the processor.

32- and 64-bit Versions

In addition to different versions (such as XP, Vista, and 7), the Windows operating system is available in 32- and 64-bit versions. As an end user of Windows, there are really only two things that are important for you to know about these two versions.

- **3 GB RAM limit:** The 32-bit version of Windows can only support a maximum of 3 gigabytes (3 GB) of RAM. Any additional RAM installed on the computer beyond this limit is simply not recognized or used.

- **Hardware drivers:** A *driver* is software that tells the operating system how to interact with and control hardware attached to the computer. With rare exceptions, a driver written for the 32-bit version of Windows will not work in the 64-bit version. Unless your hardware is quite old, however, you will usually be able to find and install a 64-bit version of a driver for it via the Internet. Many 64-bit drivers also come preinstalled on the 64-bit version of Windows.

Application Programs

An application program (or simply, an application) is software designed to help you get work done. Anything useful you can do with a computer depends on the applications you've installed on it.

Application Program Categories

Most applications can be grouped into one of four categories, as described in the following table.

Category	Description	Examples
Proprietary (Commercial)	Applications for which you must purchase a license in order to use legally	Office 2010 Suite Photoshop
Shareware	Applications you are allowed to install and use without paying for initially; if you continue to use the software, you are required or expected to pay a license fee	WinZip SnagIt PDFCreator Xnote Stopwatch
Freeware	Free applications you do not have to pay for no matter how much you use them; these applications are still copyrighted, however, which means others can't turn around and try to sell the freeware program themselves	Jing Firefox Star Office
Malware	Often called *viruses*, these are applications designed to harm your computer.	MyDoom Code Red Blaster

Types of Application Programs

The variety of application programs available for computers is almost infinite. In this course, you will learn about some of the most popular types of applications.

- Word processor (Word)
- Spreadsheet (Excel)
- Database (Access)
- Presentation (PowerPoint)
- Email/personal information (Outlook)
- Web browsing (Internet Explorer)

Anti-malware Software

One of the software categories you learned of previously is *malware*. A special type of application designed to counter malware attacks is called anti-malware, or sometimes antivirus or Internet security. Anti-malware software can counter a variety of programs such as *spyware,* Trojan horses, worms, email-borne viruses, and many others. Internet security suites add additional protections in the form of features such as *firewalls*, anti-spyware and identity theft protection, and many others.

If your computer is connected to the Internet, you need an anti-malware program to protect it.

User Files

User files are the saved products you create when you use an application program. A user file can be a letter, flyer, budget spreadsheet, presentation slide show, digital photo, video, song, or any of the other numerous creations possible with application software.

File Formats

A *file format* is a technique for storing file data. There are numerous file formats in use with computers. Each file format has specific strengths and uses for storing particular types of data. For example, the JPEG file format is well suited for storing digital photos, and most digital cameras use this file format by *default*. MP3 is another example of a popular file format; it's optimized for storing music in compact files that take up less space than most other formats.

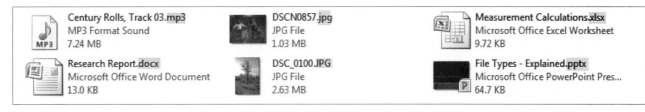

Each file type displays with its own special icon. The normally hidden filename extensions that indicate file type are shaded here.

Native File Formats

Every application has a *native file format;* a technique for storing your work in the form of a file. File formats are usually identified by the hidden extension stored at the end of the filename. For example, Microsoft Office Word 2010 uses the *.docx* format introduced with Word 2007. Word 2003 uses the older *.doc* format introduced with Word 97. Windows also uses a different file icon (picture) to indicate the two formats as shown in the following figure. Windows normally hides these filename extensions and you will rarely see them. But they work in the background to help Windows link your user files with specific application programs.

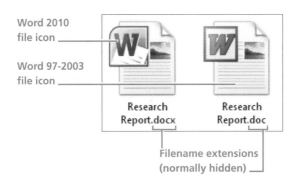

This is how Word files display when their hidden extensions are made visible. The letters after the period in each filename identify the file format. (Filename extensions were turned on temporarily to create this illustration.)

In addition to their native file formats, many programs can save and open files in other popular file formats. When you install a program, Windows learns about its native file format and also installs special icons to represent various types of files the program can create. These icons also help you identify the files visually when you scan a file list.

Links to Applications

Windows makes a link between any new file type an application needs and that application. This link tells Windows which application to start when you double-click a file of a particular type. When you install a program that uses a file type that's already in use, sometimes you will be asked to choose which program you prefer to open that type of file.

Windows uses the (normally hidden) filename extension to make the link (association) between a user file and an application program. Take care never to change the extension of a filename if the extension happens to be visible.

1.8 Concepts Review

Concepts Review	labyrinthelab.com/ob10

To check your knowledge of the key concepts introduced in this lesson, complete the Concepts Review quiz by going to the URL listed above. If your classroom is using Labyrinth eLab, you may complete the Concepts Review quiz from within your eLab course.

Reinforce Your Skills

Check Your Computer's Basic Specifications

In this exercise, you will give a command to display the basic specifications of a computer, such as its processor, RAM, and Windows version.

Before You Begin: Some computer labs have computers "locked down," so this exercise will not work. You may need to try this exercise at home.

1. If necessary, **start** and **log on** to your computer.

2. Click the **Start** button.

Win 7   Win Vista   Win XP

Windows displays the Start menu.

3. Follow the step for your version of Windows:

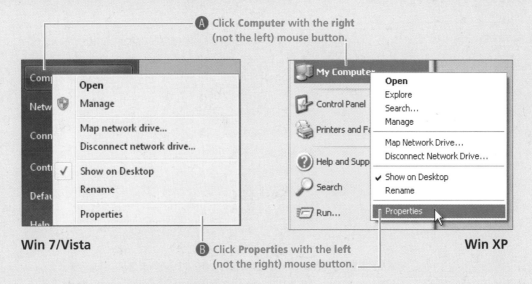

Ⓐ Click **Computer** with the **right** (not the left) mouse button.

Win 7/Vista

Ⓑ Click **Properties** with the **left** (not the right) mouse button.

Win XP

A new window appears to display the basic details of your computer.

4. Follow the steps for your version of Windows to review basic details about your computer:

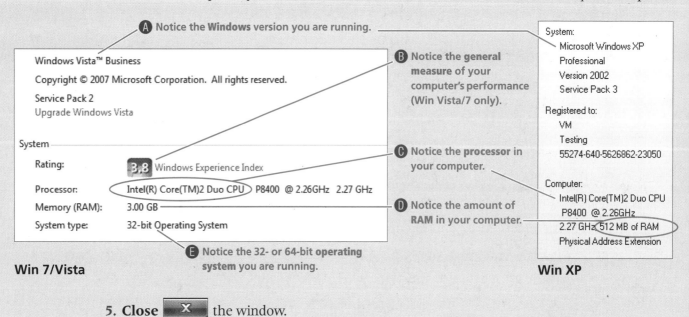

A Notice the **Windows** version you are running.

B Notice the **general measure** of your computer's performance (Win Vista/7 only).

C Notice the **processor** in your computer.

D Notice the amount of **RAM** in your computer.

E Notice the 32- or 64-bit **operating system** you are running.

Win 7/Vista

Win XP

5. Close ☒ the window.

Check Your Screen Resolution

In this exercise, you will give a command to display the resolution of your screen (monitor).

Before You Begin: Some computer labs have computers "locked down," so this exercise will not work. You may need to try this exercise at home.

1. If necessary, **start** and **log on** to your computer.

2. Point at any **clear area** of the screen, then click the **right** (not the left) mouse button to display a pop-up menu.
   In future exercises, this pop-up menu will be referred to as a context menu.

3. Follow the step for your version of Windows:

   ■ **Win 7:** Choose **Screen Resolution**.

   ■ **Win Vista:** Choose **Personalize**.

   ■ **Win XP:** Choose **Properties**.

   A new window appears to display your choices. Its appearance will vary according to the version of Windows you are running.

4. Follow the step for your version of Windows:

   ■ **Win 7:** Do **nothing** (you are already looking at the correct command).

   ■ **Win Vista: Scroll** to the bottom of the window, then click **Display Settings** as shown at right.

   ■ **Win XP:** Click the **Settings** tab.

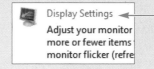

Windows displays your current resolution settings.

5. Notice the **resolution** (Win 7/Vista) or **screen resolution** (Win XP) setting.

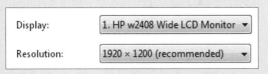

Win 7

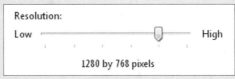

Win Vista

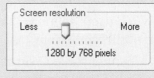

Win XP

The number displays the horizontal × vertical settings, for example 1360 × 768. On most systems, this will be your screen's native (best-looking) resolution.

6. Click the **Cancel** button to close the Settings window. (Do not change the screen resolution.)

7. (Win Vista only) **Close** [X] the Personalization window.

Program Windows

LEARNING OBJECTIVES

After studying this lesson, you will be able to:

- Log on and log off from Windows
- Identify the significant features of the Windows Desktop
- Switch users so more than one person can log on at the same time
- Start any installed Windows program
- Place program windows exactly where you want them on the screen
- Switch from one program to another

Every program you run is in a program window. You can make program windows fill the screen, disappear, or change their shape to fill just part of the screen. You can also run more than one program at the same time (called *multitasking*) and quickly switch from one running program to another. Win 7 and Win Vista also support a feature called gadgets, handy little programs to display information such as clocks, notes, and the weather. There are also methods to make locating and starting the programs you use most often easier. In this lesson, you will practice opening, positioning, and switching between program windows.

Using the Best Program

Josie is working on a report late at night. She has to submit it first thing in the morning and it has to look good. Part of the report requires some calculations. Josie works out the math on the Excel spreadsheet program, since numbers is what Excel does best. She writes her report using Word. And she creates a slide show presentation in PowerPoint using details created in the other two programs. As she works, Josie switches from program to program, copying items from one and pasting them into another. When one program is cluttering the Desktop, Josie minimizes it to clear it from the screen. For this task, the best program is all three programs. Windows makes it easy to run and use the programs together smoothly.

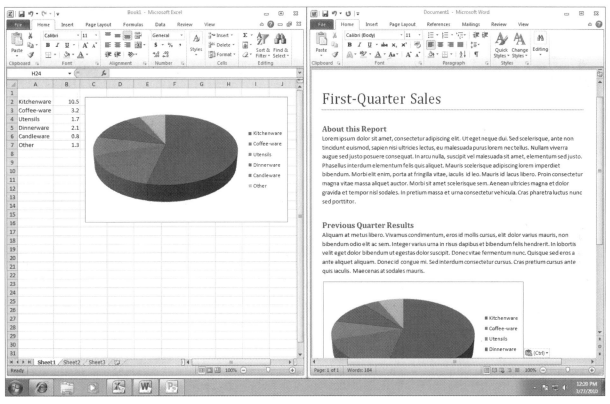

Josie arranges program windows on the screen to suit her needs.

2.1 Starting Windows

Video Lesson labyrinthelab.com/videos

The first thing your computer does when it "wakes up" is locate and load an operating system into its RAM. For this course, you will be using a version of Microsoft Windows. This book covers use of the three versions of Windows that can run Office 2010:

- Windows 7 (Win 7)
- Windows Vista (Win Vista)
- Windows XP (Win XP)

Logging On

Once Windows loads, it indicates that it's ready to log on a user. Depending on how the computer is configured, you will see one of the following.

- A Welcome screen displaying all of the usernames that can log on
- A network login screen in which a username and password must be typed
- A user's Desktop (if only one user is set up for Windows, Windows can be set up to log in that user automatically)

DEVELOP YOUR SKILLS 2.1.1
Log On to Windows

In this exercise, you will log on to Windows and view the Desktop.

1. If necessary, **switch on** the power to the computer and monitor. Ask your instructor for help if necessary.

Most Desktop computers have a power button on the front of the system unit. Most monitors also have a power button on the front.

The computer goes through its startup routine, ending with a Windows log on screen.

2. Write down your **logon information** below. Your instructor will give you this information if you do not have it already.

Username: _____

Password: _____

3. Follow the appropriate steps below:

Network Logon Prompt:

■ Follow these steps to give the Ctrl + Alt + Delete command:

Ⓐ Hold down the Ctrl and Alt keys on the keyboard.

Ⓑ Tap the Delete key.

■ Type your **username** and **password** into the boxes, and then click the **Logon** button or tap the Enter key.

The Windows Desktop appears.

Skip the rest of this exercise and continue reading the next topic.

Welcome Screen with Account Names Displayed:

■ Click the **username** for the logon account you will use.

■ Type the **password** into the Password box and **tap** the Enter key.

The Windows Desktop

Video Lesson   labyrinthelab.com/videos

The Desktop appears after you first log on to Windows. The Desktop is where all of your computing activity takes place on the screen. Depending on the version of Windows you are running, particular features will be apparent. The following figure displays significant features of a typical Win 7 Desktop.

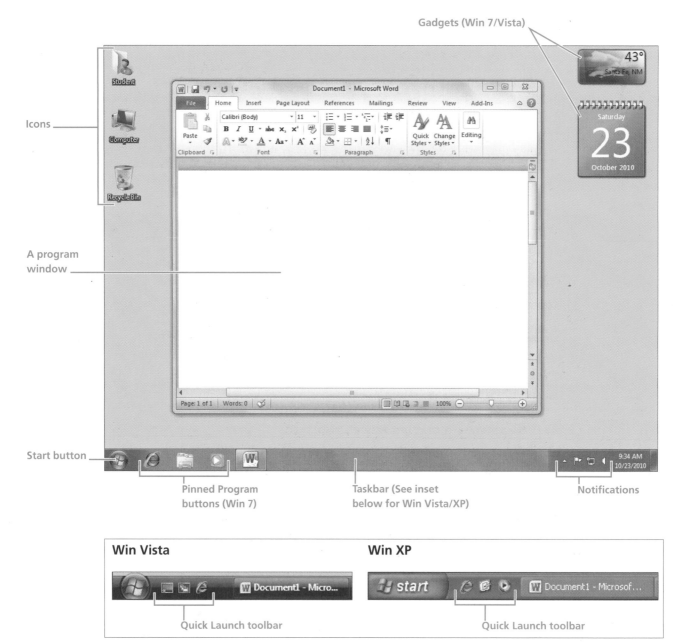

Gadgets (Win 7/Vista)

Icons

A program window

Start button

Pinned Program buttons (Win 7)

Taskbar (See inset below for Win Vista/XP)

Notifications

Win Vista

Quick Launch toolbar

Win XP

Quick Launch toolbar

Other Modes of Operation

Besides being active and logged on, you can put the computer into other modes of operation while remaining logged on. The following table gives a brief description of each mode and its use.

Mode	Description/Use
Switch User	This mode allows a user to log on while other users remain logged on as well. It keeps your programs and work open while someone else uses the computer. Later, you can switch back to being the active user.
Sleep	This mode puts the computer into a low-power mode until a key is tapped or the mouse is moved. You usually must enter a password to regain access to the Desktop. When the computer comes out of Sleep mode, all of your programs and files reappear just as they were before you put the computer to sleep.
Hibernation	This mode stores the current screen and programs onto the hard drive, then powers off the computer. The next time you power up the computer, it restores any open programs and files to their appearance when the computer went into hibernation.
Locked (Win 7/Vista)	This mode blocks view of the Desktop until you reenter your password. This is a good mode to use when you want to temporarily leave the computer on and unattended.

QUICK REFERENCE — SWITCHING BETWEEN MODES

Task	Procedure
Switch Mode (Win 7/Vista)	■ Click Start and then click the Shut Down menu button. ■ Choose the desired mode from the menu.
Switch Mode (Win XP)	■ *Switch User:* Click Start, click Log Off, and choose Switch User. ■ *Sleep/Hibernate:* Click Start, click Shut Down, and choose Sleep or Hibernate.

DEVELOP YOUR SKILLS 2.1.2
Try Switch User

In this exercise, you will try the Switch User command to temporarily free the computer for someone else to log on. Then you will log back on.

1. Follow the steps for your version of Windows:

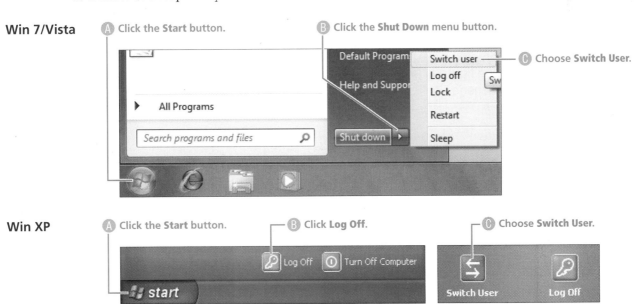

Win 7/Vista (A) Click the **Start** button.   (B) Click the **Shut Down** menu button.   (C) Choose **Switch User**.

Win XP (A) Click the **Start** button.   (B) Click **Log Off**.   (C) Choose **Switch User**.

The logon screen reappears. Now someone else can log on, or you can return to your own Windows session. In this case, we will assume you want to return to your own Windows session.

2. If necessary, use $\boxed{\text{Ctrl}}$ + $\boxed{\text{Alt}}$ + $\boxed{\text{Delete}}$ to get to a logon screen.

3. **Choose** your logon name, **type** your password, and **tap** $\boxed{\text{Enter}}$.
You are back at your own Windows session.

2.2 Starting Programs

Video Lesson labyrinthelab.com/videos

Windows gives you a variety of methods to start programs. These methods include the Start menu, the Quick Launch toolbar (Win XP/Vista), and pinning programs to the taskbar (Win 7). And, you can always start a program by double-clicking a file you created it with.

- Start menu
- Windows taskbar button (Win 7)
- Quick Launch toolbar (Win Vista/XP)
- User Files

Start Menu

When you install a new program on your computer, a folder for that program is usually created in the Start menu. If you don't recall where a program was installed, you can search for it (Win7/Vista only). Programs that you use frequently can also be "pinned" to the Start menu for easier access.

DEVELOP YOUR SKILLS 2.2.1A
Start a Program (Win 7/Vista)

Win XP Users: Skip this version of the exercise and perform the steps in Develop Your Skills on page 31.
In this exercise, you will start the Word 2010 program.

The following figure is from Win 7, but Win Vista's Start menu is identical except for minor visual differences.

1. Follow these steps to Start Word 2010:

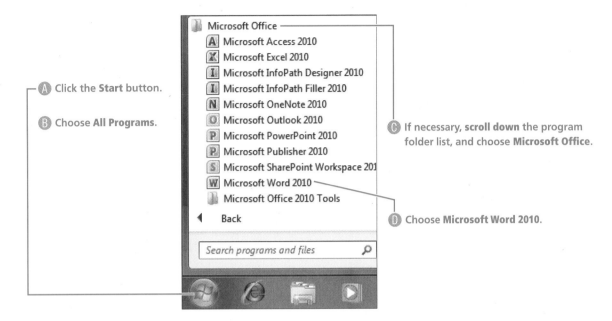

A Click the **Start** button.

B Choose **All Programs**.

C If necessary, **scroll down** the program folder list, and choose **Microsoft Office**.

D Choose **Microsoft Word 2010**.

The Word program window appears on the screen. Depending on how it was open previously, the program window may fill all or only part of the screen.

Skip the Win XP version of this exercise and continue reading the next topic.

DEVELOP YOUR SKILLS 2.2.1B
Start a Program (Win XP)

In this exercise, you will start the Word 2010 program.

1. Follow these steps to Start Word 2010:

A Click the **Start** button.

B Choose **All Programs**.

C Choose **Microsoft Office**.

D Choose **Microsoft Word 2010**.

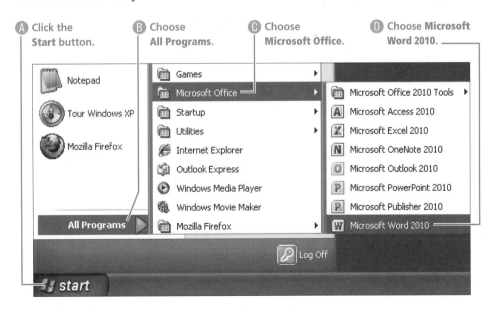

The Word program window appears on the screen.

The Windows Taskbar

Video Lesson   labyrinthelab.com/videos

The Windows taskbar along the bottom of the screen displays buttons for each active program. You can use these buttons to switch from one program to another. And the taskbar buttons also allow you to minimize program windows if you wish.

Win XP and Vista both feature a Quick Launch toolbar to which you can add favorite programs. Win 7 replaces this feature with the capability to pin programs to the taskbar itself.

Pinning Programs to the Taskbar (Win 7 Only)

Win 7 features the capability to "pin" frequently used programs directly to a spot on the taskbar. This keeps these program buttons in a stable location that's easy to access. Not only can you start the program from this taskbar button, you can also quickly view and select open program windows.

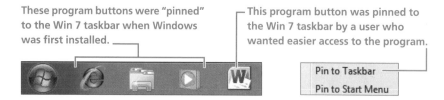

These program buttons were "pinned" to the Win 7 taskbar when Windows was first installed.

This program button was pinned to the Win 7 taskbar by a user who wanted easier access to the program.

Pin to Taskbar
Pin to Start Menu

User Files

Every file you save indicates its file type with an icon. When you double-click a user file, Windows opens the program you used to create the file, or it opens a default program for that type of file. For example, if you double-click a Word document file, Windows knows to start the Word program. If you double-click a photo file saved from your digital camera, Windows uses a default program to view the photo.

Searching for Programs

If you have numerous programs installed, it might become difficult to find a particular program you don't use very often. Win 7 and Vista have a search feature in their Start menus to help you locate such programs. You simply type the program name, and the search feature displays all Start menu entries that include that name.

Search for a Program (Win 7/Vista)

Win XP Users: Skip this exercise and continue reading the next topic.

In this exercise, you will log on to Windows and view the Desktop.

1. Follow these steps to quickly locate a program in the Start menu:

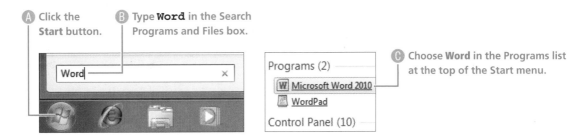

A Click the **Start** button.

B Type **Word** in the Search Programs and Files box.

C Choose **Word** in the Programs list at the top of the Start menu.

Programs (2)
W Microsoft Word 2010
WordPad
Control Panel (10)

   Windows starts another Word program window. You can also see another Word button on the taskbar if you are running Win Vista. Win 7 just shows the same Word taskbar button, but if you point at it you will see a preview of both Word windows.

2. **Close** ⊠ the new Word program window.
   The first Word window remains open, as does its taskbar button.

2.3 Controlling Program Windows

Video Lesson   labyrinthelab.com/videos

Every program you start runs in one or more program windows. You can position windows on the screen in just about any way you find convenient. Many Windows beginning users forget that they can instantly size a window to fill the entire screen, which reduces the amount of scrolling you might have to do to view everything you are working on. Program windows open with one or more buttons that help you make quick changes to their placement on the Desktop.

Program Window Features

Several features are common to virtually all program windows. The following figure points out key program window features.

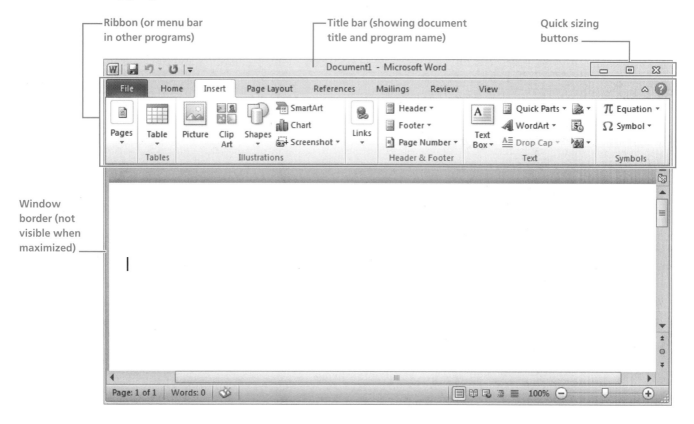

Ribbon (or menu bar in other programs)

Title bar (showing document title and program name)

Quick sizing buttons

Window border (not visible when maximized)

Quick Sizing Buttons

Most program windows have three quick sizing buttons that allow you to instantly give a commonly used window command. The center button changes its type depending on how the window is currently sized.

Command Name	Icon	Description
Close		Closes the program window and exits the program
Maximize		Makes the program window instantly fill the entire screen
Restore		Restores a maximized program window back to filling only part of the screen
Minimize		Removes the program window from the screen but leaves it running in the background

DEVELOP YOUR SKILLS 2.3.1
Use Quick Sizing Buttons

In this exercise, you will use the quick sizing buttons to control a program window.

1. Follow the appropriate step below:
    - Click the **Maximize** quick sizing button if it is visible: .
    - Continue to the next step if the window is already maximized.

    The Word program window should now fill the entire screen. It is quite useful to maximize the window area of a program you are using.

2. Click Word's **Restore** quick sizing button.
    Now the window only fills a portion of the screen.

3. **Minimize** the Word window.
    The program window disappears from the screen. However, Word is still running and any work being done in the program is still there.

4. Click once on the **Word** taskbar button for your version of Windows.

Win 7   Win XP/Vista

The Word window reappears in whichever shape it had been when minimized.

Leave the Word window open and continue reading.

Positioning and Shaping Program Windows

Video Lesson   labyrinthelab.com/videos

You can adjust the placement of restored (not maximized) program windows on the screen. There are two primary methods for changing window positions and shape:

- **Drag the title bar:** You can drag the title bar of a *restored* window to place it anywhere on the Desktop.

- **Drag window borders:** You can drag the borders of a *restored* window to change its dimensions.

Holding down the left mouse button while pointing at the title bar allows you to change a window's location.

When you point at a window border, a double-headed arrow appears to indicate you can change the window's shape.

Neither of these methods works on a *maximized* window.

Shape a Program Window

In this exercise, you will control the size and shape of a program window.

Before You Begin: Make sure that the Word window is not maximized *(does not fill the entire screen). You cannot change the shape of a window that is maximized.*

Change the Window's Location

1. Follow these steps to change the location of the Word window:

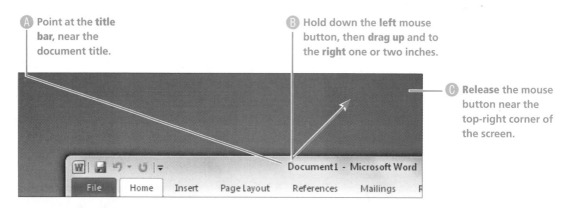

Ⓐ Point at the **title bar**, near the document title.

Ⓑ Hold down the **left** mouse button, then **drag up** and to the **right** one or two inches.

Ⓒ **Release** the mouse button near the top-right corner of the screen.

2. Drag the **Word** window by its title bar until it is near the top-left corner of the screen.

Change the Window's Shape

3. Follow these steps to change the window's shape from the corner:

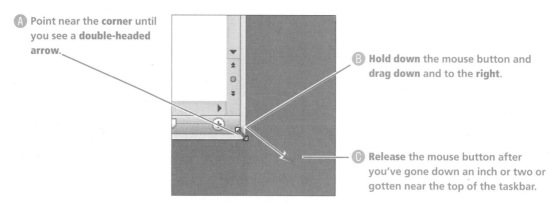

Ⓐ Point near the **corner** until you see a **double-headed arrow**.

Ⓑ **Hold down** the mouse button and **drag down** and to the **right**.

Ⓒ **Release** the mouse button after you've gone down an inch or two or gotten near the top of the taskbar.

4. **Point** at the right side border of the window until you see a **double-headed arrow**, then **hold down** the mouse button and **drag** the window narrower, similar to the figure at right.

5. Practice changing the window's **position** on the screen (by dragging the title bar) and its **shape** (by dragging on borders) until you can reliably put a window where you want it. When you finish, continue with the next topic.

Multitasking

Video Lesson   labyrinthelab.com/videos

Running more than one program at the same time is called *multitasking*. Multitasking can definitely enhance your productivity on many tasks. For example, you can view a web page in one window while you are writing about a related topic in Word. Or you might be entering data in an Excel spreadsheet while you prepare a PowerPoint screen show. Although only one window at a time is "active" all of the windows can be displaying something useful. You can switch the active window immediately as you change tasks.

Multitasking and RAM

Everything you see on the screen is taking place in RAM. The more programs you multitask, the more RAM you need to run all those programs efficiently. (Windows can run more programs than it has RAM to support, but everything will run much more slowly.) Fortunately, it is possible to install more RAM on most computers if you find your level of multitasking requires it.

DEVELOP YOUR SKILLS 2.3.3
Multitask with Three Programs

In this exercise, you will run three programs at once.

Before You Begin: The Word program should be running.

1. Use **Start→All Programs→Microsoft Office→Microsoft Excel 2010** to start the Excel spreadsheet program.
   The Excel program window appears. It may be maximized, depending on its state when the program was previously closed. Excel is now the active program.

2. Click the **upper** (not the lower) **Restore** button if the Excel program window currently fills the screen (is maximized).
   The Excel window should only cover a portion of the screen now.

3. Follow the step for your version of Windows to start Internet Explorer:

   ■ **Win 7:** Choose **Start→All Programs→Internet Explorer**. Or, click the **Internet Explorer** button on the taskbar, as shown at right.

   ■ **Win Vista/XP:** Choose **Start→Internet** (near the top of the Start menu).

   A web browser window appears and becomes the active program. Depending on its state when the program was closed, Internet Explorer might also fill the screen.

4. Click the **Restore** 🔲 button if Internet Explorer currently fills the screen (is maximized).

5. Click the **Word** button on the Windows taskbar to make it the active program.

6. Click anywhere on the **Excel** program window or **click** its button on the Windows taskbar.
   Excel immediately becomes the active program window and covers parts of the other two windows.

7. **Minimize** 🔲 the Excel window, as shown at right.
   Since it was the active program just before Excel, Word becomes active again.

8. **Minimize** 🔲 the Internet Explorer window.
   Now only the Word window remains visible on the Desktop. However, you can see the buttons for Excel and Internet Explorer on the taskbar at the bottom of the screen.

Switching Programs

Video Lesson   labyrinthelab.com/videos

When you run multiple programs, Windows offers keyboard shortcuts for switching between them. You can also clear the Desktop with a single command (effectively minimizing all program windows).

QUICK REFERENCE	SWITCHING PROGRAMS WITH WINDOWS
Task	**Procedure**
Switch programs with the keyboard	▪ Hold down the Alt key and then tap the Tab key.
	▪ Continue tapping the Tab key until the program you want to use is chosen.
	▪ Release the Alt key.
Clear the Desktop of open windows (Win 7)	▪ Click the Show Desktop button. ◁)) 7:37 PM 10/19/2010
Clear the Desktop of open windows (Win Vista/XP)	▪ Right-click a clear portion of the taskbar.
	▪ Choose Show the Desktop from the context menu.

DEVELOP YOUR SKILLS 2.3.4
Switch Program Windows

In this exercise, you will practice flipping between programs using the keyboard.

Before You Begin: Word, Excel, and Internet Explorer should be running.

Flip Between Programs

1. **Hold down** the Alt key on the keyboard and keep it held down until told to release it; then **tap** the Tab key.
   A window displaying icons for currently running programs appears in the middle of the screen.

2. Taking care to continue **holding down** the Alt key, **tap** the Tab key again.
   The highlight in the program icon display moves to the next program.

3. Still **holding down** the Alt key, **tap** the Tab key a few more times until the highlight returns to the Excel program, then **release** the Alt key.
   Excel becomes the active program.

4. Use Alt + Tab to switch back to the Word program.

Aero 3D Flip (Win 7/Vista)

Win XP Users: *Skip the rest of this exercise and continue reading the next topic.*

5. **Hold down** the **Windows** key on the keyboard and then **tap** the Tab key.
Windows displays miniatures of each open program window.

6. Still holding down the **Windows** key, **tap** the Tab key until the Internet Explorer window comes to the front of the display; then **release** the Windows key.
The newly chosen program becomes active.

Aero Desktop (Win 7)

Video Lesson labyrinthelab.com/videos

The Aero Desktop in Win 7 makes many common program window arrangements automatic. For example, you can instantly make a program window fill just half of the screen. The Aero Desktop also makes the Maximize and Restore window commands even more intuitive. The following table summarizes various features of the Aero Desktop in Win 7.

QUICK REFERENCE	USING WIN 7'S AERO DESKTOP
Task	**Procedure**
Use Aero Snap	■ *Fill half the screen:* Drag the title bar of the window until the mouse pointer touches the right or left side of the screen. ■ *Snap vertically:* Drag the bottom of a program window until it reaches the top of the taskbar to snap the rest of the window to the top of the screen. ■ *Maximize a window:* Drag the title bar of the window to the top of the screen. ■ *Restore a window:* Drag the title bar of a maximized window away from the top of the screen.
Use Aero Peek	■ *Make all windows transparent:* Point (don't click) at the Show Desktop button.
Use Aero Shake	■ *Minimize all but one window:* Point at the title bar of the program you want to keep on the screen, then hold down the mouse button while shaking it back and forth.
Use Aero Flip 3D	■ *Switch windows:* Hold down the Windows (⊞) key and then tap the Tab key. ■ Release the Tab key when the window you wish to use is in the front of the display.

DEVELOP YOUR SKILLS 2.3.5
Use Aero Desktop Features (Win 7)

Win XP/Vista Users: Skip this exercise and continue reading the next topic.

In this exercise, you will practice using the automatic window arrangement features of the Aero desktop in Windows 7.

1. **Minimize** ⊟ the Internet Explorer window.

2. **Drag** the title bar of the **Word** window to the very top of the screen.
The Word window snaps to maximized.

3. **Drag** the title bar of the **Word** window away from the top of the screen.
The Word window snaps back to restored.

4. Follow these steps to have Aero Snap make the Word window fill the left half of the screen:

A **Drag** the Word window title bar to the **left side** of the screen.

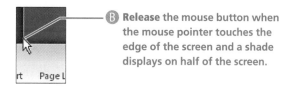

B **Release** the mouse button when the mouse pointer touches the edge of the screen and a shade displays on half of the screen.

Windows automatically shapes the Word window to fill half the screen. This can be very useful on wide-screen displays.

5. Use **Aero Snap** to make Excel fill the right half of the screen.

6. Drag the **Word** window title bar down and to the right about one inch.
Windows restores the Word window to its previous shape.

7. Point at the **Word** window title bar, then **hold down** the mouse button and **shake** the window back and forth for a couple seconds.

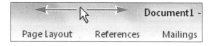

The Excel window (and any other open windows) minimizes, leaving Word the only window visible on the Desktop.

8. **Click** its taskbar button to make the **Excel** window visible again.

9. Click the **Show the Desktop** button, as shown at right.
All open windows are immediately minimized.

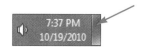

10. Click the **Show the Desktop** button again.
All previously open windows are immediately restored. Notice that Internet Explorer was not restored, since it was already minimized when you gave the Show the Desktop command in step 9.

2.4 Shutting Down Windows

Video Lesson   labyrinthelab.com/videos

It's important to shut down the computer properly. You don't want to simply press or hold down the power button. Windows has a Shut Down command that tells it to perform necessary housekeeping chores, exit out of any open program windows, and then shut off power to the computer. If your computer needs to install some updates to its software, the Shut Down command will also perform this task.

 ── The shield with exclamation point tells you that Windows needs to shut down to install software updates.

Logging Off

Logging off the computer keeps the computer running and allows others to log on later. It helps secure your computer since another user would have to know your password to log back in.

Restarting Windows

Sometimes when you install or uninstall software, you need to restart the computer. Windows has a restart command that essentially shuts down then restarts the computer. This allows any new program settings to become active.

DEVELOP YOUR SKILLS 2.4.1
Shut Down the Computer

In this exercise, you will shut down the computer.

1. **Close** ⊠ the Excel window. Choose **Don't Save** if you are asked to save any work done with Excel.
   If you've typed anything in Excel, the program will ask if you want to save it. In this case, that's not necessary.

2. **Close** ⊠ the Word window. Choose **Don't Save** if asked to save any work.
   It's always a good idea to close any open program windows before you shut down the computer. This gives you a chance to save changes to any work you've been doing with the programs.

3. Follow the steps for your version of Windows to shut down the computer:

Win 7

Ⓐ Click the **Start** button.

Ⓑ Click **Shut Down**.

Win Vista

Ⓐ Click the **Start** button.

Ⓑ Click the **Shut Down** button.

Win XP

Ⓐ Click the **Start** button.   Ⓑ Click **Turn Off Computer**.   Ⓒ Choose **Turn Off**.

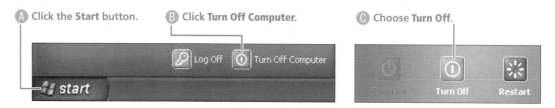

Windows goes through its shutdown routine, then powers off the computer.

2.5 Concepts Review

Concepts Review   labyrinthelab.com/ob10

To check your knowledge of the key concepts introduced in this lesson, complete the Concepts Review quiz by going to the URL listed above. If your classroom is using Labyrinth eLab, you may complete the Concepts Review quiz from within your eLab course.

Reinforce Your Skills

Multitask with Windows

In this exercise, you will practice starting programs, switching programs, and arranging program windows on the Desktop.

1. Use **Start→All Programs→Microsoft Office→Microsoft Word 2010** to start the Word program.

2. Use similar commands to start the **PowerPoint** and **Excel** Office 2010 programs.

3. **Maximize** ▣ the **Word** window.

4. Use its taskbar button to make the **PowerPoint** window active.

5. Use Alt + Tab to make the **Excel** window active.

6. **Minimize** ▬ the **Excel** and **PowerPoint** program windows.

7. Make the **Word** window fill the left half of the screen by **dragging** on its title bar and borders (or use **Aero Snap** if you are running Win 7).

8. **Restore** ▣ the **PowerPoint** window if it is maximized (fills the screen).
   You cannot adjust the size and shape of a maximized window.

9. Make the **PowerPoint** window fill the right half of the screen.

10. **Right-click** the PowerPoint button on the taskbar and choose **Close** from the context window.
    This can be a handy way to close open program windows.

11. **Close** ⊠ the **Word** window.

12. Use any method to **close** the **Excel** window.

Apply Your Skills

Configure Program Windows

In this exercise, you will arrange program windows on the Desktop.

1. Start the **Word**, **Excel**, and **PowerPoint** programs.

2. Arrange the program windows as indicated here.

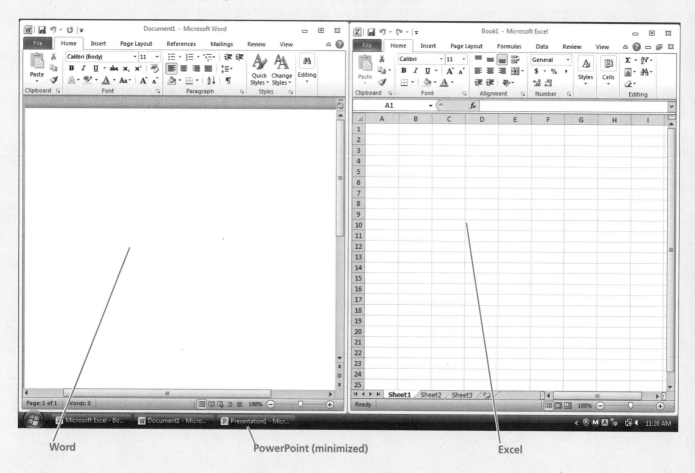

Word   PowerPoint (minimized)   Excel

3. Get your instructor's initials: _____

File Management

LEARNING OBJECTIVES

After studying this lesson, you will be able to:

- Browse files on the computer
- Open files from a folder window
- Copy and move files
- Create new folders
- Rename files and folders
- Delete and restore files using the Recycle Bin
- Back up files on a USB flash drive

When you begin working with a computer, you will have just a few files to keep track of. But as your use of the computer grows, so will the number of files you must manage. After several months, you can have more than one hundred of your own files. After a year, you can have hundreds more. Fortunately, Windows gives you a very effective tool for managing files: folders. With folders, you can group related files. You can even create folders inside of other folders. Win 7 introduces a new level of file management called the library, which can contain files and folders from more than one storage drive. In this lesson, you will practice browsing folders and libraries. You will also move and copy files from one storage location to another. This is particularly useful if you use a USB flash drive to store your coursework.

CASE STUDY

Creating Folders for a New Semester

Esmeralda is taking four courses at her community college. As she goes over the syllabi, Esmeralda notices that one of her courses will require her to submit a term paper. She decides to prepare for some of the research she must do. Esmeralda creates several folders on her computer to help her organize files as she performs the research for her term paper. She also creates a folder for each of her classes on her computer. Then she creates folders inside the class folders to further organize her files. For example, she creates Final and Drafts folders for the word processor documents she will create. Esmeralda also creates a Research folder to hold the various files, web pages, and notes she will collect. She creates a folder called Old Stuff for everything she thinks she doesn't need but does not yet want to delete. She can delete the Old Stuff folder after the term paper project is finished.

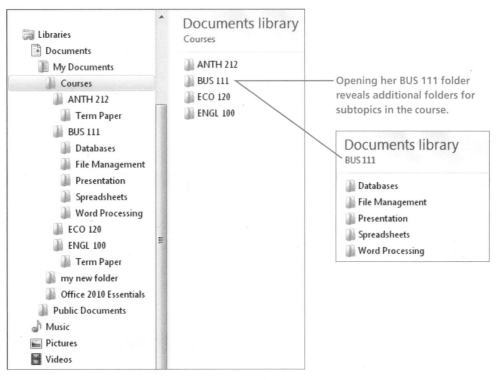

Esmeralda organizes folders for her courses this semester.

3.1 Browsing User Files

Video Lesson labyrinthelab.com/videos

You can accumulate a lot of files as you work and play with a computer. If you have a digital camera, for example, you can end up with hundreds or even thousands of photo files by the end of a year. Working at a job or studying some courses will require the creation of numerous files. There will be times when you need to locate a file you haven't looked at in months. Browsing to find the file(s) you need can become a daily activity. This topic shows you some useful methods for browsing and finding files.

How Files Are Organized

Windows uses a flexible hierarchy that is common to most personal computers. The three (or four) levels in the hierarchy are listed in the following table.

Level	Definition	Examples
Drive	This is a physical place in which you store files.	■ An internal hard drive ■ A USB flash drive
Library (Win 7)	This is a collection of folders and files on a local or network drive. Libraries can contain items from more than one drive.	■ Documents ■ Music ■ Pictures ■ Public
Folder	This is an electronic location in which you store groups of related files. It is also possible to place folders inside of other folders.	■ A folder to store all files for an application program ■ A folder to store files you type for a project
File	This is a collection of computer data that has some common purpose.	■ A letter you've typed ■ A picture you've drawn

About Libraries

Win 7 introduces the *library* to the file organization hierarchy. Libraries are essentially collections of related groups of files and folders located on one storage drive (or more). A library can bring together folders from more than one location on your computer or on a network. Win 7 sets up some basic libraries when it is first installed on a computer. You can also create new libraries if you wish.

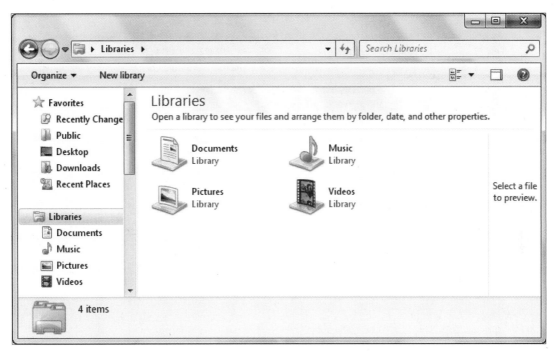

Win 7 sets up four basic libraries for each username. Each library can contain one or more folders.

Browsing Files

As you work with application programs such as Word and Excel, you will want to locate and open files you have created previously. Although you can open files from within an application program, sometimes it is more convenient to search directly through all of the files you have saved to a USB flash or hard drive. Then you can view all of the files you have saved rather than just files of the type your application program recognizes.

Computer Window Features

The following illustrations describe the major features of a typical Computer window. Take a moment to review these features before beginning the first Develop Your Skills exercise.

Win 7/Vista

The address bar displays the current location you are browsing.

The Search box allows you to search for files on your computer.

Forward and Back buttons help you navigate through the system.

The toolbar contains buttons for common tasks.

Links to frequently browsed locations are listed here. (Libraries appear in Win 7 only.)

The Computer window displays your storage drives.

Basic information about a selected location or device is displayed here.

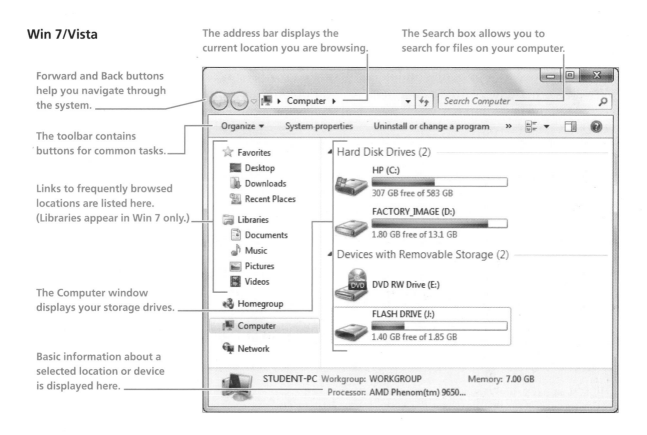

Win XP

The Search button allows you to search for files on your computer.

The address bar displays the current location you are browsing.

Forward and Back buttons help you navigate through the system.

The Task Pane contains frequently used commands.

Links to frequently browsed locations are listed here.

Here, the My Computer window is showing storage drives and document folders.

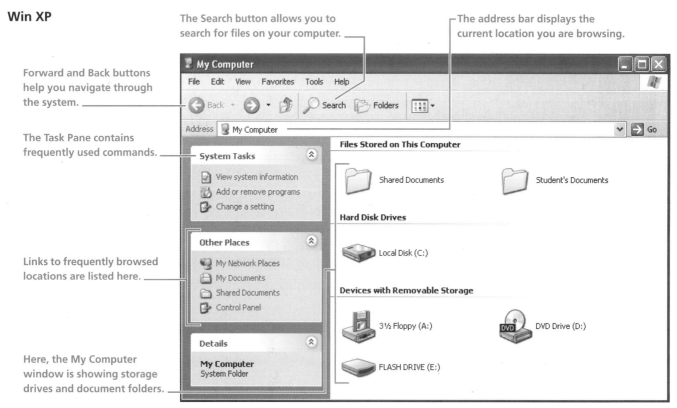

 Win XP calls this view My Computer rather than simply Computer. Throughout this lesson, Computer and Documents (as used in Win 7/Vista) will mean My Computer and My Documents if you are using Win XP.

About Drive Letters

Windows identifies each storage drive on the computer with a drive letter. When you attach a USB flash or external drive to the computer, Windows immediately assigns it the next available drive letter. Thus, your USB flash drive may have a different drive letter on different computers. This makes no difference in terms of the files you actually store on the drive.

The primary hard drive is always named drive C:.

The DVD or Blu-Ray drive is usually drive D: or E:.

This USB flash drive received the next available drive letter.

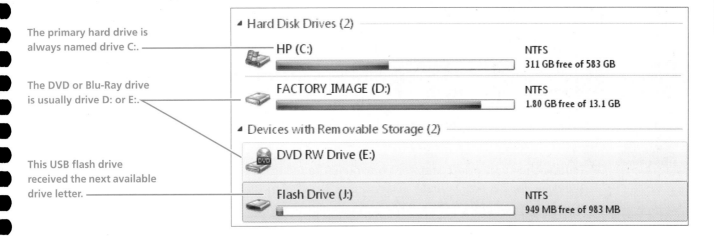

Storing Your Exercise Files

Throughout this book, you will be referred to files in your "file storage location." You can store your exercise files on various media, such as on a USB flash drive, in the Documents folder, or to a network drive at a school or company. While some figures may display files on a USB flash drive, it is assumed that you will substitute your own location for that shown in the figures. See Storing Your Exercise Files for additional information on alternative storage media. Storing Your Exercise Files is available on the student web page for this book at labyrinthelab.com/ob10.

 In Win XP, the folder is called My Documents. In Win Vista/7, it is called Documents. Throughout this lesson, we will use the word *Documents* when referring to this folder.

If you have not yet copied the student exercise files to your local file storage location, follow the instructions in Storing Your Exercise Files, located on the student web page for this book.

 Regarding Window Sizing Buttons: Different versions of Windows display different sizes and colors of window sizing buttons, even though the symbol of the button is identical. For simplicity's sake, only the *Win 7* version of such buttons will be shown. Close button examples:

Win7   Win Vista   Win XP

Open a Folder Window

In this exercise, you will open a Folder window and view the contents of your exercise folder.

Before You Begin: Navigate to the student web page for this book at labyrinthelab.com/ob10 and see the Downloading the Student Exercise Files section of Storing Your Exercise Files for instructions on how to retrieve the student exercise files for this book and to copy them to your file storage location.

1. If necessary, **start** the computer and **log on** to Windows.

2. Carefully **insert** your USB flash drive, if you are using one as your file storage location. Otherwise, skip to **step 3**.

Close ▭✕ the AutoPlay window if it appears after you insert the USB flash drive.

3. Follow the appropriate step for your file storage location:
   Windows displays the Computer folder. This shows all of the storage drives available to you in the main panel on the right side of the window.

   FLASH DRIVE (E:)

   - **USB flash drive:** Click **Start→Computer**, and then **double-click** the icon for your flash drive in the Computer window. (It may or may not have a name similar to the figure at right.) Or, **click** once to select the flash drive then **tap** the [Enter] key on the keyboard.

   - **Documents:** Click **Start→Documents**.

   - **Any other location:** Ask your instructor for help if necessary.

4. Click the **Maximize** ▣ button if the folder window is not already maximized.

5. **Double-click** the Office 2010 Brief folder. Or, **click** once to select the folder then **tap** the [Enter] key on the keyboard.
   A list of all folders for lessons in the course appears.

6. **Double-click** the Lesson 03 folder. Or, **click** once to select the folder then **tap** the [Enter] key on the keyboard.
   Windows displays the contents of the folder. You should see icons for fourteen files inside the Lesson 03 folder.

   Notice that the address bar displays where you are browsing, including the drive letter.

Leave the Lesson 03 window open.

Opening Files

Video Lesson   labyrinthelab.com/videos

When you double-click a file's icon, Windows launches the program used to create or edit that type of file and displays the file in the program window. This is a convenient way to start working with a file after you find it.

About Files

A file is a named collection of computer data. You create files by using application programs, such as Word or Excel. A typical hard disk drive has thousands of files stored on it. With most Windows programs, you use the Save command to save your work in a file. Windows displays your files in various ways that you can choose. In general, each file has a filename and an icon. The icon indicates what type of file you are viewing.

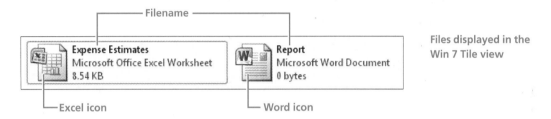

Files displayed in the Win 7 Tile view

Filename Extensions

Most Windows filenames have an extension that consists of three or four letters following a period at the end of the filename. Filename extensions identify the type of file you are working with and they are what allows Windows to launch the correct program when you double-click a file. For example, the Bonuses file is a spreadsheet document, so it has a filename extension of *.xlsx*. The .xlsx filename extension tells Windows to launch Microsoft Excel when you double-click the file. Windows application programs add this extension to the filename when you save a file. Most Windows systems hide the filename extension. But if your system is set to display it, you must type out the extension whenever you rename a file.

Windows systems normally hide this filename extension.

Do not change the extension of a filename if it is visible when you rename a file. This causes Windows to lose track of which program is configured to open the file.

Open and Close a Document File

In this exercise, you will open one of the files in the Lesson 03 folder.

Before You Begin: The Lesson 03 folder window should be open.

1. Examine the various files in the Lesson 03 window.
   Notice that the files in the Lesson 03 folder display different icons. The icon is a visual cue as to which program will open the file.

2. **Double-click** the Meeting Notes file. Or, **click** once to select the file then **tap** the [Enter] key.
   Windows starts Microsoft Word to display the file. Windows knows to start Word because Word was used to create the file originally.

3. **Click** [File] and then choose **Close** from the menu to close the file and leave Microsoft Word running. Choose **No** if you are prompted to save changes.
   The Meeting Notes file closes, but the Microsoft Word program remains open.

4. **Close** [⊠] the Microsoft **Word** program window.
   The Lesson 03 folder window should be visible again. Leave the window open.

3.2 Working with Folders

| Video Lesson | labyrinthelab.com/videos |

A *folder* is an electronic location where you store groups of related files. Folders are important tools for organizing files. You may have just a few files when you begin using a computer, but after a year or two you may have hundreds of files. What if you could only view your files in a single, long list? This would be similar to finding a book in a library that had only one long bookshelf. You could find the book eventually, but you would need to scan through many titles first. Folders help you subdivide your files into easy-to-find groups.

Folder Hierarchy

Folders form a hierarchy on a storage drive or Documents window. You can create new folders inside of other folders to add multiple layers to your file organization. Win 7 also allows you to organize groups of folders into *libraries*, but that technique is beyond the basic scope of this lesson.

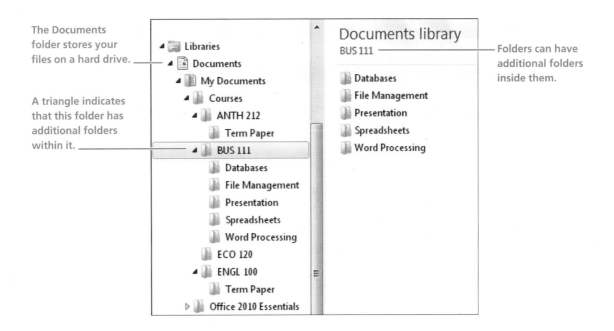

The Documents folder stores your files on a hard drive.

A triangle indicates that this folder has additional folders within it.

Folders can have additional folders inside them.

Creating Folders

You can create folders on a USB flash drive or the Documents folder on the hard drive whenever you need them. You can create a new folder while browsing in a Computer or Documents window. You can also create folders from the Save As dialog box of most Windows programs. The following figures each show the New Folder command in the Word 2010 Save As dialog box.

Win 7   **Win Vista**   **Win XP**

Word 2010 allows you to create a new folder as you save a document.

QUICK REFERENCE	CREATING FOLDERS
Task	**Procedure**
Create a folder (Win 7)	▪ Open a Computer or Folder window.
	▪ Click the New Folder button on the toolbar.
	▪ Type a name for the new folder and tap the ⌈Enter⌋ key.
Create a folder (Win Vista)	▪ Open a Computer or Folder window.
	▪ Choose Organize→New Folder from the toolbar.
	▪ Type a name for the new folder and tap the ⌈Enter⌋ key.
Create a folder (Win XP)	▪ Open My Computer, My Documents, or any folder window.
	▪ Choose File→New→Folder from the menu bar.
	▪ Type a name for the new folder and tap the ⌈Enter⌋ key.

Create Folders (Win 7/Vista)

Win XP Users: Skip this version of the exercise and perform the steps in Develop Your Skills 3.2.1B on page 57.

In this exercise, you will create three folders in the Lesson 03 folder. Later in this lesson you will move and copy files into these folders.

Before You Begin: The Lesson 03 folder should be open.

1. Follow the steps for your version of Windows to create a new folder:

Win 7   Ⓐ Click the **New Folder** button on the toolbar.

Win Vista   Ⓐ Click the **Organize** button on the toolbar.

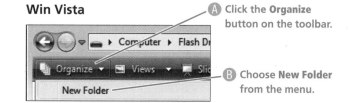

Ⓑ Choose **New Folder** from the menu.

A new folder appears. Its name is already selected, ready for you to type the new name.

2. Type **Pictures** as the new folder name and **tap** the [Enter] key.

3. **Double-click** the Pictures folder to navigate to your new folder.
   Notice that the address bar displays the folder you are viewing. This folder is empty now, but you will place files in it later.

The Pictures folder is considered a subfolder of the Lesson 03 folder. Conversely, the Lesson 03 folder is considered the parent folder of the Pictures folder.

4. Click the **Back** 🔙 button on the toolbar to return to the Lesson 03 parent folder.

5. Follow the step for your version of Windows to create another new folder:
   - **Win 7**: Click the **New Folder** button on the toolbar.
   - **Win Vista**: Choose **Organize→New Folder** from the menu bar.

6. **Name** the new folder **Spreadsheets** and **tap** the [Enter] key.

7. Create a third **subfolder** named **Documents**.

8. **Right-click** on a clear area of the folder window and choose **Refresh** from the context menu.
   If the folders weren't alphabetized before, they should be now. The top of your Lesson 03 folder should look similar to the illustration at right.

9. Follow the steps for your version of Windows to set the Tiles view:

- ■ **Win 7**: Click the **Views** menu button, as shown at right, and choose **Tiles**.

- ■ **Win Vista**: Click the **Views** menu button, as shown at right, and choose **Tiles**.

Windows changes the view to the versatile Tiles view. This shows a good-sized icon and gives additional information about each file.

Leave the Lesson 03 window open.

Skip the Win XP version of this exercise and continue reading the next topic.

DEVELOP YOUR SKILLS 3.2.1B

Create Folders (Win XP)

In this exercise, you will create three folders in the Lesson 03 folder. Later in this lesson you will move and copy files into these folders.

Before You Begin: The Lesson 03 folder should be open.

1. Follow these steps to create a new folder:

Ⓐ **Click** once on a clear area of the **Computer** window to ensure no file is selected (highlighted).

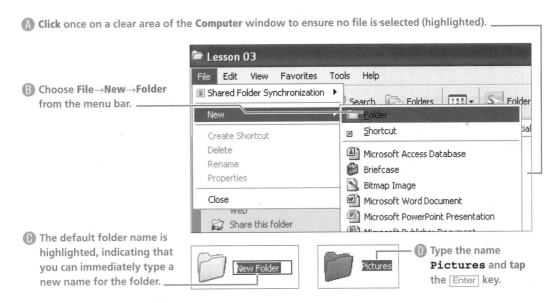

Ⓑ Choose **File→New→Folder** from the menu bar.

Ⓒ The default folder name is highlighted, indicating that you can immediately type a new name for the folder.

Ⓓ Type the name **Pictures** and tap the Enter key.

The newly named folder appears in the file list.

2. **Double-click** the Pictures folder icon to navigate to your new folder.
   Notice that the address bar displays the folder you are viewing. This folder is empty now, but you will place files in it later.

3. **Click** the [Back] button on the toolbar to return to the Lesson 03 folder.

4. Choose **File→New→Folder** from the menu bar to create a second subfolder within Lesson 03.

5. Name the folder **Spreadsheets**, then **click** a clear area in the window to deselect the folder.

6. Create a third **subfolder** named **Documents**.

7. Choose **View→Tiles** from the menu bar.
   Windows displays the files as medium-sized icons with some file information alongside.

8. Choose **View→Arrange Icons By→Name** from the menu bar.
   Windows sorts the contents of the window alphabetically by name, with the folder names coming first. Now the Lesson 03 folder should look similar to the following figure.

Leave the Lesson 03 window open.

Renaming Files and Folders

Video Lesson   labyrinthelab.com/videos

Sometimes files are created with default names like Document1 or Workbook1. It is easy to rename a file when its icon displays in a folder window. Use either of the two methods described in the following Quick Reference table to rename a file or folder in a folder window. Whichever method you use, once the folder name is highlighted, you can immediately type the new name and tap the Enter key to rename the file.

QUICK REFERENCE	RENAMING FILES AND FOLDERS
Task	**Procedure**
Rename a file or folder with the right-click method	▪ Right-click on the file or folder icon and choose Rename from the context menu. ▪ Type the new name and tap the Enter key.
Rename a file or folder with the click-pause method	▪ Left-click once on the filename under the icon. ▪ Pause about one second then click on the filename again. ▪ Type the new name and tap the Enter key.

Rename a File

In this exercise, you will rename files and folders using several methods.

1. Follow these steps to issue the Rename command with the right-click method:

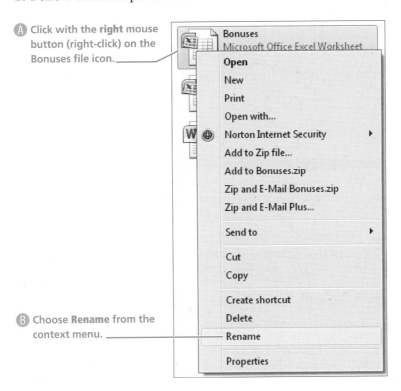

Ⓐ Click with the **right** mouse button (right-click) on the Bonuses file icon.

Bonuses
Microsoft Office Excel Worksheet

Open
New
Print
Open with...
Norton Internet Security ▶
Add to Zip file...
Add to Bonuses.zip
Zip and E-Mail Bonuses.zip
Zip and E-Mail Plus...

Send to ▶

Cut
Copy

Create shortcut
Delete
Rename

Properties

Ⓑ Choose **Rename** from the context menu.

Windows highlights the filename, ready for you to rename it.

2. Type **Bonuses Jan-June** and **tap** Enter.
   The new name replaces the old filename.

3. **Click** on a clear area of the window to **deselect** the Bonuses Jan-June file.

4. **Click** once (do not right-click) on the Bonuses Jan-June filename (not the icon) then **pause** one second and **click** again.
   The filename is highlighted and ready for editing.

5. **Tap** the left arrow ← key until the insertion point is blinking to the left of the *B* in *Bonuses*.
   The arrow keys allow you to move the insertion point without deleting any part of the filename.

6. Type **Company**, **tap** the Spacebar, and **tap** the Enter key.
   The new filename should read Company Bonuses Jan-June. *Leave the Lesson 03 window open.*

3.3 Moving and Copying Files

Video Lesson labyrinthelab.com/videos

Windows lets you move and copy files from one drive to another and from one folder to another. There are several techniques you can use to move and copy files. This lesson will teach you two methods.

- **Copy and Paste:** Copies files into a new location
- **Cut and Paste:** Moves files to a new location

QUICK REFERENCE	MOVING AND COPYING FILES WITH CUT, COPY, AND PASTE
Task	**Procedure**
Copy files with Copy and Paste	■ Select the files to be copied. ■ **Win 7/Vista:** Choose Organize→Copy from the toolbar. **Win XP:** Choose Edit→Copy from the menu bar. ■ Navigate to the location in which the files are to be copied. ■ **Win 7/Vista:** Choose Organize→Paste from the toolbar. **Win XP:** Choose Edit→Paste from the menu bar.
Move files with Cut and Paste	■ Select the files to be moved. ■ **Win 7/Vista:** Choose Organize→Cut from the toolbar. **Win XP:** Choose Edit→Cut from the menu bar. ■ Navigate to the location in which the files are to be moved. ■ **Win 7/Vista:** Choose Organize→Paste from the toolbar. **Win XP:** Choose Edit→Paste from the menu bar.

Selecting Multiple Files for Move and Copy Commands

You can move and copy a single file or dozens of files with the same command. Before you give the Cut or Copy command, select the file(s) you wish to be affected by the command. To select a single file, simply click on it. The two easiest methods of selecting multiple files are described in the following Quick Reference table. You can combine these two techniques as your needs dictate.

You can select nonconsecutive files for cut and copy commands. In this example, only the Excel spreadsheet files and a picture file are selected.

QUICK REFERENCE · SELECTING MULTIPLE FILES FOR COMMANDS

Task	Procedure
Ctrl+click technique to select several files	■ Click the first file you wish to select. ■ Press and hold the Ctrl key on the keyboard while you click any other files you wish to select. ■ Release the Ctrl key when you have made all of your selections.
Shift+click technique to select several files in a row	■ Click the first file you wish to select. ■ Press and hold the Shift key on the keyboard while you click the last file in the group that you wish to select; release the Shift key.
Deselect a selected file	■ Press and hold the Ctrl key on the keyboard while you click on the file you wish to deselect.

DEVELOP YOUR SKILLS 3.3.1

Move and Copy Files

In this exercise, you will use the Cut and Paste technique to move single files into one of your new folders. Then you will use the Copy and Paste technique to copy files into another folder.

Move a File with Cut and Paste

1. With the Lesson 03 folder open, **click** once (do not double-click) to select the Company Bonuses Jan-June file.

2. Follow the step for your version of Windows:
   - **Win 7/Vista**: Choose **Organize→Cut** from the toolbar.
   - **Win XP**: Choose **Edit→Cut** from the menu bar.

   Notice that the icon for the file you selected is "dimmed." This indicates that the file has been cut and will be moved when you give the Paste command.

3. **Double-click** to open the Spreadsheets folder.
   This navigates you to the empty Spreadsheets folder.

4. Follow the step for your version of Windows:
   - **Win 7/Vista**: Choose **Organize→Paste** from the toolbar.
   - **Win XP**: Choose **Edit→Paste** from the menu bar.

   The pasted file appears in the folder window.

5. Click the **Back** ⬅/⬅ Back button to return to the Lesson 03 folder.
   Notice that the Company Bonuses Jan-June file is no longer listed with the other files; it was moved to a different folder.

6. Repeat steps 1–4 to **cut and paste** (move) the file Expense Estimates into the Spreadsheets folder.

7. Go **back** ⬅/⬅ Back to the Lesson 03 folder.

Copy Multiple Files

In this part of the exercise, you will use the [Ctrl] key to select more than one file for the Copy and Paste commands.

8. **Click** once (do not double-click) to select the December picture file.

9. **Hold down** the [Ctrl] key and keep it held down as you **click** once to select the other three image files:
   - Giants
   - Monument Valley
   - Sea Dragon

10. **Release** the [Ctrl] key.
    Even after you release the [Ctrl] key, the four image files are selected and ready for your next command.

11. Follow the step for your version of Windows:
    - **Win 7/Vista**: Choose **Organize→Copy** from the toolbar.
    - **Win XP**: Choose **Edit→Copy** from the menu bar.

12. **Double-click** to open the Pictures folder.

13. Follow the step for your version of Windows:
    - **Win 7/Vista**: Choose **Organize→Paste** from the toolbar.
    - **Win XP**: Choose **Edit→Paste** from the menu bar.

    The files appear in the window as they are copied.

14. Go **back** / Back to the Lesson 03 folder.
    Notice the four image files are still in the Lesson 03 window because they were copied rather than moved.

    Leave the Lesson 03 window open.

Video Lesson labyrinthelab.com/videos

You can delete unneeded files and folders to free up space on a storage drive. When you delete a folder, any other folders and files inside that folder are deleted as well. However, the Delete command doesn't necessarily mean erase. Windows takes steps to help avoid the loss of files you may not have meant to delete.

What Happens to Deleted Files?

Windows does not physically erase a deleted file from the hard drive. Instead, the file is placed in the Recycle Bin. (Exception: See the warning below.) The Recycle Bin holds the deleted files until you give a command to empty it, or it runs out of the space allotted to store deleted files. If you delete files from the hard drive, you can usually recover them from the Recycle Bin.

Files and folders deleted from **USB flash drives** or a network drive *are not* sent to the Recycle Bin! They are immediately deleted when you issue the delete command.

DEVELOP YOUR SKILLS 3.4.1
Delete Files and a Folder

In this exercise, you will delete some of the files in the Lesson 03 subfolder. Then you will delete the Lesson 03 folder itself.

Before You Begin: The Lesson 03 folder should be open.

Delete Files

1. **Double-click** to open the Pictures folder.
   Windows displays the contents of the Pictures folder.

2. Follow the steps for your version of Windows to select the four files in the right panel:
   - **Win 7/Vista**: Choose **Organize→Select All** from the toolbar.
   - **Win XP**: Choose **Edit→Select All** from the menu bar.
   Windows selects all of the files in the folder.

3. **Tap** the Delete key on the keyboard.
   Windows will probably display a prompt window asking you to confirm the Delete command. This is a safeguard to protect against accidental deletions.

4. Choose **Yes** to confirm the deletion.
   The files disappear from the right panel and have been sent to the Recycle Bin. The Pictures folder is now empty.

If you deleted the picture files from a USB flash drive, the files are not sent to the Recycle Bin. (You still have copies of them in the Lesson 03 folder, however.)

5. Go **back** ⬅ / ⬅ Back to the Lesson 03 folder.

Delete a Folder

6. **Right-click** the Pictures folder, then choose **Delete** from the context menu. Choose **Yes** if Windows asks you to confirm the deletion.

    The Pictures folder disappears and is moved to the Recycle Bin. (Exception: The folder is not in the Recycle Bin if it was deleted from a USB flash drive.)

7. **Close** █X█ the Lesson 03 folder window if you use a USB flash drive to store your exercise files. Leave the window open if you store your files in the Documents folder.

 Skip the rest of this exercise if you use a USB flash drive as your file storage location. Files deleted from USB flash drives are not sent to the Recycle Bin.

View Files in the Recycle Bin

Now you will view your files from within the Recycle Bin. Any file in the Recycle Bin can be restored (undeleted) to the location from which it was deleted.

8. **Minimize** ▭ the Lesson 03 folder.

9. **Double-click** the Recycle Bin icon on the Desktop.

    The Recycle Bin folder opens to show the contents of the Recycle Bin. Depending on the type of storage location you deleted the files from, the three files deleted in step 3 may be visible.

10. Attempt to open the Giants file by **double-clicking** it.

    The file does not open. Instead, a Properties window opens. You are not able to open files if they are in the Recycle bin.

11. Click the **Cancel** button at the bottom of the Properties window to close it.

    Leave the Recycle Bin window open.

Emptying Files from the Recycle Bin

Video Lesson	labyrinthelab.com/videos

Files located in the Recycle Bin are permanently deleted from your computer when you issue an Empty Recycle Bin command, or automatically when the Recycle Bin runs out of space to keep deleted files. Depending on your computer's configuration, the Recycle Bin is set to store a certain amount of files. Once that limit is reached, the oldest files in the Recycle Bin are automatically and permanently deleted to make room for additional files.

Restoring Files from the Recycle Bin

Files cannot be opened if they are located in the Recycle Bin. If you decide you need a file you previously deleted, and it hasn't been permanently deleted from the Recycle Bin, you can restore the file to its original location by right-clicking the file and choosing Restore from the pop-up menu. The Recycle Bin also has a Restore All Items command to restore all files it presently contains.

Recovering Lost Files

There may be an occasion in the future when you accidentally empty the Recycle Bin while it's holding some valuable files you didn't intend to delete. In a situation like this, there are two important things to keep in mind.

- **Don't panic:** In most cases, the "lost" files can be recovered. Don't go into cardiac arrest! Instead, follow the second point below.

- **Get expert help:** There are experts in file recovery everywhere and most likely in your town. Do as little as possible with the storage drive from which the files were deleted and take it to a computer expert as soon as you can.

QUICK REFERENCE	DELETING AND RESTORING FILES
Task	**Procedure**
Delete a file or folder	▪ Select the file or folder in a folder window. You can select multiple files if you wish using the Ctrl and/or Shift keys. ▪ Tap the Delete key on the keyboard. Or, right-click any selected file/folder and choose Delete from the context menu.
Restore an item from the Recycle Bin	▪ Double-click the Recycle Bin on the Desktop. ▪ Select the files and/or folders you wish to restore. ▪ Click the Restore the Selected Items from the left panel of the Recycle Bin folder window.
Empty the Recycle Bin	▪ Right-click the Recycle Bin icon. ▪ Choose Empty Recycle Bin from the context menu. (Remember, this will permanently delete the contents of the Recycle Bin.)

DEVELOP YOUR SKILLS 3.4.2
Restore Files and Folders

In this exercise, you will restore the files and folders you deleted in the previous exercise.

Before You Begin: Skip this exercise if you use a USB flash drive as your file storage location.

1. If the Recycle Bin window is not already open, **double-click** the Recycle Bin icon on the Desktop.

2. Use Ctrl+click to select three files in the Recycle Bin:

   - Giants
   - Monument Valley
   - Sea dragon

   Your Recycle Bin may have more items, but we are only concerned with the files and folder deleted in the previous exercise.

3. **Right-click** any one of the three selected files (it doesn't matter which one) and choose **Restore** from the context menu, as shown at right.
   The file disappears from the right panel because it has been removed from the Recycle Bin and restored to its original location.

4. **Close** [X] the Recycle Bin window.

5. If necessary, click its button on the Windows **taskbar** to display the Lesson 03 folder.
Notice that the Pictures folder has reappeared. It was re-created when you restored the three picture files that were deleted while inside it.

6. **Double-click** to open the Pictures folder.
The three restored picture files should be visible.

7. **Close** ☒ the Pictures folder window.
The Windows Desktop is now empty.

3.5 Backing Up Your Files

Video Lesson   labyrinthelab.com/videos

USB flash drives are extremely compact and convenient. They are also easy to misplace! The last thing you want is to lose an entire semester's work on your flash drive. The best way to avoid a loss is to make regular backups of your flash drive onto your computer's hard drive. Then, at most you might lose a day or two of work—but not weeks or months.

Make a backup of your coursework files at least once a week, or even more often.

Storing Backups

Creating a special folder in your Documents folder for backups is a great idea. That way the backup is easy to find. You could even rename the backup folder with the current date each time you copy files from your flash drive. That way, you always know how long ago you made your most recent backup.

QUICK REFERENCE   BACKING UP FLASH DRIVE FILES

Task	Procedure
Create a new folder for backups	■ Open a Documents window. ■ Use the New Folder command to create a new folder. ■ Name the folder **Flash Drive Backups** and tap Enter.
Back up files from the flash drive to a hard drive	■ Carefully insert your flash drive into a USB port, open a Computer window, and then open your flash drive. ■ Use Ctrl+A from the keyboard to select all of the files and folders on the flash drive. ■ Use Ctrl+C from the keyboard to copy the selection. ■ Display the Documents folder on your computer. ■ Open the Flash Drive Backups folder. ■ Use Ctrl+V from the keyboard to paste the files and folders copied previously. (If you've previously made a backup, Windows will ask if you wish to overwrite the previous backup with this new backup.) Follow the step for your version of Windows: ■ Win 7/Vista: 　◆ Place a checkmark in the Do This for All Current Items checkbox and choose Yes. 　◆ Place a checkmark in the Do This for The Next... checkbox and choose Copy and Replace. ■ Win XP: 　◆ Choose Yes to All. ■ (Optional) Click the Back button and rename the Flash Drive Backups folder, putting today's date at the end of the folder name.

DEVELOP YOUR SKILLS 3.5.1
Back Up Files

In this exercise, you will copy all the files from your USB flash drive to a hard drive.

Before You Begin: Skip this exercise if you are not using a USB flash drive.

1. If necessary, carefully insert your **USB flash drive** into a USB port.

2. Open a **Computer** window and **double-click** to display your flash drive.

3. Follow the steps for your version of Windows to select all of the files and folders on your flash drive in the right panel:
   - **Win 7/Vista**: Choose **Organize→Select All** from the toolbar. Or, use Ctrl+A from the keyboard.
   - **Win XP**: Choose **Edit→Select All** from the menu bar. Or, use Ctrl+A from the keyboard.

   Windows highlights its selection of all of the files and folders on your flash drive.

4. Follow the step for your version of Windows:
   - **Win 7/Vista**: Choose **Organize→Copy** from the toolbar.
   - **Win XP**: Choose **Edit→Copy** from the menu bar.

5. Click **Documents** on the left navigation panel.
   Windows displays your Documents folder.

Create a Backup Folder

Now you will make a new folder to store your backup files.

6. **Create** a new folder, name it **Flash Drive Backup**, and **tap** Enter .
   The renamed folder appears in the Documents folder.

7. **Double-click** to open the Flash Drive Backup folder.
   Now that you are at the destination, you can paste the copied files.

8. Follow the step for your version of Windows:
   - **Win 7/Vista**: Choose **Organize→Paste** from the toolbar. Or, use Ctrl + V from the keyboard.
   - **Win XP**: Choose **Edit→Paste** from the menu bar. Or, use Ctrl + V from the keyboard.
   All of the files and folders from your flash drive appear in the backup folder.

9. Go **back** ← / ← Back to the Documents folder.
   You should see your Flash Drive Backup folder in the file/folder list.

Delete the Backup Files (Optional)

If you are studying on a public computer, you will want to delete your files from the Documents folder.

10. **Skip** the rest of this exercise if the files in your Documents folder will remain private. (Ask your instructor if you are unsure.)

11. **Click** once (do not double-click) to select the Flash Drive backup folder and **tap** the Delete key. Choose **Yes** if Windows asks you to confirm the deletion.

12. **Close** X the Documents window.

13. **Open** the Recycle Bin then click the **Empty the Recycle Bin** command to remove the recently deleted files and folders. Choose **Yes** when Windows asks you to confirm emptying the Recycle Bin.

14. **Close** X the Recycle Bin window.

3.6 Concepts Review

Concepts Review   labyrinthelab.com/ob10

To check your knowledge of the key concepts introduced in this lesson, complete the Concepts Review quiz by going to the URL listed above. If your classroom is using Labyrinth eLab, you may complete the Concepts Review quiz from within your eLab course.

Reinforce Your Skills

Create Folders

In this exercise, you will create a new folder on your file storage location.

1. Open a Computer window and display the location where your student files are located.

 If necessary, carefully plug in your USB flash drive now. Close the window when AutoPlay opens.

2. **Open** the Office 2010 Brief folder then open the Lesson 03 folder.

3. Follow the step for your version of Windows to create a new folder:
   - **Win 7**: Click the **New Folder** button on the toolbar.
   - **Win Vista**: Choose **Organize→New Folder** from the toolbar.
   - **Win XP**: Choose **File→New→Folde**r from the folder window menu bar.

   A new folder appears. The generic folder name is already selected, ready for you to type the new name.

4. **Name** the new folder **Folder Practice**.

5. **Double-click** to open the new Folder Practice folder.
   The newly created folder is empty.

6. **Create** five new folders inside the Folder Practice folder:

   Travel Planning

   Photos

   Backups

   Letters

   Reports

7. Go **back** ⬅/⬅ Back to the Lesson 03 folder.

Copy and Delete Files

In this exercise, you will copy files to the new Folder Practice folder, then delete them.

Before You Begin: You must complete Reinforce Your Skills 3.1 before starting this exercise.

1. If necessary, follow **steps 1 and 2** of Reinforce Your Skills 3.1 to **open** a folder window displaying the Lesson 03 folder.

Copy Files to a Folder

2. **Click** once (do not double-click) on the **December** photo to select it for the **Copy** command.

3. **Hold down** the Ctrl key, then **click** once (do not double-click) on each of the other three picture (type JPG) files (Giants, Monument Valley, Sea Dragon); **release** the Ctrl key.

 If you choose a file you don't want in the selection, hold down the Ctrl key and select it again. The reselection of a selected file drops it from the selection.

4. Follow the step for your version of Windows to give the Copy command:
   - **Win 7/Vista**: Choose **Organize→Copy** from the toolbar.
   - **Win XP**: Choose **Edit→Copy** from the menu bar.

5. Open the **Folder Practice** folder then open the **Photos** folder.

6. Follow the step for your version of Windows to give the Paste command:
   - **Win 7/Vista**: Choose **Organize→Paste** from the toolbar.
   - **Win XP**: Choose **Edit→Paste** from the menu bar.
   The four files you selected should appear in the folder.

7. Go **back** ◀/◀ Back twice to view the Lesson 03 folder.

Delete Files

8. **Click** once on a picture file to select it.

9. **Hold down** the Ctrl key, select the other three picture files again, and **release** the Ctrl key.

10. **Tap** the Delete key on the keyboard. Chose **Yes** when Windows asks you to confirm the deletion.
    The files are placed in the Recycle Bin, unless you deleted them from your flash drive. (Files deleted from a flash drive are never placed into the Recycle Bin.)

REINFORCE YOUR SKILLS 3.3
Move Files

In this exercise, you will move files from the new Reinforce Your Skills 3.1 folder back into the Lesson 03 folder.

Before You Begin: You must complete Reinforce Your Skills 3.2 before starting this exercise.

1. **Display** the Lesson 03 folder.

2. Using the Ctrl key, select the following files:
   - Destinations
   - Museums
   - Road Trips
   - Travel Expenses

3. Follow the step for your version of Windows to give the Cut command:
   - **Win 7/Vista**: Choose **Organize→Cut** from the toolbar.
   - **Win XP**: Choose **Edit→Cut** from the menu bar.

   The four files you selected appear dimmed, indicating that they have been cut for moving. They will stay in this folder until you give the Paste command.

4. **Open** the Folder Practice folder then open the Travel Planning folder.

5. Give the **Paste** command.
   The four moved files appear in the folder.

6. Go **back** ⬅/⬅ Back to view the Folder Practice folder.

Copy a Folder

You can copy folders and their contents the same way you copy/move individual files.

7. **Click** once (don't double-click) to select the Travel Planning folder.

8. **Copy** the folder.

9. **Double-click** to open the Backups folder.

10. **Paste** the folder.
    The folder you copied appears in the Backups folder.

11. **Open** the Travel Planning folder.
    All the files in the folder when you copied it are here too.

12. Go **back** ⬅/⬅ Back three times to the Lesson 03 folder.
    Notice that the files you moved in steps 2–5 are no longer listed in the Lesson 03 folder.

Apply Your Skills

Manage Files

In this exercise, you will create a new folder in your file storage location.

1. **Open** a Computer window and display your file storage location.

2. **Open** the Office 2010 Brief folder then open the Lesson 03 folder.

3. **Create** a new folder named **Manage Files**.

4. **Open** the Manage Files folder and **create** three new folders within it:

    Excel Spreadsheets

    Project Files

    Backup Files

5. Return to **viewing** the Lesson 03 folder.

Copy Files

6. Select the **Word** files in the Lesson 03 folder and **copy** them into the Project files folder in the Manage Files folder. (Hint: You will need to open *two* folders to complete this command.)

7. Return to **viewing** the Lesson 03 folder. (Go back twice.)

Move Files

8. Select the **Excel** spreadsheet file in the folder and **move** it into the Excel Spreadsheets folder that is inside the Manage Files folder.

9. Return to **viewing** the Lesson 03 folder.

Create a Backup of a Folder

10. **Copy** the Manage Files folder to the Office 2010 Brief folder on your USB flash drive or the Documents folder. (This will place your backup folder at the same level as all the lesson folders in Office 2010 Brief.)

11. **Rename** this backup folder **Manage Files 3-1**.

UNIT

Word 2010

In this unit, you will begin working with Word 2010, a powerful word processing program that allows you to do much more than just type documents. You will begin by opening Word, then opening, navigating through, and closing Word documents. Once you're comfortable with these skills, you will move on to creating your own documents and learning how to search the Help feature when you need more information. Throughout these lessons, you will learn to create and enhance business letters, memoranda, and press releases. Important basic topics in this unit include using Word's spelling checker and grammar checker, the AutoCorrect feature, the Format Painter, formatting, editing, and copying and moving text.

Working with Word Basics

In this lesson, you will get an overview of Microsoft Office Word 2010. First you will learn to start Word, and then how to work with the Word interface. You will open and close documents, navigate through a multipage document, and work with Word Help. Finally, you will exit the Word program.

LEARNING OBJECTIVES

After studying this lesson, you will be able to:
- Use and customize the Ribbon
- Use the Quick Access toolbar and the Mini toolbar
- Open and close documents
- Navigate in a document
- Use Word Help

CASE STUDY

Getting Oriented to Word 2010

My Virtual Campus

Stefanie Bentley has been promoted to marketing assistant at My Virtual Campus, a social networking technology company. My Virtual Campus sells their web application to colleges and universities, allowing students, alumni, faculty, and staff to utilize this social networking website, which is closed to the public and branded for their institution. Her first task is to create a brief summary of what their best-selling website is and how it is used. This effort will provide Stefanie a good opportunity to see just how easy Microsoft Word 2010 is to use when writing her paper, and if she runs into any problems along the way, she will appreciate how much help is at her fingertips.

My Virtual Campus

Our best-selling website, a social networking Intranet established specifically for college communities worldwide, has been gaining popularity at an extraordinary rate.

The website is useful for all types of networking opportunities; for example, social events and career prospects can be publicized, prospective students can check out the campus, professors and students can participate in extended training occasions and collaborate on special projects. It also proves useful when looking for a roommate or offering items for sale. Alumni can post job opportunities for current students and other noteworthy news, and so forth.

In general, here's how it works; you join and create a profile about yourself, choosing how much personal information to enter. Then, you can invite other people to join also. You can chat in real-time with other members, post photos to share, and most importantly, you can control what information others can see about you.

Security is taken very seriously by My Virtual Campus and every step has been taken to ensure your privacy and protect your confidential information.

[handwritten note] If you have older version of file Word a phone. Save as — (E:) drive Save as type: Word 97-2003 Document.

77

4.1 Presenting Word 2010

Video Lesson labyrinthelab.com/videos

Microsoft Office Word 2010 is a dynamic document-authoring program that lets you create and easily modify a variety of documents. Word provides tools to assist you in virtually every aspect of document creation. From desktop publishing to web publishing, Word has the right tool for the job. For these and many other reasons, Word is the most widely used word processing program in homes and businesses.

4.2 Starting Word

The method you use to start Word depends on whether you intend to create a new document or open an existing one. If you intend to create a new document, use one of the following methods to start Word:

- Click the ⊞ button, choose Microsoft Office from the All Programs menu, and then choose Microsoft Word 2010.
- Click the Microsoft Word 2010 W button on the Quick Launch toolbar located at the left edge of the taskbar. (This button may not appear on all computers.)

Use one of the following methods if you intend to open an existing Word document. Once the Word program starts, the desired document will open in a Word window.

- Navigate to the desired document using Windows Explorer or My Computer and double-click the document name.
- Click the ⊞ button and choose Documents. Choose Recently Changed under Favorites, and then double-click the desired document name.

After you start Word, the document window shows. Don't be concerned if your document window looks a little different from this example. The Word screen is customizable.

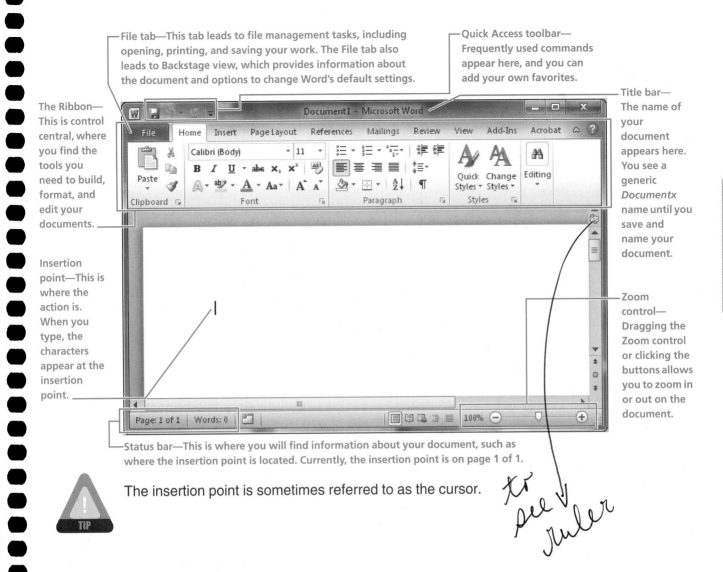

File tab—This tab leads to file management tasks, including opening, printing, and saving your work. The File tab also leads to Backstage view, which provides information about the document and options to change Word's default settings.

Quick Access toolbar—Frequently used commands appear here, and you can add your own favorites.

Title bar—The name of your document appears here. You see a generic *Documentx* name until you save and name your document.

The Ribbon—This is control central, where you find the tools you need to build, format, and edit your documents.

Insertion point—This is where the action is. When you type, the characters appear at the insertion point.

Zoom control—Dragging the Zoom control or clicking the buttons allows you to zoom in or out on the document.

Status bar—This is where you will find information about your document, such as where the insertion point is located. Currently, the insertion point is on page 1 of 1.

The insertion point is sometimes referred to as the cursor.

to see v ruler

Page layout

L

to set tabs

Start Word

In this exercise, you will experience starting Word, and you will examine the Word window.

1. If necessary, **start** your computer. The Windows Desktop appears.

2. **Click** the ⊕ button at the left edge of the taskbar, and choose **All Programs**.

3. Choose **Microsoft Office→Microsoft Word 2010** from the menu.

4. Make sure the Word window is **maximized** ▣.

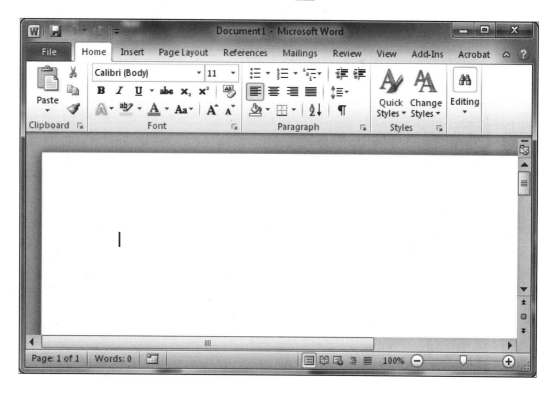

4.3 Opening Documents

Video Lesson labyrinthelab.com/videos

The Open command on the File tab displays the Open dialog box, where you can navigate to a storage location and open previously saved documents. Once a document is open, you can edit or print it.

Opening Older Word Documents

If you open a document created in a previous version of Word, 2007 and earlier, it opens in Compatibility Mode.

The term appears in the Title bar, as shown in the illustration. Older Word documents do not understand the new features in Word 2010, so those features are limited or disabled.

When an older document is open, a Convert command is available in Backstage view, which you can use to upgrade the file and make the new features of Word 2010 available.

DEVELOP YOUR SKILLS 4.3.1

Open a Document

In this exercise, you will learn the steps to open an existing document through the Open dialog box.

1. Follow these steps to open the document:

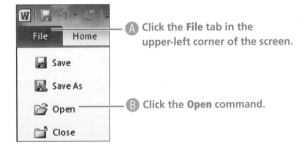

Ⓐ Click the **File** tab in the upper-left corner of the screen.

Ⓑ Click the **Open** command.

Later in this lesson, the preceding steps will be written like this: Click the [File] (or File) tab and choose Open from the menu.

2. When the **Open** dialog box appears, follow these steps to open the My Virtual Campus document:

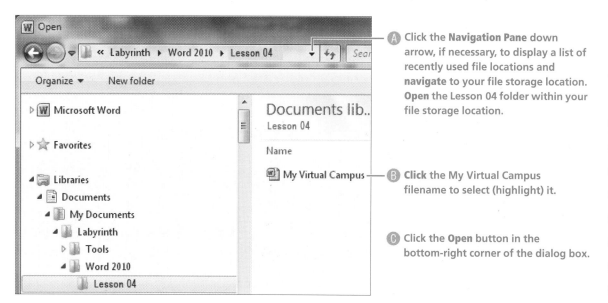

Ⓐ Click the **Navigation Pane** down arrow, if necessary, to display a list of recently used file locations and **navigate** to your file storage location. **Open** the Lesson 04 folder within your file storage location.

Ⓑ **Click** the My Virtual Campus filename to select (highlight) it.

Ⓒ Click the **Open** button in the bottom-right corner of the dialog box.

You can also double-click on a filename to open it.

3. Make sure the Word window is **maximized** 🔲.

4.4 Working with the Word 2010 Interface

Video Lesson   labyrinthelab.com/videos

The band running across the top of the screen is the Ribbon. This is where you will find the tools for building, formatting, and editing your documents. You can customize the Ribbon by adding new tabs with their own groups and commands.

The Ribbon

The Ribbon consists of three primary areas: tabs, groups, and commands. The tabs include Home, Insert, Page Layout, and so on. A group houses related commands within a tab. Groups on the Home tab, for instance, include Clipboard, Font, Paragraph, Styles, and Editing. An example of a command in the Paragraph group is Increase Indent.

Be aware that the arrangement of the buttons on the Ribbon can vary, depending on your screen resolution and how the Word window is sized. Following are two examples of how the Paragraph group might appear on the Ribbon.

(handwritten) If ribbon disappears – double click on home

Contextual Tabs

Contextual tabs appear in context with the task you are performing. As shown in the following illustration, double-clicking a clip art object in a document activates Picture Tools, with the Format tab in the foreground.

 You have to double-click the object the first time to activate the contextual tab; afterward, you only have to click the object once to reactivate it.

Dialog Box Launcher

Some groups include a dialog box launcher in the bottom-right corner of the group. This means that there are additional commands available for the group. Clicking the launcher opens the dialog box, or it may open a task pane, which, like a dialog box, houses additional commands related to the group.

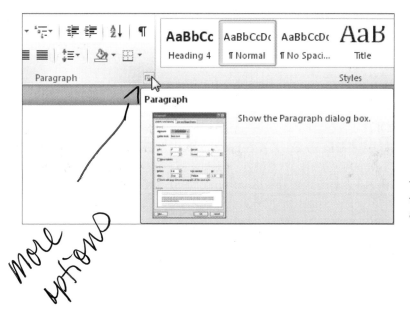

(handwritten) more options

(handwritten) tells you you're in a sub-tab

The dialog box launcher displays the dialog box or task pane available for a given command.

Live Preview with Galleries

Live Preview shows what a formatting change looks like without actually applying the format. In the following example, selecting a block of text, and then hovering the mouse pointer over a font in the font gallery, previews how the text will look. Clicking the font name applies the font to the text.

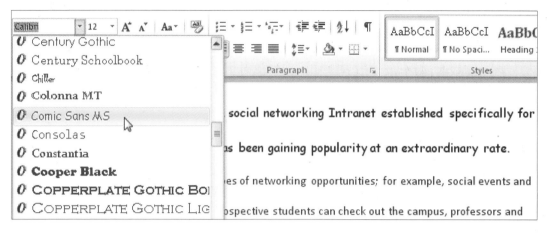

Live Preview of the Comic Sans MS Font

Hide the Ribbon

FROM THE KEYBOARD

Ctrl + F1 to hide/unhide the Ribbon

If you want more room to work, you can temporarily hide the Ribbon by double-clicking the active tab. This collapses the Ribbon, as shown in the following illustration.

Clicking a tab, such as Home, redisplays the full Ribbon temporarily. It collapses again when you click in the document. If you want the Ribbon to remain open, double-click the same tab you used to collapse it, or right-click on the Ribbon and choose Minimize the Ribbon to turn off the feature.

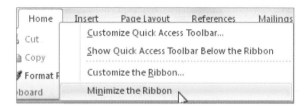

Customize the Ribbon

The Ribbon can now be customized, making it easier for you to have access to the commands that you use frequently all under one tab, if you like. You can add new groups to existing tabs or add new tabs with their own groups and commands. You can always restore the original Ribbon tabs, groups, and commands very easily.

You cannot add new commands to an existing group on the original Ribbon.

When you choose to add a new tab to the Ribbon, the new tab appears on the right of the active tab; however, you can move it at any time. The new tab includes an empty new group, ready for you to add commands to it. You use the Move Up and Move Down arrows in the Word Options dialog box to reposition existing tabs and groups.

Move Up and Move Down arrows

DEVELOP YOUR SKILLS 4.4.1
Work with the Ribbon

In this exercise, you will explore the various aspects of the Ribbon, including tabs, contextual tabs, the dialog box launcher, and Live Preview. Finally, you'll hide and unhide the Ribbon, and learn how to customize it.

Display the Insert Tab

1. Click the **Insert** tab on the Ribbon to display the commands available in that category.

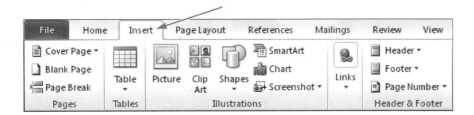

2. Take a moment to investigate some of the other tabs on the Ribbon, and then return to the **Home** tab.

Display Contextual Tabs and Use the Dialog Box Launcher

3. **Double-click** the clip art object at the top of your document to display Picture Tools on the Ribbon then **click** anywhere in the document to deselect the clip art.

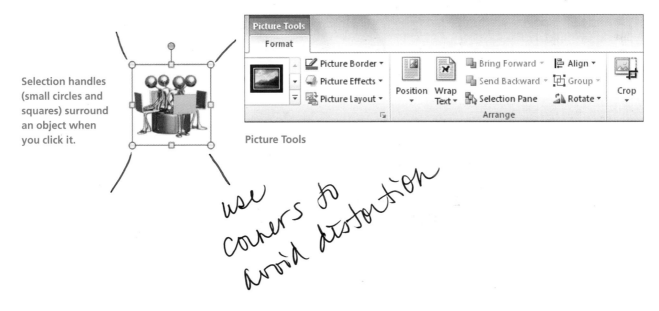

Selection handles (small circles and squares) surround an object when you click it.

Picture Tools

use corners to avoid distortion

4. Return to the **Home** tab, and hover the **mouse pointer** over the dialog box launcher in the bottom-right corner of the Font group to display the ToolTip, as shown here.

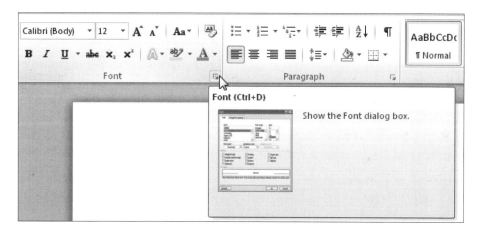

5. Click the **dialog box launcher** to open the Font dialog box.

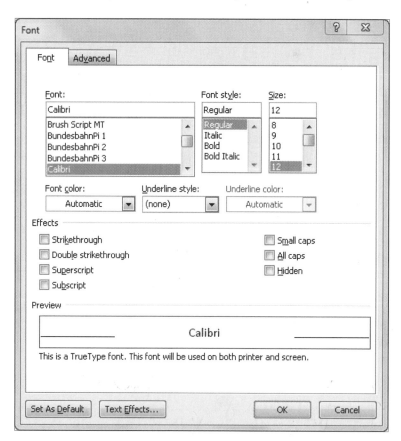

This dialog box provides additional tools for formatting text.

6. Click the **Cancel** button in the bottom-right corner to close the dialog box.

7. Position the **mouse pointer** in the white, left margin area of the second paragraph. Then, **double-click** the left mouse button to select (highlight) the entire paragraph, as shown here.
If you notice a little toolbar fade in, you can ignore it for now. It will fade away on its own.

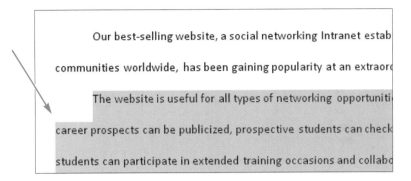

8. Follow these steps to use Live Preview:

Ⓐ Click the drop-down arrow on the **Font** list.

Ⓑ With the mouse pointer, drag the **scroll box** up to the top of the scroll bar, if necessary.

Ⓒ Slide the mouse pointer onto **Arial Black**.

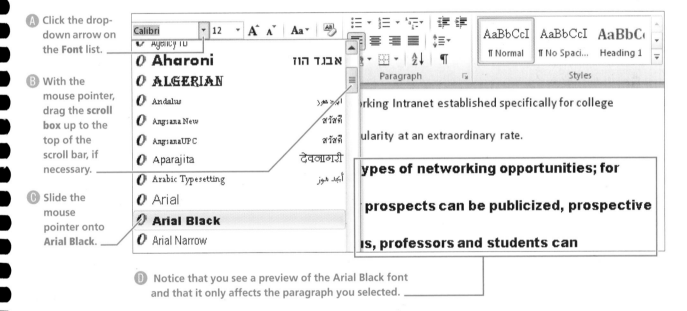

Ⓓ Notice that you see a preview of the Arial Black font and that it only affects the paragraph you selected.

9. Take a moment to **preview** a few other fonts.

10. **Click** anywhere in the document to close the font list, and **click** once again to deselect the highlighted text.

Hide/Unhide the Ribbon

11. **Double-click** the Home tab to hide the Ribbon.

12. **Right-click** the collapsed Ribbon and choose **Minimize the Ribbon** from the menu to turn off the feature.

Add a New Tab to the Ribbon

13. **Right-click** the Home tab and then choose **Customize the Ribbon**.

14. Follow these steps to add a new tab to the Ribbon:

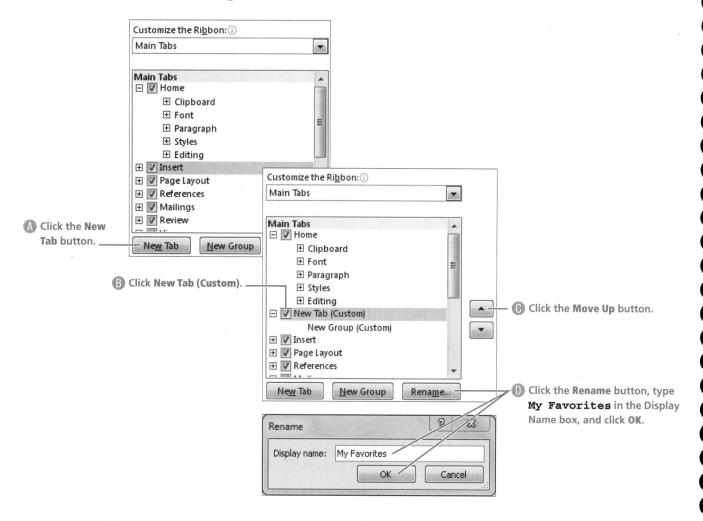

Ⓐ Click the **New Tab** button.

Ⓑ Click **New Tab (Custom)**.

Ⓒ Click the **Move Up** button.

Ⓓ Click the **Rename** button, type **My Favorites** in the Display Name box, and click **OK**.

Notice when you create a new tab, it automatically includes a new group for you to customize with commands.

15. Click **OK** again in the Word Options dialog box, and then click the new **My Favorites** tab. *Notice the new tab is to the left of the Home tab, there are currently no commands on the new tab, and there is a blank New Group awaiting commands to be added to it.*

Add a New Group to the My Favorites Tab

16. **Right-click** the My Favorites tab and choose **Customize the Ribbon**.

17. Follow these steps to add a new group:

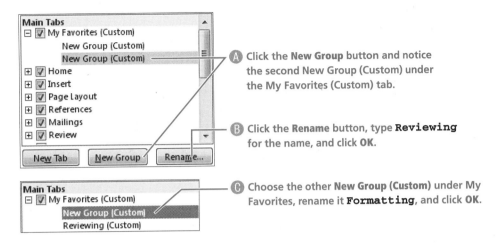

A Click the **New Group** button and notice the second New Group (Custom) under the My Favorites (Custom) tab.

B Click the **Rename** button, type **Reviewing** for the name, and click **OK**.

C Choose the other **New Group (Custom)** under My Favorites, rename it **Formatting**, and click **OK**.

Leave the Word Options box open so you can add commands to your new groups.

Add Commands to Custom Groups

18. If necessary, click the **Formatting (Custom)** group.

19. Follow these steps to add commands to the group:

A Click **Font** in the Popular Commands list on the left.

B Click the **Add>>** button in the middle to copy the command into the Formatting group.

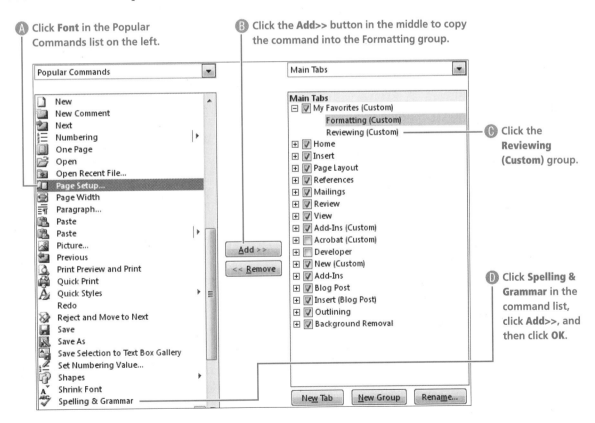

C Click the **Reviewing (Custom)** group.

D Click **Spelling & Grammar** in the command list, click **Add>>**, and then click **OK**.

Notice the Ribbon now has a new tab named My Favorites that contains two new groups, Formatting and Reviewing, each containing one command.

20. Right-click the Home Ribbon tab and choose **Customize the Ribbon**.

21. Follow these steps to delete the tab, groups, and commands you made earlier:

Ⓐ Click the **Reset** button.

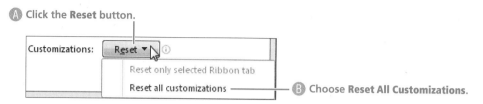

Ⓑ Choose **Reset All Customizations**.

22. Click **Yes** in the message box confirming the action, and then click **OK**.

The Quick Access Toolbar

Video Lesson   labyrinthelab.com/videos

The Quick Access toolbar in the upper-left corner of the screen contains frequently used commands. It is customizable and operates independently from the Ribbon.

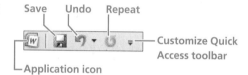

Moving the Quick Access Toolbar

You can place the Quick Access toolbar in one of two positions on the screen. The default position is in the upper-left corner. Clicking the Customize Quick Access toolbar button at the right edge of the toolbar reveals a menu from which you can choose Show Below the Ribbon.

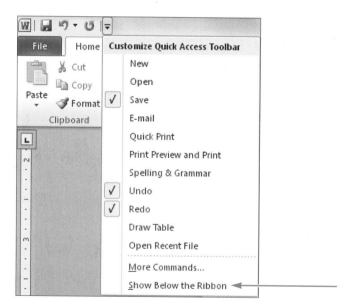

The Customize Quick Access Toolbar menu conveniently lists a series of frequently used commands that you can add to the toolbar by choosing them from the menu.

Customizing the Quick Access Toolbar

You can add buttons to and remove them from the Quick Access toolbar to suit your needs. You might want to add commands you use regularly so they are always available.

Right-click the Ribbon command you want to add (Center in this example), and choose Add to Quick Access Toolbar from the shortcut menu.

The terms shortcut, context, pop-up, and drop-down are used interchangeably when referring to a secondary menu that appears.

To remove a button from the Quick Access toolbar, right-click the button and choose Remove from Quick Access Toolbar from the shortcut menu.

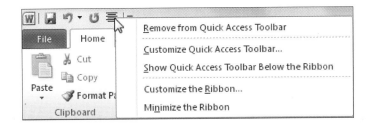

QUICK REFERENCE	WORKING WITH THE QUICK ACCESS TOOLBAR
Task	**Procedure**
Add a button to the toolbar	■ Right-click the button you want to add. ■ Choose Add to Quick Access Toolbar from the menu.
Remove a button from the toolbar	■ Right-click the button you want to remove. ■ Choose Remove from Quick Access Toolbar from the shortcut menu.
Change the location of the toolbar	■ Click the Customize Quick Access Toolbar button at the right edge of the toolbar. ■ Choose Show Below (or Above) the Ribbon.

Work with the Quick Access Toolbar

In this exercise, you will reposition the Quick Access toolbar, and then you will customize it by adding and removing buttons.

Change the Quick Access Toolbar Location

1. Follow these steps to move the Quick Access toolbar below the Ribbon:

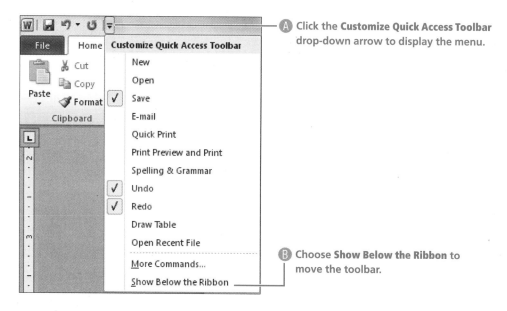

Ⓐ Click the **Customize Quick Access Toolbar** drop-down arrow to display the menu.

Ⓑ Choose **Show Below the Ribbon** to move the toolbar.

The toolbar appears below the Ribbon at the left edge of the window. Now you will return it to its original position.

2. Click the **drop-down arrow** at the right edge of the Quick Access toolbar again, and this time choose **Show Above the Ribbon**.

Add a Button to the Quick Access Toolbar

3. Make sure that the **Home** tab is in the foreground, and then follow these steps to add the Bullets button to the toolbar:

Ⓐ **Right-click** the Bullets button in the Paragraph group to display the shortcut menu.

Ⓑ Choose **Add to Quick Access Toolbar.**

The Bullets button now appears on the toolbar.

4. **Right-click** the Bullets 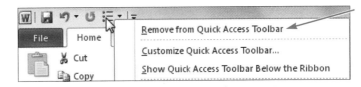 button on the Quick Access toolbar and choose the **Remove from Quick Access Toolbar** command.

The button disappears from the Quick Access toolbar.

The Mini Toolbar

| Video Lesson | labyrinthelab.com/videos |

There's another toolbar in Word, and it contains frequently used formatting commands. When you select (highlight) text, the Mini toolbar fades in. After a pause, it fades away. Make it reappear by right-clicking the selected text.

In the following example, clicking the Bold **B** button on the Mini toolbar applies the Bold feature to the selected text.

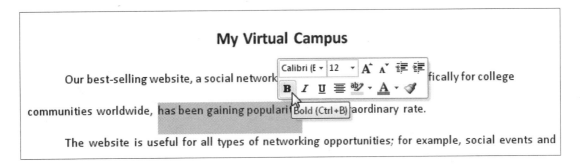

DEVELOP YOUR SKILLS 4.4.3

Use the Mini Toolbar

In this exercise, you will use the Mini toolbar to format text.

1. Follow these steps to italicize a paragraph:

Ⓐ Position the **mouse pointer** in the white margin to the left of the first paragraph and then **double-click** to select (highlight) the paragraph.

Ⓑ When the Mini toolbar fades in, click the **Italic** button.

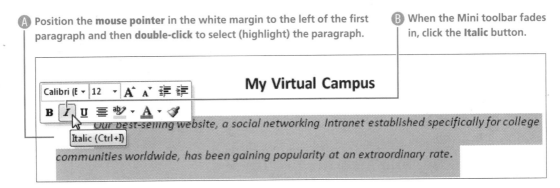

If this timid little toolbar disappears, right-click the highlighted text and it will reappear.

Microsoft Word

2. **Click** anywhere in the document to deselect the text and view the formatted paragraph.

3. Select the **first paragraph** again and click the **Italic** button to remove the formatting.

4.5 Navigating in a Word Document

Video Lesson   labyrinthelab.com/videos

If you are working in a multipage document, it is helpful to know about various techniques for moving through a document. You can navigate using the scroll bar located at the right side of the screen, or you can use keystrokes.

Navigating with the Scroll Bar

The scroll bar lets you browse through documents; however, it does not move the insertion point. After scrolling, you must click in the document where you want to reposition the insertion point. The following illustration shows the components of the scroll bar.

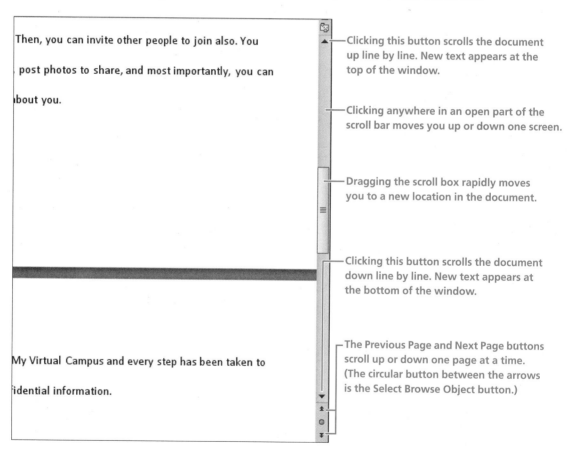

Then, you can invite other people to join also. You

post photos to share, and most importantly, you can

about you.

Clicking this button scrolls the document up line by line. New text appears at the top of the window.

Clicking anywhere in an open part of the scroll bar moves you up or down one screen.

Dragging the scroll box rapidly moves you to a new location in the document.

Clicking this button scrolls the document down line by line. New text appears at the bottom of the window.

My Virtual Campus and every step has been taken to

idential information.

The Previous Page and Next Page buttons scroll up or down one page at a time. (The circular button between the arrows is the Select Browse Object button.)

Positioning the Insertion Point

When the mouse pointer is in a text area, it resembles an uppercase "I" and it is referred to as an I-beam. The insertion point is positioned at the location where you click the I-beam and it begins flashing. Thus, wherever the insertion point is flashing, that is where the action begins.

Practice Scrolling and Positioning the Insertion Point

In this exercise, you will use the scroll bar to practice moving through a document, and then you will position the insertion point.

Scroll in the Document

1. Follow these steps to scroll in the document:

A Click the **Scroll Down** button five times, and notice that you move down the document, but the flashing insertion point does not move.

B Click the **Scroll Up** button five times to move in the other direction. Notice that you move up in the document, but the flashing insertion point still does not move.

2. Position the **I-beam** I mouse pointer in the body of the document.
Notice that while the mouse pointer looks like an I-beam when it's inside the document, it looks like a white arrow when it is in the document's left margin. The pointer must have the I-beam shape before you can reposition the insertion point.

Position the Insertion Point

3. Click the **I-beam** I anywhere in the document to position the blinking insertion point.

4. Move the **mouse pointer** into the left margin area. The white arrow shape is now visible.

5. Position the **I-beam** I in the first line of the body of the document, and click the **left** mouse button.
The insertion point appears just where you clicked. If the background is highlighted, you accidentally selected the text. Deselect by clicking the mouse pointer in the document background.

6. Click the open part of the **scroll bar** below the scroll box to move down one screen, as shown in the illustration to the right.

Use the Scroll Box and the Next Page/Previous Page Buttons

7. Drag the **scroll box** to the bottom of the scroll bar with the mouse pointer.
Notice that the insertion point is not blinking anywhere on the screen because all you have done is scroll through the document. You have not repositioned the insertion point yet.

8. Click any open part of the **scroll bar** above the scroll box, then click the **I-beam** I at the end of the text to position the insertion point on the last page.

9. Drag the **scroll box** to the top of the scroll bar, and click the **I-beam** I in front of the first word of the first paragraph.

10. Click the **Next Page** ⧨ button to move to the top of page 2.

    The insertion point moves with you when you use the Next Page and Previous Page buttons.

11. Click the **Previous Page** ⧨ button to move to the top of page 1.

Navigating with the Keyboard

Video Lesson   labyrinthelab.com/videos

Whether you use the mouse or the keyboard to navigate through a document is a matter of personal preference. Navigating with the keyboard always moves the insertion point, so it will be with you when you arrive at your destination.

The following Quick Reference table provides keystrokes for moving quickly through a document.

QUICK REFERENCE	NAVIGATING WITH THE KEYBOARD		
Press	**To Move**	**Press**	**To Move**
→	One character to the right	Page Down	Down one screen
←	One character to the left	Page Up	Up one screen
Ctrl + →	One word to the right	Ctrl + End	To the end of the document
Ctrl + ←	One word to the left	Ctrl + Home	To the beginning of the document
↓	Down one line	End	To the end of the line
↑	Up one line	Home	To the beginning of the line

DEVELOP YOUR SKILLS 4.5.2
Use the Keyboard to Navigate

In this exercise, you will use the keyboard to practice moving through a document.

Use the Arrow Keys

1. Click the **I-beam** I in the middle of the first line of the first paragraph.

2. Tap the **right arrow** → and **left arrow** ← keys three times to move to the right and left, one character at a time.

3. Tap the **down arrow** ↓ and **up arrow** ↑ keys three times to move down and then up, one row at a time.

Use Additional Keys

4. **Hold down** the Ctrl key and keep it down, then **tap** the Home key to move the insertion point to the beginning of the document. **Release** the Ctrl key.

5. Use the **arrow keys** to position the insertion point in the middle of the first line of the first paragraph.

6. **Hold down** the Ctrl key and keep it down, then tap the **left arrow** ← key three times to move to the left, one word at a time. **Release** the Ctrl key.

7. **Hold down** the `Ctrl` key and keep it down, then tap the **right arrow** `→` key three times to move to the right, one word at a time. **Release** the `Ctrl` key.

8. **Tap** the `Home` key to move to the beginning of the line.

9. **Tap** the `End` key to move to the end of the line.

10. Spend a few moments **navigating** with the keyboard. Refer to the preceding Quick Reference table for some additional keystrokes.

11. **Hold down** the `Ctrl` key then **tap** the `End` key to move the insertion point to the end of the document. **Release** the `Ctrl` key.

12. Move the **insertion point** back to the beginning of the document.

4.6 Closing Documents

Video Lesson   labyrinthelab.com/videos

You close a file by clicking the [File] tab and choosing the Close command from the menu. If you haven't saved your document, Word will prompt you to do so.

DEVELOP YOUR SKILLS 4.6.1
Close the Document

In this exercise, you will close a file.

1. **Click** the [File] tab, and then choose **Close** from the menu.

2. If Word asks you if you want to save the changes, click **Don't Save**.

3. If a blank document is open on the screen, use the same technique to **close** it.
The document window always has this appearance when all documents are closed.

4.7 Starting a New, Blank Document

Video Lesson labyrinthelab.com/videos

FROM THE KEYBOARD

Ctrl+N to start a new document

You can click the [File] tab, and then choose the New command from the menu to open a new, blank document.

DEVELOP YOUR SKILLS 4.7.1
Start a New Document

In this exercise, you will open a new, blank document. There should not be any documents in the Word window at this time.

1. **Click** the [File] tab, and then choose **New** from the menu.

2. When the New Document dialog box appears, **double-click** the Blank Document icon to display the new document.
   Now you will close the new document and try using the shortcut keystrokes to start another new document.

3. **Click** the [File] tab, and then choose **Close** from the menu.

4. **Hold down** the Ctrl key and **tap** the N on your keyboard to open a new document.

5. Leave this document **open**.

4.8 Getting Help in Word 2010

Video Lesson labyrinthelab.com/videos

The Microsoft Word Help button appears in the upper-right corner of the Word screen. Clicking the Help button opens the Word Help window where you can browse through a Table of Contents, click links to access a variety of topics, or type a term in the search box and let the system find the answer for you.

Use Word Help

In this exercise you will practice working with several Help techniques.

1. Click the **Help** button in the upper-right corner of the Word window.

2. Follow these steps for an overview of Word Help:

A Some of these toolbar buttons are like ones you may already be familiar with from using a web browser. Click the **mouse pointer** on the top frame of the Word Help window to activate it, and then **hover** the mouse pointer over buttons to see **ToolTips** describing their purpose. The Table of Contents is not visible the first time you use Help; however, you can use the Table of Contents button to display it.

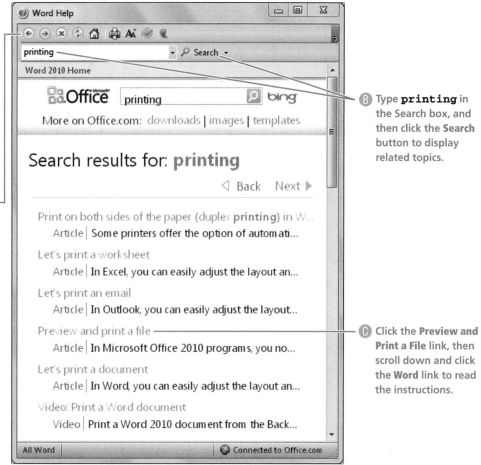

B Type **printing** in the Search box, and then click the **Search** button to display related topics.

C Click the **Preview and Print a File** link, then scroll down and click the **Word** link to read the instructions.

3. Click the **Close** button in the upper-right corner of the Word Help window.

4.9 Exiting from Word

Video Lesson   labyrinthelab.com/videos

Clicking the [File] tab and then clicking the [X Exit] button closes the Word application. It's important to exit Word in an orderly fashion. Turning off your computer before exiting Word could cause you to lose data.

You can also use the Close button in the upper-right corner of the window to close Word.

DEVELOP YOUR SKILLS 4.9.1
Exit from Word

In this exercise, you will exit from Word. Since the blank document on the screen has not been modified, you won't bother saving it.

1. **Click** the [File] tab.
2. **Click** the [X Exit] button at the bottom of the list.
3. When Word prompts you to save changes, click **Don't Save**.
   Word closes and the Windows Desktop appears.

4.10 Concepts Review

Concepts Review   labyrinthelab.com/ob10

To check your knowledge of the key concepts introduced in this lesson, complete the Concepts Review quiz by going to the URL listed above. If your classroom is using Labyrinth eLab, you may complete the Concepts Review quiz from within your eLab course.

Reinforce Your Skills

Use Word Help

In this exercise, you will work with the Word Help window to find information that can assist you as you work.

1. Click the **Microsoft Word Help** button in the upper-right corner of the Word window.

Use the Browse Word Help Window

Now you'll review opening a file in another file format.

2. Click the **File Migration** link; then scroll down and click the **Use Word to Open or Save a File in Another File Format** link and read the topic.

3. Scroll up and click the **Word 2010 Home** link at the top of the pane to return to the Browse Word Help pane.

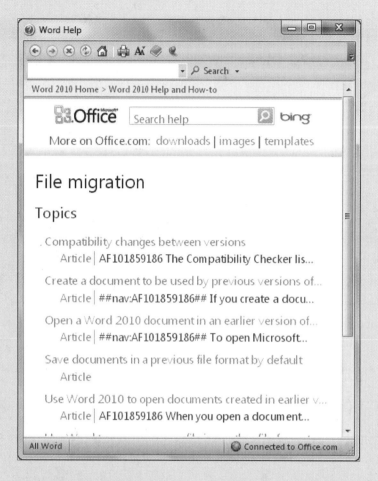

4. Click the **Creating Documents** link in the Word Help window.

5. Click the **Create a Document** link.

6. **Scroll down** to see the major topics that are covered.

Search for Help

7. Follow these steps to locate the Set the Default Font topic:

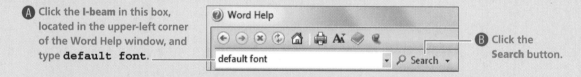

Ⓐ Click the **I-beam** in this box, located in the upper-left corner of the Word Help window, and type **default font**.

Ⓑ Click the **Search** button.

8. Click the **Set the Default Font** link in the Word Help window to view the topic.

9. **Scroll down** and take a moment to read the first few entries.

10. Click the **Close** X button in the upper-right corner of the Word Help window.

REINFORCE YOUR SKILLS 4.2

Navigate in a Document

In this exercise, you will use a letter that an exchange student in Paris wrote to his friend. It's a long letter, so it will provide good practice for navigating.

1. **Click** the **File** tab and choose **Open** from the menu.

2. When the Open dialog box appears, if necessary, **navigate** to your file storage location and **open** the Lesson 04 folder.

3. **Double-click** to open the file named rs-Exchange Student.

Navigate with the Scroll Bar

4. Click the **Next Page** ⯯ button at the bottom of the scroll bar to move to the top of page 2.

5. Click the **scroll bar** below the scroll box to move down one screen.

6. Drag the **scroll box** to the top of the scroll bar, and **click** for an insertion point at the beginning of the document.

7. Click the **Scroll Down** ⯯ button, and hold the mouse button down to scroll quickly through the document.

8. Click the **Previous Page** ⯭ button enough times to return to the top of the document.

Navigate with the Keyboard

9. Tap the **down arrow** ⬇ key twice to move to the beginning of the first paragraph.

10. **Tap** the End key to move the insertion point to the end of the line.

11. **Tap** the Home key to move to the beginning of the line.

12. **Tap** Ctrl + End to place the insertion point at the end of the document.

13. **Tap** Ctrl + Home to move to the top of the document.

14. If you press and hold the arrow keys, the insertion point moves quickly through the document. **Press and hold** the ⬇ key long enough to move to the beginning of the second paragraph.

15. **Hold down** the Ctrl key and **tap** the → key three times to move to the right, one word at a time.

16. Please leave this document **open** for the next exercise.

Work with the Quick Access Toolbar

In this exercise, you will move the Quick Access toolbar below the Ribbon, and you will customize the toolbar by adding a button to it.

Before You Begin: The rs-Exchange Student document should be open in Word.

1. Follow these steps to move the Quick Access toolbar:

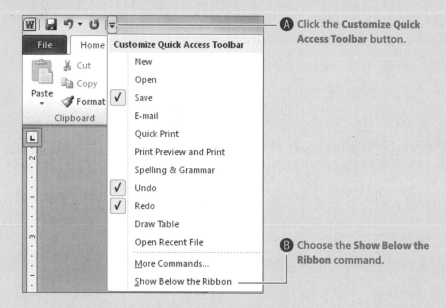

Ⓐ Click the **Customize Quick Access Toolbar** button.

Ⓑ Choose the **Show Below the Ribbon** command.

Now you will return the toolbar to its original position.

2. Click the **drop-down arrow** at the right edge of the toolbar, and choose **Show Above the Ribbon** from the menu.
   Next you'll add a button to the Quick Access toolbar.

3. Make sure you're on the **Home** tab. If not, **click** the tab to bring it to the foreground.

4. Follow these steps to add the **Clear Formatting** button to the toolbar:

Ⓐ **Right-click** the Clear Formatting button in the Font group.

Ⓑ Choose **Add to Quick Access Toolbar** from the menu.

The button now appears on the toolbar.

5. Ask your instructor to inspect your work and initial here to verify the placement of the Clear Formatting button on the toolbar. _____

Next you will remove the button you just added to the toolbar.

6. Place the mouse pointer over the **Clear Formatting** button on the Quick Access toolbar and click the **right** mouse button.

7. Choose **Remove from Quick Access Toolbar** from the menu.

8. Please leave this document **open** for the next exercise.

Microsoft Word

Apply Your Skills

Use Help to Learn About Print Preview

In this exercise, you will explore Help to learn how to preview a document before printing it.

Before You Begin: The rs-Exchange Student document should be open in Word.

1. Use Help's **Search** feature to locate information about Print Preview.

2. Open the **Print Preview** window by following the instructions in the Help window.

3. Practice using the commands in the **Zoom** group on the Ribbon to view your document in various magnifications.

4. Zoom your document to **250%**, and then ask your instructor to verify the zoom magnification and initial this step. _____

5. **Close** Print Preview, and leave this document **open** for the next exercise.

6. **Close** the Help window.

Ribbon Terminology

In this exercise, you will review terminology relating to the Ribbon. Feel free to refer back in this lesson or to use Word's Help feature to find the correct terms.

1. List the names of the tabs on the Ribbon.

_____

_____

_____

_____

_____

_____

_____

2. List three commands in the Paragraph group of the Home tab.

_____

_____

_____

3. Define contextual tabs.

_____

_____

4. Ask your instructor to verify your answers and initial this exercise. _____

5. Leave the rs-Exchange Student document open for the next exercise.

Customize the Ribbon

In this exercise, you will customize the Ribbon by adding a new tab and group.

1. Add a new **tab** named **Favorites** with a new **group** named **Formatting**.

2. Place the Favorites tab between the **Home** and **Insert** tabs on the Ribbon.

3. Place three **formatting commands** to the new Formatting group.

4. **Restore** all Ribbon defaults by removing any customizations.

5. **Close** the rs-Exchange Student document. If you are prompted to save, do not.

Microsoft Word

Critical Thinking & Work-Readiness Skills

In the course of working through the following Microsoft Office-based Critical Thinking exercises, you will also be utilizing various work-readiness skills, some of which are listed next to each exercise. Go to labyrinthelab.com/ workreadiness *to learn more about the work-readiness skills.*

4.1 Use Help

Elise Ferrer, one of My Virtual Campus' tech support specialists, has been asked to help with the company's migration from Office 2007 to Office 2010. She decides to provide a "cheat sheet" of online help tutorials to aid the employees using Word. Start Word, create a new, blank document, and use Word's Help feature to locate five basic topics for this purpose. Use a sheet of notebook paper and a pen to record the five links to the online help topics you found.

WORK-READINESS SKILLS APPLIED

- Acquiring and evaluating information
- Thinking creatively
- Knowing how to learn

4.2 Customize the Ribbon

To help the employees in the marketing department work more efficiently, Elise customizes their Ribbons by adding a custom tab. Create a new tab in Word called **Marketing** and position it before the Home tab. Create a group in the custom tab named **Marketing Tasks**. Add five commands to the Marketing Tasks group that you think might be useful for someone working in a marketing department (they will be opening, editing, and formatting documents, in addition to inserting pictures). On a sheet of notebook paper, write down the five commands you selected and explain why you think those particular commands would be helpful for someone in the marketing department. Reset the Ribbon to its default setting when you are finished.

WORK-READINESS SKILLS APPLIED

- Solving problems
- Thinking creatively
- Showing responsibility

4.3 Customize the Interface

Elise decides to customize the Word interface of her own computer to help her work more efficiently. Practice minimizing and maximizing the Ribbon. Display the Quick Access toolbar both above and below the Ribbon. Add or remove buttons from the Quick Access toolbar. On a sheet of notebook paper, draw a simple sketch of your preferred settings for the Ribbon and Quick Access toolbar. If applicable, exchange papers with a partner and configure your Word interface according to your partner's sketch. Reset the Ribbon and Quick Access toolbar to their default states when you are finished.

WORK-READINESS SKILLS APPLIED

- Managing the self
- Showing responsibility
- Participating as a member of a team

Creating and Editing Business Letters

In this lesson, you will create business letters while learning proper business document formatting. You will also learn fundamental techniques of entering and editing text, copying and moving text, and saving and printing documents. In addition, you will learn to use Word's AutoCorrect tool to insert frequently used text and control automatic formatting that is applied as you type.

LESSON OUTLINE

LEARNING OBJECTIVES

After studying this lesson, you will be able to:

- Type a professional business letter
- Save a document
- Select and edit text
- Use the AutoCorrect feature
- Set AutoFormat as You Type options
- Copy and move text
- Set Page Layout options
- Preview a document

Student Resources   labyrinthelab.com/ob10

Taking Care with Business Letters

My Virtual Campus

Rob Maloney just landed his job as a customer service representative in the Sales Department at My Virtual Campus. He is working for the sales manager, Bruce Carter. A new prospect, Richmond University, has expressed interest in the networking website that My Virtual Campus sells. Mr. Carter has asked Rob to prepare a standard letter for potential new clients, thanking them for their interest and providing information about the website.

Rob starts by referring to his business writing class textbook to ensure that he formats the letter correctly for a good first impression and a professional appearance.

November 24, 2012

Ms. Paige Daniels
Richmond University
15751 Meadow Lane
Chester Allen, VA 23333

Dear Ms. Daniels:

Travis Mayfield referred you to us after he spoke to you about our extraordinary product. I want to take this opportunity to personally thank you for considering My Virtual Campus' social-networking website for your institution. As Travis may have mentioned, we pride ourselves in providing the latest in technology as well as excellent customer service with satisfaction guaranteed.

Enclosed you will find information to review regarding the features of the website. After reading the material, please contact our sales manager, Bruce Carter, at your earliest convenience to discuss your options. Thank you again for considering our amazing website.

Sincerely,

Rob Maloney
Customer Service Representative
Sales Department

rm
Enclosures (2)
cc: Bruce Carter

5.1 Defining Typical Business Letter Styles

Video Lesson labyrinthelab.com/videos

There are several acceptable styles of business letters. The styles discussed in this text include block, modified block standard format, and modified block indented paragraphs. All business letters contain the same or similar elements, but with varied formatting. The following styles are described in this section:

- Block Style
- Modified Block Style—Standard Format
- Modified Block Style—Indented Paragraphs

Block Style

The following illustration outlines the parts of the block style business letter.

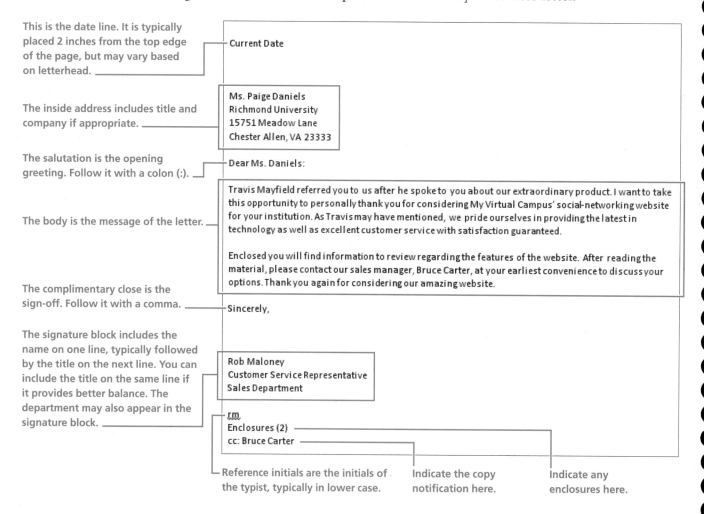

This is the date line. It is typically placed 2 inches from the top edge of the page, but may vary based on letterhead.

Current Date

The inside address includes title and company if appropriate.

Ms. Paige Daniels
Richmond University
15751 Meadow Lane
Chester Allen, VA 23333

The salutation is the opening greeting. Follow it with a colon (:).

Dear Ms. Daniels:

The body is the message of the letter.

Travis Mayfield referred you to us after he spoke to you about our extraordinary product. I want to take this opportunity to personally thank you for considering My Virtual Campus' social-networking website for your institution. As Travis may have mentioned, we pride ourselves in providing the latest in technology as well as excellent customer service with satisfaction guaranteed.

Enclosed you will find information to review regarding the features of the website. After reading the material, please contact our sales manager, Bruce Carter, at your earliest convenience to discuss your options. Thank you again for considering our amazing website.

The complimentary close is the sign-off. Follow it with a comma.

Sincerely,

The signature block includes the name on one line, typically followed by the title on the next line. You can include the title on the same line if it provides better balance. The department may also appear in the signature block.

Rob Maloney
Customer Service Representative
Sales Department

rm
Enclosures (2)
cc: Bruce Carter

Reference initials are the initials of the typist, typically in lower case.

Indicate the copy notification here.

Indicate any enclosures here.

Modified Block Style—Standard Format

The following illustration outlines the differences in the standard modified block style business letter from the block style business letter.

The date line, the complimentary close, and the signature block begin at the 3 ½ inch mark on the ruler. All other lines begin at the left margin.

November 24, 2012   ⊘ 3

Ms. Paige Daniels
Richmond University
15751 Meadow Lane
Chester Allen, VA 23333

Dear Ms. Daniels:

Travis Mayfield referred you to us after he spoke to you about our extraordinary product. I want to take this opportunity to personally thank you for considering My Virtual Campus' social-networking website for your institution. As Travis may have mentioned, we pride ourselves in providing the latest in technology as well as excellent customer service with satisfaction guaranteed.

Enclosed you will find information to review regarding the features of the website. After reading the material, please contact our sales manager, Bruce Carter, at your earliest convenience to discuss your options. Thank you again for considering our amazing website.

Sincerely,

Rob Maloney
Customer Service Representative
Sales Department

rm
Enclosures (2)
cc: Bruce Carter

Modified Block Style—Indented Paragraphs

The following illustration shows the modified block style business letter with indented paragraphs.

In this format, the first lines of the body paragraphs are indented one-half inch.

November 24, 2012

Ms. Paige Daniels
Richmond University
15751 Meadow Lane
Chester Allen, VA 23333

Dear Ms. Daniels:

    Travis Mayfield referred you to us after he spoke to you about our extraordinary product. I want to take this opportunity to personally thank you for considering My Virtual Campus' social-networking website for your institution. As Travis may have mentioned, we pride ourselves in providing the latest in technology as well as excellent customer service with satisfaction guaranteed.

    Enclosed you will find information to review regarding the features of the website. After reading the material, please contact our sales manager, Bruce Carter, at your earliest convenience to discuss your options. Thank you again for considering our amazing website.

Sincerely,

Rob Maloney
Customer Service Representative
Sales Department

rm
Enclosures (2)
cc: Bruce Carter

5.2 Inserting Text

Video Lesson   labyrinthelab.com/videos

You always insert text into a Word document at the flashing insertion point. Therefore, you must position the insertion point at the desired location before typing.

AutoComplete

Word's AutoComplete feature does some of your typing for you. It recognizes certain words and phrases, such as names of months and names of days, and offers to complete them for you, as shown here.

As you begin typing the month November, AutoComplete offers to finish typing it out.

 AutoComplete does not offer to complete the months March through July.

You accept AutoComplete suggestions by tapping ⌈Enter⌋. If you choose to ignore the suggestion, just keep typing, and the suggestion will disappear.

Using the Enter Key

You use ⌈Enter⌋ to begin a new paragraph or to insert blank lines in a document. Word considers anything that ends by tapping ⌈Enter⌋ to be a paragraph. Thus, short lines such as a date line, an inside address, or even blank lines themselves are considered paragraphs.

Tapping ⌈Enter⌋ inserts a paragraph ¶ symbol in a document. These symbols are visible when you display formatting marks.

Showing Formatting Marks

The Show/Hide ¶ button in the Paragraph group of the Home tab shows or hides formatting marks. Although they appear on the screen, you will not see them in the printed document. Marks include dots representing spaces between words, paragraph symbols that appear when you tap ⌈Enter⌋, and arrows that represent tabs.

Viewing these characters can be important when editing a document. You may need to see the nonprinting characters to determine whether the space between two words was created with the ⌈Spacebar⌋ or ⌈Tab⌋. The following illustrations show the location of the Show/Hide button and the characters that appear when you tap the ⌈Spacebar⌋, the ⌈Enter⌋ key, or the ⌈Tab⌋ key.

Show/Hide button ———

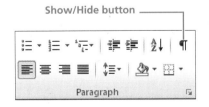

Paragraph

These symbols are paragraph marks. They appear whenever you tap ⌈Enter⌋. ——

The dots between words are inserted when you tap the ⌈Spacebar⌋. ——

Tabs are represented by small arrows. ———

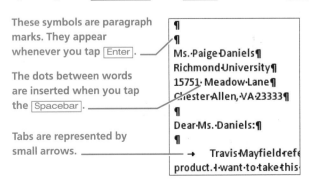

Microsoft Word

Spacing in Letters

In Word 2007, new default line spacing was introduced. This change adjusted the default line spacing to 1.15 rather than the standard single spacing and added an extra 10 points (a little more than an eighth of an inch) at the end of paragraphs. Therefore, rather that tapping Enter twice at the end of a paragraph, you just tap Enter once, and Word adds the extra spacing.

Apply Traditional Spacing Using the Line Spacing Button

When writing letters, a traditional, more compact look (without the additional spacing) is still considered appropriate. Therefore, when you begin a letter, you may wish to switch to single (1.0) spacing and remove the extra space after paragraphs by choosing the options shown in the following figure.

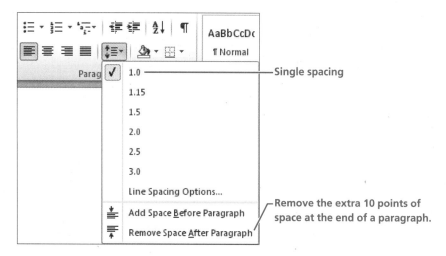

Apply these settings when you wish to type a more compact, traditional letter.

Apply Traditional Spacing Using the No Spacing Style

An alternative to using the Line Spacing button to achieve traditional spacing is to apply the No Spacing style located in the Styles group of the Home tab on the Ribbon, as shown here.

When you begin a new document, click the No Spacing icon on the Ribbon to achieve traditional spacing.

The exercises in this lesson use the Line Spacing button to set traditional spacing; however, feel free to use this alternate method instead if you prefer.

Word Wrap

If you continue typing after the insertion point reaches the end of a line, Word automatically wraps the insertion point to the beginning of the next line. If you let Word Wrap format your paragraph initially, the paragraph will also reformat correctly as you insert or delete text.

Creating an Envelope

Microsoft Word is very smart and versatile when it comes to creating envelopes. For example, when you type a business letter with the recipient's name and address at the top of it, Word recognizes this as the delivery address. Word also gives you two options: print the address directly onto the envelope or insert the envelope at the top of the document in a separate section. The latter option means you can open the letter at any time and the envelope is there, ready for you to print it.

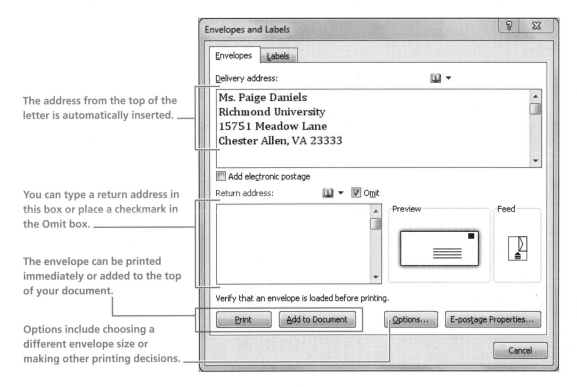

The address from the top of the letter is automatically inserted.

You can type a return address in this box or place a checkmark in the Omit box.

The envelope can be printed immediately or added to the top of your document.

Options include choosing a different envelope size or making other printing decisions.

Return Address

The Envelopes and Labels dialog box allows you to type a return address and keep it as the default. If you don't want the default return address to print on the envelope, you must ensure the Omit checkbox is unchecked in the dialog box.

If a default return address has not been established or the Return Address box is empty, clicking the Omit checkbox is not necessary. By default, the Omit checkbox is already checked.

Place a checkmark here if you have preprinted return address envelopes or labels.

When you enter a return address, you will be prompted to save it as the default so you don't have to type it each time you create an envelope.

Type a Letter and an Envelope

In this exercise, you will display formatting marks, adjust spacing, use AutoComplete, work with the [Enter] *key, and let Word Wrap do its job. Finally, you will create an envelope for the letter.*

Display Nonprinting Characters and Modify Line Spacing

1. Start **Word**. Make sure the Word window is **maximized** [□].

2. Choose **Home→Paragraph→Show/Hide** [¶] from the Ribbon, as shown to the right.
   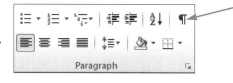
   New documents contain a paragraph symbol; you won't see it if you don't turn on the Show/Hide feature. Paragraph symbols carry formatting in them. For a new document, formatting includes default spacing of 1.15 lines and extra space at the end of a paragraph.

   In the next step, you'll select (highlight) the paragraph symbol and reformat it, changing the default line spacing to 1.0 and removing additional space after a paragraph.

3. Position the **I-beam** [I] left of the paragraph symbol, **press and hold** the mouse button, **drag** to the right to select (highlight) the paragraph symbol, and then **release** the mouse button.

4. Follow these steps to reformat the paragraph symbol:

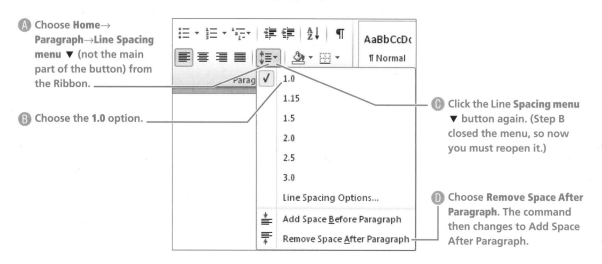

(A) Choose **Home→Paragraph→Line Spacing menu ▼** (not the main part of the button) from the Ribbon.

(B) Choose the **1.0** option.

(C) Click the Line **Spacing menu ▼** button again. (Step B closed the menu, so now you must reopen it.)

(D) Choose **Remove Space After Paragraph**. The command then changes to Add Space After Paragraph.

Turn On the Ruler and Type the Letter

5. Click the **View Ruler** [▦] button at the top of the vertical scroll bar to display the ruler.

6. **Tap** [Enter] five times to place the insertion point 2 inches from the top of the page (at approximately the 1 inch mark on the vertical ruler).

7. Start typing **Nove**, but stop when AutoComplete displays a pop-up tip.
   AutoComplete suggests the word it thinks you are typing and offers to complete it.

8. **Tap** [Enter] to automatically insert November into the letter.

9. Finish **typing** the date as **November 24, 2012**.

10. Continue **typing** the letter as shown in the following illustration, **tapping** [Enter] wherever you see a paragraph symbol.
If you catch a typo, you can tap the [Backspace] *key enough times to remove the error, and then continue typing.*

¶
¶
¶
¶
¶
November·24,·2012¶
¶
¶
¶
Ms.·Paige·Daniels¶
Richmond·University¶
15751·Meadow·Lane¶
Chester·Allen,·VA·23333¶
¶
Dear·Ms.·Daniels:¶
¶

11. **Type** the first body paragraph in the following illustration. Let Word Wrap do its thing, and then **tap** [Enter] twice at the end of the paragraph.

Travis·Mayfield·referred·you·to·us·after·he·spoke·to·you·yesterday·about·our·extraordinary·product.·I·
want·to·take·this·opportunity·to·thank·you·for·considering·My·Virtual·Campus'·social·networking·
website·for·your·institution.·As·Travis·may·have·mentioned,·we·pride·ourselves·in·providing·the·latest·in·
technology·as·well·as·excellent·customer·service.¶
¶

If you see a wavy red line, that is Word's way of telling you that a word *might* be misspelled. If a term is not in Word's dictionary, it is marked as a possible error, even if it is spelled correctly. Wavy green lines indicate possible grammatical errors. Ignore red and green wavy lines for now.

12. Continue **typing** the letter, **tapping** [Enter] where you see a paragraph symbol.

I·have·enclosed·information·for·your·review·regarding·the·various·features·of·the·website.·After·reading·
the·material,·please·contact·our·sales·manager,·ASAP,·to·discuss·your·options.·Thank·you·again·for·
considering·our·amazing·website.¶
¶
Yours·truly,¶
¶
¶
¶
Rob·Maloney¶
Customer·Service·Representative¶
Sales·Department¶

Create the Envelope

Now you will create an envelope for the letter and add it to the top of the document.

13. **Tap** [Ctrl] + [Home] to place the insertion point at the top of the document, then choose **Mailings→Create→Envelopes** from the Ribbon.

14. Follow these steps to add an envelope to the document with no return address:

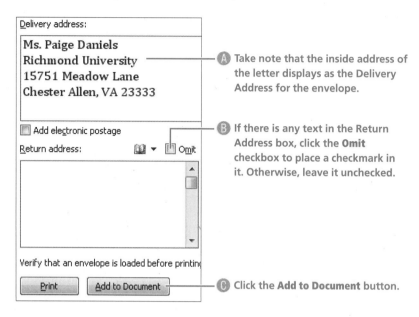

Delivery address:

Ms. Paige Daniels
Richmond University
15751 Meadow Lane
Chester Allen, VA 23333

Ⓐ Take note that the inside address of the letter displays as the Delivery Address for the envelope.

Ⓑ If there is any text in the Return Address box, click the **Omit** checkbox to place a checkmark in it. Otherwise, leave it unchecked.

☐ Add electronic postage

Return address: Omit

Verify that an envelope is loaded before printing

Print   Add to Document

Ⓒ Click the **Add to Document** button.

Notice that the envelope has been added to the top of the document. When you save the document, the envelope is saved with it so you may print it at any time.

15. Click the **Undo** 🔄 button to remove the envelope from the document.

16. Choose **Home→Paragraph→Show/Hide** ¶ to turn off the formatting marks.

Feel free to turn the Show/Hide feature on or off as you see fit throughout this course.

5.3 Saving Your Work

Video Lesson labyrinthelab.com/videos

It's important to save your documents frequently! Power outages and accidents can result in lost data. Documents are saved to storage locations such as hard drives and USB flash drives.

The Save Command

There are three primary commands used to save Word documents:

FROM THE KEYBOARD

Ctrl+S to save

- The Save 🖫 button on the Quick Access toolbar
- The File→Save command
- The File→Save As command

When you save a document for the first time, the Save As dialog box appears. The following illustration describes significant features of the new Save As dialog box.

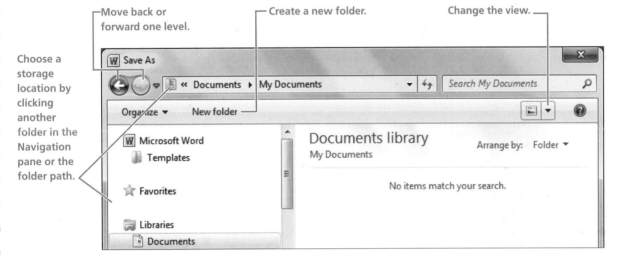

Save Compared to Save As

While the Save and Save As commands are quite similar, each has a specific use. If the document was never saved, Word displays the Save As dialog box, where you specify the name and storage location of the document. If the document was previously saved, choosing the Save command again replaces the prior version with the edited one, without displaying the Save As dialog box. You can also use Save As to save a copy of a document, giving it a new file-name and/or a new storage location.

Word's DOCX File Format

A file format is a technique for saving computer data. Word 2003 and earlier versions saved documents in the *doc* format. Word 2007 introduced a new file format: *docx*. This is important because users of Word 2003 and prior versions may not be able to read Word files in the *docx* format. However, you can choose to save your document in the older *doc* file format, thus enabling someone with an older version of Word to open the file without installing special software. Also, when you open a document created in Word 2007, the title bar displays

Compatibility Mode next to the actual title. This means certain Word 2010 features not compatible with 2007 are turned off while working in the document.

Word 2003 users can download a compatibility pack from the Microsoft website that allows them to open, edit, save, and create files in the docx file format.

DEVELOP YOUR SKILLS 5.3.1

Save the Letter

In this exercise, you will save the letter you created in the previous exercise.

1. Click the **Save**  button on the Quick Access toolbar.
   Word displays the Save As dialog box, since this is the first time you are saving this document. Once the file is named, this button will simply save the current version of the file over the old version.

2. Follow these steps to save the letter:
   Keep in mind that your dialog box may contain more files than shown here.

Ⓐ Click in the **Navigation pane,** and open the Lesson 05 folder on your file storage location.

Ⓑ Word always proposes the first line of text as the filename. Type the name **Daniels Letter** and it will replace the proposed name. (If you switched file storage locations, you may need to click in the **File Name** box, **delete** the proposed name with the Delete or Backspace key, and then **type** the new name.)

Ⓒ Click the **Save** button.

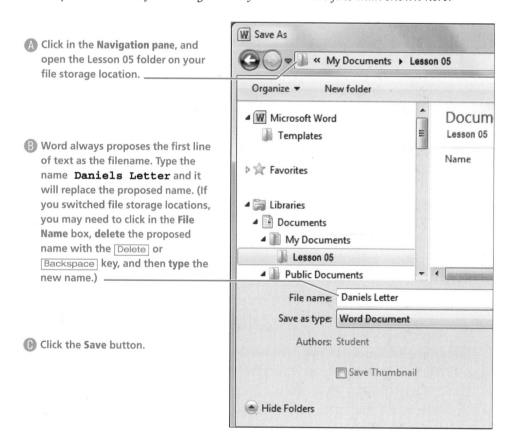

3. Leave the file **open** for the next exercise.

5.4 Selecting Text

Video Lesson   labyrinthelab.com/videos

You must select (highlight) text if you wish to perform some action on it. Suppose you want to delete an entire line. You would select the line first, and then tap ⌈Delete⌋.

Selection Techniques

Word provides many selection techniques; some use the mouse, and some use the keyboard. Use the keyboard techniques if you have difficulty controlling the mouse. Deselect text by clicking in the text area of the document or by tapping an arrow key. The following Quick Reference table illustrates various selection techniques.

QUICK REFERENCE	WORKING WITH SELECTION TECHNIQUES
Item to Be Selected	**Mouse Technique**
One word	Double-click the word.
Continuous block of text	Press and hold the left mouse button while dragging the I-beam over the desired text.
A line	Place the mouse pointer in the margin to the left of the line. Click when the pointer is shaped like an arrow.
A sentence	Hold down ⌈Ctrl⌋ and click the mouse pointer anywhere in the sentence.
One paragraph	Position the mouse pointer in the margin to the left of the paragraph and double-click, or triple-click anywhere in the paragraph.
Multiple paragraphs	Position the mouse pointer in the left margin and drag up or down when the pointer is shaped like an arrow, or drag the I-beam over the desired paragraphs.
Entire document	Triple-click in the left margin, or make sure no text is selected and then press and hold ⌈Ctrl⌋ and click in the left margin.
Nonadjacent areas	Select the first block of text, and then press and hold ⌈Ctrl⌋ while dragging over additional blocks of text.
Item to Be Selected	**Keyboard Technique**
One word	Click at the beginning of the word, and then press and hold ⌈Shift⌋+⌈Ctrl⌋ while tapping ⌈→⌋.
Continuous block of text	Click at the beginning of the text, and then press and hold ⌈Shift⌋ while tapping any arrow key. You can also click at the beginning of the text, press and hold ⌈Shift⌋, and click at the end of the selection.
A line	Press ⌈Shift⌋+⌈End⌋ to select from the insertion point to the end of the line. Press ⌈Shift⌋+⌈Home⌋ to select from the insertion point to the beginning of the line.
Entire document	Press ⌈Ctrl⌋+⌈A⌋ to execute the Select All command, or press ⌈Ctrl⌋ and click in the left margin.

Select Text

In this exercise, you will practice various selection techniques using the letter you just created. Selecting text causes the Mini toolbar to fade in. You can ignore it for now.

Select Using the Left Margin

1. Follow these steps to select text using the left margin:

Ⓐ **Point** outside the margin of the first line of the inside address.

Ⓑ **Click** once to select the entire line.

Ⓒ Make sure the pointer tilts to the **right**, and then **click** once to select this line. (Notice that the previously selected line is no longer selected.)

Ms. Paige Daniels
Richmond University
15751 Meadow Lane
Chester Allen, VA 23333

Dear Ms. Daniels:

Travis Mayfield referred you to us after he spoke to you yesterday about our extraordinary product. I want to take this opportunity to thank you for considering My Virtual Campus' social-networking website for your institution. As Travis may have mentioned, we pride ourselves in providing the latest in technology as well as excellent customer service with satisfaction guaranteed.

Ⓓ Select this paragraph by **double-clicking** in front of it, using the white selection arrow.

2. Making sure the mouse pointer tilts to the **right** ⇗, **drag** down the left margin. Be sure to **press and hold** the left mouse button as you drag. Then, **click** in the body of the document to deselect the text.

3. Move the **mouse pointer** back to the margin so it is tilting to the **right** ⇗, then **triple-click** anywhere in the left margin.
   Word selects the entire document.

4. **Click** once anywhere in the body of the document to deselect it.

Select Words

5. Point on any word with the **I-beam** Ⅰ, and then **double-click** to select it.

6. **Double-click** a different word, and notice that the previous word is deselected.

Nonadjacent Selections

You can also select multiple locations within a document.

7. **Double-click** to select one word.

8. With one word selected, **press and hold** the ⌈Ctrl⌉ key while you **double-click** to select another word, and then **release** the ⌈Ctrl⌉ key.
   Both selections are active. You can select as many nonadjacent areas of a document as desired using this technique. This can be quite useful when formatting documents.

Drag to Select

9. Follow these steps to drag and select a block of text:

Ⓐ Position the **I-beam** here, just in front of *Travis Mayfield*.... Make sure the I-beam is visible, not the right-tilting arrow.

Ⓑ **Press and hold** down the mouse button, and then **drag to the right** until the phrase *Travis Mayfield referred you to us after he spoke to you* is selected.

Ⓒ **Release** the mouse button; the text remains selected.

Travis Mayfield referred you to us after he spoke to you yesterday abo
want to take this opportunity to thank you for considering My Virtual C
website for your institution. As Travis may have mentioned, we pride o

5.5 Editing Text

Video Lesson   labyrinthelab.com/videos

Word offers many tools for editing documents, allowing you to insert and delete text and undo and redo work.

Inserting and Deleting Text

When you insert text in Word, existing text moves to the right as you type. You must position the insertion point before you begin typing.

Use Backspace and Delete to remove text. The Backspace key deletes *characters* to the left of the insertion point. The Delete key removes characters to the *right* of the insertion point. You can also remove an entire block of text by selecting it, and then tapping Delete or Backspace.

Using Undo and Redo

Word's Undo 🔄 button lets you reverse your last editing or formatting change(s). You can reverse simple actions such as accidental text deletions, or you can reverse more complex actions, such as margin changes.

FROM THE KEYBOARD
Ctrl+Z to undo the last action

The Redo 🔁 button reverses Undo. Use Redo when you undo an action and then change your mind.

The Undo menu ▾ button (see figure at right) displays a list of recent changes. You can undo multiple actions by dragging the mouse pointer over the desired items in the list. However, you must undo changes in the order in which they appear on the list.

Insert and Delete Text and Use Undo and Redo

In this exercise, you will insert and delete text. You will delete characters using both the Backspace *and* Delete *keys, and you will select and delete blocks of text. You will also use the Undo and Redo buttons on the Quick Access toolbar.*

1. In the first line of the first paragraph, **double-click** the word *yesterday,* as shown to the right, and then **tap** Delete to remove the word.

    > spoke to you yesterday about
    > for considering My Virtual Car

2. Click with the **I-beam** (not the right-tilted arrow) at the beginning of the word *thank* in the second line of the first paragraph of the first paragraph, type **personally**, and then **tap** the Spacebar.

3. Position the **insertion point** at the end of the first paragraph between the word *service* and the period at the end of the sentence.

4. **Tap** the Spacebar, and type **with satisfaction guaranteed**.

5. **Drag** to select the first three words of the second paragraph and then type **Enclosed you will find** to replace the selected text.

6. In the same line, position the **insertion point** after the word *your* and **tap** Backspace until the words *for your* are deleted, then type **to**.

7. **Double-click** the word *various* in the same line and **tap** Delete to remove it.

8. In the next line, **double-click** *ASAP,* and type **Bruce Carter, at your earliest convenience,** in its place.

9. Move the **mouse pointer** into the margin to the left of *Yours truly.*
   Remember, the mouse pointer is a white, right-tilted arrow when it's in the left margin.

10. **Click** once to select the line, and then type **Sincerely,** in its place.

Use Undo and Redo

11. You've decided that you prefer *Yours truly,* so click the **Undo** button on the Quick Access toolbar until you return to *Yours truly.*

12. Well, maybe *Sincerely* is better after all. Click the **Redo** button on the Quick Access toolbar until you return to *Sincerely.*

Save Your Changes

13. Click the **Save** button on the Quick Access toolbar to save your changes.

14. Leave the document **open** for the next exercise.

5.6 Working with AutoCorrect

Video Lesson   labyrinthelab.com/videos

AutoCorrect is predefined text used for automatically correcting common spelling and capitalization errors. You may have noticed AutoCorrect changing the spelling of certain words while working through the last exercise.

The AutoCorrect feature corrects more than spelling errors. For example, you can set up an AutoCorrect entry to insert the phrase *as soon as possible* whenever you type *asap* and tap the Spacebar or certain other characters such as a Tab, Comma, or Period. AutoCorrect will also capitalize a word it thinks is the beginning of a sentence.

DEVELOP YOUR SKILLS 5.6.1
Use AutoCorrect

In this exercise, you will type some terms that AutoCorrect will fix for you.

1. **Tap** Ctrl + End to move the insertion point to the end of the document.

2. If necessary, **tap** Enter a few times to provide some space to practice.

3. **Type** the word **teh** and **tap** the Tab key.
   AutoCorrect corrects the mistake and capitalizes the word because it thinks it is the first word of a sentence.

4. **Type** the word **adn** and **tap** the Spacebar.

5. Now **select** and Delete the words you were just practicing with.

AutoCorrect Options Smart Tag

Video Lesson   labyrinthelab.com/videos

Word uses smart tags, small buttons that pop up automatically, to provide menus of options that are in context with what you are doing at the time. One of those smart tags is the AutoCorrect Options smart tag.

If Word automatically corrects something that you don't want corrected, a smart tag option allows you to undo the change. For example, when Word automatically capitalizes the first C in the cc: line, you can quickly undo the capitalization, as shown here.

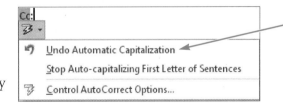

You will see many smart tags as you work. If you do not want to use a smart tag, you can ignore it and it will disappear on its own.

Microsoft Word

Use the AutoCorrect Smart Tag

In this exercise, you will use the AutoCorrect Options smart tags.

1. Choose **Home→Paragraph→Show/Hide** ¶ to display formatting marks.
    The reference initials should appear on the second blank line following the signature block. Make sure two paragraph symbols appear, as shown here.

2. If necessary, position the **insertion point** and use Enter to create the blank line(s).

3. Position the **insertion point** next to the second paragraph symbol, and type **rm** as the reference initials, and then **tap** Enter.
    Notice what happened. Autocorrect capitalized the R, and it should not be capitalized.

4. Position the **mouse pointer** over the R, and you should see a small blue rectangle just below the R. Then **drag down** a little, and the AutoCorrect Options screen tip appears.

5. Click the **AutoCorrect Options** smart tag to display the menu shown below. (This is a delicate mouse move, so you may need to try it a couple of times.)

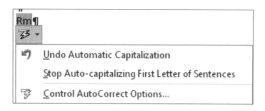

6. Choose **Undo Automatic Capitalization** from the menu.
    Notice that Word marks the initials with a wavy red line, indicating it's a possible spelling error. You can just ignore it.

7. Make sure the **insertion point** is on the blank line below the initials. Then **type** the enclosures notification, **Enclosures (2)**, and **tap** Enter.

8. **Save** 💾 the document and leave it **open** for the next exercise.

Setting AutoCorrect Options

Video Lesson labyrinthelab.com/videos

To display the AutoCorrect dialog box, choose the File tab to display the Backstage view and then click the Options tab at the bottom of the Navigation pane to open the Word Options window. The AutoCorrect Options button on the Proofing page opens the AutoCorrect dialog box.

When you create AutoCorrect entries in Word, the entries are also available for use in Microsoft Excel, PowerPoint, and Access.

In addition to correcting spelling errors, AutoCorrect makes these changes. Removing a checkmark from one of the checkboxes turns the feature off. _____

This checkbox turns the AutoCorrect feature on or off. _____

Use the Replace and With boxes to create customized AutoText entries. _____

The AutoCorrect table contains AutoCorrect terms that are built into Word as well as your customized entries. _____

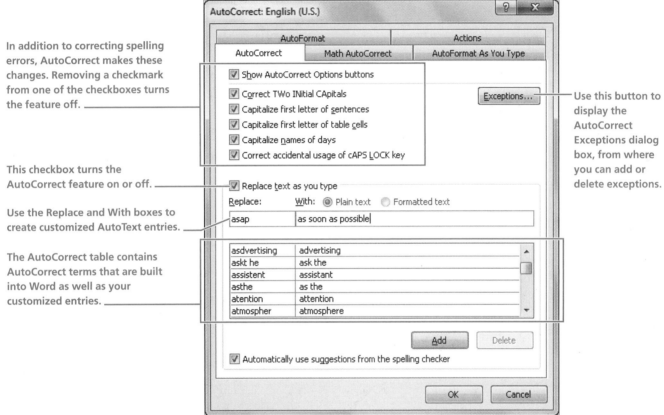

Use this button to display the AutoCorrect Exceptions dialog box, from where you can add or delete exceptions.

Customizing AutoCorrect

Word's AutoCorrect feature also lets you automatically insert customized text and special characters, and it is useful for replacing abbreviations with full phrases. For example, you could set up AutoCorrect to insert the name of your company whenever you type an abbreviation for it. You can also customize AutoCorrect by deleting entries that are installed with Word; however, please do not delete any in this classroom.

Do not create an AutoCorrect entry with an abbreviation you may want to use on its own; for example, if you used *USA* as an abbreviation for *United States of America,* you could not use *USA* alone because every time you typed it, it would be replaced with *United States of America.*

Create a Custom AutoCorrect Entry

In this exercise, you will create a custom AutoCorrect entry. It's now time for the copy notification, and you plan to copy Bruce Carter. Since you work for him, you know you'll need to type his name frequently, so it's a perfect candidate for a custom AutoCorrect entry.

1. Click the **File** tab and then click Options at the bottom of the Navigation pane.

2. When the Word Options window opens, follow these steps to display the AutoCorrect dialog box:

Ⓐ Choose **Proofing** from the menu.   Ⓑ Click the **AutoCorrect Options** button. ───

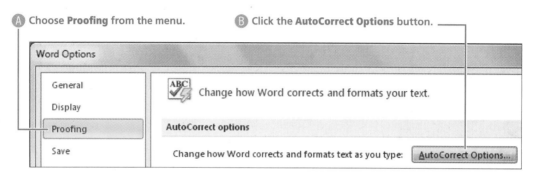

3. When the AutoCorrect dialog box appears, follow these steps to add a custom AutoCorrect entry:

Ⓐ Type **bmc** in the Replace box. ───

Ⓑ Type **Bruce Carter** in the With box. ───

Ⓒ Click the **Add** button. ───

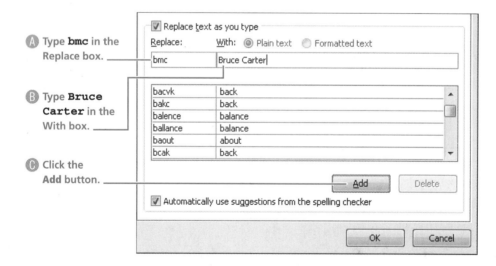

4. Click **OK** twice.

5. Type **cc:** and **tap** the ⎴Spacebar⎴.

6. Use the **AutoCorrect Options** smart tag to undo the automatic capitalization.
   Now you can try out the new AutoCorrect item you added in step 3.

7. Type **bmc** and **tap** ⎴Enter⎴ to automatically type the sales manager's name.

Delete the Custom AutoCorrect Entry

You can easily remove AutoCorrect entries, whether they are new custom entries you added or default entries you did not create originally.

8. Click the **File** tab and then click **Options** at the bottom of the Navigation pane.

9. Choose **Proofing** from the menu, and then click the **AutoCorrect Options** button in the right-hand pane.

10. Type **bmc** in the Replace box, which scrolls the list to Bruce Carter.

11. Click the **Delete** button in the bottom-right corner of the dialog box.

12. Click **OK** twice.

13. **Save** the letter and leave it **open** for the next exercise.

Setting AutoFormat As You Type Options

Video Lesson   labyrinthelab.com/videos

One of the tabs in the AutoCorrect dialog box is AutoFormat As You Type. You may have noticed certain formatting taking place automatically; this is happening because certain options are already set for you. For example, AutoFormat will replace a typed hyphen (-) with a dash (–), an ordinal (1st) with superscript (1st), or a fraction (1/2) with a fraction character ($\frac{1}{2}$). AutoFormat can also create an automatic bulleted list when you start a line with an asterisk (*), a hyphen (-), or a greater than symbol (>) followed by a space or a tab. Likewise, it creates a numbered list when you start a line with a number followed by a period or a tab.

You can control the formatting that happens automatically as you type by placing or removing checkmarks.

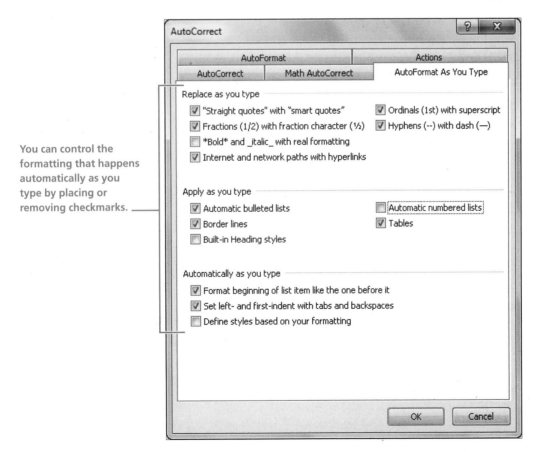

Turn On Automatic Numbering

In this exercise, you will turn on the option that automatically creates a numbered list when you begin a sentence with a number.

1. Click the **File** tab and then click the **Options** tab at the bottom of the Navigation pane.

2. Click **Proofing** on the left and then click the **AutoCorrect Options** button.

3. Follow these steps to turn on automatic numbering:

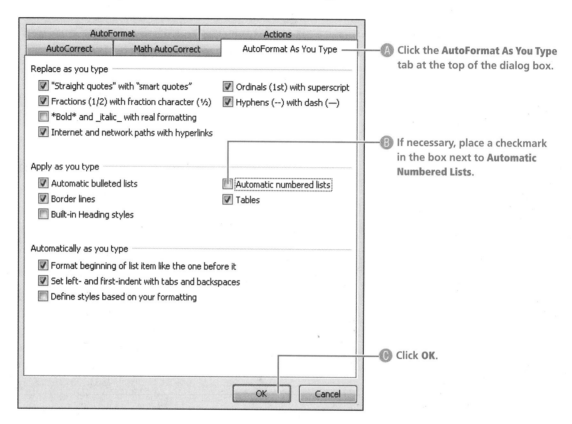

A Click the **AutoFormat As You Type** tab at the top of the dialog box.

B If necessary, place a checkmark in the box next to **Automatic Numbered Lists.**

C Click **OK.**

4. Click **OK** again in the Word Options dialog box to close it.

5. Click the **Save** 🖫 button and leave the document **open** for the next exercise.

5.7 Copying and Moving Text

Video Lesson labyrinthelab.com/videos

Cut, Copy, and Paste allow you to copy and move text within a document or between documents. The Cut, Copy, and Paste commands are conveniently located on the Ribbon in the Clipboard command group at the left side of the Home tab.

The following table describes these commands.

QUICK REFERENCE	USING CUT, COPY, AND PASTE	
Command	**Description**	**How to Issue the Command**
Cut	The Cut command removes selected text from its original location and places it on the Clipboard.	Click the Cut button.
Copy	The Copy command places a copy of selected text on the Clipboard, but it also leaves the text in the original location.	Click the Copy button.
Paste	The Paste command pastes the most recently cut or copied text into the document at the insertion point location.	Click the Paste button.

Working with the Clipboard

The Clipboard lets you collect multiple items and paste them into another location in the current document or into a different document. It must be visible on the screen to collect the items; otherwise, only one item at a time is saved for pasting. The Clipboard can hold up to 24 items. When the items you cut or copy exceed 24, the Clipboard automatically deletes the oldest item(s).

The dialog box launcher that displays the Clipboard task pane is located on the Home tab of the Ribbon.

The following illustration points out the main features of the Clipboard.

In this area, the number of items currently on the Clipboard is displayed.

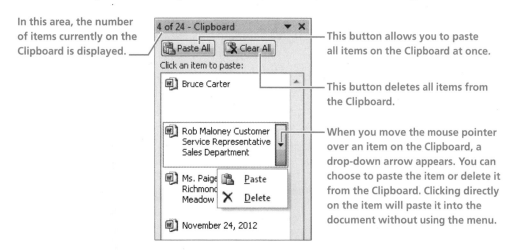

This button allows you to paste all items on the Clipboard at once.

This button deletes all items from the Clipboard.

When you move the mouse pointer over an item on the Clipboard, a drop-down arrow appears. You can choose to paste the item or delete it from the Clipboard. Clicking directly on the item will paste it into the document without using the menu.

Use Cut, Copy, and Paste

In this exercise, you will move and copy information and work with the Clipboard.

1. If necessary, choose **Home→Paragraph→Show/Hide** ¶ from the Ribbon to display the formatting marks.

Copy and Paste Using the Clipboard

2. Choose **Home→Clipboard→dialog box launcher** ⬏ from the Ribbon.

3. Tap ⌈Ctrl⌉+⌈Home⌉, then position the **mouse pointer** in the margin to the left of the date and then **click** to select the line.

4. Choose **Home→Clipboard→Copy** 🖹 from the Ribbon.

5. Tap ⌈Ctrl⌉+⌈End⌉ to move the insertion point to the bottom of the document.

6. Follow these steps to paste the date at the bottom of the document:

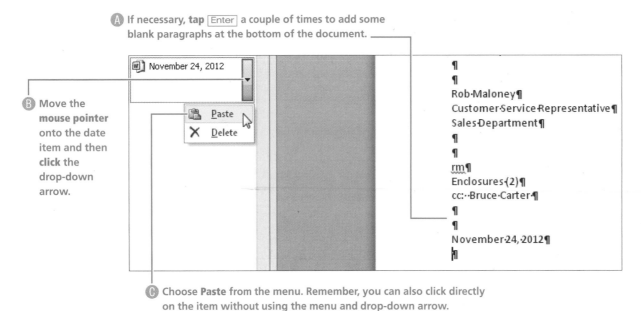

Ⓐ If necessary, **tap** ⌈Enter⌉ a couple of times to add some blank paragraphs at the bottom of the document.

Ⓑ Move the **mouse pointer** onto the date item and then **click** the drop-down arrow.

Ⓒ Choose **Paste** from the menu. Remember, you can also click directly on the item without using the menu and drop-down arrow.

Notice the Paste Options smart tag that popped up at the bottom of the pasted text.

7. Click the **smart tag** to view its menu and then click anywhere in the document to close the menu.

8. Tap ⌈Esc⌉ to dismiss the smart tag.

If you don't tap ⌈Esc⌉, the button will disappear on its own.

9. Click **Undo** ↩ to undo the paste.

Move the Inside Address

10. **Scroll up** to the top of the letter, position the **mouse pointer** in the margin to the left of the first line of the inside address, and then **drag** to select all four lines.

11. **Tap** Ctrl + X to cut the text.
Notice that using the keyboard shortcut to cut text also puts the item on the Clipboard.

12. **Tap** Ctrl + End to move the insertion point to the bottom of the document.

13. Click the **inside address** on the Clipboard to paste it at the insertion point.

14. Click **Undo** twice to undo the move and place the address back at the top of the letter.

15. Click the **Close** ☒ button on the Clipboard task pane.

16. Click the **Save** 🖫 button to save the changes.

Editing with Drag and Drop

Video Lesson	labyrinthelab.com/videos

Drag and drop produces the same result as cut, copy, and paste. It is efficient for moving or copying text a short distance within the same page. You select the text you wish to move and then drag it to the desired destination. If you press and hold Ctrl while dragging, the text is copied to the destination.

Drag and drop does not place the selection on the Clipboard.

DEVELOP YOUR SKILLS 5.7.2
Use Drag and Drop

In this exercise, you will use drag and drop to move and copy text.

1. Make sure there are a couple of **blank lines** at the bottom of your document.

2. If necessary, **scroll** so that you can see both the bottom of the document and the *Rob Maloney* line in the signature block.

Drag and Drop Move

3. **Select** the *Rob Maloney* line, and then **release** the mouse button.

4. Place the **mouse pointer** in the highlighted text.
The pointer now looks like a white arrow.

5. **Press and hold** the mouse button, and follow these steps to move the text:

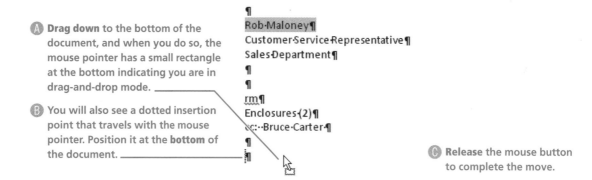

Ⓐ **Drag down** to the bottom of the document, and when you do so, the mouse pointer has a small rectangle at the bottom indicating you are in drag-and-drop mode. _____

Ⓑ You will also see a dotted insertion point that travels with the mouse pointer. Position it at the **bottom** of the document. _____

Rob·Maloney¶
Customer·Service·Representative¶
Sales·Department¶
¶
¶
rm¶
Enclosures·(2)¶
c:··Bruce·Carter·¶
¶
¶

Ⓒ **Release** the mouse button to complete the move.

Now you will undo the move and repeat the process, but this time you'll copy the text.

6. Click the **Undo** button to undo the move.

Drag and Drop Copy

7. Make sure the *Rob Maloney* line is still selected.

8. Place the **mouse pointer** inside the selected text, **press and hold** the Ctrl key and **drag** the text to the bottom of the document, **release** the mouse button, and then **release** the Ctrl key.
Holding the Ctrl key while dragging is what causes the action to be a copy instead of a move. For this reason, you must release the mouse button before the Ctrl key; otherwise, the action will become a move.

9. Click **Undo** to undo the copy.

10. Leave the document **open** for the next exercise.
Soon you will learn to switch between documents so you can copy information from one document to another.

5.8 Switching Between Documents

Video Lesson <u>labyrinthelab.com/videos</u>

There are several techniques for switching between documents. In the next exercise, you
will use the taskbar at the bottom of the screen for switching documents. When you have multiple documents open, they will appear as buttons on the taskbar. Clicking a button displays that document in the foreground. In the following illustration, Daniels Letter is the active document. The active document button is lighter than the others.

Viewing Open Documents on the Taskbar

When several documents are open at the same time, they may share one taskbar button. A small image of each open document displays on the screen when you hover the mouse pointer over the taskbar button. You can click the image to display the full document on the screen.

Image of
open Word
documents

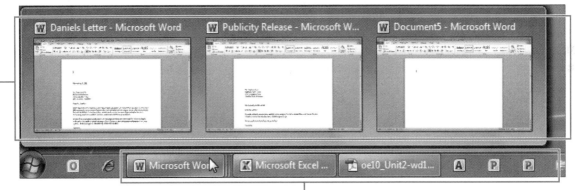

Taskbar buttons for open programs (Notice the
Word button has three documents stacked on it.)

Your buttons may be different from the ones shown in the preceding illustration, depending on which program buttons are displayed on your computer's taskbar.

Switch and Copy Between Documents

In this exercise, you will copy and paste between two documents, using the taskbar buttons to switch between the documents.

1. **Open** the Publicity Release document in the Lesson 05 folder.

2. Follow these steps to switch to the Daniels Letter:

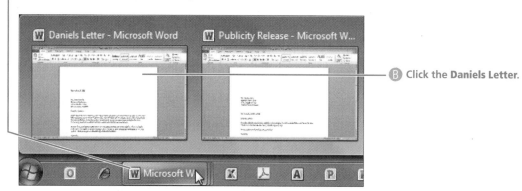

Ⓐ Hover the **mouse pointer** over the Microsoft Word taskbar button to display small images of the documents.

Ⓑ Click the **Daniels Letter**.

Copy and Paste the Inside Address

3. **Select** the four lines of the inside address and **tap** Ctrl + C to copy the text.

4. Hover the **mouse pointer** over the Microsoft Word taskbar button again and **click** the image of the Publicity Release document to switch to it.

5. Select the **first three lines**, as shown to the right.

6. **Tap** Ctrl + V to paste the address over the selected text in this document.

> YOUR·NAME¶
> ADDRESS¶
> CITY,·STATE··ZIP¶

Paste the Sales Manager's Name Multiple Times

7. Using the **taskbar**, switch back to the Daniels Letter, and then **select** *Bruce Carter* in the second line of the second paragraph.

8. **Tap** Ctrl + C to copy his name.

9. Using the **taskbar** button, **switch** back to the Publicity Release document.

10. **Select** *SALES MANAGER* in the salutation and then **tap** Ctrl + V to paste *Bruce Carter*. *Notice that the salutation does not look exactly right; it should be a title with a last name. You will fix that in just a moment.*

11. **Select** *SALES MANAGER* in the first paragraph and then **tap** Ctrl + V to paste *Bruce Carter* again.

Once you have copied text, you can paste it multiple times without copying the text again.

12. **Double-click** *Bruce* in the salutation and type **Mr**.

13. **Select** and **copy** *Paige Daniels* at the top of the letter; **paste** it over *YOUR NAME* at the bottom of the document.

14. **Save** 🖫 the changes you made in this document and then **close** it.

15. **Save** 🖫 the changes to Daniels Letter, but leave it **open** for the next exercise.

5.9 Using Page Layout Options

Video Lesson   labyrinthelab.com/videos

The three most commonly used layout options are margins, page orientation, and paper size. All of these are located in the Page Setup group on the Page Layout tab of the Ribbon.

Setting Margins

Margins determine the amount of white space between the text and the edge of the paper. You can set margins for the entire document, a section, or for selected text. The Margins gallery displays preset top, bottom, left, and right margins. The Custom Margins option at the bottom of the gallery opens the Page Setup dialog box.

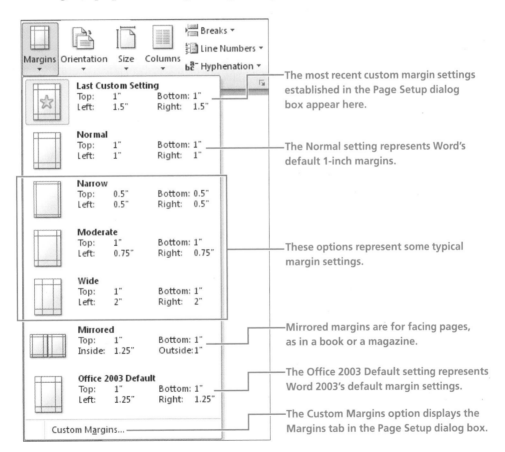

The most recent custom margin settings established in the Page Setup dialog box appear here.

The Normal setting represents Word's default 1-inch margins.

These options represent some typical margin settings.

Mirrored margins are for facing pages, as in a book or a magazine.

The Office 2003 Default setting represents Word 2003's default margin settings.

The Custom Margins option displays the Margins tab in the Page Setup dialog box.

Task	Procedure
Change margins from the Margins gallery	■ Choose Page Layout→Page Setup→Margins from the Ribbon. ■ Choose predefined margin settings from the gallery.
Set custom margins	■ Choose Page Layout→Page Setup→Margins from the Ribbon. ■ Choose the Custom Margins command at the bottom of the gallery. ■ Enter settings for top, bottom, left, and right margins.

DEVELOP YOUR SKILLS 5.9.1
Set Page Layout Options

In this exercise, you will use the Margins gallery and the Page Setup dialog box to change the document's margins.

1. Choose **Page Layout→Page Setup→Margins** ⊞ from the Ribbon to display Word's Margins gallery.

2. Choose **Narrow** from the gallery and observe the impact on your document.

3. Click the **Margins** ⊞ button again to reopen the gallery and choose **Wide** to see how that affects the document.

4. Open the gallery again; change the margins back to the **Normal** (default) setting.

5. Click the **dialog box launcher** ⊡ at the bottom-right corner of the Page Setup group to open the Page Setup dialog box.
   You can also open the dialog box using the Custom Margins command at the bottom of the Margins gallery.

6. If necessary, click the **Margins** tab at the top of the dialog box.
   Notice the options for changing the top, bottom, left, and right margins.

7. Use the **spinner controls** (up/down arrows) to change the left and right margins to **1.5 inches**.

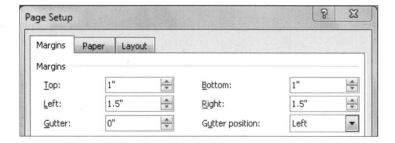

8. Click **OK**; notice the change in your document's margins.

9. Click the **Margins** ⊞ button to display the gallery and choose Normal.

10. **Save** 🖫 the document and leave it **open** for the next exercise.

Setting the Page Orientation

Video Lesson   labyrinthelab.com/videos

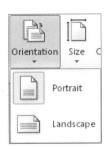

The page orientation determines how the text is laid out on the paper. The options are vertically (Portrait) or horizontally (Landscape). The default orientation is Portrait. Some common uses for a landscape orientation include brochures, flyers, wide tables, and so forth. The Orientation options are located on the Page Layout tab of the Ribbon.

Setting the Paper Size

Most documents use the standard letter size paper. However, Word supports the use of many other paper sizes, including legal, and also allows you to create custom sizes.

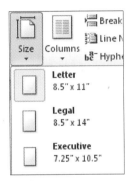

QUICK REFERENCE	SETTING PAGE ORIENTATION AND PAPER SIZE
Task	**Procedure**
Change the page orientation	■ Choose Page Layout→Page Setup→Orientation from the Ribbon. ■ Choose the desired page orientation.
Change the paper size	■ Choose Page Layout→Page Setup→Size from the Ribbon. ■ Choose the desired size from the menu, or choose the More Paper Sizes command to create a custom paper size.

Microsoft Word

Change the Orientation and Paper Size

In this exercise, you will experiment with the page orientation and paper size options.

View Landscape Orientation

1. If necessary, click the **Maximize** ▣ button.

2. Choose **View→Zoom→One Page** 🔲 from the Ribbon.
   The page is currently in the default orientation of Portrait (vertical). Viewing the entire page allows you to see this clearly.

3. Choose **Page Layout→Page Setup→Orientation** 📄 from the Ribbon.

4. Choose **Landscape** from the menu.
   The page layout changes to horizontal.

5. Click the **Orientation** 📄 button again and choose **Portrait** to change the page back to a vertical layout.

View Paper Size Options

6. Choose **Page Layout→Page Setup→Size** 📄 from the Ribbon and switch to Legal.
   Notice the paper and envelope sizes available on the menu. The More Paper Sizes command at the bottom of the menu opens the Page Setup dialog box, where you can set a custom paper size if you wish.

7. Choose **Size** 📄 again and switch back to **Letter**.

8. Choose **View→Zoom→100%** 📄 from the Ribbon to have a larger view of the document.

9. **Save** 💾 the document and leave it **open** for the next exercise.

5.10 Working with Combined Print and Print Preview

Video Lesson labyrinthelab.com/videos

In Word 2010, the Print and Print Preview commands have been combined and are available in Backstage view. The left section is all about the printer and the current page layout options, while the right section is a preview of your document that shows how it will look when printed. You can experiment with different options and see the results immediately.

To display the Print options and Print Preview, choose File→Print.

You can no longer edit while previewing a document.

These options allow you to choose a different printer, view the printer properties, and set the number of copies to print.

Print

Copies: 1

Print

Printer ⓘ

HP LaserJet 4050 Series ...
Offline

Printer Properties

Settings

Print All Pages
Print the entire document

Pages: ⓘ

Print One Sided
Only print on one side o...

Collated
1,2,3   1,2,3   1,2,3

Portrait Orientation

Letter
8.5" x 11"

November 24, 2012

Ms. Paige Daniels
Richmond University
15751 Meadow Lane
Chester Allen, VA 23333

Dear Ms. Daniels:

Travis Mayfield referred you to us after he spoke to you about our extraordinary product. I want to take this opportunity to personally thank you for considering My Virtual Campus' social networking website for your institution. As Travis may have mentioned, we pride ourselves in providing the latest in technology as well as excellent customer service with satisfaction guaranteed.

Enclosed you will find information to review regarding the features of the website. After reading the material, please contact our sales manager, Bruce Carter, at your earliest convenience to discuss your options. Thank you again for considering our amazing website.

Sincerely,

Rob Maloney
Customer Service Representative
Sales Department

rm
Enclosures (2)
cc: Bruce Carter

These options allow you to change various page layout options and see the proposed change on the right in the preview section.

Experiment with Print and Print Preview

In this exercise, you will set printing and page layout options and preview the results.

1. Choose **File→Print**.

Explore Print Options

2. Follow these steps to print multiple copies of the current page:

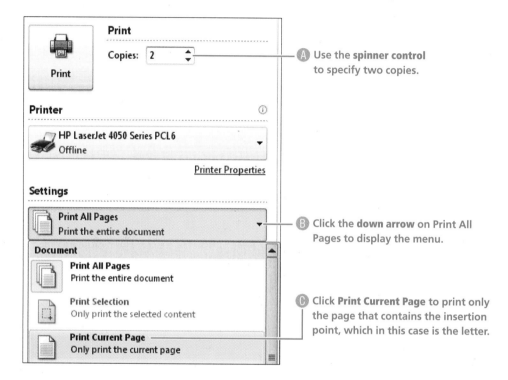

Ⓐ Use the **spinner control** to specify two copies.

Ⓑ Click the **down arrow** on Print All Pages to display the menu.

Ⓒ Click **Print Current Page** to print only the page that contains the insertion point, which in this case is the letter.

Preview Page Setting Changes

3. Follow these steps to preview the document with a different margin setting:

Ⓐ Click the **down arrow** on the Normal Margins setting.

Ⓑ Choose **Office 2003 Default**.

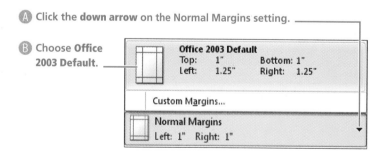

Notice the difference in the margins in the preview.

4. Switch back to the **Normal** margin setting.

5. Change the Orientation to **Landscape** and preview the change in the document.

6. Switch back to the **Portrait** orientation.

7. Click the **File** tab to close Backstage view and return to the document.

8. **Save** 🖫 and **close** the document.

5.11 Concepts Review

Concepts Review   labyrinthelab.com/ob10

To check your knowledge of the key concepts introduced in this lesson, complete the Concepts Review quiz by going to the URL listed above. If your classroom is using Labyrinth eLab, you may complete the Concepts Review quiz from within your eLab course.

Reinforce Your Skills

Create a Block-Style Letter

In this exercise, you will practice using traditional spacing for a business letter and letting Word Wrap and AutoComplete take effect. You should control the AutoCorrect feature as needed.

1. If necessary, **tap** Ctrl + N to start a new blank document.

2. Use the **Show/Hide** ¶ button to display formatting marks.

3. Select the **paragraph symbol**, change the line spacing to **1.0**, and then **remove** the space after paragraphs. (You will need to open the menu twice to do this.)

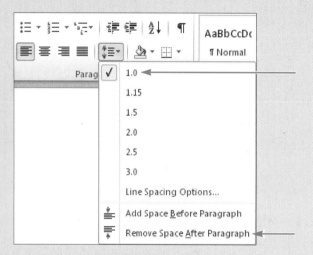

4. **Type** the following letter, **tapping** Enter wherever you see a paragraph symbol. Notice the five paragraph symbols at the top of the document. They position the date at approximately 2 inches from the top of the page.

```
¶
¶
¶
¶
¶
January·11,·2012¶
¶
¶
¶
Ms.·Courtney·Thompson¶
Service·Manager¶
Statesboro·Software·Services¶
810·Ivanhoe·Way¶
Statesboro,·GA·30458¶
¶
Dear·Ms.·Thompson:¶
¶
I·would·like·to·take·this·opportunity·to·thank·you·for·your·excellent·customer·service.·You·were·patient,·
courteous,·and·very·helpful.·The·installation·assistance·you·provided·was·invaluable.¶
¶
I·have·already·put·your·program·to·good·use.·As·you·know,·application·programs·can·boost·personal·
productivity.·Your·program·allows·me·to·manage·my·business·much·more·effectively.·I·am·enclosing·the·
$45·fee·you·requested.·Please·send·me·a·receipt·and·a·catalog.¶
¶
Sincerely,¶
¶
¶
¶
Blake·Evans¶
Administrative·Assistant¶
¶
be¶
Enclosure¶
```

5. Position the **insertion point** just in front of the sentence starting *I am enclosing the $45*, and **tap** ⌐Enter⌐ twice to create a new paragraph.

6. Position the **insertion point** at the end of the second paragraph, just in front of the paragraph symbol.

7. **Tap** ⌐Delete⌐ twice to remove the two paragraph symbols separating the new paragraph from the following paragraph.

8. If necessary, **tap** the ⌐Spacebar⌐ to insert a space between the combined sentences.

9. Position the **insertion point** at the end of the first paragraph before the paragraph mark, and **tap** the ⌐Spacebar⌐ if there is no space at the end of the sentence.

10. **Type** this sentence: **I also appreciate the overnight delivery.**

11. Add an **envelope**, without a return address, to the top of the letter.

12. **Save** the letter in the Lesson 05 folder, name it **rs-Thompson Letter**, and then **close** it.

Use the Clipboard and Drag and Drop

In this exercise, you will open a document from your file storage location and use the Clipboard to rearrange paragraphs. You will use drag and drop to move blocks of text.

1. **Open** the rs-Professional Contacts document in the Lesson 05 folder.
    Notice that the document contains a list of professional contacts. In the next few steps, you will use the Clipboard to reorganize the contacts by profession: all the attorneys will be grouped together, followed by the designers, and then the bookkeepers.

2. Choose **Home→Clipboard→dialog box launcher** ⬚ from the Ribbon to display the Clipboard.

3. If necessary, click the **Clear All** button to clear the Clipboard.

4. **Select** the first attorney contact, *David Roberts, Attorney,* by clicking in front of the contact in the left margin.
    This will select the entire paragraph, including the paragraph mark.

5. Choose **Home→Clipboard→Cut** ✂ from the Ribbon.
    The item appears on the Clipboard.

6. **Select** the next attorney, *Lisa Wilson,* and **Cut** ✂ it to the Clipboard.

7. **Cut** the remaining attorney contacts to the Clipboard. Use **Undo** ↩ if you make a mistake. However, be careful because even if you use Undo, the item you cut will remain on the Clipboard.

8. Now **Cut** ✂ the designer contacts to the Clipboard.
    The bookkeeper contacts should now be grouped together in the document.

9. **Tap** Enter to position the insertion point on a new line below the bookkeeper contacts.

10. Click the **Paste All** button on the Clipboard to paste the attorney and designer contacts.
    Notice that the contacts are pasted in the order they were cut, thus grouping the attorneys together and the designers together.

Create Headings

11. Click to place the **insertion point** in front of the first bookkeeper contact, and **tap** Enter twice to create blank lines.

12. Click the **blank line** above the first bookkeeper and type **Bookkeepers**.

13. Use this technique to create headings for attorneys and designers.

Use Drag and Drop

14. Select the *Attorneys* heading, the four attorneys, and the blank line below by **dragging** in the left margin and then **releasing** the mouse button.

15. Position the **mouse pointer** on the selection, and **drag up** until the dotted insertion point is just in front of the Bookkeepers heading.

16. **Release** the mouse button to move the attorneys block above the bookkeepers.

17. Now move the designers above the bookkeepers.

18. **Close** the Clipboard, and then **save** and **close** the file.

REINFORCE YOUR SKILLS 5.3
Edit a Document

In this exercise, you will edit a document that is marked up for changes.

1. Choose **File→Open**.

2. **Open** the rs-Maine document in the Lesson 05 folder.
   You will edit this document during this exercise. Notice that this document contains formatting that you have not yet learned about. For example, the title is centered and bold, and the paragraphs are formatted with double line spacing. This document is already formatted like this because it is a report.

   ■ If only one or two characters require deletion, then position the **insertion point** in front of the character(s) and use ⌈Delete⌉ to remove them.

   ■ If one or more words require deletion, then select the text and use ⌈Delete⌉ to remove the selected text.

   ■ If a word or phrase needs to be replaced with another word or phrase, then select the desired text and type the replacement text.

   ■ Use **Undo** ⌈↺⌉ if you make mistakes.

3. When you have finished, **save** the changes and **close** the document.

MAINE – THE PINE TREE STATE

Maine is recognized as one of the most ~~healthy~~ *healthful* states in the nation with temperatures averaging 70°F and winter temperatures averaging 20°F. It has 3,~~7~~*5*00 miles of coastline, is about 320 miles long and 210 miles wide, with a total area of 33,215 square miles or about as big as all of the other five New England States combined. It comprises 16 counties with 22 cities, 424 towns, 51 plantations, and 416 unorganized townships. Aroostook county is so large (6,453 square miles) that it covers an area greater than the combined size of Connecticut *and Rhode Island*.

Maine abounds in natural assets—542,629 acres of state and national parks, including the 92-mile Allagash Wilderness Waterway, Acadia National Park (second most visited national park in the United States), and Baxter State Park (location of Mt. Katahdin and the northern end of the Appalachian Trail). Maine has one mountain ~~which~~ *that* is approximately one mile high—Mt. Katahdin (5,268 ft. above sea level) and also claims America's first chartered city: York, 1641.

Maine's blueberry crop is the largest ~~blueberry crop~~ in the nation—98% of the low-bush blueberries. Potatoes rank third in acreage and third in production nationally. Maine is nationally famed for its shellfish; over 46 million pounds of ~~shellfish~~ *lobster* were harvested *in the United States* in 1997. The total of all shellfish and fin fish harvested was approximately 237 million pounds with a total value of $273 million *in 1997* ~~during the 1997 fishing season.~~

Apply Your Skills

Create a Modified Block-Style Letter

In this exercise, you will practice the skills needed to create a modified block-style letter. You'll turn on the ruler to ensure the correct spacing for the date, the complimentary close, and the signature block.

1. **Start** a new blank document.
   You will create an AutoCorrect entry for Back Bay Users Group to use in your letter.

2. Click the **File** tab and then click the **Options** button at the bottom of the Navigation pane.

3. In the Options window, choose **Proofing** from the menu on the left.

4. Click the **AutoCorrect Options** button.

5. When the AutoCorrect dialog box appears, type **bbug** in the **Replace** box.

6. Type **Back Bay Users Group** in the **With** box.

7. Click the **Add** button, and then click **OK** twice.

8. If necessary, click the **View Ruler** 🔲 button at the top of the vertical scroll bar to display the ruler.

9. Create the **modified block-style** business letter shown in the illustration on the next page.

10. Follow these guidelines as you type your letter.
    - Change to **single-spacing** and remove the **after-paragraph spacing**.
    - Space down the proper distance from the top of the page.
    - Use ⌈Tab⌉ to align the date, closing, and signature block at **3 inches** on the ruler. (You'll need to **tap** ⌈Tab⌉ six times to indent the lines at 3 inches.)
    - Use correct spacing between paragraphs.
    - Use your **AutoCorrect** shortcut in the first paragraph, rather than typing Back Bay Users Group.

```
                          Today's Date




Mrs. Suzanne Lee
8445 South Princeton Street
Chicago, IL 60628

Dear Mrs. Lee:

Thank you for your interest in the Back Bay Users Group. We will be holding an orientation for new
members on the first Thursday in April at our headquarters.

Please let us know if you can attend by calling the phone number on this letterhead. Or, if you prefer,
you may respond in writing or via email.

                          Sincerely,




                          Jack Bell
                          Membership Chair

XX
```

11. **Save** 💾 the letter to the Lesson 05 folder on your file storage location as **as-Lee Letter**.

12. **Hide** the ruler using the same button you used to display it.

13. **Delete** the AutoCorrect entry you created in this exercise.

14. **Preview** the letter, then preview how it would look in Landscape orientation with **Narrow** margins.

15. Restore to **Portrait** orientation and **Normal** margins.

16. **Print** the letter if your computer is connected to a printer, and then **save** and **close** the document.

Use the Clipboard and Drag and Drop

In this exercise, you will use the Clipboard and the drag-and-drop technique to rearrange items in a list.

1. **Open** as-Animals in the Lesson 05 folder in your file storage location.

2. Open the **Clipboard**, and use the **Clear All** button, if necessary, to empty it.

3. Use the **Home→Clipboard→Cut** ✄ button to place all the animals on the Clipboard, and then cut all the vegetables to the Clipboard.

4. Position the **insertion point** below the list of minerals, and then use the **Paste All** button to paste the animals and vegetables back in the document.

5. Use the ⎡Enter⎤ key to put two blank lines between groups and an extra blank line above the minerals, and then **type** an appropriate title at the top of each group.

6. Use **drag and drop** to arrange the groups in this order: Animals, Vegetables, Minerals. Remember, when selecting the text, include the blank line below the group.

7. **Save** 💾 the file and **close** it.

Edit a Document

In this exercise, you will use your editing skills to make specified changes to a letter.

1. **Open** the as-Wilson Letter document in the Lesson 05 folder in your file storage location.

2. **Edit** the document, as shown in the illustration at the end of this exercise.

3. Use Enter to push the entire document down, so that the date is positioned at approximately the **1-inch** mark on the vertical ruler.

4. If necessary, use Tab to move the date, complimentary close, and signature block to the **3-inch** position on the ruler. This will convert the letter from block style to modified block style.

5. When you finish, **save** 💾 the changes, **print** the letter, and **close** the document.

Today's Date

~~Ms. Cynthia Wilson~~ Mr. Roosevelt Jackson
~~118 Upper Terrace~~ 8 Spring street
~~Freehold, NJ 08845~~ Martinville, NJ 08836

Dear ~~Ms. Wilson~~:
    Mr. Jackson
                                          back
Thank you for your recent letter concerning back injuries in your office. Yes, ∨ injuries are a common problem for office workers today. It was estimated by the U. S. Bureau of Labor Statistics that in one year over ~~490~~,000 employees took time from work due to back injuries.
       580

Encourage your office employees to make certain their work surface is at a ~~suitable~~ height. They should also be encouraged to take frequent breaks from their desks.   comfortable

Please
~~Feel free to~~ contact my office if you would like more information.

Sincerely,

Elaine Boudreau
Ergonomics Specialist

Critical Thinking & Work-Readiness Skills

In the course of working through the following Microsoft Office-based Critical Thinking exercises, you will also be utilizing various work-readiness skills, some of which are listed next to each exercise. Go to labyrinthelab.com/workreadiness *to learn more about the work-readiness skills.*

5.1 Create a Business Letter

Stefanie Bentley, the marketing assistant for My Virtual Campus, has received an email from Mary Jones, the student life coordinator from Magnolia College (3000 College Lane, Anywhere, Iowa 22222) asking what's different about the My Virtual Campus service compared to other similar services. Write a response in business letter format stating that My Virtual Campus has the most flexible set of solutions and that you can demonstrate these solutions in an online meeting. Suggest a time and date two weeks from today, and mention that you have enclosed a brochure. Save the letter as **ct-Magnolia** to your Lesson 05 folder. Close the file.

> **WORK-READINESS SKILLS APPLIED**
> - Writing
> - Serving clients/customers
> - Organizing and maintaining information

5.2 Use AutoCorrect and AutoFormat

After two weeks with no response from Mary at Magnolia College, Stefanie decides to send a follow-up letter. Create another business letter addressed to Mary (her title and contact details shown above) asking for confirmation that she received your earlier letter and suggesting another time for a meeting. Configure Word's AutoCorrect options to automatically replace **mvc** with *My Virtual Campus* and test it to make sure *mvc* is automatically corrected. Save your document to your Lesson 05 folder as **ct-Follow Up**. Delete the custom Auto-Correct entry so other students can perform this exercise on the same computer later.

> **WORK-READINESS SKILLS APPLIED**
> - Writing
> - Serving clients/customers
> - Applying technology to a task

5.3 Combine and Switch Between Documents

Stefanie decides to blend content from multiple documents so she has a single tool she can use for marketing purposes. Open the files ct-MVC Description Rev 1 and ct-MVC Description Rev 2 from the Lesson 05 folder. Cut, paste, drag and drop, and use any other editing techniques to combine the two descriptions into a single, complete description of My Virtual Campus. You will have to decide which document will contain the updated edits. Save that document to your Lesson 05 folder as **ct-MVC Description Final**.

> **WORK-READINESS SKILLS APPLIED**
> - Thinking creatively
> - Making decisions
> - Organizing and maintaining information

Creating a Memorandum and a Press Release

LESSON OUTLINE

LEARNING OBJECTIVES

After studying this lesson, you will be able to:

- Insert dates and symbols
- Insert and delete page breaks
- Work with proofreading tools
- Use Research options
- Work with formatting features
- Search using the Navigation pane and Find and Replace

In this lesson, you will expand on the basic Word skills you've developed. You will create a memo and a press release and then apply character formatting. You will also get experience with Word's proofing and editing tools, including Spelling & Grammar check. Finally, you will find synonyms in Word's thesaurus and explore other research options.

Preparing a Memorandum

My Virtual Campus continues to grow and is constantly adding the newest advancements in technology. Brett Martin is the public relations representative, and she regularly issues press releases to members and potential customers, trumpeting forthcoming upgrades. Brett creates a memorandum to which she attaches her latest press release announcing the launch of MyResume, which is being integrated into the website. Memorandums are used for internal communication within a company or organization, whereas business letters are used for external communication. Brett understands the importance of protecting the corporation's proprietary information, so she uses the appropriate trademark designations in her documents.

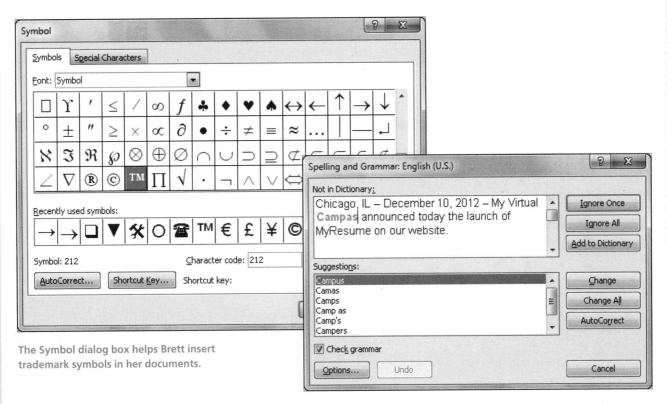

The Symbol dialog box helps Brett insert trademark symbols in her documents.

The Spelling and Grammar tool is a powerful proofreading aid.

6.1 Typing a Memorandum

Video Lesson   labyrinthelab.com/videos

There are a variety of acceptable memorandum styles in use today. All memorandum styles contain the same elements but with varied formatting. The style shown in the following figure is a traditional memorandum style with minimal formatting.

The introduction includes headings such as Memo To: and From:. Use a double space between paragraphs, or use the new Microsoft spacing, which automatically adds space after a paragraph. This means you only need to tap Enter once between paragraphs.

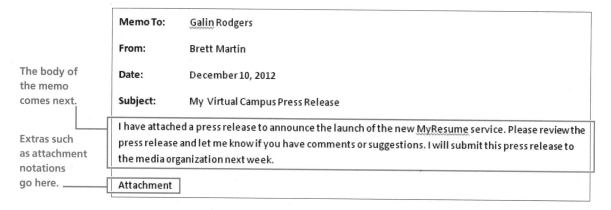

Memo To: Galin Rodgers

From: Brett Martin

The body of the memo comes next.

Date: December 10, 2012

Subject: My Virtual Campus Press Release

Extras such as attachment notations go here.

I have attached a press release to announce the launch of the new MyResume service. Please review the press release and let me know if you have comments or suggestions. I will submit this press release to the media organization next week.

Attachment

Introducing Default Tabs

The Tab key moves the insertion point to the nearest tab stop. In Word, the default tab stops are set every $1/2$ inch, thus the insertion point moves $1/2$ inch whenever you tap the Tab key. In this lesson, you will use Word's default tab settings.

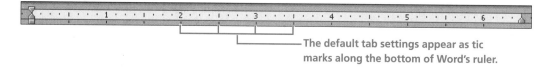

The default tab settings appear as tic marks along the bottom of Word's ruler.

A quick way to turn the ruler on and off is to click the View Ruler button at the top of the scroll bar.

Inserting and Formatting the Date

You use the Insert→Text→Insert Date and Time 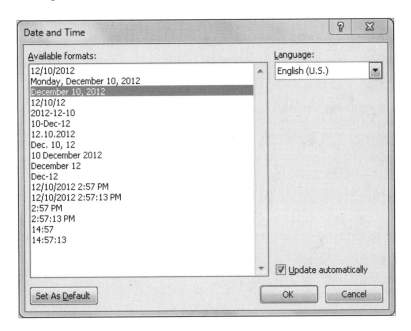 command on the Ribbon to display the Date and Time dialog box. Word lets you insert the current date in a variety of formats. For example, the date could be inserted as 12/10/12, December 10, 2012, or 10 December 2012.

FROM THE KEYBOARD

Alt + Shift + D
to insert a date

The Update Automatically Option

You can insert the date and time as text or as a field. Inserting the date as text has the same effect as typing the date into a document. Fields, however, are updated whenever a document is saved or printed. For example, imagine you create a document on December 10, 2012, and you insert the date as a field. If you open the document the next day, the date will automatically change to December 11, 2012. The date and time are inserted as fields whenever the Update Automatically box is checked, as shown here.

DEVELOP YOUR SKILLS 6.1.1

Set Up a Memo and Insert the Date

In this exercise, you will create a memo and insert the date automatically. You will also try out Word's 1.15 line spacing and the extra space following paragraphs.

Set Up a Memo

1. **Start** a new blank document. Make sure the Word window is **maximized** ▣ .

2. If necessary, click the **View Ruler** button at the top of the vertical scroll bar to turn on the ruler.

3. **Tap** Enter twice to space down to approximately 2 inches from the top of the page (1-inch mark on the vertical ruler).
   Using Word's default spacing, you don't have to tap Enter as many times as you did in the previous lesson to position the insertion point at 2 inches.

Microsoft Word

4. Type **Memo To:** and **tap** the Tab key.
   Notice that the insertion point moves to the next $^1/_2$-inch mark on the ruler.

5. If necessary, choose **Home→Paragraph→Show/Hide** ¶ from the Ribbon to display formatting marks.
   Notice the arrow formatting mark that represents the tab.

6. Type **Galin Rodgers** and **tap** Enter once.
   Notice that the word Galin has a red wavy underline, indicating it is not in Word's dictionary.

7. Type **From:** and **tap** Tab twice.
   It is necessary to Tab twice to align the names. The first tab aligns the insertion point at the $^1/_2$-inch mark on the ruler; the second aligns the insertion point at the 1-inch position.

8. Type **Brett Martin** and **tap** Enter once.

9. Type **Date:** and **tap** Tab twice.

Choose a Date Format and Insert the Date

10. Choose **Insert→Text→Insert Date and Time** 📆 from the Ribbon to display the Date and Time dialog box.

11. Follow these steps to insert the date:

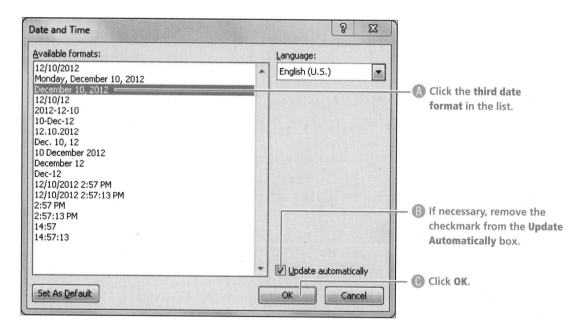

Leaving the Update Automatically box checked instructs Word to insert the date as a field, which means the original date would be lost if you opened and saved the document at a later date. In this instance, you do not want the date to change.

12. Choose **Home→Paragraph→Show/Hide** ¶ to turn off the paragraph marks.

13. Complete the remainder of the memorandum, as shown in the following illustration, using the ⌈Tab⌉ to align the text in the Subject line. Bear in mind that you only need to **tap** ⌈Enter⌉ once between paragraphs.

Memo To: Galin Rodgers

From: Brett Martin

Date: December 10, 2012

Subject: My Virtual Campus Press Release

I have attached a press release to announce the launch of the new MyResume service. Please review the press release and let me know if you have comments or suggestions. I will submit this press release to the media organization next week.

Attachment

---

14. Click the **View Ruler** 🔳 button at the top of the scroll bar to turn off the ruler.

15. Click the **Save** 💾 button, and save the document in Lesson 06 folder as **Martin Memo**.

16. Leave the memorandum **open**, as you will modify it throughout this lesson.

Inserting Symbols

Video Lesson   labyrinthelab.com/videos

Word lets you insert a variety of symbols, typographic characters, and international characters not found on the keyboard. You insert symbols via the Symbol dialog box. The following illustration shows how you access the Symbol dialog box. You can also use shortcut key combinations to insert certain symbols; for example, type (c), (r), or (tm) to insert the copyright, registered trademark, or trademark symbols, respectively.

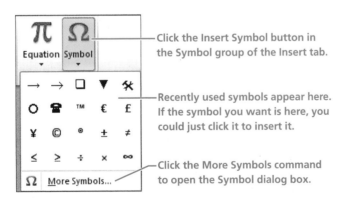

Click the Insert Symbol button in the Symbol group of the Insert tab.

Recently used symbols appear here. If the symbol you want is here, you could just click it to insert it.

Click the More Symbols command to open the Symbol dialog box.

The Special Characters tab displays commonly used special characters, such as the registered trademark (®) symbol and various punctuation symbols.

You can choose from several fonts, each displaying a different set of characters in the dialog box. Some fonts, such as Wingdings, contain interesting and fun symbols.

You can look up or set an AutoCorrect entry (or a keyboard shortcut) that may be used to insert a symbol rather than opening this dialog box.

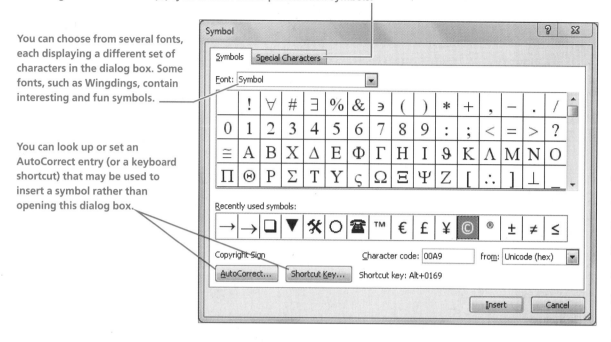

Insert Symbols

In this exercise, you will add a trademark symbol and a registered trademark symbol to your document.

1. Position the **insertion point** to the right of *My Virtual Campus* on the *Subject:* line.

2. Click **Insert→Symbols→Insert Symbol** Ω from the Ribbon, and choose the **More Symbols** command at the bottom of the menu.

3. When the Symbol dialog box appears, click the **Special Characters** tab.

4. Choose the **registered trademark symbol** (an R inside a circle), and then click the **Insert** button.
   The ® symbol is inserted in the document, and the Symbol dialog box remains open. Word leaves the dialog box open in case you wish to insert additional symbols.

5. Position the **insertion point** to the right of *MyResume* in the main paragraph.
   You may need to drag the dialog box out of the way in order to see the word. To do that, position the mouse pointer on the blue title bar at the top of the dialog box, press and hold the mouse button, drag the dialog box out of the way, and then release the mouse button.

6. Click the **trademark** (™) symbol from Special Characters and then click **Insert**.
   The trademark (™) symbol indicates that a company claims a phrase or icon as its trademark but has not received the federal protection accompanying the registered trademark (®) symbol.

7. Click the **Symbols** tab in the Symbol dialog box, and choose different fonts from the Font list to see other sets of symbols.

8. When you finish experimenting, click the **Close** button to close the dialog box.

9. Click the **Save** 💾 button to save the changes.

6.2 Working with Page Breaks

Video Lesson labyrinthelab.com/videos

If you are typing text and the insertion point reaches the bottom of a page, Word automatically breaks the page and begins a new page. This is known as an automatic page break. The location of automatic page breaks may change as text is added to or deleted from a document. Automatic page breaks are convenient when working with long documents that have continuously flowing text. For example, imagine you were writing a novel and you decided to insert a new paragraph in the middle of a chapter. With automatic page breaks, you could insert the paragraph and Word would automatically repaginate the entire chapter.

You force a page break by choosing Insert→Pages→Page Break 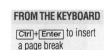 from the Ribbon. A manual page break remains in place unless you remove it. You insert manual page breaks whenever you want to control the starting point of a new page.

FROM THE KEYBOARD
Ctrl+Enter to insert a page break

 If you are working on a first draft or a document you suspect will go through revisions, it is not a good idea to insert manual page breaks because the pages will not repaginate correctly and you may end up with unwanted blank pages.

Removing Manual Page Breaks

In Draft view, a manual page break appears as a horizontal line, including the phrase *Page Break*. You can also see the page break line in Print Layout view if you turn on the Show/Hide feature. You can remove a manual page break by positioning the insertion point on the page break line and tapping Delete, as shown in the illustration to the right.

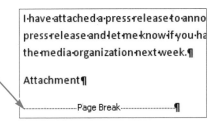

Displaying the Word Count

Microsoft Word tracks the number of words, pages, characters, paragraphs, and lines as you type them in a document. The number of words is displayed on the Word Count button on the Status bar; the other counts are available when you double-click the Word Count button.

You may need to count the number of words in a certain paragraph, a certain page, and so forth. To check these statistics, you need to first select the text; you can even select sections of text that are not connected to each other. The word count appears on the Status bar, which shows the number of selected words and the total number of words in the document. For example, a 42-word selection in a document that contains 60 words would display as 42/60.

Page: 1 of 2 | Words: 42/60 ——— Word Count button on Status bar

 Select nonadjacent sections by highlighting the first selection, holding down the Ctrl key, and then selecting the additional sections.

Work with Page Breaks

In this exercise, you will practice using manual page breaks. You will insert a page break, thereby creating a new page so you can copy and paste the press release information from another document into your new page.

Insert a Page Break

1. Make sure you are in **Print Layout** view. If you are not sure, click the **View** tab and choose **Print Layout** from the Document Views group at the left edge of the Ribbon. (If the button is highlighted, you are already in Print Layout view.)

2. **Tap** Ctrl + End to position the insertion point at the bottom of the document and, if necessary, **tap** Enter to generate a blank line below the *Attachment* line.

3. Choose **Insert→Pages→Page Break** from the Ribbon.

4. Select the body paragraph and view the **Word Count** button the Status bar.
   Notice that the numbers 42/60 represent the number of words selected and total number in the document.

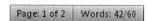

5. If necessary, **scroll** to see the bottom portion of page 1 and the top of page 2.

Remove the Page Break

6. **Scroll** up until the *Attachment* line is visible.

7. If necessary, click **Home→Paragraph→Show/Hide** ¶ to display formatting marks and see the page break.

8. **Click** to the left of the page break line, and tap Delete.

9. Try **scrolling** down to the second page and you will see that it is gone.

Reinsert the Page Break

10. Check to see that the **insertion point** is just below the *Attachment* line, and **tap** Ctrl + Enter to reinsert the page break.
    This shortcut keystroke is useful when you use page breaks frequently.

11. Click **Home→Paragraph→Show/Hide** ¶ to hide the formatting marks.
    The insertion point should be positioned at the top of the second page.

12. Click **File→Open** and, if necessary, navigate to your file storage location and **open** Press Release from the Lesson 06 folder.
    Notice that a number of phrases are flagged by the spelling checker (red wavy underlines) and grammar checker (green wavy underlines) in the document. You will take care of those in the next exercise.

13. In the Press Release document, **tap** Ctrl + A to select the entire document.

14. **Tap** Ctrl + C to copy the document.
    Now you will switch to your memo.

15. On the taskbar, click the **Martin Memo** button to switch back to that document.

16. Make sure your **insertion point** is at the top of page 2.

17. Choose **Home→Clipboard→Paste** from the Ribbon.
    The press release is pasted on page 2 of your document. Now you will switch back to the press release and close it.

18. Use the **taskbar** button to switch to Press Release.

19. Choose **File→Close** to close the file.
    The Martin Memo should now be in the foreground.

20. **Save** the file and leave it **open** for the next exercise.

6.3 Working with Proofreading Tools

Video Lesson   labyrinthelab.com/videos

Word's powerful Spelling and Grammar tool helps you avoid embarrassing spelling and grammar errors. Whether you choose to use the default on-the-fly checking, where Word marks possible errors as you type, or you choose to save proofing tasks until you've completed your document content, these tools can help polish your writing. However, these tools are proofreading aids, not the final word. You still need to involve human judgment in a final round of proofing, such as making sure you don't overuse a particular word. The Thesaurus can aid in finding alternate words for you.

- Spelling checker
- Grammar checker
- Research Task Pane

Using the Spelling Checker

Word checks a document for spelling errors by comparing each word to the contents of its built-in dictionary. Word also looks for double words such as *the the,* and a variety of capitalization errors. If you start the spelling checker in the middle of the document, when it reaches the end, a message appears asking if you want to go back and start spell checking from the beginning of the document.

Word can automatically check your spelling as you type. It flags spelling errors by underlining them with wavy red lines. You can correct a flagged error by right-clicking the error and choosing a suggested replacement word or other option from the menu that pops up.

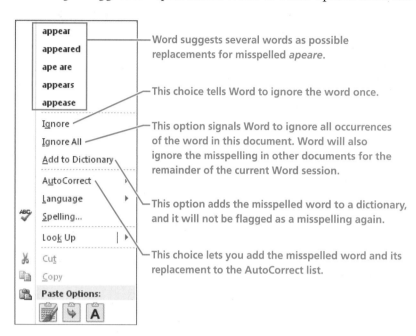

Word suggests several words as possible replacements for misspelled *apeare*.

This choice tells Word to ignore the word once.

This option signals Word to ignore all occurrences of the word in this document. Word will also ignore the misspelling in other documents for the remainder of the current Word session.

This option adds the misspelled word to a dictionary, and it will not be flagged as a misspelling again.

This choice lets you add the misspelled word and its replacement to the AutoCorrect list.

Working with Word's Dictionaries

The main Word dictionary contains thousands of common words; however, it may not include proper names, acronyms, technical terminology, and so forth. When you run the spelling checker and it comes across a word not found in the main dictionary, it marks the word as a possible spelling error. If that word is one that you use often in your writing, you can add it so the spelling checker recognizes it the next time and does not mark it as an error.

Dictionary Options

When the Suggest from Main Dictionary Only checkbox is unchecked, the spelling checker will search for words in the custom dictionaries; however, if that option is checked, it will only search the main dictionary. Adding a word during spell checking adds that word to a custom dictionary. The dictionary options are found on the Proofing page in the Word Options dialog box.

Choose whether Word includes suggestions from custom dictionaries or only the main dictionary.

Access the list of words added to the custom dictionaries.

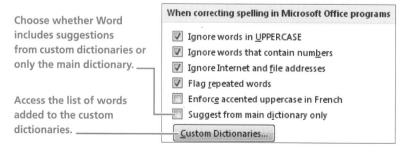

 The options you set for custom dictionaries in Microsoft Word apply to all Office programs.

Remove a Word from a Custom Dictionary

You may add a word to a custom dictionary and then realize it was a mistake. This is not a problem because you can remove it using the Custom Dictionaries dialog box. You simply open the custom dictionary, display the word list, and choose which word to delete.

Choose a word from the list to delete.

Display the list of words currently in the custom dictionary.

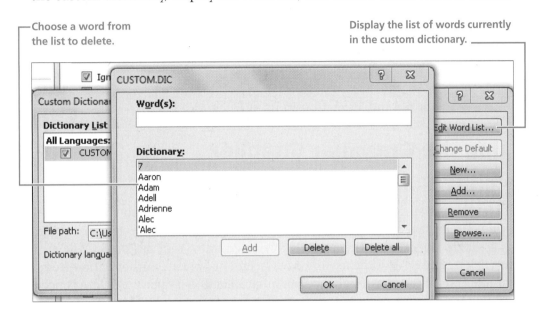

Use Automatic Spelling Checker

In this exercise, you will use the Ignore All option on the spelling checker pop-up menu to remove the red underlines from all occurrences of the words MyResume. *You will also delete a repeated word.*

Spellcheck Using Ignore All

1. Notice that the word *MyResume* in the first line of page 2 has a wavy red underline. This word appears a number of times in the document.
   MyResume *is spelled correctly; it's just that it does not appear in Word's dictionary. As a result, Word flags it as a possible spelling error.*

2. Follow these steps to have the spelling checker ignore all occurrences of *MyResume* and thereby remove the wavy red underline wherever the term appears:

Ⓐ **Right-click** the first occurrence of *MyResume*, and a pop-up menu appears. (The Mini toolbar also shows up, but you can disregard it.)

Ⓑ Choose **Ignore All** from the menu. This removes the red wavy underline from all occurrences of *MyResume*, thus making the document cleaner and easier to work with.

Work with Double Word Errors

Word flagged a double word error in the first paragraph of the press release.

3. **Right-click** the word *our* with the wavy red line, and choose the **Delete Repeated Word** command from the menu.

4. **Save** 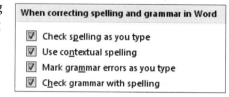 your file and leave it **open** for the next exercise.

Using the Grammar Checker

> **Video Lesson**   labyrinthelab.com/videos

Word has a sophisticated grammar checker that can help you with your writing skills. Like the spelling checker, the grammar checker can check grammar as you type. The grammar checker flags errors by underlining them with wavy green lines. You can correct a flagged error by right-clicking the error and choosing a replacement phrase or other option from the pop-up menu. Be careful when using the grammar checker. It isn't perfect. There is no substitute for careful proofreading.

Grammar checking is active by default. Grammar checking options are available by clicking the File tab, then clicking the Options tab to display the Word Options window. You can enable or disable the feature by checking or unchecking the boxes shown in the figure to the right.

When correcting spelling and grammar in Word

- ☑ Check spelling as you type
- ☑ Use contextual spelling
- ☑ Mark grammar errors as you type
- ☑ Check grammar with spelling

The Spelling and Grammar Dialog Box

FROM THE KEYBOARD

F7 to start the Spelling & Grammar check

Choose Review→Proofing→Spelling and Grammar [ABC] from the Ribbon to display the Spelling and Grammar dialog box. You may prefer to focus on your document's content and postpone proofing until you're done. You can use the Spelling and Grammar dialog box for that purpose.

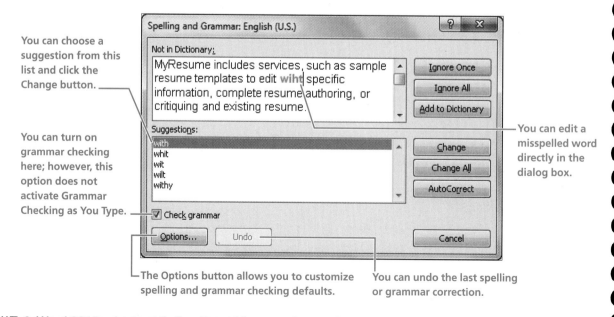

You can choose a suggestion from this list and click the Change button.

You can turn on grammar checking here; however, this option does not activate Grammar Checking as You Type.

You can edit a misspelled word directly in the dialog box.

The Options button allows you to customize spelling and grammar checking defaults.

You can undo the last spelling or grammar correction.

Use the Spelling and Grammar Dialog Box

In this exercise, you will make corrections to the Martin Memo using the Spelling and Grammar dialog box. If you do not see any text underlined in green, the grammar checking options are turned off on your computer. If you see the green grammar check lines in your document, follow the steps to turn the feature on anyway, so you will know where to locate the feature in the future.

1. Click the **File** tab and then click the **Options** tab to display the Word Options window.

2. Choose **Proofing** from the menu on the left.

3. Follow these steps to turn on grammar checking:

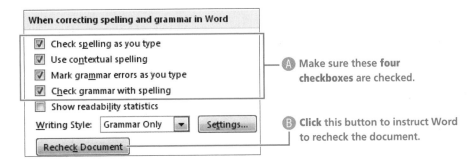

4. When the message box appears, choose **Yes** to dismiss the message, then click **OK** to close the window.
   Since you clicked Recheck Document, notice that MyResume has wavy red lines again.

5. Position the **insertion point** at the beginning of the first line on page 2.

6. Choose **Review→Proofing→Spelling and Grammar** ![ABC] from the Ribbon.
   The Spelling and Grammar dialog box appears, and MyResume is noted as a possible spelling error.

7. Click the **Add to Dictionary** button.
   You will delete MyResume from the Custom Dictionary a little later in this exercise.

8. The next error is a simple typo; the suggestion with is correct, so click the **Change** button.
   Now Word points out a possible grammatical error.

Use the Grammar Checker

9. Follow these steps to correct the grammatical error:

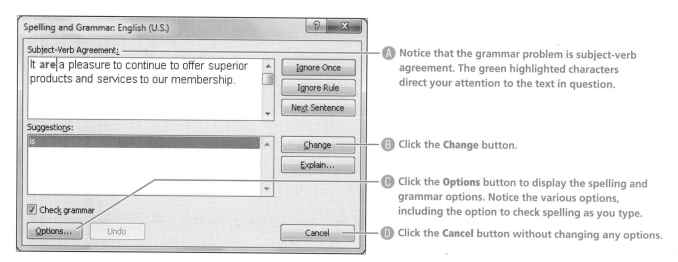

(A) Notice that the grammar problem is subject-verb agreement. The green highlighted characters direct your attention to the text in question.

(B) Click the **Change** button.

(C) Click the **Options** button to display the spelling and grammar options. Notice the various options, including the option to check spelling as you type.

(D) Click the **Cancel** button without changing any options.

10. The next error is a spelling error, and the suggestion *Delivery* is correct, so click the **Change** button.

11. Finish checking the rest of the press release using your own good judgment regarding what changes to make. When *Galin* is flagged, click the **Ignore Once** button.

12. When the message appears indicating that the spelling and grammar check is complete, click **OK**.

Remove a Word from the Custom Dictionary

You will now delete the name MyResume *that you added to the dictionary earlier in this exercise.*

13. Click **File→Options**.

14. Click the **Proofing** tab in the Navigation pane.

15. Follow these steps to display the word list in the Custom Dictionary:

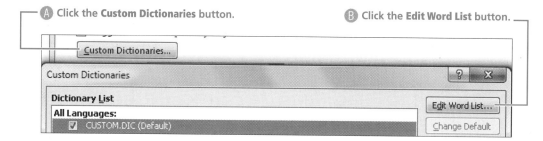

(A) Click the **Custom Dictionaries** button.

(B) Click the **Edit Word List** button.

16. Follow these steps to delete *MyResume* from the word list:

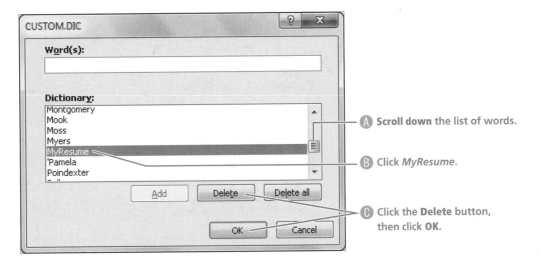

A **Scroll down** the list of words.

B Click *MyResume*.

C Click the **Delete** button, then click **OK**.

17. Click **OK** two more times to close the remaining windows.

18. **Save** 💾 the file and leave it **open** for the next exercise.

Using the Thesaurus to Find a Synonym

Video Lesson labyrinthelab.com/videos

FROM THE KEYBOARD

Alt +click the word to look up for Thesaurus

A thesaurus contains words that have the same meaning as another word (synonyms). You can quickly see a list of synonyms for a word by simply right-clicking the word and choosing Synonyms. For a more extensive list with additional options, you can display the Research task pane by choosing Thesaurus from the bottom of the context menu or from the Proofing group on the Review tab of the Ribbon.

The Thesaurus also contains antonyms, which are words meaning the opposite of other words.

Using the Research Task Pane

The Research task pane goes beyond displaying a list of alternate words. As you know, a word can have different meanings depending upon the context in which it is used. For example, the word *certain* can be used to mean *sure*, *clear*, *particular*, or *some*. Using the Thesaurus in the Research task pane, you can look up those additional synonyms by clicking any word displayed in the results list.

In addition to displaying words from the Thesaurus, the Research task pane also provides access to other references, such as a dictionary, business and financial sites, and research sites.

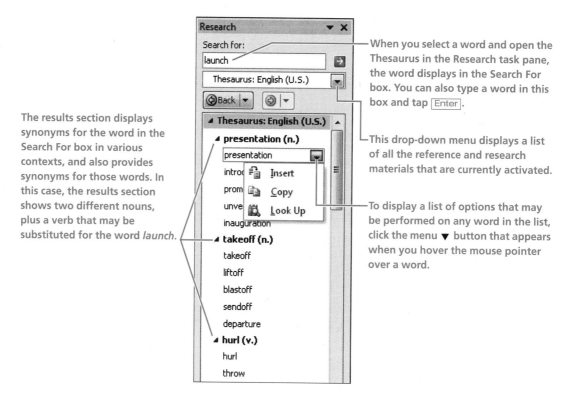

The results section displays synonyms for the word in the Search For box in various contexts, and also provides synonyms for those words. In this case, the results section shows two different nouns, plus a verb that may be substituted for the word *launch*.

When you select a word and open the Thesaurus in the Research task pane, the word displays in the Search For box. You can also type a word in this box and tap [Enter].

This drop-down menu displays a list of all the reference and research materials that are currently activated.

To display a list of options that may be performed on any word in the list, click the menu ▼ button that appears when you hover the mouse pointer over a word.

Research Task Pane Options

Word already includes a long list of services in the Research task pane, though you may wish to add your favorites to the list. Certain services in the list are currently activated; however, you can choose which ones to activate and deactivate. When you perform a search, only the services that are currently activated will be researched.

DEVELOP YOUR SKILLS 6.3.3
Use the Thesaurus

In this exercise, you will use the context menu to replace a word with a synonym, and you will experiment with the Thesaurus in the Research task pane. Finally, you will activate and deactivate services in the Research Options.

Choose a Synonym from the Menu

1. **Scroll** to view the press release page.

2. **Right-click** the word *launch* in the first sentence of the *Announcement* paragraph.

3. Follow these steps to replace the word with a synonym:

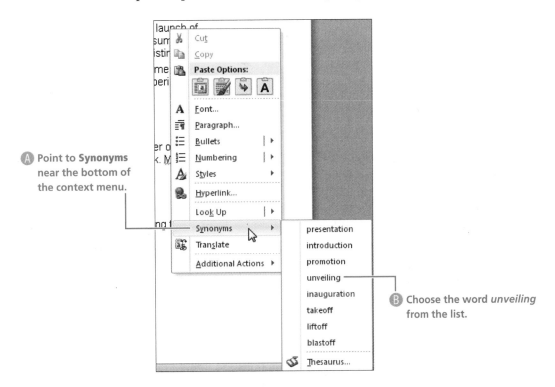

Ⓐ Point to **Synonyms** near the bottom of the context menu.

Ⓑ Choose the word *unveiling* from the list.

Notice that the word launch *in the first paragraph has been changed to* unveiling.

Look Up Synonyms in the Research Task Pane

4. Choose **Review→Proofing→Thesaurus** from the Ribbon.

5. Follow these steps to insert an alternate word for *unveiling*:

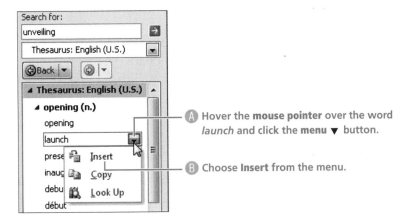

Ⓐ Hover the **mouse pointer** over the word *launch* and click the **menu ▼** button.

Ⓑ Choose **Insert** from the menu.

6. While the Research task pane is still displayed, **click** any word in the results section to view synonyms for that word.

7. Choose **Research Options** from the bottom of the Research task pane.

8. Click the **checkbox** next to Diccionario de la Real Academia Espanola.

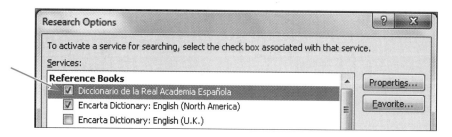

9. Before clicking OK, scroll down through the list to view the available services which may or may not be activated.

   Please do not activate or deactivate services unless are instructed to do so in the classroom.

10. Click the **menu ▼** button in the Research task pane to display the list of currently activated services.

    Notice that the list now includes the Spanish dictionary you just activated.

11. Choose **Research Options** again and remove the **checkmark** from the checkbox to deactivate the Diccionario de la Real Academia Espanola; click **OK**.

12. Click the **Close ✖** button in the upper-right corner of the Research task pane.

6.4 Formatting Text

Video Lesson   labyrinthelab.com/videos

FROM THE KEYBOARD
Ctrl+B for bold
Ctrl+U for underline
Ctrl+I for italics

You can format text by changing the font, size, and color, or by applying various enhancements, including bold, italics, and underline. You can change the text formatting before you start typing, or you can select existing text and then make the changes. When you tap Enter, Word continues to use the same formatting until you change it. Two common methods for formatting text include using the Font dialog box or the commands on the Ribbon.

Clearing Text Formatting

Once you have applied formatting, it is very easy to remove. Any selection can be returned to plain text with one click of the Clear Formatting command. You find the Clear Formatting command in the Font group on the Home tab of the Ribbon.

TIP

Changes to the font case are not affected by the Clear Formatting command.

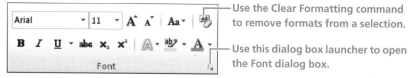

Use the Clear Formatting command to remove formats from a selection.

Use this dialog box launcher to open the Font dialog box.

The following illustration describes the Font dialog box.

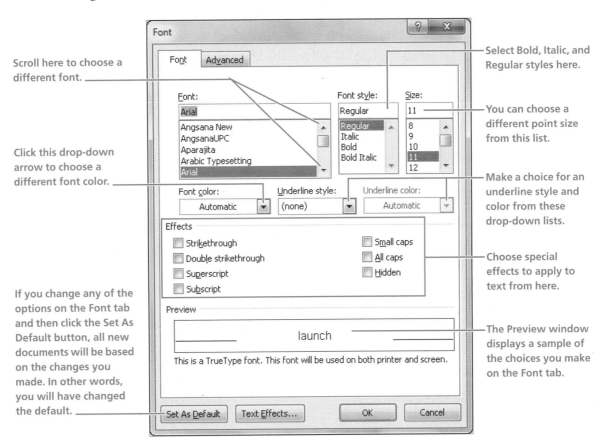

Scroll here to choose a different font.

Click this drop-down arrow to choose a different font color.

If you change any of the options on the Font tab and then click the Set As Default button, all new documents will be based on the changes you made. In other words, you will have changed the default.

Select Bold, Italic, and Regular styles here.

You can choose a different point size from this list.

Make a choice for an underline style and color from these drop-down lists.

Choose special effects to apply to text from here.

The Preview window displays a sample of the choices you make on the Font tab.

Microsoft Word

6.5 Working with Fonts and Themes

Fonts determine the appearance of the text. There are many fonts installed with Word; some are appropriate for business while others add a more whimsical, personal touch.

A theme is a set of formatting selections including colors, graphic elements, and fonts, all designed to blend well together. The theme-related font choices include one font for body text and one for headings. You will see the actual names of the theme fonts listed in the Font drop-down menu on the Ribbon, but you will see only their generic names, +Body and +Heading, in the Font dialog box. Various themes use different sets of theme fonts.

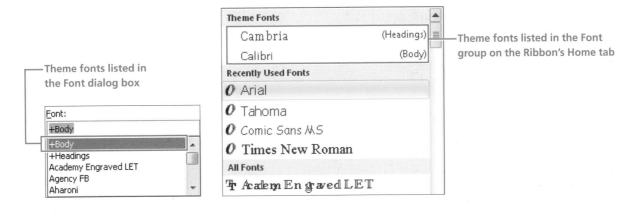

Theme fonts listed in the Font dialog box

Theme fonts listed in the Font group on the Ribbon's Home tab

Changing the Font Case

FROM THE KEYBOARD
Shift + F3 to change font case

Font cases include lowercase, uppercase, sentence case, and capitalize each word. Before beginning to type, if you want the text in uppercase, you can tap the Caps Lock key and all text will be capitalized until you tap the key again. Many times though, you may want to change the case after you've already typed the text. In this situation, all you have to do is select the text and apply a different font case. You can change the font case by using the Change Case command in the Font group on the Home tab of the Ribbon or by using Shift + F3 to toggle through the uppercase, lowercase, and capitalize each word commands.

DEVELOP YOUR SKILLS 6.5.1
Format Text

In this exercise, you will use elements from the Font group on the Ribbon, format the text, change the case, and clear formatting.

Format the Press Release Title Lines

1. **Scroll** to the top of the second page.

2. Position the **mouse pointer** in the left margin, and **drag down** to select the first three heading lines.

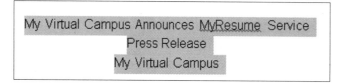

3. Choose **Home→Font→dialog box launcher** ⌐ to display the Font dialog box.

4. Follow these steps to change the font and font size:

Ⓐ Scroll down and choose **Arial** from the Font list.

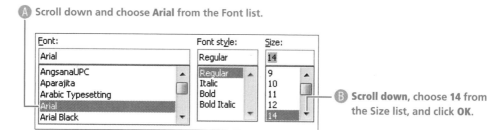

Ⓑ **Scroll down**, choose **14** from the Size list, and click **OK**.

Add Text Enhancements

5. With the three lines still selected, **tap** Ctrl + B and then **tap** Ctrl + U to apply bold and underline enhancements to the headings.

6. Click the **Underline** U button to remove that enhancement.

7. Follow these steps to apply bold formatting to multiple selections at the same time:

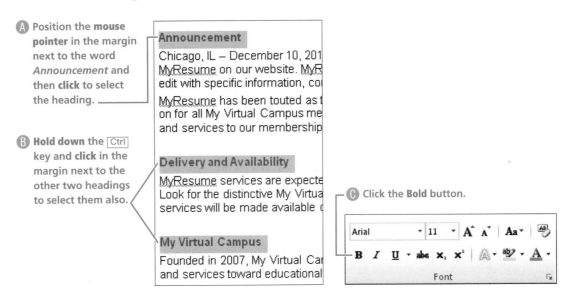

Ⓐ Position the **mouse pointer** in the margin next to the word *Announcement* and then **click** to select the heading.

Ⓑ **Hold down** the `Ctrl` key and **click** in the margin next to the other two headings to select them also.

Ⓒ Click the **Bold** button.

Change the Font Case

8. At the top of the first page, position the **insertion point** at the beginning of the first line, and then **click and drag** over *Memo To*.

9. **Press and hold down** the `Shift` key and **tap** `F3`.
   Notice that the text changed to all uppercase with one tap. If you continued holding down the `Shift` key and tapped `F3` again, it would change to all lowercase, followed by Capitalize Each Word with an additional tap.

10. **Double-click** the word *From*, and then choose **Home→Font→Change Case** **Aa** from the Ribbon.

11. Choose **UPPERCASE** from the drop-down menu.

12. Using either method above, change the words *Date* and *Subject* to **uppercase**.
    Don't panic here! The reason that the subject text moved to the next half-inch tab stop is because the word Subject *got bigger when you changed it to uppercase—it's an easy fix.*

13. Position the **insertion point** after the colon and **tap** `Delete` once to remove the extra tab stop.

Clear Formatting from Selected Text

14. Position the **mouse pointer** in the left margin, and then **triple-click** to select the entire document.

15. Choose **Home→Font→Clear Formatting** from the Ribbon.
    Notice that all formatting is removed from the entire document, including all font changes and text alignments, etc.

16. Click the **Undo** button to restore all the formatting.

17. **Save** your file and leave it **open** for the next exercise.

The Format Painter

Video Lesson   labyrinthelab.com/videos

The Format Painter 🖌️ lets you copy text formats from one location to another. This is convenient if you want the same format(s) applied to text in different locations. The Format Painter copies all text formats, including the font, font size, and color. This saves time and helps create consistent formatting throughout a document. The Format Painter is located in the Clipboard group on the Home tab, and it also appears on the Mini toolbar.

QUICK REFERENCE	COPYING TEXT FORMATS WITH THE FORMAT PAINTER
Task	**Procedure**
Copy text formats with the Format Painter	■ Select the text with the format(s) you wish to copy.
	■ Click the Format Painter once if you want to copy formats to one other location, and double-click if you want to copy to multiple locations.
	■ Select the text at the new location(s) that you want to format. If you double-clicked in the previous step, the Format Painter will remain active, allowing you to select text at multiple locations. You can even scroll through the document to reach the desired location(s).
	■ If you double-clicked, then click the Format Painter button to turn it off.

DEVELOP YOUR SKILLS 6.5.2
Use the Format Painter

In this exercise, you will change the format applied to a heading and use the Format Painter to copy formats from one text block to another.

1. **Scroll** to page 2, if necessary, and **select** the heading *Announcement* just above the first large paragraph of text.

2. When the Mini toolbar appears, follow these steps to apply color to the heading line:

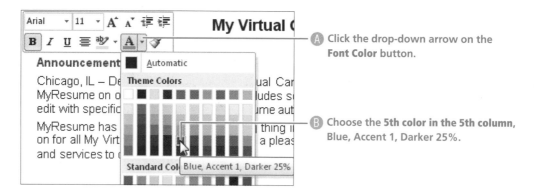

Ⓐ Click the drop-down arrow on the **Font Color** button.

Ⓑ Choose the **5th color in the 5th column**, Blue, Accent 1, Darker 25%.

Notice that the color you selected is in the Theme Colors category. These are the theme colors for Word's default *theme.*

3. Keep the text selected and the Mini toolbar active, and follow these steps to apply additional formats to the text:

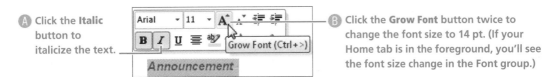

A Click the **Italic** button to italicize the text.

B Click the **Grow Font** button twice to change the font size to 14 pt. (If your Home tab is in the foreground, you'll see the font size change in the Font group.)

Copy Formats to One Location

4. Make sure the heading *Announcement* is selected.

5. Click the **Format Painter** button on the Mini toolbar.
   A paintbrush icon is added to the I-beam mouse pointer once it is positioned over the document.

6. Drag the **mouse pointer** across the *Delivery and Availability* heading, and then **release** the mouse button.
   The 14 pt italic blue formats should be copied to the heading. The animated paintbrush icon also vanishes because you clicked the Format Painter button just once in the previous step. If you want to copy formats to multiple locations, you must double-click the Format Painter.

7. Make sure the *Delivery and Availability* heading is still selected.

8. Click the **Format Painter** button on the Ribbon and then **select** the last heading, *My Virtual Campus*, to copy the format again.

Copy Formats to More Than One Location

9. **Scroll up** to the top of page 1.

10. **Click** and **drag** over *MEMO TO:* and then click the **Bold** button.
    Be sure to include the colon in the MEMO TO: selection so it is formatted also.

11. Make sure *MEMO TO:* is still selected, and then **double-click** the **Format Painter** on the Ribbon.

12. **Drag** over *FROM:* to apply the formatting from *MEMO TO:*.

13. **Drag** over *DATE:* and *SUBJECT:* to format these headings also.

14. Choose **Home→Clipboard→Format Painter** to turn it off.

15. **Save** your file and leave it **open** for the next exercise.

6.6 Working with Find and Replace

Video Lesson   labyrinthelab.com/videos

FROM THE KEYBOARD
Ctrl + F for Find
Ctrl + H for Replace

Word's Find command lets you search a document for a particular word or phrase. You can also search for text formats, page breaks, and a variety of other items. Find is often the quickest way to locate a phrase, format, or item in a document.

The Find and Replace commands appear in the Editing group at the right end of the Home tab.

Searching with the Navigation Pane

The Find command now displays the new Navigation pane on the left side of the screen. You can search for text or other objects in your document, and the items found will conveniently display in the results area, giving you a quick view of everywhere they appear in the document.

Browse Options

By default, the Find command searches for text; however, with a click of the magnifying glass, you can choose to search for other objects, such as graphics, tables, footnotes, and so forth. At the top of the results window are three tabs that allow you to browse the results by the headings, the pages, or the word(s) you typed in the search box.

When you perform a search, the results are displayed in the navigation pane and are also highlighted in the actual document. You can scroll through the document, locating each instance, or simply click any of the results in the navigation pane to jump to that instance in the document.

The magnifying glass displays a menu of search options, including objects such as tables or graphics, which you may search for instead of text.

Type the text that you are searching for here.

These three buttons control what displays in the results section: headings, pages, or the search text entered.

The search results display all instances of the word *announce* as they appear throughout the document.

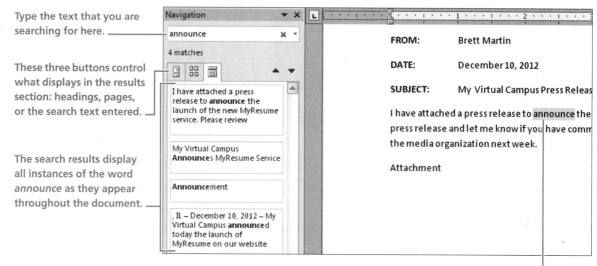

The search results are also highlighted in the document.

Using the Find and Replace Dialog Box

The Replace option in the Editing group on the Home tab displays the Find and Replace dialog box, where you can enter text, an object, or formatting you are searching for and the replacement for the found text, object, or format.

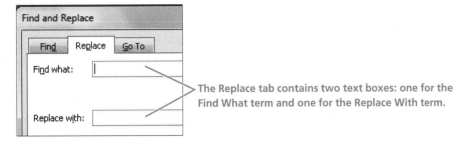

The Replace tab contains two text boxes: one for the Find What term and one for the Replace With term.

If you have already searched for text using the Navigation pane, the text automatically appears in the Find What text box in the Find and Replace dialog box.

Click the Go To button to display a menu of of specific places to jump to.

You type the term you are searching for here.

Click this button if it is labeled More. (The button name toggles between More and Less.) Clicking More displays the bottom half of the dialog box. Clicking Less closes the bottom half.

Notice that the Find and Replace tabs appear within the same dialog box.

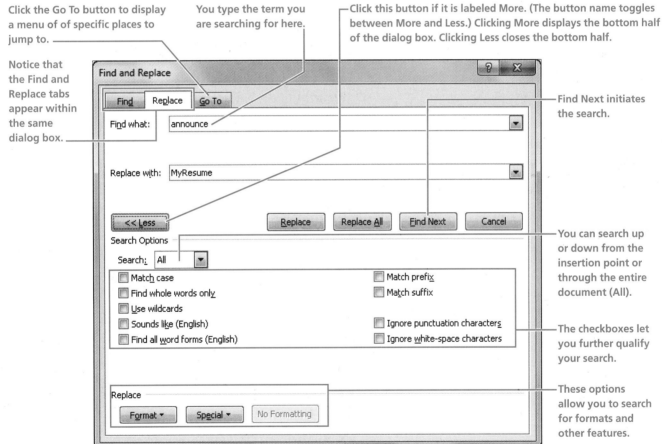

Find Next initiates the search.

You can search up or down from the insertion point or through the entire document (All).

The checkboxes let you further qualify your search.

These options allow you to search for formats and other features.

Finding and Replacing Formats

You may want to replace the formats in a document. Perhaps you formatted certain elements with a particular font and now you want to use a different font. Find and Replace finds the formatted elements for you and automatically replaces them.

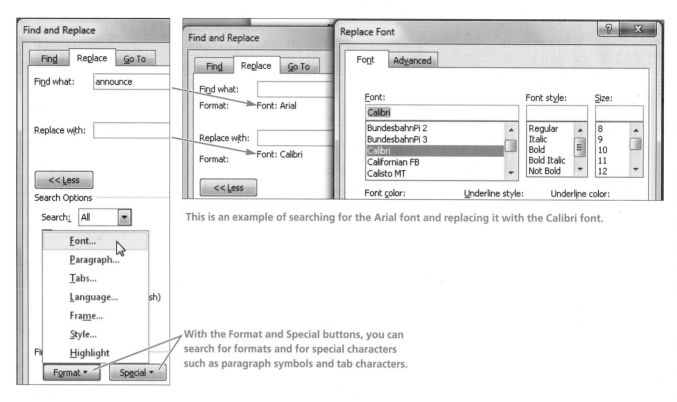

This is an example of searching for the Arial font and replacing it with the Calibri font.

With the Format and Special buttons, you can search for formats and for special characters such as paragraph symbols and tab characters.

DEVELOP YOUR SKILLS 6.6.1
Use Find and Replace

In this exercise, you will search with the Navigation pane, use Find and Replace, and explore some special search options.

Find a Word

1. Position the **insertion point** at the top of page 2, and make sure no text is selected.

2. Choose **Home→Editing→Find** 📖.

3. Follow these steps to find all occurrences of *website*:

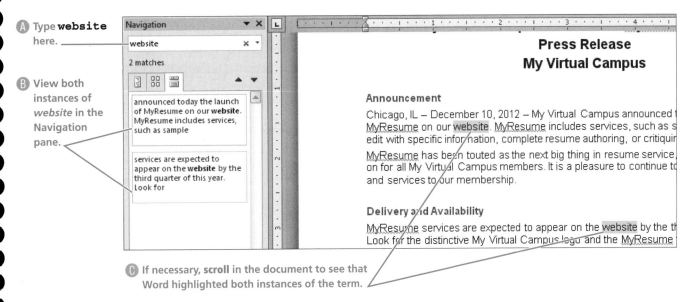

A Type **website** here.

B View both instances of *website* in the Navigation pane.

C If necessary, **scroll** in the document to see that Word highlighted both instances of the term.

4. **Scroll** to the top of the document, and position the **insertion point** anywhere in the first line of the memo.

Find Another Word

5. Click in the **Navigation pane** search box, delete *website*, and type **Announce** (with a capital A) in its place.
   Notice that Word located announce *in the first paragraph of the memo and that* announce *has a lowercase* a, *even though you typed it in uppercase.*

6. Click the second instance in the **Navigation pane** results list and notice that *Announces* is highlighted in the first heading line of the press release.
   Notice that Word found Announce, *even though it is part of* Announces. *By default, the search feature is not case sensitive and doesn't recognize the difference between a whole word and part of a word. You will change this, however, in the next few steps.*

Use the Match Case Option

Now you will use the Find Options and Additional Search Commands menu to display the Find and Replace dialog box, and then use Match Case.

7. Follow these steps to display the Find and Replace dialog box:

A Click the **Find Options and Additional Search Commands menu** ▼ button next to the Search Document box and choose **Advanced Find** from the drop-down menu. Notice that the Navigation pane is no longer the active window since you opened the Find and Replace dialog box.

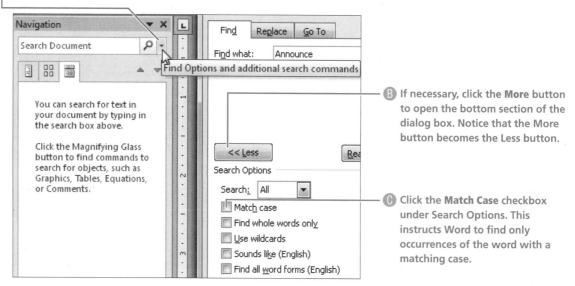

B If necessary, click the **More** button to open the bottom section of the dialog box. Notice that the More button becomes the Less button.

C Click the **Match Case** checkbox under Search Options. This instructs Word to find only occurrences of the word with a matching case.

8. Click the **Find Next** button, and Word locates the capitalized word *Announcement*.

9. Click **Find Next** again, and Word indicates that the entire document has been searched. *Word skipped over* announced *in lowercase in the next line.*

10. Click **OK** in the message box.

11. Uncheck the **Match Case** checkbox.

Search for a Whole Word

12. If necessary, **scroll** to the top of the document, and place the **insertion point** anywhere in the first line of the memo.

13. Check the **Find Whole Words Only** checkbox.

14. Click **Find Next** twice, and on the second click Word indicates that the entire document was searched.
    Notice that this time the search did not locate Announces, Announcement, *or* announced.

15. Click **OK** in the message box, and then uncheck the **Find Whole Words Only** checkbox.

16. Delete the word *Announce* in the **Find What** box.

Search for Text Formats

17. Click the **Format** button at the bottom of the dialog box.
    The Format button lets you search for specific fonts, paragraph formats, and other formats.

18. Choose **Font** from the list.

19. Choose **Bold** from the Font Style list, and click **OK**.
Font: Bold *should appear below the Find What box.*

20. Click the **Find Next** button, and Word selects a word in bold face type.

21. Click the **Less** button to collapse the bottom portion of the dialog box, and then click the **Cancel** button to close the dialog box.

Use Replace

22. Position the **insertion point** at the top of the document, and make sure no text is selected.

23. **Press** Ctrl + H to display the Find and Replace dialog box.
Notice that the Replace tab is active in the dialog box. The shortcut keystrokes that you use determine which tab displays when the dialog box appears. Make sure the insertion point is in the Find What text box.

24. Click the **More** button to expand the dialog box, and then click the **No Formatting** button at the bottom of the dialog box.
You need to turn off the Bold formatting option so Find will no longer limit it's results to finding words with Bold formatting.

25. Click the **Less** button to collapse the dialog box.
The Marketing Department decided to change the name of My Virtual Campus' new feature from MyResume to ResumePlus.

26. Type **MyResume** in the Find What box, and then type **ResumePlus** in the Replace With box.

27. Click the **Find Next** button to locate the first occurrence of *MyResume*.

28. Click the **Replace** button to make the replacement.
Word moves to the next occurrence of MyResume.

Use Replace All

29. Click the **Replace All** button to make all the changes at once.
The message box informs you that Word made seven replacements.

Use Replace All with caution. You should be confident about the replacements Word will make before you use this feature. Using Replace allows you to monitor each replacement.

30. Click **OK** to dismiss the message, and then **close** the Find and Replace dialog box and observe the *ResumePlus* replacements.

31. **Save** 🖫 and **close** the file.

6.7 Concepts Review

Concepts Review   labyrinthelab.com/ob10

To check your knowledge of the key concepts introduced in this lesson, complete the Concepts Review quiz by going to the URL listed above. If your classroom is using Labyrinth eLab, you may complete the Concepts Review quiz from within your eLab course.

Reinforce Your Skills

Create a Memorandum

In this exercise, you will create a memorandum. You will also apply character formatting.

1. Follow these guidelines to create the memorandum shown at the end of this exercise:
   - **Position** the line *MEMO TO:* approximately 2 inches down from the top of the page.
   - Apply **bold** to the lead words *MEMO TO:*, *FROM:*, *DATE:*, and *SUBJECT:*.
   - Apply **bold** formatting to the time and date in the body paragraph.
   - Type your **initials** at the bottom of the memo.

2. **Save** 💾 the memo in the Lesson 06 folder as **rs-Alexander Memo**, and then **close** it.

MEMO TO:	Trevor Alexander
FROM:	Linda Jackson
DATE:	Today's Date
SUBJECT:	Monthly Sales Meeting

Our monthly sales meeting will be held in the conference room **at 10:00 a.m.** on **Thursday, January 24**. Please bring your sales forecast for February and be prepared to discuss any important accounts that you wish to. I will give you a presentation on our new products that are scheduled for release in March. I look forward to seeing you then.

xx

Use the Spelling Checker and Find and Replace

In this exercise, you will practice using the Find and Replace feature and then spell check the document.

1. **Open** rs-Birds of Prey from the Lesson 06 folder.

2. **Spell check** the document, making the appropriate changes.

3. Use the **Navigation pane** to highlight all instances of *Birds*.

4. Display the **Find and Replace** dialog box from the Navigation pane.

5. **Replace** all occurrences of *Birds of Prey* with *Bird Watcher*.
   Word automatically italicizes the phrase Bird Watcher *because* Birds of Prey *was italicized.*

6. **Save** 💾 the document, and then **close** it.

Apply Your Skills

Edit a Business Letter

In this exercise, you will get more practice with Find and Replace and the spelling checker feature. You will also make some formatting changes and practice moving text.

1. **Open** as-Ota Letter from the Lesson 06 folder.
   This letter is set up with traditional letter spacing.

2. **Spell check** the document, making any necessary changes.

3. Use **Find and Replace** to replace all occurrences of *bill* with *account*.

4. Use **Find and Replace** to replace all occurrences of *payment* with *check*.

5. Select the entire document, change the font to **Times New Roman**, and change the font size to **12 points**.

6. Use ⌷Enter⌷ to start the date line at approximately the 2-inch position.

7. Replace *Today's Date* with the current date.

8. Move the **address block** from the bottom of the letter to the space between the last body paragraph and the complimentary close *Sincerely*. If necessary, **insert** or **remove** hard returns until there is a double space between the address block and the last body paragraph and between the address block and the complimentary close *Sincerely*.

9. Insert your typist's **initials** below the signature block.

10. **Save** 🖫 the changes, and then **close** the document.

Use the Spelling Checker and Find and Replace

In this exercise, you will practice using the spelling checker and the Find and Replace feature.

1. **Open** as-Collarbone from the Lesson 06 folder.

2. **Spell check** the document. Use your best judgment to determine which replacement words to use for incorrectly spelled words.

3. Use **Find and Replace** to make the following replacements. Write the number of replacements in the third column of the table.

Word	Replace With	Number of Replacements
breaks	fractures	_____
collarbone	clavicle	_____
movement	range-of-motion	_____

4. **Print** the document when you have finished.

5. **Save** 💾 the changes, and then **close** the document.

Format Characters and Insert Special Characters

In this exercise, you will try out various character formats and insert special characters. Then you will insert and delete a page break.

1. **Open** as-Formatting from the Lesson 06 folder.

2. Follow the instructions in the exercise document to format lines and insert special characters.

3. **Capitalize** and **underline** the title at the top of the document.

4. **Save** 💾 the document and **close** it.

Critical Thinking & Work-Readiness Skills

In the course of working through the following Microsoft Office-based Critical Thinking exercises, you will also be utilizing various work-readiness skills, some of which are listed next to each exercise. Go to labyrinthelab.com/ workreadiness to learn more about the work-readiness skills.

6.1 Use Dates and Symbols

Brett has received positive feedback from early users of MyResume and her press release. She writes a memo to her manager, Rick Smith, reporting some of the feedback. Open ct-Feedback Memo (Lesson 06 folder). Insert a complete and appropriate heading for a memorandum at the top of the document, including To, From, Date, and Subject. Be sure to use the tab stops so the information is nicely formatted and aligned. Add the trademark symbol (™) after *MyResume*. Use Find and Replace to replace all instances of *we have* with **we've**. Save the file to your Lesson 06 folder as **ct-Feedback Final**.

WORK-READINESS SKILLS APPLIED
- Writing
- Serving clients/ customers
- Communicating information

6.2 Use Page Breaks and Proofreading Tools

Start with the ct-Feedback Final document you created in the previous exercise and save it to your Lesson 06 folder as **ct-Feedback Points**. Add a final sentence to the first page explaining that specific feedback is on the next page. Insert a page break after the last paragraph and add at least five points of positive feedback from users of MyResume, the online resume builder. Use the spelling and grammar checker throughout the memo, making corrections as necessary. Save your changes.

WORK-READINESS SKILLS APPLIED
- Writing
- Thinking creatively
- Communicating information

6.3 Rewrite and Reformat a Memorandum

Start with the ct-Feedback Points document you created in the previous exercise and save it to your Lesson 06 folder as **ct-Feedback Rewrite**. Use the tools on the Navigation pane to find the first instance of the word *positive* and then replace the word with a synonym you found using the Research task pane. Find and replace the word *potential* with a synonym. Replace at least one other word with a synonym using the Research task pane. Save your changes.

WORK-READINESS SKILLS APPLIED
- Solving problems
- Selecting technology
- Applying technology to a task

U N I T

3

Excel 2010

n this unit, you will be introduced to the essential Excel 2010 features. You will begin by reviewing the Ribbon interface. Next, you will move on to create worksheets by entering and editing data in them. You will also edit worksheets with Cut, Copy, and Paste commands, drag and drop, and the automated features AutoFill and AutoComplete. When working with formulas and functions, you will learn about point mode and absolute, relative, and mixed references.

Microsoft Excel

Exploring Excel 2010

LEARNING OBJECTIVES

After studying this lesson, you will be able to:

- Explain ways Excel can help your productivity
- Navigate around the Excel window
- Enter text and numbers into cells
- Distinguish between a text and a number entry in a cell
- Save and "save as" workbooks

In this lesson, you will develop fundamental Excel skills. This lesson will provide you with a solid understanding of Excel so you are prepared to master advanced features later. You will learn how to navigate around a worksheet, enter various types of data, and select cells.

Building a Basic Spreadsheet

Welcome to Green Clean, a janitorial product supplier and cleaning service contractor to small businesses, shopping plazas, and office buildings. Green Clean uses environmentally friendly cleaning products and incorporates sustainability practices wherever possible, including efficient energy and water use, recycling and waste reduction, and reduced petroleum use in vehicles. In addition to providing green cleaning services, the company also sells its eco-friendly products directly to customers.

Throughout this unit, you will follow the steps with Green Clean employees as they use essential Excel features to complete tasks and projects.

Nicole Romero works as a payroll assistant at Green Clean. She needs to create a list of hours that cleaning service employees worked during the weekend (Friday through Sunday). Nicole's manager has asked her to compile the data from employee time sheets and report hours on a daily basis. Nicole decides that Excel is the right tool for this task and proceeds to organize the data in a worksheet, shown in the following illustration.

	A	B	C	D	E
1	Service Employees Weekend Hours Worked				
2					
3	Alton Mall		Friday	Saturday	Sunday
4		Barnes	6	6	6
5		Chau	8	8	8
6		Lee	4	0	4
7		Olsen	4	3	0
8		Total Hrs			
9	Century Bank				
10		Garcia	3	5	0
11		Kimura	3	4	0
12		Tan	3	5	0
13		Total Hrs			
14	Newport Medical				
15		Kowalski	8	6	8
16		Silva	6	6	0
17		Wilson	5	2	5
18		Total Hrs			

Notice that Excel makes it easy for you to organize your data in columns and rows. The "Total Hrs" rows have been included in the example, although you will not learn how to create formulas to calculate totals in this lesson.

7.1 Presenting Excel 2010

Video Lesson labyrinthelab.com/videos

Microsoft Office Excel is an electronic spreadsheet program that allows you to work with numbers and data much more efficiently than the pen-and-paper method. Excel is used in virtually all industries and many households for a variety of tasks such as:

- Creating and maintaining detailed budgets
- Keeping track of extensive customer lists
- Performing "what-if" scenarios and break-even analyses
- Determining the profitability of a business or sector
- Creating tables to organize information
- Tracking employee information
- Producing detailed charts to graphically display information
- Creating invoices or purchase orders
- Determining the future value of an investment, the present value of an annuity, or the payment for a loan
- Working with reports exported from small business accounting software programs such as Intuit's QuickBooks®

As you can see from this list, Excel is not just used to crunch numbers. It is a very powerful program that is used not only to work with numbers but also to maintain databases. If you have started a database in Excel, you can even import it into Microsoft Access (the program in the Microsoft Office Suite that is specialized for working with databases). Many people may use Excel to track their databases rather than Access because of its ease of use and because Access is not included in all of the Microsoft Office editions. If you are tracking multiple databases that you wish to include in reports and data queries, you will want to consider utilizing Access, though, as it really is designed to work with multiple tables of data.

Throughout the Excel lessons, the terms *spreadsheet* and *worksheet* will be used interchangeably.

7.2 Exploring the Excel Program Window

Video Lesson labyrinthelab.com/videos

When you launch Excel, you will see a blank workbook displayed. The window is filled with many objects and a space for you to create your spreadsheet. Using the figures that follow, you will have an opportunity to learn the names of some of the objects that you can see on your screen.

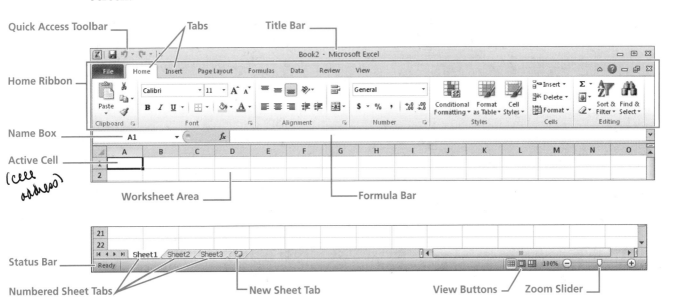

Using Worksheets and Workbooks

Excel displays a blank workbook the moment you start the program. A workbook is composed of worksheets. A workbook is similar to a paper notebook with several sheets of paper. You enter text, numbers, formulas, charts, and other objects in worksheets. By default, Excel displays three worksheets in a new workbook, each accessible by a separate tab at the bottom of the screen. The maximum number of worksheets you can insert is limited only by the amount of memory available on your computer.

In this example, the sheet tabs are named so that you can
organize data for each season as well as track annual information.

A worksheet has a grid structure with horizontal rows and vertical columns. A new worksheet has 16,384 columns and 1,048,576 rows. However, at any given time only a small number of the rows and columns are visible in the worksheet window. The intersection of each row and column is a cell. Each cell is identified by a reference. The reference is the column letter followed by the row number. For example, A1 is the reference of the cell in the top-left corner of the worksheet. So, this is called cell A1.

The name of the cell will be displayed in the Name Box.

Ctrl + home takes back to A1

Mousing Around in Excel

The shape of the mouse pointer will change as you move it around the Excel window. The shape of the pointer will let you know what will happen if you click over that spot.

Mouse Pointer Shape	Function
✛	Click to select a cell. Click and drag to select multiple cells.
➕	The fill handle pointer; dragging this pointer will copy the cell contents or the next values in a data series to adjacent cells.
⬉	Allows you to perform a variety of tasks when clicked, such as issue a command from the Ribbon or select a new tab.
✥	The move pointer; if you drag with this, it will move cell contents from one location to another.
↕ ⬌ ⬂	The resize pointers; dragging one of these pointers will allow you to change the height, width, or both dimensions of objects such as pictures, shapes, or charts.
➡ ⬇	Select a row or column.
I	Click with the I-beam pointer to enter text, such as in the Formula Bar.

Scrolling Along in a Worksheet

There are two scroll bars visible in the Excel window, both vertical and horizontal. They allow you to see other areas of the worksheet without changing which cell is active. There are three ways to use the scroll bars to view other areas of your spreadsheet.

Click between an arrow and the scroll box to move one "screen view" at a time.

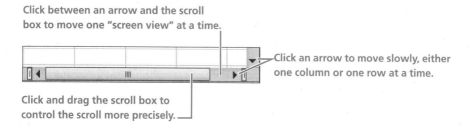

Click an arrow to move slowly, either one column or one row at a time.

Click and drag the scroll box to control the scroll more precisely.

Navigating in a Worksheet

When you have a cell selected, it is surrounded by a thick line, which indicates that it is the active cell. You can change the active cell by clicking in another cell or by using the keyboard. This is important because data is entered into the active cell. The vertical and horizontal scroll bars let you navigate through a worksheet; however, scrolling does not change which cell is active. After scrolling, you will have to select which cell is to be active, either by clicking or using one of the keystrokes listed below.

You may type a cell reference in the Name Box and then tap ⌈Enter⌋ to navigate to that cell.

Keystroke(s)	How the Highlight Moves
→ ← ↑ ↓	One cell right, left, up, or down
Home	Beginning of current row
Ctrl + Home	Home cell, usually cell A1
Ctrl + End	Last cell in active part of worksheet
Page Down	Down one visible screen
Page Up	Up one visible screen
Alt + Page Down	One visible screen right
Alt + Page Up	One visible screen left
Ctrl + G	Displays Go To dialog box—enter cell reference and click OK

DEVELOP YOUR SKILLS 7.2.1
Move the Selection and Explore the Excel Window

In this exercise, you will practice selecting the active cell in a worksheet so that you can become comfortable enough with the program to begin to create a worksheet.

1. Start Excel by choosing **Start** →**All Programs**→**Microsoft Office**→**Microsoft Office Excel 2010**.

2. **Maximize** the window, if necessary.

Navigate with the Mouse

3. Slide the **mouse pointer** over the screen and notice the thick **cross shape** ✚ when it is in the worksheet area.
   If you click with this pointer shape, you will select a cell.

4. Click the **cross-shaped pointer** on any cell and notice that the cell becomes active.

5. Move the selection five times by **clicking** in various cells.

Navigate with the Keyboard

Now that you have practiced using the mouse, it is time to learn how to use the keyboard to move about a worksheet. You should use the keys on your keyboard that are between the main part and the numeric keypad on the far right.

6. Use the →, ←, ↑, and ↓ keys to position the highlight in **cell F10**.

7. **Tap** the Home key and see that the highlight moves to cell A10.
   The Home key always makes the cell in column A of the current row active.

8. **Press** Ctrl + Home to make A1 the active cell.

9. **Tap** the Page Down key two or three times.
   Notice that Excel displays the next 25 or so rows (one "visible" screen's worth) each time you tap Page Down.

10. **Press** and **hold down** the ↑ key until A1 is the active cell.

Use the Scroll Bars

The scroll bars allow you to see other areas of the Excel worksheet area without changing which cell is active.

11. Click the **Scroll Right** ▶ button on the horizontal scroll bar until columns AA and AB are visible.
    Excel labels the first 26 columns A–Z and the next 26 columns AA–AZ. A similar labeling scheme is used for the remaining columns out to the final column, XFD.

12. Click the **Scroll Down** ▼ button on the vertical scroll bar until row 100 is visible.
    Notice that the highlight has not moved. To move the highlight, you must click in a cell or use the keyboard.

13. Take a few minutes to practice **scrolling** and **moving** the selection.

Use the Go To Command

As you learned in the preceding keystroke navigation table, you can use Ctrl + G *to display the Go To box, where you can go to a specific cell by entering the desired cell reference in the Reference box and clicking OK. You can use* Ctrl + Home *to select cell A1.*

14. **Press** Ctrl + G to display the Go To dialog box.

15. Type **g250** in the Reference box and click **OK**.
    Notice that cell references are not case sensitive.

16. Use the **Go To** command to move to two or three different cells.

17. **Press** Ctrl + Home to return to cell A1.

Navigate with the Name Box

18. Click the **Name Box** at the left of the Formula Bar.

19. Type **ab9** and **tap** Enter.

20. **Press** Ctrl + Home to return to cell A1.

Explore the Excel Window

Now that you have learned how to select cells and move around in the window, it is time to explore the Excel window a bit further.

21. Follow these steps to explore the Excel window:

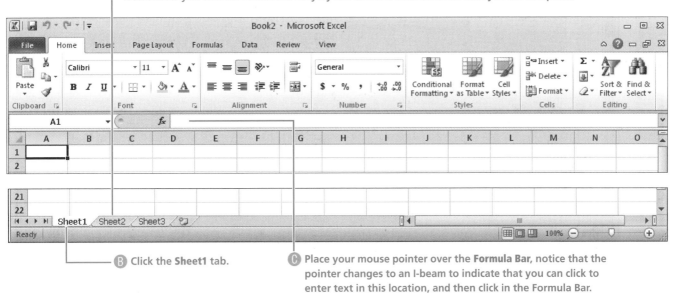

Ⓐ Click the **Sheet2** tab and notice that a different blank worksheet appears. The number of worksheets you can have is limited only by the amount of available memory in the computer.

Ⓑ Click the **Sheet1** tab.

Ⓒ Place your mouse pointer over the **Formula Bar**, notice that the pointer changes to an I-beam to indicate that you can click to enter text in this location, and then click in the Formula Bar.

22. Select any cell **other than** A1, the currently active cell, to exit the Formula Bar.

23. Select **cell A1**.
Leave the Excel window open.

Microsoft Excel

Video Lesson   labyrinthelab.com/videos

You can begin entering data the moment Excel is started. Data is entered into the active cell (the cell with the thick line around it). Text and numbers are used for different purposes in a worksheet. For instance, text entries cannot be used in calculations, whereas number entries can. Text is used for descriptive headings and entries that require alphabetic characters or a combination of alphabetic and numeric characters and spaces. Numbers can be entered directly or can be calculated using formulas. Excel recognizes the data you enter and decides whether the entry is text, a number, or a formula that performs a calculation.

Data Types

Entries are defined as one of two main classifications: constant values or formulas. Constant values can be text, numeric, or a combination of both. The one thing that makes an entry constant is that the value does not change when other information changes. Conversely, formula entries display the results of calculations, and a result can change when a value in another cell changes.

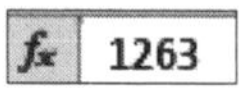

fx 1263	fx =SUM(C5:C8)
This entry is a constant value; it will not change as other cells are updated.	When a formula entry is used, it will refer to one or more cells and will change as the indicated cells are updated.

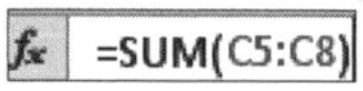

Completing Cell Entries

Text and numbers are entered by positioning the highlight in the desired cell, typing the desired text or number, and completing the entry. You can use Enter, Tab, or any of the arrow keys (→, ←, ↑, ↓) to complete an entry. The position of the active cell following a cell entry depends on the method by which you complete the entry.

[handwritten note in margin: change # in formula not cell or double click in cell]

Entry Completion Method	Where the Active Cell Will Appear
Enter	It will move down to the next cell.
Tab	It will move to the next cell to the right.
→ ↑ ↓ ←	It will move to the next cell in the direction of the arrow key.
Esc	The entry will be deleted and the current cell will remain active.

The Enter and Cancel Buttons

The Enter ✓ and Cancel ✗ buttons appear on the Formula Bar whenever you enter or edit an entry. The Enter button completes the entry and keeps the highlight in the current cell. The Cancel button cancels the entry, as does the Esc key.

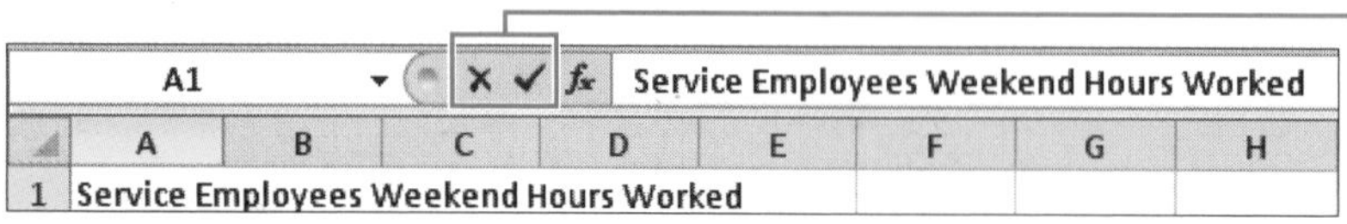

The Cancel and Enter buttons appear when an entry is being entered or edited.

| A1 ▾ | ✗ ✓ fx | Service Employees Weekend Hours Worked |

	A	B	C	D	E	F	G	H
1	Service Employees Weekend Hours Worked							

Deleting and Replacing Entries

You can delete an entire entry after it has been completed by clicking in the cell and tapping Delete. Likewise, you can replace an entry by clicking in the cell and typing a new entry. The new entry will replace the original entry.

Long Text Entries

Text entries often do not fit in a cell. These entries are known as long entries. Excel uses the following rules when deciding how to display long entries:

- If the cell to the right of the long entry is empty, then the long entry displays over the adjacent cell.

- If the cell to the right of the long entry contains an entry, then Excel shortens, or truncates, the display of the long entry.

Keep in mind that Excel does not actually change the long entry; it simply truncates the display of the entry. You can always widen a column to accommodate a long entry.

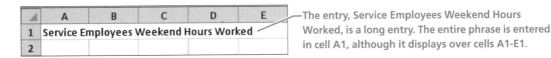

The entry, Service Employees Weekend Hours Worked, is a long entry. The entire phrase is entered in cell A1, although it displays over cells A1-E1.

DEVELOP YOUR SKILLS 7.3.1
Enter Text

In this exercise, you will enter text into your worksheet.

Type a Long Entry

First, you will have the opportunity to see how text can flow over empty cells to the right of its "home" cell.

1. Make **cell A1** active by clicking the **mouse pointer** ✛ in it.

2. Type **Service Employees Weekend Hours Worked** and **tap** Enter.
   The text is entered in the cell and the highlight moves down to cell A2. Excel moves the highlight down when you tap Enter *because most people enter data column by column. Notice that the entry displays over cells B1, C1, D1, and E1. The long entry would not display over these cells if they contained data.*

3. Click **cell A1** and note the appearance of the Formula Bar.

Notice that the Formula Bar displays the name of the active cell (A1) as well as its content. In this example, the cell's content is the title, Service Employees Weekend Hours Worked. The title is a long entry because it is wider than cell A1. Cells B1-E1 are empty so the long entry is displayed over them. Keep in mind, however, that the entire entry belongs to cell A1. This concept will be demonstrated in the next few steps.

Verify that the Entry Belongs to Cell A1

4. **Tap** the → key to make cell B1 active.

5. Look at the **Formula Bar** and notice that cell B1 is empty.
   The long entry belongs to cell A1 even though it is displayed over cells A1–E1.

Microsoft Excel

6. Click in **cell C3**.

7. Type **Friday** and **tap** →️ once.
   Notice that the entry is completed and the highlight moves to cell D3. You can always use the arrow keys to complete an entry and move the highlight in the desired direction.

8. Type **Wednesday** in cell D3 and **tap** →️.

9. Type **Sunday** in cell E3 and **tap** ←️.
   Notice that the display of Wednesday *is shortened, or truncated.*
   However, the Wednesday entry is still contained in its entirety in cell D3.
   A long entry is always truncated when the cell to the right contains text, a number, or a formula.

Friday	Wednesd:	Sunday

10. Type **Saturday** in cell D3 and **tap** Enter.
    The new entry in cell D3 replaces the previous entry.

11. **Enter** the remaining text entries shown in the following illustration.
    If Excel proposes any entries for you as you type, simply continue typing. Leave the workbook open for the next exercise.

	A	B	C	D	E
1	Service Employees Weekend Hours Worked				
2					
3	Alton Mall		Friday	Saturday	Sunday
4		Barnes			
5		Chau			
6		Lee			
7		Olsen			
8		Total Hrs			
9	Century Bank				
10		Garcia			
11		Kimura			
12		Tan			
13		Total Hrs			
14	Newport Medical				
15		Kowalski			
16		Silva			
17		Wilson			
18		Total Hrs			

7.4 Working with Numbers

Video Lesson   labyrinthelab.com/videos

Number entries can contain only the digits 0–9 and a few other characters. Excel initially right-aligns numbers in cells, although you can change this alignment. The following table lists characters that Excel accepts as part of a number entry.

Valid Characters in Number Entries
The digits 0–9
The following characters: + – ( ) , / $ % . *

Entering numbers using the numeric keypad is very quick. The keypad is designed like a calculator. It includes its own decimal point and an Enter key.

Number Formats

It isn't necessary to type commas, dollar signs, and other number formats when entering numbers. It's easier to simply enter the numbers and use Excel's formatting commands to add the desired number format(s). You will not format numbers in this lesson.

Decimals and Negative Numbers

You should always type a decimal point if the number you are entering requires one. Likewise, you should precede a negative number entry with a minus (–) sign or enclose it in parentheses ( ).

DEVELOP YOUR SKILLS 7.4.1
Enter Numbers

In this exercise, you will practice entering numbers and canceling entries before completion.

Use the Enter Button

1. Position the highlight in **cell C4**.

2. Type **6** but don't complete the entry.

3. Look at the Formula Bar and notice the **Cancel** ☒ and **Enter** ☑ buttons.
   These buttons appear whenever you begin entering or editing data in a cell.

4. Click the **Enter** ☑ button to complete the entry.
   Notice that the highlight remains in cell C4. You can use the Enter button to complete entries, though it is more efficient to use the keyboard when building a worksheet. This is because the highlight automatically moves to the next cell. The Enter button is most useful when editing entries.

Use the Cancel Button and the [Esc] Key

5. Position the highlight in cell C5 and type **8**, but don't complete the entry.

6. Click the **Cancel** [X] button on the Formula Bar to cancel the entry.

7. Type **8** again, but this time **tap [Esc]** on the keyboard.
   The [Esc] key has the same effect as the Cancel button.

8. Type **8** once again, and this time **tap [↓]**.
   Notice that Excel right-aligns the number in the cell.

9. **Enter** the remaining numbers shown in the illustration at right.

To use the numeric keypad to enter numbers, the [number lock] light must be on. If it's not, press the [Num Lock] key on the keypad.

⊿	A	B	C	D	E
1	Service Employees Weekend Hours Worked				
2					
3	Alton Mall		Friday	Saturday	Sunday
4		Barnes	6	6	6
5		Chau	8	8	8
6		Lee	4	0	4
7		Olsen	4	3	0
8		Total Hrs			
9	Century Bank				
10		Garcia	3	5	0
11		Kimura	3	4	0
12		Tan	3	5	0
13		Total Hrs			
14	Newport Medical				
15		Kowalski	8	6	8
16		Silva	6	6	0
17		Wilson	5	2	5
18		Total Hrs			

10. Take a minute to verify that you have correctly entered all the numbers.
    It is so important for you to be accurate when you are entering data into Excel. Learning how to use complex formulas and functions will not do you any good if your original data is inaccurate!

7.5 Understanding Save Concepts

Video Lesson   labyrinthelab.com/videos

One important lesson to learn is to save your workbooks early and often! Power outages and careless accidents can result in lost data. The best protection is to save your workbooks every 10 or 15 minutes or after making significant changes. Workbooks are saved to file storage locations such as a USB drive, the Documents folder, a shared network drive, and websites on the Internet.

The Save Command

The Save [💾] button on the Quick Access toolbar or the File tab on the Ribbon initiates the Save command. If a document has been saved previously, Excel replaces the original version with the new, edited version. If a document has never been saved, Excel displays the Save As dialog box. The Save As dialog box lets you specify the name and storage location of the document. You can also use the Save As dialog box to make a copy of a document by saving it under a new name or to a different location. Your filenames can have up to 255 characters, including spaces. Your filenames, however, should be descriptive but brief enough to manage your files and share them on networks and the Internet effectively.

Save As Options

In Excel, you are given multiple options as to how to save your workbook. How you save a workbook depends on how it will be used and who will be using it. If you are collaborating with someone who has a version earlier than Excel 2007 installed, you will need to save the file in the Excel 97-2003 Format. If you wish to publish your workbook and do not wish for others to make changes to it, you may save it as a PDF file for viewing in the Adobe Reader program. The default format is the Excel Workbook format, which is great to use if everyone who will be utilizing the file has Excel 2010 or 2007 installed.

The Save As command allows you to save a spreadsheet or entire workbook in various formats to use data in earlier versions of Excel or other applications.

Excel Workbook
Excel Macro-Enabled Workbook
Excel Binary Workbook
Excel 97-2003 Workbook
XML Data
Single File Web Page
Web Page
Excel Template
Excel Macro-Enabled Template
Excel 97-2003 Template
Text (Tab delimited)
Unicode Text
XML Spreadsheet 2003
Microsoft Excel 5.0/95 Workbook
CSV (Comma delimited)
Formatted Text (Space delimited)
Text (Macintosh)
Text (MS-DOS)
CSV (Macintosh)
CSV (MS-DOS)
DIF (Data Interchange Format)
SYLK (Symbolic Link)
Excel Add-In
Excel 97-2003 Add-In
PDF
XPS Document
OpenDocument Spreadsheet

Locating Workbooks

The Save As dialog box lets you locate workbooks on your local drives and in network locations. The Documents folder in the hard drive of your local computer usually is the default location for saving a workbook. You must change the location if you do not want to save there. Once you save to or open a workbook from a different location, the default changes to that location. Always check the Save As dialog box for the current drive and folder before finishing the save.

Issuing Commands from the Keyboard

There are many times when it is more convenient to issue a command from the keyboard than to chase it down with your mouse. These commands are termed keyboard shortcuts and can help you to be more efficient as you can enter these commands "on the fly" without removing your fingers from the keyboard. In this book, you will see keyboard shortcuts displayed in a special feature called From the Keyboard. Whenever you issue a keyboard command, you will first hold down the shortcut key (Ctrl, Alt, or Shift) and then tap the additional key to issue the command. This approach is similar to holding down the Shift key and then tapping a letter to make it capital. Throughout this book, you will be asked to use Ctrl + S to save your worksheet.

FROM THE KEYBOARD
Ctrl+S to save

QUICK REFERENCE	SAVING A WORKBOOK
Task	**Procedure**
Save for the first time	■ Click Save 🖫 on the Quick Access toolbar.
	■ Name the workbook and choose the location in which to save it.
	■ Click Save.

Task	Procedure
Save changes in the workbook	■ Click Save  on the Quick Access toolbar.
Save in a new location or with a new name	■ Choose File→Save As . ■ Change the name of the workbook, the file storage location, or both. ■ Click Save.
Save the workbook in the Excel 97-2003 Format	■ Choose File→Save As . ■ Enter the filename and navigate to the desired file storage location. ■ Choose Excel 97-2003 from the Save as Type list. ■ Click Save.

DEVELOP YOUR SKILLS 7.5.1

Save the Workbook

In this exercise, you will save the workbook created in the previous exercises to your file storage location.

1. Click the **Save** 💾 button on the Quick Access toolbar.
   The Save As dialog box appears because this is the first time you are saving the workbook.

2. Notice that the proposed name Book1 is highlighted in the File Name box.
   The name may be Book2 or something similar. You may need to select the name to highlight it if you clicked elsewhere in the dialog box.

3. **Type** the name **Weekend Hours Worked** and it will replace the proposed name.

File name:	Weekend Hours Worked
Save as type:	Excel Workbook

4. Choose the Lesson 07 folder in your file storage location by **navigating** to the correct drive and folder.
   See the online document, Storing Your Exercise Files, for specific instructions for your operating system.

5. Click **Save** or **tap** [Enter].
   Notice that the filename appears in the Title Bar of the window to indicate that the workbook is saved.

Weekend Hours Worked - Microsoft Excel

6. Choose **File→Exit** ⊠ to close Excel.

7.6 Concepts Review

Concepts Review	labyrinthelab.com/ob10

To check your knowledge of the key concepts introduced in this lesson, complete the Concepts Review quiz by going to the URL listed above. If your classroom is using Labyrinth eLab, you may complete the Concepts Review quiz from within your eLab course.

Reinforce Your Skills

Create a Workbook

In this exercise, you will create a workbook. You will start Excel and then enter text and numbers that contain two decimal places.

Start Excel and Enter Text

1. Start Excel by selecting **All Programs→Microsoft Office→Microsoft Office Excel 2010** from the Start menu.
   Notice that a blank workbook with three worksheets is displayed when you open Excel.

2. Enter text in **rows 1 through 9** as shown in the following illustration.
   Use the Tab *and* Enter *keys as necessary to enter the data. Type the customer's name and address in cells B5, B6, and B7.*

	A	B	C	D	E
1	Order Tracking Sheet				
2					
3	Order No.	1552			
4					
5	Sold to:	Empire Dry Cleaning			
6		1833 Franklin Highway			
7		Huntington, WV 25716			
8					
9	Item	In Stock?	Quantity	Price	Discount

Enter Decimal and Negative Numbers

3. In **cells A9 through E14**, enter the data shown in the illustration at right.
   Type a decimal point (.) in the Price numbers and Discount numbers. Type a minus (–) sign before the Discount numbers.

	A	B	C	D	E
9	Item	In Stock?	Quantity	Price	Discount
10	A423	Y	2	63.95	-3.15
11	A321	Y	4	28.95	0
12	D928	N	16	5.85	-0.59
13	S251	N	8	3.09	-0.31
14	B444	Y	20	8.77	-0.88

Save the Workbook

4. Choose **Save** 💾 on the Quick Access toolbar.

5. **Type** the filename **rs-Order Tracking** and **navigate** to the Lesson 07 folder in your file storage location.

6. Click **Save** or **tap** Enter .
   The workbook will be saved in the location that you specified. Leave the workbook open.

Explore the Excel Window and Save and Close Your Workbook

In this exercise, you will take a look at the features of the Excel window before saving the changes and closing your new workbook.

1. **Click** to display the Data tab of the Ribbon.
   Look at the types of commands available. Many of them will be covered in later lessons of this book.

2. Select the **View** tab of the Ribbon.

3. Click the **Minimize the Ribbon** button at the upper-right corner of the window to hide the Ribbon.

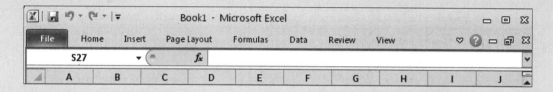

4. **Double-click** the Home tab to display the Ribbon once again.
   Notice that the Home tab is displayed because you chose it to redisplay the Ribbon.

5. Click **cell C5**, and then look at the **Formula Bar**.

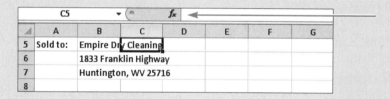

There is nothing displayed because the entire entry is contained in cell B5 and is simply spilling over cell C5 because it is empty.

6. **Type** your name, and then click the **Enter** ✔ button.
   Your name will now appear in cell C5, and the customer name in cell B5 will be truncated.

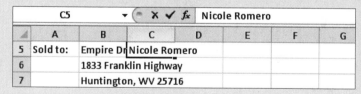

7. **Tap** Delete.
   Your name will be deleted, and the customer name from B5 will once again spill over the cells to the right.

8. Select **cell A16** and **enter** your first and last names.

9. Use Ctrl + S to save the changes to the workbook.
   The workbook saves to your same file storage location as before.

10. Choose **File→Exit** to close Excel.

Apply Your Skills

Create a New Workbook

In this exercise, you will create a new worksheet and then save and close the workbook.

1. Start **Excel**.
   A new, blank workbook appears.

2. Create the **worksheet** shown in the following illustration and **type** your first and last names in **cell D1**.
   Proofread all data. You will not create formulas to calculate totals in this exercise.

	A	B	C	D	E
1	Green Clean Q1 Expenses			Student Name	
2					
3	Item		January	February	March
4	Building	Lease	3000	3000	3000
5		Utilities	1689	1572	1646
6		Phone	250	242	329
7		Insurance	8696	0	0
8		Total			
9					
10	Equipment		1211	506	4890
11					
12	Salaries	Mgmt	4500	4500	4500
13		Full time	20658	19777	21422
14		Part time	24656	25980	25316
15		Total			
16					
17	Supplies	Office	1963	2432	1784
18		Vehicle	872	944	903
19		Total			
20					
21	Other	Fuel			
22		Marketing	500	300	200
23		Uniforms	63	101	83
24		Misc	162	471	65
25		Total			

3. **Save** the workbook with the name **as-Q1 Expenses** in **your** Lesson 07 folder and then **exit** Excel.

Critical Thinking & Work-Readiness Skills

In the course of working through the following Microsoft Office-based Critical Thinking exercises, you will also be utilizing various work-readiness skills, some of which are listed next to each exercise. Go to labyrinthelab.com/workreadiness *to learn more about the work-readiness skills.*

7.1 Enter Missing Data into a Worksheet

WORK-READINESS SKILLS APPLIED

- Listening
- Reading
- Showing responsibility

Nicole's manager at Green Clean mentions the importance of the spreadsheet for daily reporting of timesheet hours for employees. Hearing this, Nicole realizes that doing a good job every day on this report will be appreciated. She decides from now on to double-check that she has transferred the numbers correctly before she shows it to her manager. Sure enough, she sees that Tan's Friday number should have been 4, and that Silva's Saturday number should have been 3. Open ct-Timesheet Hours (Lesson 07 folder), enter the corrections, and save the corrected workbook as **ct-Timesheet Hours Revised**.

7.2 Enter New Data into a Worksheet

WORK-READINESS SKILLS APPLIED

- Serving clients/customers
- Solving problems
- Showing responsibility

Nicole begins to understand that mileage for employees driving to jobs is a big concern. Trying to anticipate her manager's needs, she decides that a handy reminder of the mileage to each customer might be useful. Using Google Maps and MapQuest, she figures out the mileage from Green Clean headquarters to each of the locations. The distances are as follows: Alton Mall, 10 miles; Century Bank, 12.5 miles; and Newport Medical, 24 miles. She wants to get her manager's feedback before going any further with her idea. Open ct-Timesheet Hours Revised, if necessary, and insert these values in column B next to each facility. Do not be concerned that the column A entries do not display completely. Save the edited worksheet as **ct-Mileage** in your Lesson 07 folder. Close the workbook but do not exit Excel.

7.3 Use the Numeric Keypad

WORK-READINESS SKILLS APPLIED

- Solving problems
- Managing the self
- Selecting technology

Now that she has proven she can create accurate spreadsheets, Nicole is asked to put together additional spreadsheets. Nicole sees that streamlining the way she does data entry will help her handle her workload. She decides to practice using the numeric keypad. Create a new, blank workbook. Practice data entry, reading numbers from various exercises in this lesson and entering the data down a column of the blank worksheet using the numeric keypad. Practice until you feel comfortable. (There is no need to save your work.) Why should Nicole (and you) pay attention to speed as well as accuracy when creating spreadsheets? Type your answer in a Word document named **ct-Questions** saved to your Lesson 07 folder.

Editing, Viewing, and Printing Worksheets

LEARNING OBJECTIVES

After studying this lesson, you will be able to:

- Use a variety of techniques to select, move, and copy cells and ranges
- Clear cell contents, including formatting
- Complete cell entries automatically
- Work with various Excel views and the zoom feature
- Print your worksheet

In this lesson, you will expand on basic skills in Excel. You will learn various methods of editing worksheets: replacing and deleting entries, using Undo and Redo, working with AutoFill, and more. You will also learn about printing Excel worksheets and working with different views. When you have finished this lesson, you will have developed the skills necessary to produce carefully edited and proofed worksheets.

Student Resources   labyrinthelab.com/ob10

Creating a Basic List in Excel

Ken Hazell is the human resources manager of Green Clean, a janitorial product supplier and cleaning service contractor. He realizes that Excel can be used as a simple database to maintain lists of employees, product inventory, or other items. He and other managers use Excel's view options to work with data and preview how the worksheet will look when printed.

Green Clean				
Management and Support Roster				
Name	Phone	Position	Employment Date	On Call
Tommy Choi	619-555-3224	President		
Mary Wright	858-555-3098	VP, Sales and Marketing	5/22/2007	Monday
Derek Navarro	619-555-3309	VP, Operations	3/30/2009	Tuesday
Isabella Riso-Neff	858-555-0211	Risk Management Director	4/13/2009	Wednesday
Kenneth Hazell	619-555-3224	Human Resources Director	7/17/2006	Thursday
D'Andre Adams	760-555-3876	Facilities Services Manager	12/7/2005	Friday
Talos Bouras	858-555-1002	Sales Manager	5/10/2004	Saturday
Michael Chowdery	858-555-0021	Purchasing Manager	10/26/2009	Sunday
Ahn Tran	760-555-0728	Office Manager	6/26/2006	
Jenna Mann	951-555-0826	Administrative Assistant	3/15/2010	
Nicole Romero	858-555-4987	Payroll Assistant	5/25/2009	
Amy Wyatt	619-555-4016	Customer Service Rep	8/17/2009	

Ken will use this spreadsheet to organize the management and support employees' phone numbers, dates of employment, and the evening that each manager is on call in case of emergency.

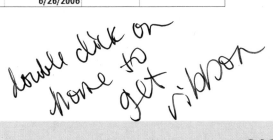

	A	B	C	D	E
			Click to add header		
1	Green Clean				
2	Management and Support Roster				
3					
4	Name	Phone	Position	Employment Date	On Call
5	Tommy Choi	619-555-3224	President		
6	Mary Wright	858-555-3098	VP, Sales and Marketing	5/22/2007	Monday
7	Derek Navarro	619-555-3309	VP, Operations	3/30/2009	Tuesday
8	Isabella Riso-Neff	858-555-0211	Risk Management Director	4/13/2009	Wednesday
9	Kenneth Hazell	619-555-3224	Human Resources Director	7/17/2006	Thursday
10	D'Andre Adams	760-555-3876	Facilities Services Manager	12/7/2005	Friday
11	Talos Bouras	858-555-1002	Sales Manager	5/10/2004	Saturday
12	Michael Chowdery	858-555-0021	Purchasing Manager	10/26/2009	Sunday
13	Ahn Tran	760-555-0728	Office Manager	6/26/2006	

Ken previews the worksheet in Page Layout view prior to printing it.

double click on home to get ribbon

8.1 Opening Workbooks

Video Lesson   labyrinthelab.com/videos

FROM THE KEYBOARD

Ctrl+O to open

The File→Open command displays the Open dialog box. The Open dialog box lets you navigate to any file storage location and open previously saved workbooks. Once a workbook is open, you can browse it, print it, and make editing changes. The organization and layout of the Open dialog box are similar to those of the Save As dialog box.

DEVELOP YOUR SKILLS 8.1.1
Open the Workbook

In this exercise, you will open a workbook that lists various employees.

1. Start **Excel**.

2. Click the **File** tab on the Ribbon and choose the **Open** command. *The Open dialog box is displayed.*

In future lessons, this command will be written, Choose File→Open.

3. **Navigate** to your file storage location (such as a USB flash drive).

4. **Double-click** the Lesson 08 folder to open it.

5. Select the Management Roster workbook and click **Open**.

You can also double-click a document in the Open dialog box to open it.

8.2 Editing Entries

Video Lesson   labyrinthelab.com/videos

You can edit the active cell by clicking in the Formula Bar and making the desired changes. You can also double-click a cell and edit the contents directly there. This technique is known as in-cell editing.

Replacing Entries

Editing an entry is efficient if the entry is so long that retyping it would be time-consuming. Editing can also be helpful when working with complex formulas and other functions that are difficult to re-create. If the entry requires little typing, however, it is usually easier to simply retype it. If you retype an entry, the new entry will replace whatever is contained in the cell.

Deleting Characters

Use the Delete and Backspace keys to edit entries in the Formula Bar and within a cell. The Delete key removes the character to the right of the insertion point, while the Backspace key removes the character to the left of the insertion point.

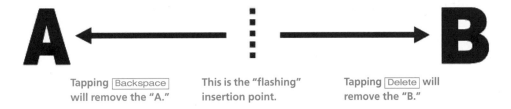

Tapping Backspace will remove the "A."	This is the "flashing" insertion point.	Tapping Delete will remove the "B."

Edit Entries

In this exercise, you will use the Formula Bar to revise the contents of cell A2. You will also edit cells B3 and B15 directly in the cells.

Edit in the Formula Bar

1. Click **cell A2** to select it.

2. Follow these steps to edit cell A2 using the Formula Bar:

Ⓐ Click in the **Formula Bar** just to the right of the word *List*.

Ⓑ Tap Backspace four times to remove the word *List*, and then type **Roster**.

Ⓒ Click the Enter button.

Replace an Entry

3. Click **cell D4**.

4. Type **Employment Date** and **tap** Enter.
The entry Employment Date *replaces the entry* Starting Date. *Notice that the cell formatting (underlining the word) has been applied to the new entry as well. Also note that the new entry is cut off or truncated because the cell to the right contains an entry.*

Use In-Cell Editing

5. **Double-click** cell A8 (the cell with the name Isabella Riso).

6. Use the mouse or the → key to position the flashing **insertion point** to the right of the last name, Riso.

7. Type **–Neff**, and then **tap** Enter to complete the change.
The entry should now read Isabella Riso-Neff.

8. Click the **Save** 🖫 button to update the changes.
Clicking the Save button automatically saves changes to a workbook that has previously been saved.

Microsoft Excel

8.3 Selecting Cells and Ranges

Video Lesson   labyrinthelab.com/videos

FROM THE KEYBOARD

Ctrl + A to select all

Ctrl + Spacebar to select a column

Shift + Spacebar to select a row

When you want to change something in a worksheet—for instance, move, copy, delete, format, or print specific data—you must first select the cell(s). The most efficient way to select cells is with the mouse, though you can also use the keyboard method. You can select one or many cells. A group of contiguous (adjacent) cells is called a range. Entire columns or rows may be selected by clicking or dragging the column headings (such as A, B, C) or row headings (such as 1, 2, 3).

Excel Ranges

Each cell has a reference. For example, A1 refers to the first cell in a worksheet. Likewise, a range reference specifies the cells included within a range. The range reference includes the first and last cells in the range separated by a colon (:). For example, the range A4:E4 includes all cells between A4 and E4 inclusive. The following illustration highlights several ranges and their corresponding range references.

	A6	▼	f_x	Mary Wright		
	A	**B**	**C**	**D**	**E**	
Range A1:A2 → 1	Green Clean					
2	Management and Support Roster					
3						
Range A4:E4 → 4	Name	Phone	Position	Employment Date	On Call	
5	Tommy Choi	619-555-3224	President			
6	Mary Wright	858-555-3098	VP, Sales and Marketing	5/22/2007		
7	Derek Navarro	619-555-3309	VP, Operations	3/30/2009		
Range A6:D10 → 8	Isabella Riso-Neff	858-555-0211	Risk Management Director	4/13/2009		
9	Kenneth Hazell	619-555-3224	Human Resources Director	7/17/2006		
10	D'Andre Adams	760-555-3876	Facilities Services Manager	12/7/2005		
11	Talos Bouras	858-555-1002	Sales Manager	5/10/2004		
12	Michael Chowdery	858-555-0021	Purchasing Manager	10/26/2009		
13	Ahn Tran	760-555-0728	Office Manager	6/26/2006		
14	Jenna Mann	951-555-0826	Administrative Assistant	3/15/2010		

The selected ranges in the worksheet are shaded, as displayed above. In addition, the first cell in the last range selected, A6, shows no shading and has an outline around it. This cell display indicates that it is the active cell, which is displayed in the Name Box and Formula Bar.

The following Quick Reference table describes selection techniques in Excel.

QUICK REFERENCE	SELECTING CELLS AND RANGES
Techniques	**How to Do It**
Select a range	Drag the mouse pointer over the desired cells.
Select several ranges	Select a range, and then press Ctrl while selecting additional range(s).
Select an entire column	Click a column heading or press Ctrl + Spacebar .

Techniques	How to Do It
Select an entire row	Click a row heading or press Shift + Spacebar.
Select multiple columns or rows	Drag the mouse pointer over the desired column or row headings.
Select an entire worksheet	Click the Select All button ◢ at the top-left corner of the worksheet or press Ctrl + A.
Select a range with Shift	Position the highlight in the first cell you wish to select, press Shift, and click the last cell in the range.
Extend or decrease a selection with Shift	Press Shift while tapping an arrow key.

DEVELOP YOUR SKILLS 8.3.1
Practice Making Selections

In this exercise, you will practice selecting multiple ranges and entire rows and columns using the mouse. You will also use the Shift and Ctrl keys to practice selecting cell ranges.

Click and Drag to Select a Range

1. Position the **mouse pointer** ✛ over **cell A4**.

2. **Press** and **hold down** the left mouse button while dragging the mouse to the right until the **range A4:E4** is selected, and then **release** the mouse button.
   Notice that for each range that is selected, the corresponding row and column headings are displayed in orange.

3. **Click** once anywhere in the worksheet to deselect the cells.

Select Multiple Ranges

4. Follow these steps to select two ranges:

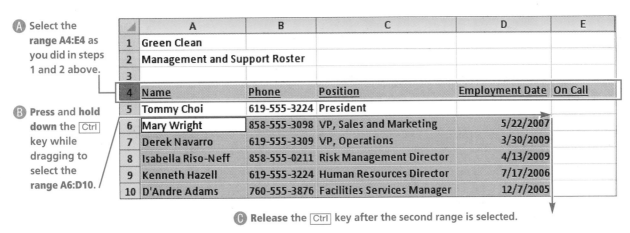

Ⓐ Select the range A4:E4 as you did in steps 1 and 2 above.

Ⓑ **Press** and **hold down** the Ctrl key while dragging to select the range A6:D10.

Ⓒ **Release** the Ctrl key after the second range is selected.

Both the A4:E4 and A6:D10 ranges are selected now. The Ctrl key lets you select more than one range at the same time.

Microsoft Excel

5. **Press** and **hold down** the ⌊Ctrl⌋ key while you select another range, and then **release** the ⌊Ctrl⌋ key.

You should now have three ranges selected.

6. Make sure you have **released** the ⌊Ctrl⌋ key, and then **click** once anywhere on the worksheet to deselect the ranges.

The highlighting of the previous selections disappears.

Select Entire Rows and Columns

7. Follow these steps to select various rows and columns:

Ⓐ Click the **column A** heading to select the entire column.

Ⓑ Position the mouse pointer on the **column C** heading and drag to the right until **columns C, D, and E** are selected.

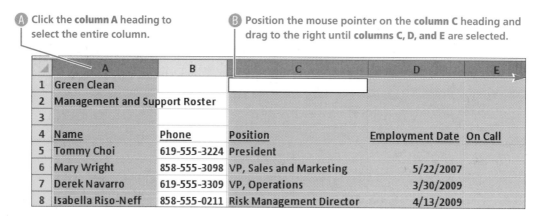

Column A will be deselected because you were not holding down the ⌊Ctrl⌋ key.

Ⓒ Click the **Select All** button to select the entire worksheet.

Ⓓ Click the **row 1** heading to select the entire row.

Ⓔ Drag the mouse pointer down over the headings from **row 6 to row 10** to select them.

Only rows 6–10 will be selected because you did not hold down ⌊Ctrl⌋.

Use Keyboard Techniques

8. Follow these steps to use keyboard techniques to select cells:

Ⓐ Click **cell A4.**

	A	B	C	D	E
4	Name	Phone	Position	Employment Date	On Call
5	Tommy Choi	619-555-3224	President		
6	Mary Wright	858-555-3098	VP, Sales and Marketing	5/22/2007	
7	Derek Navarro	619-555-3309	VP, Operations	3/30/2009	
8	Isabella Riso-Neff	858-555-0211	Risk Management Director	4/13/2009	
9	Kenneth Hazell	619-555-3224	Human Resources Director	7/17/2006	
10	D'Andre Adams	760-555-3876	Facilities Services Manager	12/7/2005	
11	Talos Bouras	858-555-1002	Sales Manager	5/10/2004	
12	Michael Chowdery	858-555-0021	Purchasing Manager	10/26/2009	
13	Ahn Tran	760-555-0728	Office Manager	6/26/2006	
14	Jenna Mann	951-555-0826	Administrative Assistant	3/15/2010	
15	Nicole Romero	858-555-4987	Payroll Assistant	5/25/2009	
16	Amy Wyatt	619-555-4016	Customer Service Rep	8/17/2009	

Ⓑ **Press** and **hold down** the Shift key and click **cell E16** to select the range **A4:E16.**

Ⓒ Click **cell A12.**

	A	B	C	D
12	Michael Chowdery	858-555-0021	Purchasing Manager	10/26/2009
13	Ahn Tran	760-555-0728	Office Manager	6/26/2006
14	Jenna Mann	951-555-0826	Administrative Assistant	3/15/2010
15	Nicole Romero	858-555-4987	Payroll Assistant	5/25/2009
16	Amy Wyatt	619-555-4016	Customer Service Rep	8/17/2009

Ⓓ **Press** and **hold down** the Shift key, and then **tap** → three times and ↓ four times.

The range A12:D16 is selected. Notice that the Shift *key techniques give you precise control when selecting. You should use the* Shift *key techniques if you find selecting with the mouse difficult or if you have a large range to select that is not entirely visible on your screen.*

9. Take a few moments to practice selection techniques. See if you can select a specific portion of a worksheet.

8.4 Working with Cut, Copy, and Paste

Video Lesson   labyrinthelab.com/videos

FROM THE KEYBOARD
Ctrl + C to copy
Ctrl + X to cut
Ctrl + V to paste

The Cut, Copy, and Paste commands are available in all Office suite applications. With Cut, Copy, and Paste, you can move or copy cells within a worksheet, between worksheets, or between different Office applications. For example, you could use the Copy command to copy a range from one worksheet and the Paste command to paste the range into another worksheet. Cut, Copy, and Paste are most efficient for moving or copying cells a long distance within a worksheet or between worksheets. Cut, Copy, and Paste are easy to use if you remember the following guidelines:

- You must select cells before issuing a Cut or Copy command.
- You must position the highlight at the desired location before issuing the Paste command. The highlight's position is important because the range you paste will overwrite any cells in the paste area.

You need only to select the upper-left cell of the destination range before pasting a copied range. It is not necessary to select the entire destination range.

Marquee and Paste Options Button

A marquee (animated dashed line) surrounds the selected cell(s) after you choose the Cut or Copy command. The marquee disappears upon the next action you take after pasting.

The Paste Options button displays at the lower-right corner of the destination cell(s) after a paste action. Its drop-down list allows you to customize what will be pasted, such as only the cell contents or their formatting. The button disappears upon the next action you take. You will not work with paste options in this lesson.

Tap the Esc key to remove the marquee manually.

You can also right-click on a cell or range of cells in order to get a shortcut menu specific to the selection. The Cut, Copy, and Paste commands are available on this menu as well. There are many ways to issue commands; your job is to simply figure out which method works best for you!

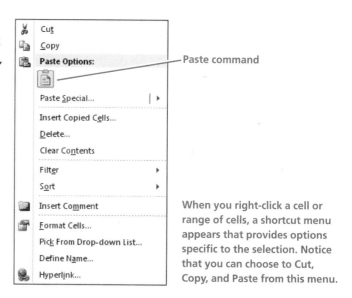

Paste command

When you right-click a cell or range of cells, a shortcut menu appears that provides options specific to the selection. Notice that you can choose to Cut, Copy, and Paste from this menu.

The Office Clipboard

The Office Clipboard lets you collect items from any Office worksheet or program and paste them into any other Office document. For example, you can collect a paragraph from a Word document, data from an Excel worksheet, and a graphic from a PowerPoint slide and then paste them all into a new Word document. The Office Clipboard can also be used within a single application like Excel to collect several items and then paste them as desired. The Office Clipboard can hold up to 24 items.

The Office Clipboard containing a copied graphic and two text blocks

How It Works

You can place multiple items on the Office Clipboard using the standard Cut and Copy commands; however, the Office Clipboard task pane must first be displayed. It is displayed by clicking the launcher button in the Clipboard area of the Home tab. Once text or other objects are on the Clipboard, you may paste any item to one or more selected cells in a worksheet.

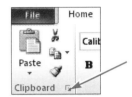

Moving and Copying Cells via Drag and Drop

Drag and Drop produces the same results as Cut, Copy, and Paste. However, Drag and Drop is usually more efficient if you are moving or copying entries a short distance within the same worksheet. If the original location and

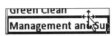

The mouse pointer changes to a four-pointed arrow as you point at the dark line surrounding the selected cell or range. Dragging the selection will move it to another location in the worksheet.

new destination are both visible in the current window, then it is usually easier to use Drag and Drop. With Drag and Drop, you select the cells you wish to move or copy, and then you point to the dark line around the selected range and drag the range to the desired destination. If you press the Ctrl key while dragging the selected area, the cells are copied to the destination. Drag and Drop does not place items on the Office Clipboard, however, so you will want to use either the Cut or the Copy command if you wish to work with the Office Clipboard.

Editing Cells via Right-Dragging

Right-dragging is a variation of the drag and drop technique. Many beginners have trouble using drag and drop because they have difficulty controlling the mouse. This difficulty is compounded if they are trying to copy entries using drag and drop. This is because copying requires the Ctrl key to be held while the selected range is dragged. With the right-drag method, the right mouse button is used when dragging. When the right mouse button is released at the desti-

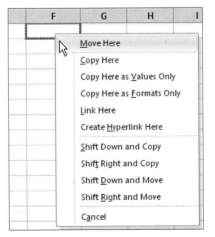

When you right-drag and drop, you will receive a pop-up menu at the destination so that you can choose whether to move or copy the data. You may cancel the action and then repeat the right-drag and drop if the indicated destination is not what you wanted.

nation, a pop-up menu appears. The pop-up menu gives you several options including Move, Copy, and Cancel. This approach provides more control because there is no need to use the Ctrl key when copying and you have the option of canceling the move or copy.

Command	Explanation	Procedure
Cut	The Cut command removes entries from selected cells and places them on the Office Clipboard.	▪ Select what you wish to move. ▪ Choose Home→Clipboard→Cut ✂ from the Ribbon, or press Ctrl+X.
Copy	The Copy command also places entries on the Office Clipboard, but it leaves a copy of the entries in the original cells.	▪ Select what you wish to copy. ▪ Choose Home→Clipboard→Copy 📋 from the Ribbon or press Ctrl+C.
Paste	The Paste command pastes entries from the Office Clipboard to worksheet cells beginning at the highlight location.	▪ Click once where you wish the clipboard contents to be pasted. ▪ Choose Home→Clipboard→ Paste from the Ribbon, or press Ctrl+V.

DEVELOP YOUR SKILLS 8.4.1
Move and Copy Selections

In this exercise, you will have the opportunity to use the Cut, Copy, and Paste commands as well as drag and drop to move and copy selections.

Copy and Paste

1. Click **cell A1** to select it.

2. Display the **Home** tab, locate the **Clipboard** command group, and click the **Copy** 📋 button on the Ribbon.
   A marquee will surround the selection that you have copied and placed on the clipboard.

3. Click **cell C2**.

4. Choose **Home→Clipboard→Paste** 📋 from the Ribbon to **paste** the selection in cell C2.
   The Paste command consists of two parts. Make certain to click the button in the upper part. If you accidentally click the drop-down arrow in the lower part of the command, you may still choose Paste from the list.

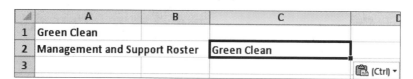

◢	A	B	C	D
1	Green Clean			
2	Management and Support Roster		Green Clean	
3				📋 (Ctrl) ▾

The contents of cell A1 will remain there as well as appear in cell C2 when you choose to copy the selection. Notice the marquee surrounding the cell that is being copied and the Paste Options button that appears to the lower right of the cell in which the selection was pasted.

Cut and Paste

5. **Right-click** cell C2.

   When you right-click a cell, a shortcut menu appears with options specific to the cell, as well as the Mini toolbar.

6. Choose **Cut** from the shortcut menu.

7. **Right-click** cell E2 and choose **Paste** under Paste Options from the shortcut menu.

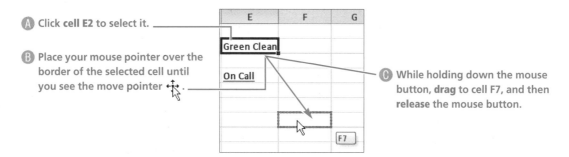

Cell C2 will now be empty because the contents were moved to cell E2.

Drag and Drop

8. Follow these steps to move the contents of cell E2 via the drag-and-drop method:

Ⓐ Click **cell E2** to select it.

Ⓑ Place your mouse pointer over the border of the selected cell until you see the move pointer.

Ⓒ While holding down the mouse button, **drag** to cell F7, and then **release** the mouse button.

When you drag a cell with this method, Excel shows what cell the selection will be dropped into by displaying it on a ScreenTip as well as placing a highlight around the cell.

Right-Drag a Selection

9. Select **cell E4**, and then place your mouse pointer over the border of the selected cell until you see the move pointer as shown at right.

10. Start **dragging** with the **right** (not the left) mouse button. Keep the right mouse button held down until told to release it in the next step.

11. Drag down to **cell F5**, and then **release** the right mouse button.
    A pop-up menu appears, listing your choices for the right-drag.

12. Choose **Copy Here** from the pop-up menu.
    The contents of cell E4 remain in the cell and are copied to the destination cell, F5. Do not save, but keep the workbook open. In the next exercise, you will undo some recent actions.

8.5 Using Undo and Redo

Video Lesson   labyrinthelab.com/videos

Excel's Undo button lets you reverse actions that have occurred in Excel. You can reverse simple actions such as accidentally deleting a cell's content or more complex actions such as deleting an entire row. Most actions can be undone, but those that cannot include printing and saving workbooks. The Undo command can become your best friend when you have to undo an action that you are not sure how you issued. Don't you wish life had an undo button at times?

The Redo button reverses an Undo command. Use Redo when you undo an action but then decide to go through with that action after all. The Redo button will be visible on the Quick Access toolbar only after you have undone an action.

Undoing Multiple Actions

FROM THE KEYBOARD

Ctrl+Z to undo
Ctrl+Y to redo

Clicking the arrow on the Undo button displays a list of actions that can be undone. You can undo multiple actions by dragging the mouse over the desired actions. However, you must undo actions in the order in which they appear on the drop-down list. For example, you cannot skip the first and second items to undo only the third item.

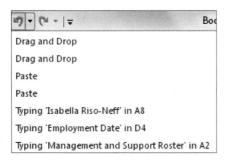

When you click the arrow on the Undo button, you will see a list of previous actions with the most recent at the top.

Limitations to "Undoing"

In Excel, there are times when the Undo command will not work. If you click the File tab on the Ribbon and choose any command (such as saving a workbook), it cannot be undone. When an action cannot be undone, Excel will change the Undo ScreenTip to "Can't Undo."

QUICK REFERENCE	UNDOING AND REDOING ACTIONS
Task	**Procedure**
Undo the last action	■ Click the Undo button on the Quick Access toolbar or tap Ctrl+Z.
Undo a series of actions	■ Click the drop-down arrow on the Undo button to display a list of previous actions.
	■ Choose the last command that you wish to have undone.
Redo an undone action	■ Click the Redo button on the Quick Access toolbar.

Reverse Actions

In this exercise, you will delete the contents of a column and then use Undo to reverse the deletion. When you do, the original data will display in the column again. You will also use Redo to reverse an Undo command.

Delete the Column Contents

1. Click the **column A** heading to select the entire column.

2. **Tap** Delete.
   All of the contents in column A have been deleted! There are many times that you will use Undo in order to reverse an action you did not wish to make.

Use Undo and Redo

3. Click **Undo** 🔄 to restore the entry.

4. Follow these steps to undo the last four commands from the previous section:

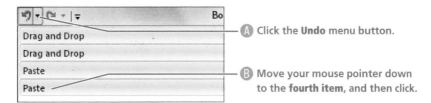

Ⓐ Click the **Undo** menu button.

Ⓑ Move your mouse pointer down to the **fourth item**, and then click.

Excel undoes your last four commands.

5. Click the **Redo** 🔄 button four times to restore the four actions that you "undid."

6. Use Ctrl + S to save the changes, but don't close the workbook.
   You must hold down the Ctrl key first and then tap the S to issue the Save command.

8.6 Clearing Cell Contents and Formats

Video Lesson   labyrinthelab.com/videos

FROM THE KEYBOARD

Delete to clear cell contents

In Excel, you can format cell content by changing the font style, size, and color. You can also add enhancements such as bold, italics, and underline. Cells with numeric data can be formatted as currency, dates, times, percents, and more. In this lesson, you will learn how to clear existing formatting.

Clicking the Clear  button displays a menu that lets you clear content, formats, and comments from cells. The submenu also contains a Clear All option that clears all of these items from the selected cell(s).

Clicking the Clear button in the Editing group of the Home ribbon will display a menu that shows all of the options for clearing cell contents.

Excel's Options for Clearing Cells

Clear Contents	Clearing the content has the same effect as tapping the Delete key. The cell contents are deleted, but any format applied to the cell remains and will be in effect when new data is entered in the cell.
Clear Formats	The clear Formats option removes all text and number formats, leaving unformatted entries in the cell(s).
Clear Comments	You can insert comments in cells to document your worksheet. The Clear Comments option also removes comments from the selected cells.
Clear Hyperlinks	Clearing a hyperlink leaves the entry in the cell but removes its link to a workbook object, a web address, or an external document.
Clear All	This command will clear everything listed above.

One of the most useful functions of Excel's Clear command is removing numeric value formats. Once a cell is formatted as a particular numeric format, such as a date or currency, Excel remembers that formatting even if the cell contents are deleted.

QUICK REFERENCE CLEARING CELL CONTENTS AND FORMATTING

Task	Procedure
Clear the contents of a cell	■ Select the cell or range that you wish to clear. ■ Choose Home→Editing→Clear  from the Ribbon. ■ Choose Clear Contents from the resulting menu.
Clear the formatting from a cell	■ Select the cell or range that you wish to clear. ■ Choose Home→Editing→Clear  from the Ribbon. ■ Choose Clear Formats from the resulting menu.
Clear contents and formatting from a cell	■ Select the cell or range that you wish to clear. ■ Choose Home→Editing→Clear  from the Ribbon. ■ Choose Clear All from the resulting menu.

Clear Cell Contents and Formatting

In this exercise, you will use the Clear command to delete cell contents and cell formats.

1. Click **cell F5**.

2. Choose **Home→Editing→Clear** ⬜▾ from the Ribbon and choose **Clear Formats**.
   The contents of the cell were underlined, a type of formatting. When you choose to clear only the formats, the contents will remain and only the formatting is removed. Notice that the contents are no longer underlined.

3. Click the **Undo** ⬜ button on the Quick Access toolbar.

4. Ensure that **cell F5** is selected, click the **Clear** ⬜▾ button, and choose **Clear All**.

5. **Type** your name and **tap** [Enter].
   Notice that the contents are no longer underlined in cell F5 because you cleared "all" (formatting and contents) from it.

6. Use [Ctrl]+[Z] to undo the typing of your name.

7. Click **cell F7** and **tap** [Delete].
   The entry Green Clean is deleted. The [Delete] key functions the same as if you had clicked the Clear button and chosen Clear Contents. Any formatting will remain in the cell.

8. **Save** ⬜ the workbook.

8.7 Using Auto Features

Video Lesson	labyrinthelab.com/videos

Excel offers "auto" features that help you to work more efficiently. AutoFill allows you to quickly fill a range of cells. AutoComplete makes it easy to enter long entries by typing an acronym or a series of characters, which are "converted" to the desired entry.

Working with AutoFill

AutoFill allows you to quickly extend a series, copy data, or copy a formula into adjacent cells by selecting cells and dragging the fill handle. If the selected cell does not contain data that AutoFill recognizes as a series, the data will simply be copied into the adjacent cells. The fill handle is a small black square at the bottom-right corner of the selected cell or cell range. A black cross appears when you position the mouse pointer on the fill handle. You can drag the fill handle to fill adjacent cells to accomplish the following:

■ **Copy an entry**—If the entry in the active cell is a number, a formula, or a text entry, the fill handle copies the entry to adjacent cells.

■ **Expand a repeating series of numbers**—If you select two or more cells containing numbers, Excel assumes you want to expand a repeating series. For example, if you select two cells containing the numbers 5 and 10 and drag the fill handle, Excel will fill the adjacent cells with the numbers 15, 20, 25, etc.

- **AutoFill of date entries**—If the active cell contains any type of date entry, Excel will determine the increment of the date value and fill in the adjacent cells. For example, if the current cell contains the entry May and you drag the fill handle, AutoFill will insert the entries Jun, Jul, and Aug in the adjacent cells.

The following table and illustrations provide examples of series that AutoFill can extend.

Selected Cells	Extended Series
Mon	Tue, Wed, Thu
Monday	Tuesday, Wednesday, Thursday
Jan	Feb, Mar, Apr
January	February, March, April
Jan, Apr	Jul, Oct, Jan
1, 2	3, 4, 5, 6
100, 125	150, 175, 200
1/10/11	1/11/11, 1/12/11, 1/13/11
1/15/11, 2/15/11	3/15/11, 4/15/11, 5/15/11
1st Qtr	2nd Qtr, 3rd Qtr, 4th Qtr

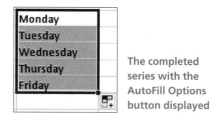

The fill handle is located at the bottom-right corner of the active cell.

If the active cell contains a date entry such as Monday, AutoFill automatically fills the adjacent cell with the next item in the series (Tuesday).

The completed series with the AutoFill Options button displayed

AutoComplete vs. AutoFill

The AutoComplete feature is useful when you want the same entry repeated more than once in a column. AutoFill allows you to select a cell and fill in entries either by completing a series or copying the source cell, whereas AutoComplete works within a cell as you type. If the first few characters you type match another entry in the column, then AutoComplete will offer to complete the entry for you. You accept the offer by tapping Tab or Enter, or reject the offer by typing the remainder of the entry yourself.

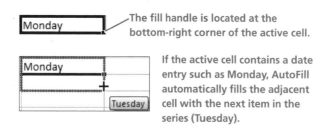

In this situation, a "c" was typed and the AutoComplete feature kicked into gear, suggesting that you may be interested in completing the entry as *Customer Service Rep* because you have already typed that entry earlier in the column. In order to accept *Customer Service Rep* as the entry, you would simply tap Tab to move to the next cell.

AutoComplete will complete the entry "case sensitive" to match capitalization from the existing column entry.

Use the AutoComplete and AutoFill Features

In this exercise, you will enter two new employees in the worksheet and use AutoComplete to aid in your entries. In addition, you will look at how to use AutoFill to complete a series of the days of the week.

Use AutoComplete

1. Click **cell A17** and type **Brian Simpson**, and then **tap** ⌐Tab⌐ to move to the next cell to the right.

2. Type **858-555-3718** and **tap** ⌐Tab⌐.

3. Type **c** and notice that Excel suggests *Customer Service Rep* as the entry. **Tap** ⌐Tab⌐ to accept the suggestion and move to the next cell to the right.
Notice that the entry will be capitalized just as it is in the cell above.

4. **Type** today's date, and then **tap** ⌐Enter⌐.
Notice that when you tap ⌐Enter⌐, *the highlight moves to cell A18 where you can begin typing the next entry of the list.*

5. Type **Leisa Malimali** and **tap** ⌐Tab⌐.

6. Type **619-555-4017** and **tap** ⌐Tab⌐.

7. Type **S** in **cell C18**.
Excel will suggest Sales Manager *from a previous row. In this case, Leisa is a sales assistant, so you will need to continue typing your entry. Make sure that you have typed a capital* S *as it will not pull from the previous entries.*

8. Continue typing **ales Assistant** and **tap** ⌐Tab⌐.
Excel will replace the AutoComplete suggestion with the entry that you type, Sales Assistant.

9. **Type** today's date and **tap** ⌐Enter⌐.

Use AutoFill to Expand a Series

In this section of the exercise, you will fill in the column showing the manager responsible for being on emergency call each evening.

10. Click **cell E6**.

11. Type **Monday**, and then click the **Enter** ✔ button.

    Now that cell E6 contains Monday, Excel will recognize it as the beginning of the series, Tuesday, Wednesday, Thursday, and so forth. E6 will remain the active cell.

12. Follow these steps to fill the adjacent cells:

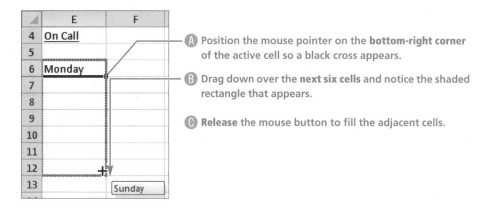

Ⓐ Position the mouse pointer on the **bottom-right corner** of the active cell so a black cross appears.

Ⓑ Drag down over the **next six cells** and notice the shaded rectangle that appears.

Ⓒ **Release** the mouse button to fill the adjacent cells.

Excel recognizes days of the week (Monday), quarters (1st Qtr, Quarter 1, First Quarter), months (January), and other date values as the beginning of a series. You can expand any of these series with the fill handle.

13. Click in the **Name Box** to the left of the Formula Bar, type **A1**, and **tap** Enter.

14. **Save** 💾 the changes and leave the workbook **open**.

Auto Fill Options

Video Lesson   labyrinthelab.com/videos

The Auto Fill Options 📑 button appears below your filled selection after you fill cells in a worksheet. A menu of fill options appears when you click the button.

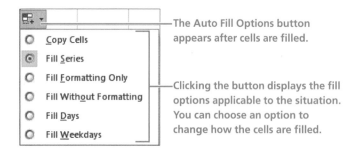

The Auto Fill Options button appears after cells are filled.

Clicking the button displays the fill options applicable to the situation. You can choose an option to change how the cells are filled.

If you choose Fill Without Formatting, you can fill cells without copying the formatting from the original cell. Fill Formatting Only copies the formatting but not the contents from the source cells.

Use Auto Fill Options

In this exercise, you will use Auto Fill Options to fill a data series without applying the source cell's formatting. You also will fill by applying only the formatting so that you may enter different data in cells.

1. Click the **Sheet2** tab at the bottom of the window.

2. With **cell A1** selected, **drag** the fill handle to **cell D1**.

	A	B	C	D
1	Year 1-Q1	Year 1-Q2	Year 1-Q3	Year 1-Q4

   The data series expands to Year 1 – Q4, and the bold and shaded formatting from cell A1 is applied to the other series cells.

3. Click the **Auto Fill Options** button at the lower-right corner of cell D1 and choose **Fill Without Formatting**.
   The formatting is removed from B1:D1.

4. **Deselect** the cells to view the actual formatting.

5. Select the **range A1:D1**.

6. **Drag** the fill handle in D1 down to **D7**.

7. Click the **Auto Fill Options** button and choose **Fill Formatting Only**.
   The contents are removed from A2:D7, but the formatting is still applied.

8. Enter numbers of your choice in **cells A2:D2**.
   Notice that the formatting matches that of A1:D1.

	A	B	C	D
1	Year 1-Q1	Year 1-Q2	Year 1-Q3	Year 1-Q4
2	222	333	444	555

9. Select the **Sheet1** tab of the workbook.

10. **Save** the changes and leave the workbook **open**.

8.8 Exploring the Many Views of Excel

Video Lesson labyrinthelab.com/videos

Changing the view in Excel does not change how the worksheet will print. For instance, if you change the zoom to 300%, the worksheet will appear much larger on the screen but will still print normally. There are other views in Excel that will aid you in working with your file and assist you in making changes to the final printed worksheet. This lesson will cover Page Layout view and Zoom. Remember that your Ribbon may appear differently, depending on the size of your Excel window. There is an additional view option, Page Break Preview, that allows you to set where pages will break when printed.

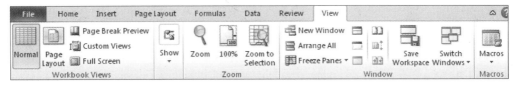

The View tab on the Ribbon provides options to view your workbook, show or hide screen items, control the zoom, and view multiple areas of the workbook at once.

Working in Page Layout View

Page Layout view allows you to see how your spreadsheet will appear when you print it, page by page. You may edit your worksheet in this view. You also can add headers and footers with text, page numbering, and other items that print at the top and bottom of every page. You may use either the View ribbon or the view buttons in the lower-right corner of the worksheet window to switch between the Normal and Page Layout views.

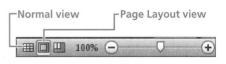

The view buttons displayed in the lower-right corner of the worksheet window

Zooming the View

The Zoom control lets you zoom in to get a close-up view of a worksheet and zoom out to see the full view. Zooming changes the size of the onscreen worksheet but has no effect on the printed worksheet. You can zoom from 10% to 400%.

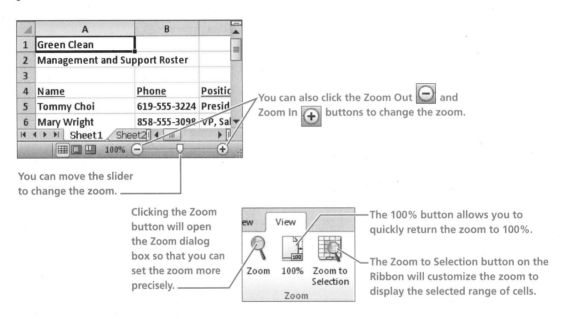

You can move the slider to change the zoom.

You can also click the Zoom Out and Zoom In buttons to change the zoom.

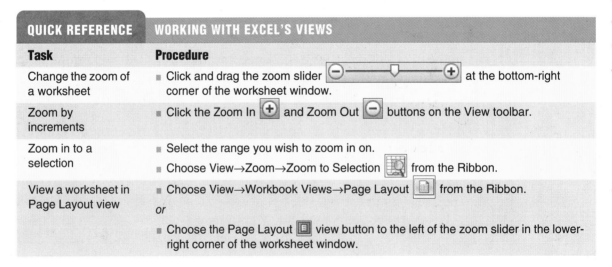

Clicking the Zoom button will open the Zoom dialog box so that you can set the zoom more precisely.

The 100% button allows you to quickly return the zoom to 100%.

The Zoom to Selection button on the Ribbon will customize the zoom to display the selected range of cells.

QUICK REFERENCE	WORKING WITH EXCEL'S VIEWS
Task	**Procedure**
Change the zoom of a worksheet	■ Click and drag the zoom slider at the bottom-right corner of the worksheet window.
Zoom by increments	■ Click the Zoom In and Zoom Out buttons on the View toolbar.
Zoom in to a selection	■ Select the range you wish to zoom in on. ■ Choose View→Zoom→Zoom to Selection from the Ribbon.
View a worksheet in Page Layout view	■ Choose View→Workbook Views→Page Layout from the Ribbon. *or* ■ Choose the Page Layout view button to the left of the zoom slider in the lower-right corner of the worksheet window.

Change Views and Use the Zoom Control

In this exercise, you will practice using commands to change the zoom and switch between Page Layout and Normal views.

Change the Zoom

1. Follow these steps to adjust the zoom percentage:

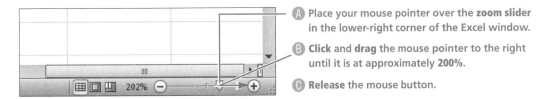

Ⓐ Place your mouse pointer over the **zoom slider** in the lower-right corner of the Excel window.

Ⓑ **Click** and **drag** the mouse pointer to the right until it is at approximately **200%**.

Ⓒ **Release** the mouse button.

2. Click the **Zoom Out** ⊖ button several times until the zoom displays **100%**.

3. Drag to select the **range A1:C18**.

4. Choose **View→Zoom→Zoom to Selection** 🔍 from the Ribbon.

5. Choose **View→Zoom→100%** from the Ribbon.

Switch Between Page Layout and Normal Views

6. Choose **View→Workbook Views→Page Layout View** from the Ribbon.
This view displays the worksheet as if printed on paper so that you may check that it fits on one page before printing.

7. Choose **View→Workbook Views→Normal View** from the Ribbon.

8. Click the **Page Layout** button on the toolbar at the left of the zoom slider in the lower-right corner of the worksheet window.
The view buttons allow you to quickly toggle between views. The workbook may be printed from either Page Layout or Normal view.

Check That Data Fit on One Page

9. **Scroll down** to view the bottom of the page and then **scroll up** to the top of the page.

10. Scroll to the **right**.
The grayed areas will not print. They indicate which rows and columns would extend to additional printed pages if data were in them. Notice that all data in range A1:E18 do fit on one page.

11. **Scroll back** to the left so that columns A–E are in view

Edit in Page Layout View

12. **Delete** the contents of **cell A1**.
You may edit the worksheet in Page Layout view just as you would in Normal view.

13. **Undo** ↺ the change.

14. **Save** 💾 the workbook.
The current workbook view is saved and would reappear the next time the workbook is opened. Leave the workbook open for the next exercise.

Microsoft Excel

8.9 Printing Worksheets

Video Lesson   labyrinthelab.com/videos

Excel gives you several ways to print your work. The method you choose depends on what you want to print. When you display the Print tab on the File menu, Backstage view displays a column of print options. The Print dialog box, familiar to users of previous Excel versions, has been eliminated. You may print specified pages, a selected range, or all data in the entire workbook. Additional choices include printing multiple copies and collating document pages in sets.

The Quick Print button can be added to the Quick Access toolbar. When clicked, it will print one copy of the entire worksheet. For large workbooks in which you frequently want to print only a certain selection, you can print a selection or set a print area. Before printing, you can preview in Backstage view or Page Layout view to see what is going to be printed. Additional page setup options such as changing the print orientation, printing column headings on every page, setting the print area, and many others are accessible from Backstage view or the Page Layout ribbon.

The light gridlines displayed around cells in Normal and Page Layout views do not print.

Print Preview

You have learned to use Page Layout view to preview the worksheet prior to printing. This view lets you see exactly how a worksheet will look when printed. Previewing can save time, paper, and wear and tear on your printer. It is especially useful when printing large worksheets and those with charts and intricate formatting. It is always wise to preview a large or complex worksheet before sending it to the printer.

In previous Excel versions, users also could display a separate Print Preview screen. Now, to save you time when you are ready to print, the Print tab of Backstage view displays a preview along with print options. The preview displays the overall look of the page that will be printed. You will usually need to zoom in to read any text. Scroll bars allow you to navigate to various areas of the zoomed-in page. The print preview is a very valuable tool for looking at how your worksheet will look when printed, but you are not able to edit your worksheet when you are in print preview mode (you will want to use Page Layout view for this purpose).

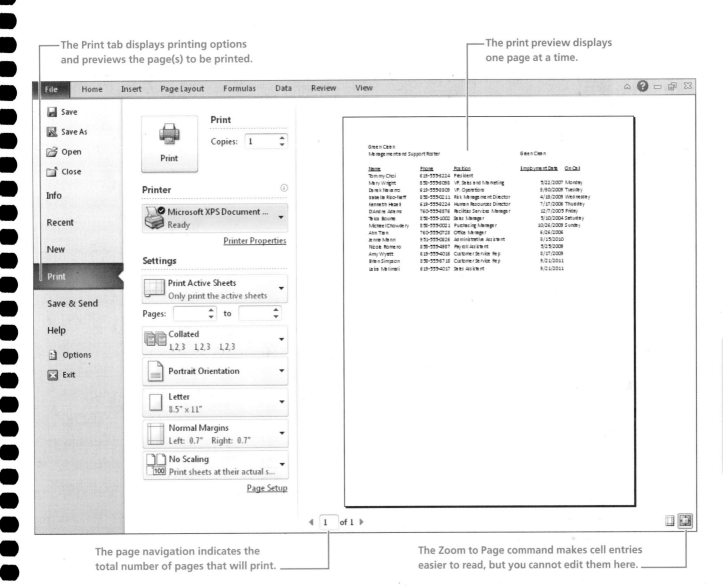

The Print tab displays printing options and previews the page(s) to be printed.

The print preview displays one page at a time.

The page navigation indicates the total number of pages that will print.

The Zoom to Page command makes cell entries easier to read, but you cannot edit them here.

Print the Worksheet

You can customize your Quick Access toolbar to include the Quick Print button, which sends the entire worksheet to the current printer using whatever print options are currently in effect. You must use the Print command on the File menu if you want to change printers, adjust the number of copies to be printed, or set other printing options such as printing only selected cells. The following illustration explains the most important options available in the Print tab of Backstage view.

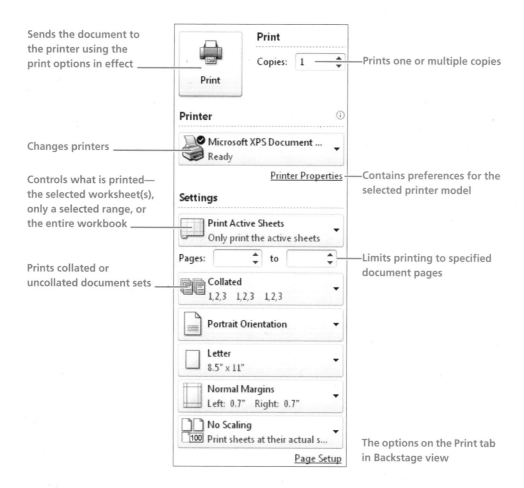

Sends the document to the printer using the print options in effect

Changes printers

Controls what is printed—the selected worksheet(s), only a selected range, or the entire workbook

Prints collated or uncollated document sets

Print

Copies: 1 —Prints one or multiple copies

Printer

Microsoft XPS Document ...
Ready

Printer Properties —Contains preferences for the selected printer model

Settings

Print Active Sheets
Only print the active sheets

Pages: to —Limits printing to specified document pages

Collated
1,2,3   1,2,3   1,2,3

Portrait Orientation

Letter
8.5" x 11"

Normal Margins
Left: 0.7"   Right: 0.7"

No Scaling
Print sheets at their actual s...

Page Setup

The options on the Print tab in Backstage view

Printing Selections

FROM THE KEYBOARD

Ctrl + P to print

Many times you will want to print only a range of cells. You can do this by selecting the desired cells, choosing the Print command, choosing to print the selection, and clicking Print. You may also use this technique to print nonadjacent selections within a worksheet. Nonadjacent selections print on separate pages.

To print a selection, you must select the cell range before issuing the Print command.

QUICK REFERENCE	PRINTING IN EXCEL
Task	**Procedure**
Preview how a worksheet will appear when printed	▪ Choose File→Print or display Page Layout view.
Print a worksheet using default settings	▪ Add the Quick Print ⊞ button on the Quick Access toolbar, if necessary. ▪ Click the Quick Print ⊞ button on the Quick Access toolbar.

Task	Procedure
Open the Print tab in Backstage view to make changes to printing options before printing	▪ Choose File→Print.
Close the Print tab of Backstage view without printing	▪ Tap the Esc key or choose any tab from the Ribbon.
Print a selection	▪ Highlight the selection you wish to print. ▪ Choose File→Print. ▪ Under Settings, choose Print Selection from the Print What list. ▪ Click Print.

DEVELOP YOUR SKILLS 8.9.1
Preview and Print a Worksheet

In this exercise, you will preview the worksheet you have been working on in the Print tab of Backstage view and send it to the printer.

Preview How Your Worksheet Will Print

1. Choose **File→Print**.

   The File tab of Backstage view displays, and a preview of page 1 displays at the right of the window. Notice that the page navigation option at the bottom-left corner of the preview indicates that you are viewing page 1 of 1 page total in the document.

2. Click the **Zoom to Page** 🖾 button at the lower-right corner of the preview to zoom in on your worksheet.

3. Use the **scroll bars** to view the zoomed-in view.

4. Click the **Zoom to Page** 🖾 button again to zoom out.

Print Your Worksheet

5. Look at the options available at the left of the File tab of Backstage view, and then click **Print** at the top-left corner of the options to print the worksheet.

6. **Tap** Ctrl + S to save the changes and close the workbook.

8.10 Concepts Review

Concepts Review labyrinthelab.com/ob10

To check your knowledge of the key concepts introduced in this lesson, complete the Concepts Review quiz by going to the URL listed above. If your classroom is using Labyrinth eLab, you may complete the Concepts Review quiz from within your eLab course.

Microsoft Excel

Reinforce Your Skills

Edit a Worksheet

In this exercise, you will edit a worksheet. This exercise demonstrates that sometimes it is easier to replace entries, whereas at other times it is easier to edit them.

Replace Several Entries

1. Start **Excel** and choose **File→Open**  from the Ribbon.

2. **Navigate** to the Lesson 08 folder in your file storage location and **open** rs-Customers.

3. Select **cell B4**.

4. Type **Ralph** and **tap** [Enter].
   Notice that it is easy to replace the entry because the name Ralph is easy to type.

5. **Replace** the name *Calvin* in **cell B6** with the name **Stephen**.

Edit Using the Formula Bar

6. Select **cell D4**.

7. Click in the **Formula Bar** just in front of the telephone prefix *333*.

8. **Tap** [Delete] three times to remove the prefix.

9. Type **222** and **complete** ✔ the entry.

10. **Change** the area code in cell D8 from *814* to **914**.
    In these entries, it was easier to edit than to retype entire phone numbers.

Use In-Cell and "Your Choice" Editing

11. **Double-click** cell E4.

12. Use → or ← to position the **insertion point** in front of the word *Lane*.

13. **Tap** [Delete] four times to remove the word *Lane*.

14. Type **Reservoir** and complete the entry.

15. Edit the next five addresses using either the Formula Bar or in-cell editing. The required changes appear bold in the following table.

Cell	Make These Changes
E5	2900 **Carleton** Drive, San Mateo, CA 94401
E6	**2300** Palm Drive, Miami, FL 33147
E7	888 Wilson Street, **Concord**, CA 94565
E8	320 Main Street, **Pittsburgh**, PA 17951
E9	**5120** 132nd Street, Los Angeles, CA **90045**

16. **Save** the workbook.
    Leave the workbook open as you will use it for Reinforce Your Skills 8.2

Use AutoComplete and AutoFill

In this exercise, you will add data to the worksheet you created in the previous exercise by using AutoComplete and AutoFill. You also will use Auto Fill Options to restrict a fill action.

Before You Begin: You must have completed Reinforce Your Skills 8.1 and the rs-Customers workbook should be open.

Use AutoComplete

1. Select **cell B10**, and type **ja**.
   Notice that AutoComplete does not suggest an entry when you only type a "j" as there are two "j" entries in the column.

2. **Tap** Tab to accept the suggested entry of Jack.

3. Using the following figure, complete the customer's information, using **AutoComplete** in column F.

⊿	A	B	C	D	E	F
9		Judy	Alioto	(213) 222-3344	132nd Street, Los Angeles, CA 95544	West
10		Jack	LaRue	(360) 444-0489	359 Peninsula Avenue, Port Angeles, WA 98363	West

Use AutoFill to Extend a Series

4. Select **cell A4**.
   Before using AutoFill, you must first select the cell that you will be using as the basis for the fill information.

5. Place your mouse pointer over the **fill handle** at the bottom-right corner of the selected cell, **drag** down through cell A10, and then **release** the mouse button when the ScreenTip shows C-07.

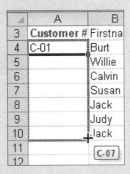
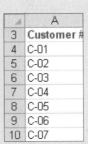

Notice that Excel recognizes C-01 as the beginning of a series (C-02, C-03, C-04, …).

Microsoft Excel

Enter Additional Customers

6. Enter the following three customers, in rows 11–13, into the list, using **AutoFill** and **AutoComplete** when possible.

	A	B	C	D	E	F
10	C-07	Jack	LaRue	(360) 444-0489	359 Peninsula Avenue, Port Angeles, WA 983	West
11	C-08	Edgar	Martinez	(206) 111-1111	11 Mariners Way Seattle, WA 98101	West
12	C-09	Trevor	Hoffman	(619) 555-1111	51 Camino de Padres, San Diego, CA 92101	West
13	C-10	Derek	Jeffries	(212) 222-5555	2 York Avenue, New York, NY 10002	East

Use an Auto Fill Option

7. Select **cell A3**.
   You will apply its bold and blue text formatting to the other column labels.

8. **Drag** the fill handle in cell A3 to the right through cell F3, and then **release** the mouse button.

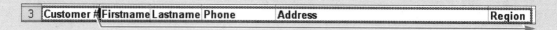

| 3 | Customer # | Firstname | Lastname | Phone | Address | | Region |

The cells are filled with Customer # because both the contents and formatting are copied by default.

9. Click the **Auto Fill Options** ⊞ button at the lower-right corner of cell F3 and choose **Fill Formatting Only** from the list.
   The contents of range B3:F3 return to their former entries and only the formatting is applied.

10. **Deselect** the cells by clicking on any other cell.

11. Use [Ctrl] + [S] to **save** your workbook. Leave the workbook open for the next exercise.

Move and Copy Cell Contents

In this exercise, you will use the workbook from Reinforce Your Skills 8.2 and move and copy the contents of cells.

Before You Begin: You must have completed Reinforce Your Skills 8.1 and Reinforce Your Skills 8.2, and the rs-Customers workbook should be open.

Use Keyboard Shortcuts

1. Select **cell E1**.

2. Choose **Home→Clipboard→Cut** ✄ from the Ribbon.

3. Select **cell A1**, and choose **Home→Clipboard→Paste** 📋 from the Ribbon.

4. Select the range **A11:F11**, and **copy** the range using the keyboard command Ctrl + C.

5. Select **cell A14**, and paste the range using Ctrl + V.
   This approach can come in handy if you have a new entry that is very similar to an existing one!

6. Use Ctrl + Z to **undo** the Paste command.

Copy Using the Context Menu

7. Select **cell D6**.

8. Taking care to avoid the fill handle, **point** at the dark line surrounding the cell, press the **right** mouse button, and **drag** down to cell D7.
   The pop-up, or context, menu appears when you release the mouse button.

9. Choose **Copy Here** from the shortcut menu.
   The phone number from cell D6 is copied to cell D7.

10. Edit the last four digits of the phone number in cell D7 to **3535**.

11. Use Ctrl + Home to return to cell A1.

12. **Close** ⊠ the workbook, choosing to **save** your workbook.

Microsoft Excel

Preview and Print a Worksheet

In this exercise, you will use the workbook from Reinforce Your Skills 8.3 to preview and then print a selection from the workbook.

Before You Begin: You must have completed Reinforce Your Skills 8.1, 8.2, and 8.3, and the rs-Customers workbook should be open.

Preview in Page Layout View

1. Click the **Page Layout** button on the toolbar at the left of the zoom slider in the lower-right corner of the worksheet window.

2. Look at the Status Bar at the bottom-left corner of the **Page Layout** window to verify that the worksheet fits on one page.
   The Status Bar should indicate Page: 1 of 1.

3. Check the overall look of data on the page.
   Some text in the Address column is truncated (cut off). Normally you would correct any problem discovered during the preview, but you may leave the text as is in this lesson.

Cancel a Print

4. Choose **File→Print**.
   A preview displays at the right of the Print tab in Backstage view.

5. Take a moment to look at the print options but **do not** change them.

6. **Tap** the Esc key to cancel the print and return to Page Layout view.

Print a Selection

7. Click the **Normal view** button on the toolbar at the left of the zoom slider in the lower-right corner of the worksheet window.
   You will print just the last names and phone numbers in the next steps. You could have selected the range in Page Layout view also.

8. Select the **range C3:D13**.

9. Use ⎡Ctrl⎤+⎡P⎤ to display the Print tab of Backstage view.

10. Follow these steps to print the selected range:

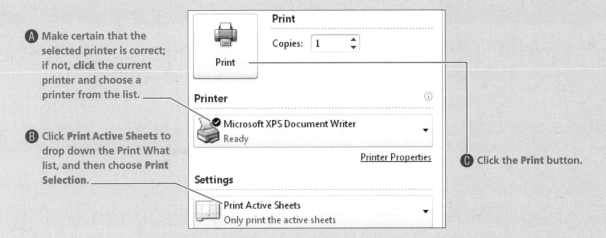

Ⓐ Make certain that the selected printer is correct; if not, **click** the current printer and choose a printer from the list.

Ⓑ Click **Print Active Sheets** to drop down the Print What list, and then choose **Print Selection**.

Ⓒ Click the **Print** button.

Only the selected range prints. Excel displays a page break (dashed line) to the right of column F in Normal view to indicate the edge of page 1.

11. **Scroll down** to view the page break at the bottom of the page (after row 52, depending on your printer).
These page breaks disappear from Normal view when the workbook is closed, but Page Layout view always shows you the page break locations.

12. Use ⎡Ctrl⎤+⎡Home⎤ to go to cell A1.

13. **Save** 🖫 the changes and **close** the workbook.

Microsoft Excel

Apply Your Skills

Edit a Worksheet and Use Page Layout View

In this exercise, you will edit a worksheet in both Normal and Page Layout views. You will also use AutoFill to extend a series.

1. **Open** the workbook named as-Bonuses from the Lesson 08 folder in your file storage location.

2. Edit the title in **cell A1** to read **Site Safety Bonuses**.

3. **AutoFill** the months February through June in **cells C3:G3**.

4. **Edit** the label in **cell A3** to **Employee Name**.

5. **Change** the name Garcia, H. in **cell A5** to **Wilson, T**.

6. View the worksheet in **Page Layout view**.

7. While in Page Layout view, **edit** the label in **cell A8** to read **Grand Total** and **complete** the entry.

8. **AutoFill** just the contents without the formatting from the range **F4:F7** to **G4:G7**. *The values in range G4:G7 should appear black when you are done.*

9. Change the entry in **cell G4** to **300**.

10. **Save** the changes and **close** the workbook.

Select, Move, and Copy in a Worksheet

In this exercise, you will practice selecting various ranges and cells in order to move and copy them.

1. **Open** the workbook named as-Carpet Products from the Lesson 08 folder in your file storage location.

2. Select **A6:D19**; try using the Shift technique.

3. Place your **mouse pointer** over the edge of the selection until you see the move pointer, and then **click** and **drag up** until the top left of the selection is in row 3.
   The selection will now be contained in the range A3:D16.

4. Select **B3:D3** and issue the **Cut** command.

5. Click **cell B4** and issue the **Paste** command.

6. **Copy** the contents of **B4:D4** into **B12:D12**.

7. **Save** the workbook and leave it **open** for the next exercise.

	A	B	C	D
1	Green Clean			
2	Carpet Products			
3				
4	CARPET CLEANING SOLUTIONS	Type	Size	Price
5	EarthWise Carpet Cleaner	Concentrate	64 ounces	$17.50
6	EarthWise Carpet Cleaner		32 ounces	$9.85
7	EarthWise Carpet Cleaner	Spray	16 ounces	$4.50
8	GBS All Purpose Carpet	Liquid	120 ounces	$11.95
9	GBS Dry Powder Cleaner	Powder	16 ounces	$4.25
10	Taz Carpet and Upholstery	Liquid	Gallon	$7.95
11				
12	CARPET STAIN REMOVERS	Type	Size	Price
13	EarthWise Carpet Stain Remover	Concentrate	64 ounces	$9.95
14	EarthWise Carpet Stain Remover	Concentrate	32 ounces	$5.50
15	EarthWise Carpet Stain Remover	Spray	16 ounces	$4.65
16	Carpet Bright Stain Eliminator	Spray	32 ounces	$7.35

Work with Undo, Clear, and AutoComplete

In this exercise, you will work with the workbook from Apply Your Skills 8.2 to clear formatting, undo commands, and use AutoComplete.

Before You Begin: You must have completed Apply Your Skills 8.1 and 8.2, and the as-Carpet Products workbook should be open.

1. Select **column D** by clicking the column header.

2. Choose **Home→Editing→Clear→Clear Formats** from the Ribbon.
   Notice that the numbers remain in column D, but they are no longer formatted as currency.

3. Click the **Undo** button on the Quick Access toolbar to bring back the cleared formatting.

4. Click **cell B6** and type **c**, observing the AutoComplete option that appears.

5. Tap [Enter] to accept the AutoComplete suggestion.

6. Select the **range A10:D10** and **tap** [Delete] to clear the contents of the cells.

7. Choose **File→Print**.

8. Check the print preview in the **Print** tab of Backstage view to make certain that the worksheet will print on one page.

9. **Print** the worksheet.

10. **Save** the changes to the workbook and **exit** from Excel.

	A	B	C	D
1	Green Clean			
2	Carpet Products			
3				
4	CARPET CLEANING SOLUTIONS	Type	Size	Price
5	EarthWise Carpet Cleaner	Concentrate	64 ounces	$17.50
6	EarthWise Carpet Cleaner	Concentrate	32 ounces	$9.85
7	EarthWise Carpet Cleaner	Spray	16 ounces	$4.50
8	GBS All Purpose Carpet	Liquid	120 ounces	$11.95
9	GBS Dry Powder Cleaner	Powder	16 ounces	$4.25
10				
11				
12	CARPET STAIN REMOVERS	Type	Size	Price
13	EarthWise Carpet Stain Remover	Concentrate	64 ounces	$9.95
14	EarthWise Carpet Stain Remover	Concentrate	32 ounces	$5.50
15	EarthWise Carpet Stain Remover	Spray	16 ounces	$4.65
16	Carpet Bright Stain Eliminator	Spray	32 ounces	$7.35

Critical Thinking & Work-Readiness Skills

In the course of working through the following Microsoft Office-based Critical Thinking exercises, you will also be utilizing various work-readiness skills, some of which are listed next to each exercise. Go to labyrinthelab.com/ workreadiness to learn more about the work-readiness skills.

8.1 Edit and Replace Entries

Ken asks Jenna Mann to update the birthday list for Green Clean employees. Jenna finds the current birthday list in a Microsoft Excel file. She decides to contact each employee personally, as an excuse to introduce herself, as well as to verify the dates. Open ct-Birthdays (Lesson 08 folder) and make these edits: change Mary Wright's birthday to March 2; delete all information for Michael Tsang and Joe Smith; change Mary Jones to **Amy Wyatt** and her birthday of June 26; and add Alan Sedgwick and his birthday of September 25 at the end of the list. Save the file as **ct-Birthday Update**. If working in a group, discuss why a company might want to recognize birthdays. If working alone, type your answer in a Word document named **ct-Questions** saved to your Lesson 08 folder.

WORK-READINESS SKILLS APPLIED

- Making decisions
- Showing responsibility
- Knowing how to learn

8.2 Edit and Print a Workbook

Ken decides to add a column to Jenna's birthday worksheet for monthly highlights (a job completed, a customer compliment, etc.) at the November employee meeting. Open ct-Birthday Update, if necessary. Add a column labeled **Highlight** and add the following:

```
Mary Wright - Congratulations on deal with Hall Properties;
Amy Wyatt - Congratulations on recent marriage; Jenna Mann -
Thanks for updating birthday list; Talos Bouras - Happy
birthday!; Michael Chowdery - Welcome, will report to Derek.
```

Proofread your work and correct as necessary. Print preview the birthday list with the new column. Print the document. Save the file as **ct-Birthday Highlights** in your Lesson 08 folder.

WORK-READINESS SKILLS APPLIED

- Acquiring and using information
- Exercising leadership
- Interpreting and communicating information

8.3 Rearrange Data and use Auto Features

Ken wants an employee roster. Also, every employee has a quarterly "green" project to complete and Ken would like to track these. Open ct-Birthdays Highlights, if necessary. Select just the employee names and copy them to the Clipboard. Open ct-Employee Roster (Lesson 08 folder), and paste the names into column B. Select the names Kenneth Hazell through Alan Sedgwick, and move the names up one cell to eliminate the blank cell. Label column A as **Empoyee #**. Create a unique number for each employee in the Employee # column, starting with EN-001. Then, assign each employee randomly to one of the following: **Light Bulb Replacement, Product Improvement, Commute Reduction**. Save file as **ct-Employee Roster and Project** in your Lesson 08 folder and close all files.

WORK-READINESS SKILLS APPLIED

- Organizing and maintaining information
- Seeing things in the mind's eye
- Showing responsibility

Working with Formulas and Functions

LEARNING OBJECTIVES

After studying this lesson, you will be able to:

- Create formulas to calculate values, utilizing the proper syntax and order of operations
- Employ a variety of methods to use statistical functions that determine the sum, average, count, maximum, and minimum of a range of numbers
- Use relative, absolute, and mixed cell references in formulas
- Modify and copy formulas
- Display the formulas contained within cells rather than the resulting values

The magic of the Excel spreadsheet lies in its ability to crunch numbers and make sense of data. The heart of this magic lies in the formulas and functions that are used for this number crunching. In this lesson, you will be introduced to creating and modifying basic formulas and functions in Excel. You will learn how to reference cells in formulas as well as how to use another automated feature of Excel, AutoSum.

Creating a Spreadsheet with Formulas

Green Clean earns revenue by selling janitorial products and contracts for cleaning services. Talos Bouras is a sales manager. He wants to set up a workbook with two worksheets, one to track commissions and the other to report how the projected profit would change based on costs and an increase or decrease in sales. He will create the necessary formulas for the workbook calculations.

green clean

	A	B	C	D	E	F
1	**Sales Department**					
2	*First Quarter Commissions*					
3						
4	*Sales Team Member*	*January*	*February*	*March*	*Qtr 1 Total*	*Sales*
5	Talos Bouras	250	486	415	**1151**	28775
6	Leisa Malimali	74	88	101	**263**	6575
7	Brian Simpson	389	303	422	**1114**	27850
8	Amy Wyatt	346	381	502	**1229**	30725
9	**Monthly Total**	**1059**	**1258**	**1440**	**3757**	
10						
11	Average	264.75	314.5	360	939.25	
12	Maximum	389	486	502	1229	
13	Minimum	74	88	101	263	
14	Count	4	4	4	4	
15	Goal					30000

The Qtr 1 Commissions worksheet sums the monthly totals for all team members and each team member's quarterly sales. Formulas also calculate the monthly average, maximum, minimum, and item count.

	A	B	C	D	E
1	**Sales Department**				
2	*Projected Net Profit*				
3		*Base*	*2%*	*5%*	*-5%*
4	**Product Sales**	$ 53,200	54,264	55,860	50,540
5	Contracts	241,000	245,820	258,111	245,205
6	**Total Revenue**	$ 294,200	$ 300,084	$ 313,971	$ 295,745
7					
8	Fixed Operating Cost	101,400	101,400	101,400	101,400
9	Marketing Expense	15,000	15,000	15,000	15,000
10	Commissions	27,824	28,380	29,721	28,058
11	**Total Costs**	$ 144,224	$ 144,780	$ 146,121	$ 144,458
12					
13	**Gross Profit**	$ 149,976	$ 155,304	$ 167,850	$ 151,287
14	**Net Profit**	$ 138,353	$ 143,267	$ 154,841	$ 139,562
15	**Gross Profit vs. Revenue**	51.0%	51.8%	53.5%	51.2%
16					
17	Contracts	482			
18	Average Contract	500	Marketing	15,000	
19	Product Commission Rate	7%	Fixed Cost	101,400	
20	Contract Commission Rate	10%	Tax Rate	7.75%	

The Profit Projection worksheet reports the effect of various sales projections and costs on net profit. When Talos changes the numbers in rows 17–20, the formulas recalculate the results in rows 4–15 automatically.

Microsoft Excel

9.1 Working with Formulas and Functions

Video Lesson labyrinthelab.com/videos

A formula is simply a math problem done in Excel. You can add, subtract, multiply, divide, and group numbers and cell contents in order to make your data work for you. A function is a prewritten formula that helps to simplify complex procedures, both for numbers and for text. For instance, a function can be used to sum a group of numbers, to determine the payment amount on a loan, and to convert a number to text.

Using AutoSum to Create a SUM Formula

FROM THE KEYBOARD

Alt + = for Autosum

The power of Excel becomes apparent when you begin using formulas and functions. The most common type of calculation is summing a column or row of numbers. In fact, this type of calculation is so common that Excel provides the AutoSum feature specifically for this purpose.

The **Σ** button on the Home tab, also known as Sum, automatically sums a column or row of numbers. When you click AutoSum, Excel starts the formula for you by entering =SUM() and proposes a range of adjacent cells within parentheses. Excel will first look upward for a range to sum, and if a range is not found there, it will next look left. You can accept the proposed range or drag in the worksheet to select a different range. You can see the formula, such as =SUM(B5:B8), in the Formula Bar as you edit cell contents. Then, the calculation result displays in the cell after you complete the entry. Empty cells in the sum range are ignored in the calculation.

If your Excel window is smaller, the button may be displayed like this: **Σ ▾**.

	A	B	C	D
	SUM	▾	X ✓ fx	=SUM(B5:B8)
1		**Sales Department**		
2		*First Quarter Commission*		
3				
4	*Sales Team Member*	*January*	*February*	*Mar*
5	Talos Bouras	250	486	
6	Leisa Malimali	74	88	
7	Brian Simpson	389	303	
8	Amy Wyatt	346	381	
9	**Monthly Total**	=SUM(B5:B8)		
10		SUM(**number1**, [number2], ...)		

The Formula Bar displays the formula.

Excel proposes to sum the range B5:B8 above the formula cell. A flashing marquee surrounds the range.

The formula is being created in cell B9.

January
250
74
389
346
1059

The result displays after you complete the entry.

AVERAGE, COUNT, COUNTA, MAX, and MIN Functions

The AutoSum button does not stop at simply summing a group of numbers. The following statistical functions are also available on the AutoSum drop-down list: average, count numbers, maximum, and minimum.

An additional Count command equal to the COUNTA function in formulas is available on the Status Bar. The following table describes these functions. The COUNTA function counts all nonblank cells in the specified range. At times, you will want use COUNTA to count all entries, whether or not they contain numbers. You could use the Count Numbers command, equal to the COUNT function, when it is important to identify any non-number cells as possible errors.

AutoSum and/or Status Bar Function	How Function Appears in Formula	Description
Sum	SUM	Adds the values in the cells indicated in the formula
Average	AVERAGE	Averages the values in the cells indicated in the formula by dividing the sum total by the number of values
Count Numbers or Numerical Count	COUNT	Counts the number of values in the cells indicated in the formula; cells containing text and blank cells are ignored
Count	COUNTA	Counts the number of nonblank cells in the cells indicated in the formula; cells containing text are included; empty cells are ignored
Max or Maximum	MAX	Returns the maximum (highest) value in the cells indicated in the formula
Min or Minimum	MIN	Returns the minimum (lowest) value in the cells indicated in the formula

Once you have entered a formula in a cell, you can use AutoFill to copy it to adjacent cells.

Status Bar Functions and Customization

The Status Bar, which is displayed at the bottom of the Excel window, allows you to view information about a range of numbers without actually inserting a function formula in the worksheet. You can customize the Status Bar to display the following functions: Average, Count, Numerical Count, Minimum, Maximum, and Sum. To customize the Status Bar, right-click anywhere on it and click to add or remove features. Other than functions, you can also customize additional features of the Status Bar, such as Zoom, Signatures, Overtype Mode, and Macro Recording.

The range B5:B8 is selected in the worksheet.

◢	A	B	C
1		**Sales Depa**	
2		*First Quarter Con*	
3			
4	*Sales Team Member*	*January*	*February*
5	Talos Bouras	250	486
6	Leisa Malimali	74	88
7	Brian Simpson	389	303
8	Amy Wyatt	346	381
9	**Monthly Total**	1059	1258

By default, Excel displays in the Status Bar the average, count of values, and sum of the selected range.

Right-clicking the Status Bar displays a menu from which you can add items to or delete them from the Status Bar.

Customize Status Bar

✓	Cell Mode	Ready
✓	Signatures	Off
✓	Information Management Policy	Off
✓	Permissions	Off
	Caps Lock	Off
	Num Lock	Off
✓	Scroll Lock	Off
✓	Fixed Decimal	Off
	Overtype Mode	
✓	End Mode	
	Macro Recording	Not Recording
✓	Selection Mode	
✓	Page Number	
✓	Average	264.75
✓	Count	4
	Numerical Count	
	Minimum	
	Maximum	
✓	Sum	1059
✓	Upload Status	
✓	View Shortcuts	
✓	Zoom	100%
✓	Zoom Slider	

QUICK REFERENCE | **USING AUTOSUM AND THE STATUS BAR FUNCTIONS**

Task	Procedure
AutoSum a range of cells	■ Click in the cell where you want the sum to appear.
	■ Choose Home→Editing→AutoSum Σ from the Ribbon.
	■ If the proposed range is correct, tap Enter or click the AutoSum button to complete the function.
	■ If the proposed range is incorrect, click and drag to select the correct range before tapping Enter.
AutoSum across columns or down rows	■ Select the cell range in the row below or column to the right of the data where you want the sums to appear.
	■ Choose Home→Editing→AutoSum Σ from the Ribbon.
Use Status Bar functions	■ Right-click the Status Bar and add or remove the desired functions, if necessary.
	■ Drag to select the range of cells to which you wish to apply the function.
	■ Look at the Status Bar at the bottom of your Excel window to view the average, count of values, and sum of the selected range.

Use AutoSum and Status Bar Functions

In this exercise, you will use AutoSum to calculate the monthly commission total for the sales team as well as the quarterly total for each sales team member. You will also explore the functions on the Status Bar.

Open an Excel File

1. Start **Excel**.

2. **Open** the Commissions workbook from the Lesson 09 folder in your file storage location.
   Take a look at the workbook. There are two tabs at the bottom of the window: Qtr 1 Commissions and Profit Projection. You will first work with the commissions worksheet to calculate monthly and quarterly commission totals. You also will find the average, maximum, minimum, and count of numbers for each month.

Use AutoSum

3. With the Qtr 1 Commissions worksheet displayed, select **cell B9**.

4. Choose **Home→Editing→Sum** $\boxed{\Sigma}$ from the Ribbon.
   Excel displays a marquee (marching ants) around the part of the spreadsheet where it thinks the formula should be applied. You can change this selection as necessary.

5. Follow these steps to complete the Sum formula.

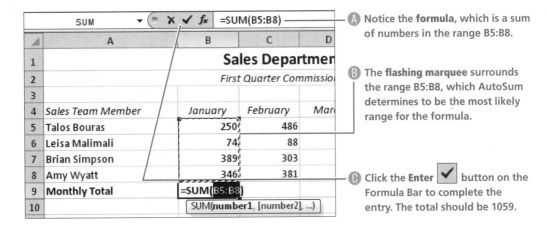

Ⓐ Notice the **formula**, which is a sum of numbers in the range B5:B8.

Ⓑ The **flashing marquee** surrounds the range B5:B8, which AutoSum determines to be the most likely range for the formula.

Ⓒ Click the **Enter** ✔ button on the Formula Bar to complete the entry. The total should be 1059.

Override the Range AutoSum Proposes

6. Select **cell E7** and choose **Home→Editing→Sum** Σ from the Ribbon.
   Notice that, as there are no values above cell E7, Excel looked to the left to find a range to sum, B7:D7. Now, assume that you wanted only cells B7:C7 to be summed.

7. Follow these steps to override the proposed range:

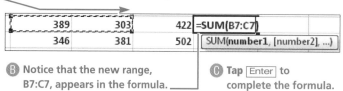

Ⓐ Position the mouse pointer on **cell B7;** **drag** to the right to select the **range B7:C7.**

389	303		422	=SUM(B7:C7)
346	381		502	SUM(**number1**, [number2], ...)

Ⓑ Notice that the new range, B7:C7, appears in the formula.

Ⓒ Tap Enter to complete the formula.

8. **Undo** ↩ the formula.

Use AutoFill to Extend a Formula

You can use AutoFill to extend a formula just as you would use it to extend a series of days in the week.

9. Follow these steps to AutoFill the formula in cell B9 into the cells to its right:

Ⓐ Select **cell B9.**

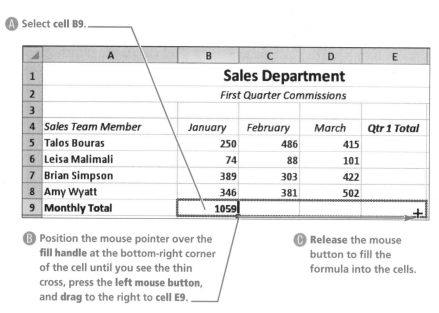

◢	A	B	C	D	E
1		**Sales Department**			
2		*First Quarter Commissions*			
3					
4	*Sales Team Member*	*January*	*February*	*March*	*Qtr 1 Total*
5	Talos Bouras	250	486	415	
6	Leisa Malimali	74	88	101	
7	Brian Simpson	389	303	422	
8	Amy Wyatt	346	381	502	
9	Monthly Total	1059			

Ⓑ Position the mouse pointer over the **fill handle** at the bottom-right corner of the cell until you see the thin cross, press the **left mouse button**, and **drag** to the right to **cell E9.**

Ⓒ **Release** the mouse button to fill the formula into the cells.

Cell E9 displays 0 because the cells above it are empty. You can create formulas that include empty cells and then enter data later.

Calculate the Quarterly Totals

10. Select the **range E5:E8**.

11. Choose **Home→Editing→Sum** $\boxed{\Sigma}$ from the Ribbon.
Excel created a formula in each cell of the selected range without requiring you to complete the formulas.

12. **Delete** the formulas in **range B9:E9** and **range E5:E8**.
The data are returned to their original state. Next you will create all formulas at once by selecting the data and the empty cells to the right and below the data.

Qtr 1 Total
1151
263
1114
1229
3757

Sum Columns and Rows Simultaneously

13. Select the **range B5:E9** and click **Sum** $\boxed{\Sigma}$.
The formula results appear in B9:D9 and E5:E9. This procedure is the most efficient to use when the data are arranged in this way.

Explore Statistical Functions with AutoSum

14. Select **cell B11**.

15. On the Home ribbon in the Editing group, click the **drop-down arrow** at the right of the **AutoSum** button.

16. Choose **Average** from the drop-down menu.
Excel proposes the range B5:B10, which is incorrect.

17. Select the correct **range B5:B8** and **tap** $\boxed{\text{Enter}}$ to complete the entry.
The result should equal 264.75.

18. Select **cell B12**.

19. Choose **Home→Editing** $\boxed{\Sigma \text{ AutoSum} \blacktriangledown}$ **menu ▼→Max** from the Ribbon.
Max means Maximum.

20. Select the correct **range B5:B8** and **tap** $\boxed{\text{Enter}}$ to display the highest value in the range you chose.

21. Select **cell B13** and choose **Home→Editing→AutoSum menu ▼→Min** from the Ribbon.
Min means Minimum, or the lowest value.

22. Correct the range to **B5:B8** and then click **Enter** $\boxed{\checkmark}$ on the Formula Bar to complete the entry.

23. Select **cell B14** and choose **Home→Editing** $\boxed{\Sigma \text{ AutoSum} \blacktriangledown}$ **menu ▼** from the Ribbon.

24. Choose **Count Numbers** from the menu, correct the range to **B5:B8**, and click **Enter** on the Formula Bar to complete the entry.

    Notice that the function COUNT is used in the formula. This function counts all cells in the range that contain a number. You can use this function to check that all cells have a number.

25. Select **cell B6** and **delete** the contents.

    The formula recalculates the count as 3 and recalculates the average because one cell in the range is now blank.

26. **Undo** ↰ the deletion.

Use Status Bar Functions

27. Select the **range B5:B8**.

28. Look at the Status Bar in the lower-right corner of the window to see the **sum value** displayed.

	B	C
✓ *fx*	=COUNT(B5:B8	
	January	*February*
	250	486
	74	88
	389	303
	346	381
	1059	1258
	264.75	314.5
	389	486
	74	88
	=COUNT(B5:B8	
	COUNT(**value1**, [value2], ...)	

Average: 264.75   Count: 4   Sum: 1059

29. **Save** 💾 the workbook and keep it **open** for the next exercise.

9.2 Creating Formulas

Video Lesson   labyrinthelab.com/videos

You have already learned how to compute totals with AutoSum. AutoSum provides a convenient method for summing a range of numbers. However, you will need to use many other types of formulas in Excel. In fact, many worksheets, such as financial models, require hundreds or even thousands of complex formulas.

Beginning Character in Formulas

As you saw in the AutoSum discussion in the previous section, functions begin with an equals (=) sign. If you are typing a formula in a cell, it is recommended that you also begin it with an equals (=) sign, even though you can begin it with a plus (+) or a minus (–) sign. It is best to adopt one method in order to create consistency.

Cell and Range References

Formulas derive their power from the use of cell and range references. For example, in the previous exercise, you used AutoSum to insert the formula =SUM(B5:B8) in cell B9. Because the range reference (B5:B8) was used in the formula, you were able to copy the formula across the row using the fill handle. There are two important benefits to using references in formulas.

■ When references are used, formulas can be copied to other cells.

■ Because a reference refers to a cell or a range of cells, the formula results are automatically recalculated when the data is changed in the referenced cell(s).

Do not type results of calculations directly into cells. Always use formulas.

The Language of Excel Formulas

Formulas can include the standard arithmetic operators shown in the following table. You can also use spaces within formulas to improve their appearance and readability. Notice that each formula in the table begins with an equals (=) sign. Also, keep in mind that each formula is entered into the same cell that displays the resulting calculation.

QUICK REFERENCE	USING ARITHMETIC OPERATORS IN FORMULAS	
Operator	**Example**	**Comments**
+ (addition)	=B7+B11	Adds the values in B7 and B11
– (subtraction)	=B7–B11	Subtracts the value in B11 from the value in B7
* (multiplication)	=B7*B11	Multiplies the values in B7 and B11
/ (division)	=B7/B11	Divides the value in B7 by the value in B11
^ (exponentiation)	=B7^3	Raises the value in B7 to the third power (B7*B7*B7)
% (percent)	=B7*10%	Multiplies the value in B7 by 10% (0.10)
( ) (grouping)	=B7/(C4–C2)	Subtracts the value in C2 from the value in C4 and then divides B7 by the subtraction result

When typing a cell reference in a formula, you can simply type the column letter in lowercase and Excel will capitalize it for you.

"Please Excuse My Dear Aunt Sally"

Excel formulas follow the algebraic hierarchy. This means that the formula completes operations in a specific order. You can memorize this hierarchy with the mnemonic "Please Excuse My Dear Aunt Sally":

Please	Parentheses (grouping symbols)
Excuse	Exponents
My	Multiplication
Dear	Division
Aunt	Addition
Sally	Subtraction

To control the order of operations, you can use parentheses to cause Excel to add or subtract before multiplying or dividing. Take a look at the following examples to see how the order of operations works with and without parentheses and how the resulting value will be different.

=53+ 7*5 = 53+35 = 88   Multiplication then addition

=(53+7)*5 = (60)*5 = 300   Parentheses then multiplication

Use the Keyboard to Create Formulas

In this exercise, you will use the keyboard to enter formulas into the spreadsheet.

1. Click the **Profit Projection** sheet tab at the bottom of the Excel window.

   | ◄ ◄ ► ►| | **Qtr 1 Commissions** / Profit Projection ◄

2. Select **cell B5** and view its formula in the Formula Bar.
   This formula multiplies the number of contracts (B17) by the average contract revenue (B18).

3. Select **cell B6** and use **AutoSum** to sum the sales in the **range B4:B5**.

4. Select **cell B11** and **sum** the costs in the **range B8:B10**.
   The total costs result is not correct, but you will enter data in cells B9 and B10 in the next exercise.

5. Select **cell B13**, the Gross Profit for the Base column.

6. Type **=B6-B11** in the cell, and then **tap** ⌨Enter to complete the formula.
   In order to calculate the gross profit, you need to subtract the total costs (B11) from total revenue (B6).

7. Select **cell B15**, Gross Profit vs. Revenue.

8. Type **=b13/b6** in the cell, and then **tap** ⌨Enter to complete the formula.
   Formulas are not case sensitive. Notice that regardless of whether you type the cell references as upper- or lowercase, the formula will work properly. In this worksheet, the cell has been formatted to display a percentage for you.

9. **Save** 🖫 the workbook and keep it **open** for the next exercise.

9.3 Using Cell References in Formulas

Video Lesson   labyrinthelab.com/videos

A cell reference identifies which cell or range of cells contains the values to use in a formula. Cell references are one of three types: relative, absolute, or mixed. All formulas use the relative cell reference unless you specifically instruct Excel to use another type. You used relative cell references in the formulas you created in the last exercise. As this lesson continues, you will learn about the other two types of cell references.

Relative Cell References

A relative cell reference means the cell is *relative* to the cell that contains the formula. For example, when you create a formula in cell C3 to calculate A3 minus B3 (=A3–B3), Excel finds that the first value is two cells to the left of the formula. The second value is one cell to the left of the formula.

When you copy a formula, the cell references update automatically and refer to new cells relative to the new formula cell. For example, if you copied the formula mentioned in the previous paragraph down to cell C4, the new formula would be A4 minus B4 (=A4–B4). The first and second values are still relative to the same number of cells to the left of the formula cell.

⊿	A	B	C	D	E
11	Total Costs	=SUM(B8:B10)	=SUM(C8:C10)	=SUM(D8:D10)	=SUM(E8:E10)
12					
13	Gross Profit	=B6-B11	=C6-C11	=D6-D11	=E6-E11

Notice that when a formula utilizing relative cell references in column B is copied through to column E, the cells referenced in the copied formulas will refer to cells relative to where they are pasted.

Point Mode

One potential danger that can occur when typing formulas is accidentally typing the incorrect cell reference. This is easy to do, especially if the worksheet is complex. Point mode can help you avoid this problem. With point mode, you can insert a cell reference in a formula by clicking the desired cell as you are typing the formula. Likewise, you can insert a range reference in a formula by dragging over the desired cells. You will use point mode in the next exercise.

Absolute Cell References

You have been using relative references thus far in this course. Relative references are convenient because they update automatically when formulas are moved or copied. In some situations, you may not want references updated when a formula is moved or copied. You must use absolute or mixed references in these situations. Absolute references always refer to the same cell, regardless of which cell the formula is moved or copied to. You can refer to cells on other worksheets or in other workbooks as well.

Creating Absolute References

You create absolute references by placing dollar signs in front of the column and row components of the reference, for example, $C$1. You can type the dollar signs as you enter a formula or add them later by editing the formula. The following illustration shows an example of how absolute references are used in formulas.

⊿	A	B	C	D	E
14	Net Profit	=B13*(1-$D$20)	=C13*(1-$D$20)	=D13*(1-$D$20)	=E13*(1-$D$20)

Cell B14 displays a formula that has both a relative cell reference (B13) and an absolute cell reference ($D$20).

When copied to cell C14, the relative cell reference will refer to the cell relative to where it is pasted (C13), but the absolute cell reference will remain the same.

Mixed References

You can mix relative and absolute references within a reference. For example, the reference $C1 is a combination of an absolute reference to column C and a relative reference to row 1. Mixed references are useful when copying many types of formulas.

Using the [F4] Function Key

You make a reference absolute or mixed by typing dollar signs while entering the reference. You can also use the [F4] function key to insert the dollar signs. You may do so right after typing the cell reference or by clicking for an insertion point in the cell reference in the Formula Bar. The first time you tap [F4], dollar signs are placed in front of both the column and row components of the reference. If you tap F4 again, the dollar sign is removed from the column component, thus creating a mixed reference. If you tap F4 a third time, a dollar sign is placed in front of just the column component and removed from the row component. One more tap of F4 will return you to a relative cell reference. The following table indicates what happens to a cell reference when its formula is copied and pasted to the next column or row.

Cell Reference	Type	Copy-and-Paste Action	Result When Pasted
B6	Relative	One column to the right	C6
B6	Relative	One row down	B7
$B$6	Absolute	One column to the right	$B$6
$B$6	Absolute	One row down	$B$6
$B6	Mixed	One column to the right	$B6
$B6	Mixed	One row down	$B7
B$6	Mixed	One column to the right	C$6
B$6	Mixed	One row down	B$6

What-If Analysis

Another great advantage to using cell references in formulas is that it allows you to perform what-if analyses. A what-if analysis is as simple as changing the value in a cell that is referenced in a formula and observing the overall change in the data. You can perform these simple analyses at any time by replacing the value(s) in referenced cells. The Undo command can come in very handy when performing a what-if analysis as it provides a quick way to return the worksheet to the original values. If you wish to perform an extensive what-if analysis and not worry about losing your original data, you may wish to save your workbook under a different name as a "practice" file.

DEVELOP YOUR SKILLS 9.3.1
Create Formulas Using Cell References

In this exercise, you will use absolute cell references to create formulas that can be copied to other cells.

Enter a Formula Using Point Mode

1. Select **cell B9** and type **=** to begin a formula.

2. Select **cell D18** and **tap** the F4 function key.

If you have a keyboard that uses the function keys for other purposes, you may have to tap the F Lock key to be able to utilize F4 for absolute or mixed references in Excel.

Tapping F4 will make the D18 cell reference an absolute by adding the $ symbol to both the column and row references. Take a look at the Formula Bar and you will see $D$18. A formula can consist of just one cell reference. In this case, you want the marketing expense always to reflect the value in cell D18.

3. **Tap** Enter to complete the formula.

Calculate the Commissions Using Order of Operations

You will enter a more complex formula to calculate the total commissions for product sales and contract sales. You want Excel to perform calculations in the following order. First, multiply product sales (B4) by their commission rate (B19). Second, multiply contract sales (B5) by their commission rate (B20). Last, add the two products together.

4. Select **cell B10** and type **=** to begin a formula.

5. Select **cell B4** and type *****.

6. Select **cell B19** and **tap** F4.

7. Type **+** to continue the formula.

8. Select **cell B5** and type *****.

9. Select **cell B20** and **tap** F4.

10. Click the **Enter** ✔ button to complete the formula.
    The result should equal 27,824. You have used point mode to create a formula containing both relative and absolute cell references. Notice how the formula appears in the Formula Bar: =B4 * $B$19 + B5 * $B$20. No matter where you copy and paste this formula, the formula always will reference the commission rates in cells B19 and B20.

Calculate the Net Profit Using Parentheses

You will create the formula =B13 * (1 - $D$20) to calculate the net profit. The gross profit in cell B13 will be multiplied by a factor that takes into account a tax on profits. The calculation in parentheses means "100% minus 7.75%," or 92.25%. The gross profit in cell B13 then will be multiplied by 92.25%.

11. Select **cell B14** and type **=** to begin a formula.

12. Select **cell B13** and type ***(1–** to continue the formula.

13. Select **cell D20** and **tap** F4.

14. Type **)** and **tap** Enter to complete the formula.
    The result should be $138,353.

Project a Sales Increase

You will create the formula =$B$4 * (1 + C$3) to project a 2 percent increase over the base product sales. The sales in cell B4 will be multiplied by (100% + 2%), or 102%. Notice that, when the formula is copied across the row later, the absolute reference will always refer to $B$4 as the base sales. The percentage of increase or decrease will change from C$3 to D$3 or E$3, the corresponding percentage over each column.

15. Select **cell C4** and type **=** to begin a formula.

16. Select **cell B4** and **tap** F4.

17. Type ***(1+** to continue the formula.

18. Select **cell C3** and **tap** F4 two times to create the C$3 mixed cell reference.

19. Type **)** and **tap** Enter to complete the formula.
    The result should equal 54,264.

20. Select **cell C5**.

21. Repeat the above procedure to project a **2 percent increase** for base contract sales.
    The result should equal 245,820.

22. **Save** 💾 the changes.

23. Compare your worksheet formulas and their results with the following illustrations.

	A	B	C	D	E
1		Sales Department			
2		Projected Net Profit			
3		Base	2%	5%	-5%
4	Product Sales	$ 53,200	$ 54,264		
5	Contracts	$ 241,000	$ 245,820		
6	Total Revenue	$ 294,200	$ 300,084	$ -	$ -
7					
8	Fixed Operating Cost	$ 101,400			
9	Marketing Expense	$ 15,000			
10	Commissions	$ 27,824			
11	Total Costs	$ 144,224			
12					
13	Gross Profit	$ 149,976			
14	Net Profit	$ 138,353			
15	Gross Profit vs. Revenue	$ 1			
16					
17	Contracts	$ 482			
18	Average Contract	$ 500	Marketing	$ 15,000	
19	Product Commission Rate	7%	Fixed Cost	$ 101,400	
20	Contract Commission Rate	10%	Tax Rate	7.75%	

	A	B	C	D	E
1		Sales Department			
2		Projected Net Profit			
3		Base	0.02	0.05	-0.05
4	Product Sales	53200	=$B$4*(1+C$3)		
5	Contracts	241000	=B5*(1+C$3)		
6	Total Revenue	=SUM(B4:B5)	=SUM(C4:C5)	=SUM(D4:D5)	=SUM(E4:E5)
7					
8	Fixed Operating Cost	=D19			
9	Marketing Expense	=$D$18			
10	Commissions	=B4*$B$19+B5*$B$20			
11	Total Costs	=SUM(B8:B10)			
12					
13	Gross Profit	=B6-B11			
14	Net Profit	=B13*(1-$D$20)			
15	Gross Profit vs. Revenue	=B13/B6			

Video Lesson labyrinthelab.com/videos

You can modify and copy formulas in much the same way that you edit and copy cells.

Modifying Formulas

You can edit a formula either in the Formula Bar or by double-clicking the formula cell to complete an in-cell edit. If you select a cell and enter a new formula, it replaces the previous contents of the cell.

When you select a formula to edit it, you will see colored lines around all of the cells that are referenced by the formula. This feature can help you to visually determine whether the formula is correct.

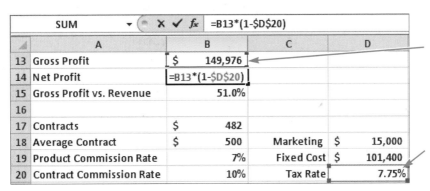

	A	B	C	D
13	Gross Profit	$ 149,976		
14	Net Profit	=B13*(1-$D$20)		
15	Gross Profit vs. Revenue	51.0%		
16				
17	Contracts	$ 482		
18	Average Contract	$ 500	Marketing	$ 15,000
19	Product Commission Rate	7%	Fixed Cost	$ 101,400
20	Contract Commission Rate	10%	Tax Rate	7.75%

The formula in B14 is selected for editing (as indicated by the insertion point in the cell). Excel graphically displays the cells that are being referenced by the formula, B13 and D20.

Circular References

You may inadvertently use a circular reference when creating or editing a formula. A circular reference occurs when the formula refers to its own cell or to another formula that refers to that cell. For example, a formula in cell C6 is =B6*C6. Excel cannot complete the calculation because cell C6 is the formula cell, not a reference to a value. When Excel displays a Circular Reference Warning message, you may either click OK to read the circular reference help topic or click Cancel to close the warning. Either option allows the circular reference to remain in the formula until you correct the formula.

You must correct the formula manually after you close Help or the Circular Reference Warning message.

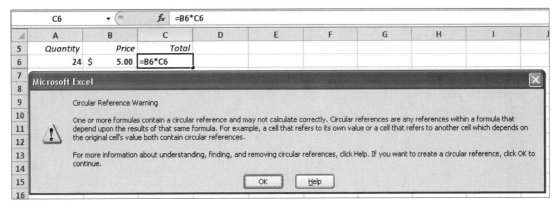

Copying Formulas

You can use either the Copy and Paste commands with formulas or AutoFill in order to copy them to new cells. You can copy formulas to one cell at a time or to a range of cells using either method.

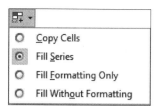

If you use Auto Fill, the Auto Fill Options button will appear once you have released the mouse button. Clicking this button will allow you to customize your fill. The Fill Series option displays in the list if you AutoFill a value but does not display for a formula.

You can change what was copied in the cells through AutoFill by clicking the Auto Fill Options button and choosing a different option.

DEVELOP YOUR SKILLS 9.4.1
Modify and Copy Formulas

In this exercise, you will use techniques to modify and copy formulas in order to complete your profit projection.

Modify Formulas and Correct a Circular Reference

1. Select **cell B8**, and then follow these steps to edit the formula in the Formula Bar:

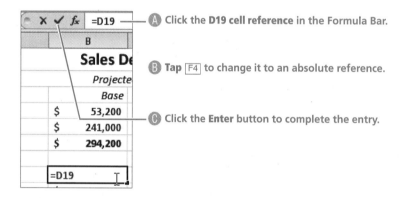

A Click the **D19 cell reference** in the Formula Bar.

B Tap F4 to change it to an absolute reference.

C Click the **Enter** button to complete the entry.

2. **Double-click** cell C6 to begin an in-cell edit.
   Notice that the cell references are displayed in color in the formula and on the worksheet.

3. Follow these steps to complete an in-cell edit:

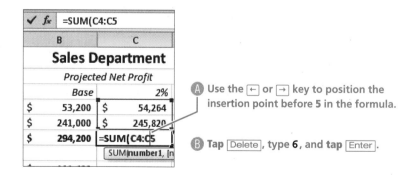

A Use the ← or → key to position the insertion point before **5** in the formula.

B Tap Delete, type **6**, and tap Enter.

Excel displays a Circular Reference Warning message because you referred to C6, the formula cell itself.

4. Choose **OK** in the Circular Reference Warning message.

5. **Undo** 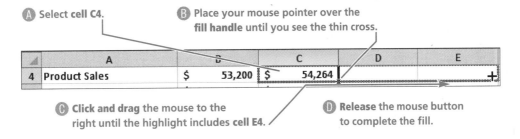 the change.

Use Copy and Paste Commands to Copy a Formula

6. Select **cell B14** and then use Ctrl + C to **copy** the formula.

7. Select **cell C14** and then use Ctrl + V to **paste** the formula in the new cell.
   This method works great if you need to copy a formula to just one cell. You can use these commands to copy a formula to a range of cells as well.

8. Select the **range D14:E14** and then use Ctrl + V.
   The formula that you copied in step 6 is now pasted to the range of cells selected.

9. **Tap** Esc to cancel the marquee around cell B14.

10. Select **cell D14** and look at the formula in the Formula Bar.

D14	▼	*fx*	=D13*(1-$D$20)	
◢	A	B	C	D
13	Gross Profit	$ 149,976		
14	Net Profit	$ 138,353	$ -	$ -

Notice that the relative cell reference now indicates cell D13, whereas the absolute cell reference is still looking to cell D20.

Use AutoFill to Copy Formulas

11. Follow these steps to copy the formula from cell C4 to the range D4:E4.

Ⓐ Select cell C4. Ⓑ Place your mouse pointer over the **fill handle** until you see the thin cross.

◢	A	B	C	D	E
4	Product Sales	$ 53,200	$ 54,264		+

Ⓒ **Click and drag** the mouse to the right until the highlight includes **cell E4**. Ⓓ **Release** the mouse button to complete the fill.

12. Use **AutoFill** to copy the formula from **cell C5** to the **range D5:E5**.
    Next, you will use AutoFill to copy formulas from B8:B15 all the way through C8:E15.

13. Select the **range B8:B15**.

14. Place your mouse pointer over the **fill handle** at the bottom right of the selected range.

15. When you see the thin cross ✛, **drag** to the **right** until the highlight includes the cells in **column E** and then release the mouse.

	A	B	C	D	E
8	Fixed Operating Cost	$ 101,400	$ 101,400	$ 101,400	$ 101,400
9	Marketing Expense	$ 15,000	$ 15,000	$ 15,000	$ 15,000
10	Commissions	$ 27,824	$ 28,380	$ 29,215	$ 26,433
11	Total Costs	$ 144,224	$ 144,780	$ 145,615	$ 142,833
12					
13	Gross Profit	$ 149,976	$ 155,304	$ 163,295	$ 136,657
14	Net Profit	$ 138,353	$ 143,267	$ 150,639	$ 126,066
15	Gross Profit vs. Revenue	51.0%	51.8%	52.9%	48.9%
16					

16. **Deselect** the filled range.

Make it a habit to deselect highlighted cells after performing an action. This step will help avoid unintended changes to cell contents.

17. **Save** 💾 the changes and leave the workbook **open**.

9.5 Displaying and Printing Formulas

Video Lesson labyrinthelab.com/videos

FROM THE KEYBOARD

Ctrl+` to show formulas

Excel normally displays the results of formulas in worksheet cells. However, you may need to display the actual formulas from time to time. Displaying formulas, especially in complex financial worksheets, can help you understand how a worksheet functions, enabling you to "debug" the worksheet and locate potential problems.

To display formulas, you will use the Show Formulas command on the Formulas tab of the Ribbon. You can edit a formula in this view, but you will need to show values again to see the result. To view the values once again, choose Show Formulas again.

While formulas are displayed, Excel automatically widens columns to show more of the cell contents. You can print the formula display as you would any other worksheet. You may wish to switch to landscape orientation, which prints the worksheet across the wide edge of the paper.

Depending on your monitor size, the buttons may appear as only icons, without the text descriptors, or as large buttons.

B	C	D
Sales Department		
Projected Net Profit		
Base	0.02	0.05
53200	=$B$4*(1+C$3)	=$B$4*(1+D$3)
=B17*B18	=$B$5*(1+C$3)	=$B$5*(1+D$3)
=SUM(B4:B5)	=SUM(C4:C5)	=SUM(D4:D5)
=$D$19	=$D$19	=$D$19
15000	15000	15000
=B4*$B$19+B5*$B$20	=C4*$B$19+C5*$B$20	=D4*$B$19+D5*$B$20
=SUM(B8:B10)	=SUM(C8:C10)	=SUM(D8:D10)
=B6-B11	=C6-C11	=D6-D11
=B13*(1-$D$20)	=C13*(1-$D$20)	=D13*(1-$D$20)
=B13/B6	=C13/C6	=D13/D6

When you choose to show formulas, you will see the formulas in the cells rather than the values as before. If a cell does not contain a formula, the contents will be visible in this view.

QUICK REFERENCE | **VIEWING AND PRINTING FORMULAS**

Task	**Procedure**
Display or hide the formulas in a workbook	■ Choose Formulas→Formula Auditing→Show Formulas 🔣 from the Ribbon.
Change paper orientation to print across the wide edge	■ Choose Page Layout→Page Setup→Orientation→Landscape from the Ribbon.
Print displayed formulas	■ Choose File→Print. ■ Choose any desired options in the Print tab and click Print.

DEVELOP YOUR SKILLS 9.5.1

Display Formulas in a Worksheet

In this exercise, you will display the formulas in the profit projection worksheet to see how it is constructed and to be able to troubleshoot any potentially inaccurate formulas.

1. Choose **Formulas→Formula Auditing→Show Formulas** 🔣 from the Ribbon.
   Take a look at the worksheet. You can use this feature to examine your formulas more closely.

2. Choose **Formulas→Formula Auditing→Show Formulas** 🔣 from the Ribbon.
   The values will be displayed once again.

9.6 Using Formula AutoComplete

Video Lesson   labyrinthelab.com/videos

Excel includes a feature that assists you in creating and editing formulas. Formula AutoComplete will jump into action once you have typed an equals (=) sign and the beginning letters of a function in a cell. It works by displaying a list of functions beginning with the typed letters below the active cell.

Functions Defined

A function is a predefined formula that performs calculations or returns a desired result. Excel has more than 400 built-in functions. You construct functions using a set of basic rules known as syntax. Fortunately, most functions use the same or similar syntax. This syntax also applies to the MIN, MAX, AVERAGE, COUNT, and COUNTA functions.

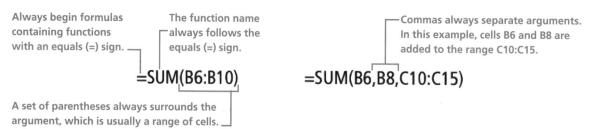

Always begin formulas containing functions with an equals (=) sign.

The function name always follows the equals (=) sign.

Commas always separate arguments. In this example, cells B6 and B8 are added to the range C10:C15.

$=SUM(B6:B10)$ $=SUM(B6,B8,C10:C15)$

A set of parentheses always surrounds the argument, which is usually a range of cells.

QUICK REFERENCE	USING FORMULA AUTOCOMPLETE TO ENTER A FORMULA INTO A CELL
Task	**Procedure**
Use Formula AutoComplete	▪ Type an equals (=) sign and begin typing the desired formula.
	▪ Double-click the formula once you see it in the list.
	▪ Select the range to which you wish to apply the formula.
	▪ Type a closed parenthesis,), to finish the formula.
	▪ Complete the entry.

DEVELOP YOUR SKILLS 9.6.1
Use Formula AutoComplete

In this exercise, you will have an opportunity to use the Formula AutoComplete feature to create a formula.

1. Display the **Qtr 1 Commissions** worksheet by clicking the sheet tab.

2. Select **cell C11**.

3. Type **=ave** and observe the list that results.

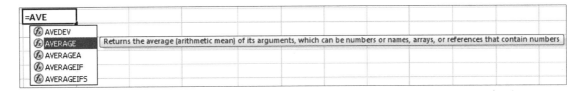

When you use Formula AutoComplete, Excel will show you a list of functions that begin with the letters you type in. If you click on a function in the list, a ScreenTip will describe the function.

4. **Double-click** AVERAGE in the list.
Excel will fill in the function name for you. It will be up to you to select the range next.

5. Drag to select **cells C5:C8** as the range for the formula.

You do not include total rows or columns when completing most functions.

6. **Tap** Enter to complete the function.
Notice that Excel added the parenthesis at the end of the formula for you. The result should be 314.5.

7. Select **cell C11** and use the fill handle to **copy** the function to the **range D11:E11**.

	A	B	C	D	E
11	Average	264.75	314.5	360	939.25
12	Maximum	389			

You now have the average commission for each month and the entire quarter.

8. **Save** 💾 the changes and leave the workbook **open**.

9.7 Using Insert Function

Video Lesson labyrinthelab.com/videos

The Insert Function f_x button displays the Insert Function dialog box. This dialog box provides access to all of Excel's built-in functions. It allows you to locate a function by typing a description or searching by category. When you locate the desired function and click OK, Excel displays the Function Arguments box. The Function Arguments box helps you enter arguments in functions. The Insert Function box and the Function Arguments box are shown in the following illustrations.

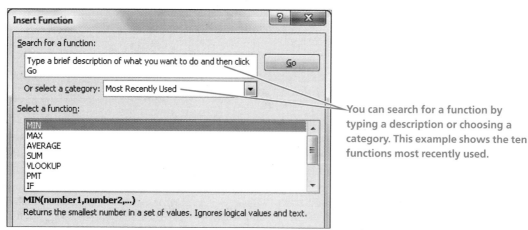

You can search for a function by typing a description or choosing a category. This example shows the ten functions most recently used.

The Function Arguments box appears when you choose a function and click OK.

You can type the argument (typically a range) in this box or select the desired range in the worksheet.

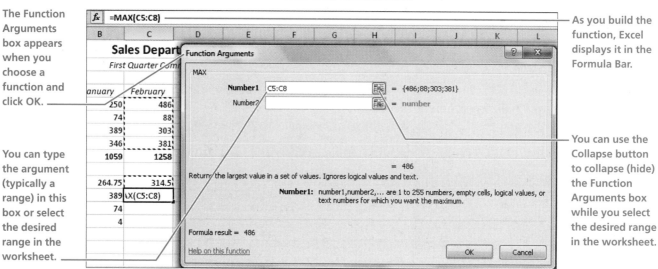

As you build the function, Excel displays it in the Formula Bar.

You can use the Collapse button to collapse (hide) the Function Arguments box while you select the desired range in the worksheet.

The Function Arguments dialog box can be moved by dragging its title bar to view the desired range on the worksheet.

QUICK REFERENCE	USING INSERT FUNCTION TO ENTER A FUNCTION IN A CELL
Task	**Procedure**
Create a function using the Insert Function command	■ Select the cell(s) in which you wish to enter a function.
	■ Click the Insert Function f_x button on the Formula Bar.
	■ Choose the desired function and click OK.
	■ Select the range to which you wish to apply the function.
	■ Click OK.

Use Insert Function

In this exercise, you will complete the commissions worksheet by using the Insert Function command to create both the maximum and minimum functions.

1. Select **cell C12**.

2. Follow these steps to create the Maximum function:

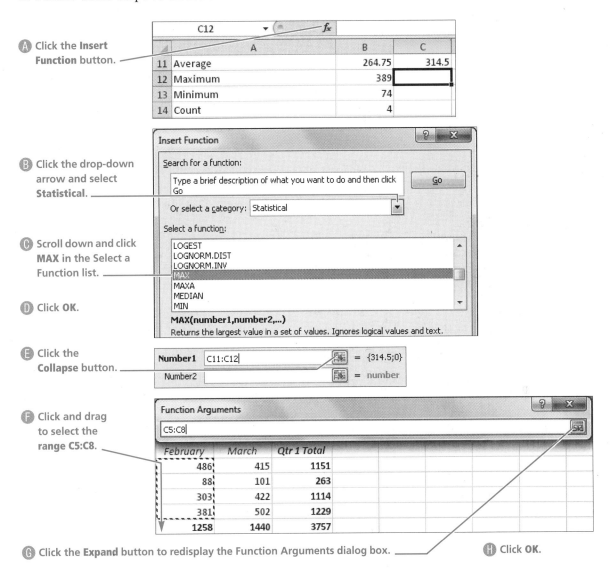

A Click the **Insert Function** button.

B Click the drop-down arrow and select **Statistical**.

C Scroll down and click **MAX** in the Select a Function list.

D Click **OK**.

E Click the **Collapse** button.

F Click and drag to select the range **C5:C8**.

G Click the **Expand** button to redisplay the Function Arguments dialog box.

H Click **OK**.

3. Using the procedure from **step 2**, create the **Minimum** function in **cell C13**.

4. Create the **Count** function in **cell C14**.

5. Select the **range C12:C14** and **copy** the formulas to the **range D12:E14**.

	A	B	C	D	E
11	Average	264.75	314.5	360	939.25
12	Maximum	389	486	502	1377
13	Minimum	74	88	101	263
14	Count	4	4	4	12

6. **Save** 🖫 the changes and **close** ⊠ the workbook.

9.8 Concepts Review

Concepts Review   labyrinthelab.com/ob10

To check your knowledge of the key concepts introduced in this lesson, complete the Concepts Review quiz by going to the URL listed above. If your classroom is using Labyrinth eLab, you may complete the Concepts Review quiz from within your eLab course.

Reinforce Your Skills

REINFORCE YOUR SKILLS 9.1

Use the AutoSum Function

In this exercise, you will use AutoSum to compute totals.

1. **Open** the rs-Benefit Plan workbook from the Lesson 09 folder in your file storage location.

2. Select **cell C10**, and then choose **Home→Editing→Sum** Σ from the Ribbon.
   Notice that Excel proposes the formula =SUM(C8:C9). Excel proposes this incorrect formula because there are empty cells in the range you are to sum.

3. **Drag** the mouse pointer over the **range C5:C9**.
   The flashing marquee will surround the range C5:C9.

4. **Complete** the entry.
   The total should equal 650.

5. Use the techniques described in the preceding steps to compute the **totals** in **cells E10, G10**, and **I10**.

6. **Save** 💾 the changes to your workbook and **close** it.

Amount	Con
100	
350	
200	
=SUM(C5:C9)	

REINFORCE YOUR SKILLS 9.2

Create Simple Formulas

In this exercise, you will create formulas using the keyboard as well as the point-and-click method.

1. **Open** the rs-Orders and Returns workbook from the Lesson 09 folder in your file storage location.

2. Select **cell B18**.

3. Type **=**.

4. Select **cell B4** and and type **+**.

5. Select **cell B9** and type **+**.

6. Select **cell B14** and **tap** ⎵Enter⎵.

7. Use **AutoFill** to copy the formula to **cells C18** and **D18**.

8. Using the techniques described in the preceding steps, create a formula in **cell B19** that **totals** the exchanges from all three sales categories.

9. Create another formula in **cell B20** that **totals** the returns from all three sales categories.

10. Use **AutoFill** to copy the formulas into the appropriate cells.

11. Take a few minutes to examine the formulas in the Formula Bar.

12. **Save** 💾 the changes and **close** the workbook.

Use Formula AutoComplete, AutoFill, and Display Formulas

In this exercise, you will calculate averages by using the Formula AutoComplete feature. You will also display formulas and preview them in Page Layout View. You will explore the Landscape and Portrait print settings.

Use AutoComplete

1. **Open** the rs-Service Contracts workbook from the Lesson 09 folder in your file storage location.

2. Select **cell A10** and **edit** the label to read **Green Clean Service Contracts – Prior Year**.

3. Select **cell B2** and use **AutoFill** to copy the series Qtr 2, Qtr 3, and Qtr 4 into the **range C2:E2**.

4. Select **cell B8**.

5. Begin **typing** the formula **=aver**, and then **tap** ⸤Tab⸥ to choose **AVERAGE** as the function.

6. Drag to select **B3:B6**, and then **tap** ⸤Enter⸥.
   The result should equal 33.

7. Use the **fill handle** to copy the formula across **row 8**.

8. Select **cell B17**.

9. Use **Formula AutoComplete** to average the **range B12:B15**.
   The result should equal 23.5. Remember that, you can type the function name and arguments in lowercase and Excel will convert them to uppercase.

10. Use the **fill handle** to copy the formula across **row 17**.

11. Select **cell B20**.

12. Use **point mode** to enter the formula =B7-B16, and **complete** the entry.
    The result should equal 38.

13. Use the **fill handle** to copy the formula across **row 20**.

Display Formulas and Preview in Page Layout View

14. Use ⸤Ctrl⸥+⸤`⸥ to display the worksheet formulas.
    The grave accent ` key is above the ⸤Tab⸥ key.

15. Choose **View→Workbook Views→Page Layout** ⬚ from the Ribbon.

16. Take a few minutes to look at the way the data and formulas display.
    Notice that Excel widened the columns so that most of the cell contents display. In this view, the worksheet fits on two pages.

17. Choose **Page Layout→Page Setup→Orientation→Landscape** from the Ribbon.
    Landscape orientation prints across the wide edge of the paper, which is useful for printing the formula view. Now the formulas fit on one page.

18. Choose **Page Layout→Page Setup→Orientation→Portrait** from the Ribbon.
    Portrait orientation prints across the narrow edge of the paper, which is acceptable for printing this worksheet while formulas are hidden.

19. Click the **Normal View** button in the view toolbar at the bottom-right corner of the window.

20. Use Ctrl + ` to **hide** the formulas.

21. **Save** 💾 the changes and **close** the workbook.

Use Absolute References and Perform a What-If Analysis

In this exercise, you will create a worksheet that calculates commissions as total sales multiplied by the commission rate. You will change the commission rate to see the impact this change has on the total sales. You will use an absolute reference when referencing the commission rate.

1. Start a **new** workbook, and set up the worksheet shown to the right. **Type** all numbers as shown.

	A	B	C
1	January Commission Report		
2			
3	Commission Rate		5%
4			
5		Sales	Commission
6	Bouras	44000	
7	Malimali	17000	
8	Simpson	41000	
9	Wyatt	36000	

2. Select **cell C6**, and **enter** the formula **=B6*$C$3** in the cell.
   The result should be 2200. Cell C3 needs an absolute reference because you will copy the formula down the column and because the new formulas must also reference C3.

3. Use the **fill handle** to copy the formula down the column to **cells C7 through C9**.

4. Select **cell C3**, and change the percentage to **3%**.
   By this time, you should see the benefit of setting up values first (such as the commission rate) and referencing them in formulas. This step allows you to perform what-if analyses. In most cases, you will need absolute references when referencing variables in this manner. Absolute references are necessary whenever you copy a formula that references a variable in a fixed location.

5. **Save** 💾 as **rs-January Commissions** in the Lesson 09 folder and continue with the next exercise.

	A	B	C
1	January Commission Report		
2			
3	Commission Rate		3%
4			
5		Sales	Commission
6	Bouras	44000	1320
7	Malimali	17000	510
8	Simpson	41000	1230
9	Wyatt	36000	1080

Microsoft Excel

Use COUNT and COUNTA Functions

In this exercise, you will create formulas using the COUNT and COUNTA functions.

Before You Begin: You must have completed Reinforce Your Skills 9.4 and the rs-January Commissions workbook should be open.

1. Type **Count** in **cell A11**.

2. Type **CountA** in **cell A12**.

3. Select **cell B11** and begin **typing** the formula **=cou**.

4. Read the description of the COUNT function in the list that appears.
   The COUNT function counts the cells containing numbers in the specified range.

5. **Tap** Tab to select **COUNT** in the list.

6. Drag to select **B5:B9** and **tap** Enter.
   The result should equal 4. The label in cell B5 is ignored.

7. Select **cell B12** and repeat the above procedure, this time selecting the **COUNTA** function.
   The result should equal 5, including the label in cell B5. The COUNTA function counts all nonblank cells in the specified range.

8. Select **cell B7** and **delete** the contents.
   The result is one less for both the COUNT and COUNTA formulas. Any blank cells are ignored.

9. Leaving **cell B7** as blank, **save** 🖫 the changes, and **close** the workbook.

◢	A	B	C
1	January Commission Report		
2			
3	Commission Rate		3%
4			
5		Sales	Commission
6	Bouras	44000	1320
7	Malimali		0
8	Simpson	41000	1230
9	Wyatt	36000	1080
10			
11	Count	3	
12	CountA	4	

Apply Your Skills

Create Simple Formulas

In this exercise, you will develop a worksheet with simple formulas.

1. **Open** the as-Credit Lines workbook from the Lesson 09 folder in your file storage location.

2. Follow these guidelines to create the following worksheet:
   - **Enter** all remaining text and number entries.
   - Use **formulas** in **columns D** and **F** to calculate subtotals and new balances. Calculate each **subtotal** as the previous balance plus new charges. Calculate each **new balance** as the subtotal minus the payment amount.
   - Use **AutoSum** to calculate totals for the **range B10:F10**.

	A	B	C	D	E	F
1	Green Clean - Credit Lines					
2						
3	Customer	Previous Balance	New Charges	Subtotal	Payment Amount	New Balance
4	Abel Printing Inc.	104	50		154	
5	Charley's Restaurant	230	85		315	
6	Hightower Electric	58	116		0	
7	Mendez Foods	423	320		423	
8	Ota Beverage Supply	140	65		0	
9	Sara Yang, CPA	97	43		100	
10	Total Credit					

3. Issue the command to display the **formulas**.
   Notice that the column widths are automatically increased to accommodate the width of the formulas. This will cause the worksheet to print on two pages.

4. Display **Page Layout** view to preview how formulas will print; **print** the formulas.

5. **Hide** the formulas and then display **Normal view**.

6. **Save** 💾 the changes and **close** the workbook.

Use AutoSum, MIN, and MAX

In this exercise, you will create a new worksheet that includes text and numbers. You will enter formulas and functions. Finally, you will save, print, and close the workbook.

1. Follow these guidelines to create the worksheet shown:

   - **Enter** the text and numbers as shown in the following illustration.

   - Use the **generic formulas** shown below to calculate the interest charge in column E and the new balance in column F. Use **parentheses** in the Interest Charge formula to change the order of the calculation. You want Excel to subtract the payments from the beginning balance and then multiply the result by 1.5%. **Don't type** the words *Beginning Balance, Charges,* etc., in the formulas; use the appropriate cell references. Use **Auto-Fill** to extend the formulas from **row 4 through row 9**.

     Interest Charge = 1.5% * (Beginning Balance – Payments)

     New Balance = Beginning Balance + Charges – Payments + Interest Charge

   - Use **AutoSum** to calculate the totals in **row 10**.

   - Use the **MAX** and **MIN** functions to calculate the highest and lowest numbers in **rows 11** and **12**.

	A	B	C	D	E	F
1	Green Clean - Accounts Receivable					
2						
3	Customer	Beg. Bal.	Charges	Payments	Interest	New Balance
4	R202	2000	2300	1000		
5	R314	2450	100	2450		
6	R572	5400	2190	3000		
7	W016	3450	500	1450		
8	W215	100	3400	100		
9	W264	1600	600	0		
10	Totals					
11	Highest					
12	Lowest					

2. Display the formulas in **Page Layout** view.

3. Change to **Landscape** orientation; **print** the formulas.
   The formulas will print on one page.

4. **Hide** the formulas and then display **Normal view**.

5. **Save** 💾 with the name **as-Accounts Receivable** in the Lesson 09 folder and **close** the workbook.

Use Absolute References

In this exercise, you will create formulas using absolute references.

1. **Open** the as-Jan Price Change workbook from the Lesson 09 folder.

2. Follow these guidelines to complete the following worksheet:

   ■ **Enter** the text entries as shown. Enter the numbers in **column B** and the percentage in **cell B3**.

   ■ Use the **generic formula** shown below to calculate the discounted price in **cell C6**. Use an **absolute reference** when referring to the discount rate in **cell B3**. Remember that you are calculating the discounted price, so your formula must subtract the discount rate in **cell B3** from 1.

   Discounted Price = Original Price * (1 – Discount Rate)

   ■ **Copy** the formula in **cell C6** down the column.

   Cell C6 was formatted for you so it displays the price with two decimal places.

3. Change the percentage in **cell B3** to **10%**, and watch the worksheet recalculate.

4. Change the percentage in **cell B3** back to **15%**, and watch the worksheet recalculate.

5. **Print** the worksheet.

6. **Display** the formulas; **print** the formulas.
   The formulas will print on one page.

7. **Hide** the formulas and then make certain Normal view is displayed.

8. **Save** 🖫 the changes and **close** the workbook.

	A	B	C
1	January Price Changes		
2			
3	January Discount Rate	15%	
4			
5		Original Price	Discounted Price
6	Bamboo Ware Plates	3.65	
7	Biograde Garbage Bags, 25	1.89	
8	Biograde Garbage Bags, 50	3.69	
9	Biograde Garbage Bags, 100	6.89	
10	Green Earth Scrub Pads	2.25	
11	Reusable Cloths, 2 dozen	2.49	
12	Reusable Cloths, 4 dozen	4.69	

Microsoft Excel

Create a Financial Report

In this exercise, you will create a worksheet by entering data, creating formulas, and using absolute references. You will also save, print a section of, and close the workbook.

1. **Open** the as-Projected Net Profit workbook from the Lesson 09 folder.

2. Use these guidelines to create the financial report at right:

◢	A	B	C	D	E
1	Projected Net Profit				
2					
3		Q1	Q2	Q3	Q4
4	Revenue	345000	390000	480000	500000
5					
6	Employee Costs				
7	Capital Expenditures				
8	Manufacturing				
9	Marketing & Sales				
10	Total Costs				
11					
12	Gross Profit				
13	Net Profit				
14					
15	Employee Costs	18%			
16	Capital Expenditures	22%			
17	Manufacturing	17%			
18	Marketing & Sales	16%			
19	Tax Rate	40%			

   - **Type** the headings, labels, and numbers as shown in the illustration to the right. Use **AutoFill** whenever possible to copy cells or complete a series (for example, with the Q1, Q2, Q3, and Q4 headings).

   - Use a **formula** to calculate the employee costs in **cell B6**. The formula should calculate the revenue in **cell B4** multiplied by the percentage in **cell B15**. Use a **mixed reference** to refer to the revenue in **cell B4** and an **absolute reference** to refer to the cost percentage in **cell B15**. Use **formulas** to calculate the other costs in the **range B7:B9**. Each formula should multiply the revenue in **row 4** by the related cost percentage in **rows 16–18**.

   - Use **AutoSum** to calculate the total cost in **cell B10**.

   - Calculate the **gross profit** in **cell B12** as **Revenue – Total Costs**.

   - Calculate the **net profit** in **cell B13** as **Gross Profit * (1 – Tax Rate)**. Once again, use an **absolute reference** when referring to the tax rate in **cell B19**.

   - Copy the cost and profit formulas from Q1 across the rows to Q2, Q3, and Q4. You must use the correct cell references in formulas to get the correct results for this exercise.

3. Perform a **what-if analysis** on your worksheet by changing the employee costs percentage in **row 15** to **25%**. Make certain that the report recalculates correctly when the value is changed.

4. Display the formulas in **Page Layout** view.

5. Change to **Landscape** orientation; **print** the formulas.
   The formulas will print on one page.

6. **Hide** the formulas and then display **Normal view**.

7. Select the **range A3:E13** and **print** just that area.

8. **Save** 💾 the changes and **close** the workbook.

Use the SUM and AVERAGE Functions

In this exercise, you will create formulas to total the safety incidents in a six-month period and calculate the average number of incidents per month.

1. **Open** the as-Safety Goal workbook from the Lesson 09 folder.

2. Enter **January** in **cell A6**; **AutoFill** down **column A** to display the months January through June.

3. Enter the data in the **range B5:B11** and **cells C5**, **A12**, and **A14**, referring to the illustration at the end of this exercise.

4. **Sum** the total safety incidents for January through June in **cell B12**.

5. Use the **AVERAGE** function to create a formula in **cell B14** that finds the average number of safety incidents per month during January through June.

6. **Display** and **print** the worksheet formulas.

7. **Save** 🖫 the changes and **close** the workbook.

	A	B
1	Green Clean	
2	Safety Scores	
3	Operations Department	
4	January-June	
5		Incidents
6	January	0
7	February	3
8	March	1
9	April	2
10	May	0
11	June	0
12	Total	6
13		
14	Average Incidents	1

Microsoft Excel

Critical Thinking & Work-Readiness Skills

In the course of working through the following Microsoft Office-based Critical Thinking exercises, you will also be utilizing various work-readiness skills, some of which are listed next to each exercise. Go to labyrinthelab.com/ workreadiness to learn more about the work-readiness skills.

9.1 Calculate Totals

WORK-READINESS SKILLS APPLIED

- Reasoning
- Evaluating information
- Using computers to process information

Sales manager Talos Bouras needs to analyze his customer base so he knows where his best chances for new sales contacts will be. Open ct-Customer Base (Lesson 09 folder). Calculate the number of projects and total billings for each company type listed in column A. Save your changes as **ct-Customer Base Totals** in the Lesson 09 folder. Which company type has the largest billings? Which customer type has the largest billing per company? If working in a group, discuss these questions. If working alone, type your answers in a Word document named **ct-Questions** saved to your Lesson 09 folder.

9.2 Create Formulas to Calculate Averages

WORK-READINESS SKILLS APPLIED

- Reasoning
- Using arithmetic/ mathematics
- Thinking creatively

Talos Bouras also wants to know the average number of projects and average billings per company type. He is thinking of adding a new type of customer—health care—to his base, but first he wants to be sure that the new customer type will perform at least as well as his current average customer type. Open ct-Customer Base Totals, if necessary, and calculate these averages. Do not be concerned about formatting the formula results. Save the file in your Lesson 09 folder as **ct-Customer Base Averages**. If Talos wants the average of total billings per customer to rise over time, what categories of customers should he pursue and which should he deemphasize? Why would knowing his average number of projects and billings help him make decisions in the future? If working in a group, discuss these questions. If working alone, type your answers in a Word document named **ct-Questions2** saved to your Lesson 09 folder.

9.3 Use Absolute Cell References

WORK-READINESS SKILLS APPLIED

- Reasoning
- Thinking creatively
- Using arithmetic/ mathematics

Green Clean is raising prices across the board by 4.5 percent in the new year. Open ct-Customer Base Averages, if necessary. Use an absolute reference to calculate the new amount of billings for each company if increased by 4.5 percent. (Hint: Calculate total billings plus 4.5 percent of total billings.) In another column, calculate each company type if the billings are increased to 7.5 percent. Save the file as **ct-Customer Base Projections**. What factors go into deciding to raise prices and commit to a 7.5 percent target increase in billings? If working in a group, discuss this question. If working alone, type your answer in a Word document named **ct-Questions3** saved to your Lesson 09 folder.

U N I T

4

PowerPoint 2010

In this unit, you will be introduced to PowerPoint 2010, a powerful program for creating slide show presentations. You will begin by creating a basic presentation, applying PowerPoint's built-in color schemes and layout templates, and running and printing a presentation. You will then apply advanced text formatting and learn an alternate way to create slide content with the Outline pane.

Creating and Delivering a Presentation

LEARNING OBJECTIVES

After studying this lesson, you will be able to:
- Apply a document theme to a new presentation
- Insert new slides
- Add text to a slide
- Manage bulleted items
- View a slide show

In this lesson, you will create a PowerPoint presentation for the iJams music distribution company. Throughout the lesson, you will be using many PowerPoint features to develop the presentation. You will be working with document themes, text layout styles, and Microsoft Word outlines. By the end of the lesson, your presentation will be ready for delivery. Equipped with the tips and techniques for a successful presentation, you will practice its delivery to the JamWorks trade show.

Creating a Presentation

iJams is an online music distribution company that sells physical CDs in addition to downloadable music. Unsigned musicians send in an existing CD or MP3 files of their original material, and then iJams duplicates the CDs on demand as orders come in and makes the MP3s available for immediate purchase or download. Musicians can also send in digital files of CD artwork, and iJams will print full color CD inserts and other supporting materials. Additionally, iJams sells promotional items branded for artists such as T-shirts, stickers, and mouse pads.

Carthic Maddix, owner of iJams, has been invited to make a presentation representing his firm to the JamWorks trade show. Carthic's goal is to introduce iJams to trade show attendees and entice them with a promotional offer. Carthic decides to use PowerPoint with his new netbook computer and video projection system to develop and deliver his presentation. Carthic chose PowerPoint because it is easy to learn and seamlessly integrates with his other Microsoft Office applications. Carthic's dynamic speaking abilities, coupled with PowerPoint's robust presentation features, are sure to win over the trade show attendees.

Slides from the iJams presentation

10.1 Presenting PowerPoint

Video Lesson   labyrinthelab.com/videos

PowerPoint 2010 is an intuitive, powerful presentation graphics program that enables you to create dynamic, multimedia presentations for a variety of functions. Whether you are developing a one-on-one presentation for your manager or a sophisticated presentation for a large group, PowerPoint provides the tools to make your presentation a success. PowerPoint allows you to project your presentation in a variety of ways. Most presentations are delivered via a computer projection display attached to a notebook computer. There are also other ways to deliver presentations. For example, you can deliver a presentation as an online broadcast over the Internet or save it as a video to be emailed or distributed on CD.

PowerPoint provides easy-to-use tools that let you concentrate on the content of your presentation instead of focusing on the design details. Using PowerPoint's built-in document themes, you can rapidly create highly effective professional presentations.

Starting PowerPoint

The method you use to start PowerPoint depends in large part on whether you intend to create a new presentation or open an existing presentation. To create a new presentation, use one of the following methods. After the PowerPoint program has started, you can begin working in the new presentation that appears.

- Click the ⊞ button, and then choose All Programs→Microsoft Office→Microsoft Office→PowerPoint 2010.
- Navigate to the desired document by using Windows Explorer or Computer and double-click the presentation.

DEVELOP YOUR SKILLS 10.1.1
Start PowerPoint

In this exercise, you will start PowerPoint.

1. **Click** the ⊞ button.

2. Choose **All Programs→Microsoft Office→Microsoft Office PowerPoint 2010**.
   PowerPoint will open, and the PowerPoint program window will appear.

Navigating the PowerPoint Window

Video Lesson   labyrinthelab.com/videos

The PowerPoint 2010 program window, like most other Microsoft Office programs, groups commands on the Ribbon. The following illustration provides an overview of the program window.

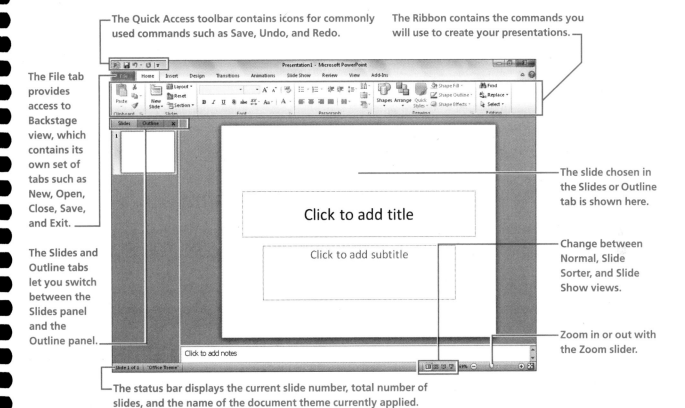

The Quick Access toolbar contains icons for commonly used commands such as Save, Undo, and Redo.

The Ribbon contains the commands you will use to create your presentations.

The File tab provides access to Backstage view, which contains its own set of tabs such as New, Open, Close, Save, and Exit.

The Slides and Outline tabs let you switch between the Slides panel and the Outline panel.

The slide chosen in the Slides or Outline tab is shown here.

Change between Normal, Slide Sorter, and Slide Show views.

Zoom in or out with the Zoom slider.

The status bar displays the current slide number, total number of slides, and the name of the document theme currently applied.

Inserting Text

PowerPoint slides have placeholders set up for you to type in. For example, the title slide currently visible on the screen has placeholders for a title and subtitle. You click in the desired placeholder to enter text on a slide. For example, to enter the title on a slide, you click in the title placeholder and then type the text. Do not press the Enter key; the placeholders are already formatted with word wrap. The placeholders also are already formatted with font and paragraph settings to make a cohesive presentation. As you will see shortly, it's easy to make changes to the formatting of slides by applying a theme.

Home → layout to make new template

3-7 slides

trip to Hawaii?

Type a Title Slide

In this exercise, you will enter a title and subtitle for the presentation.

1. Follow these steps to add a title and subtitle:

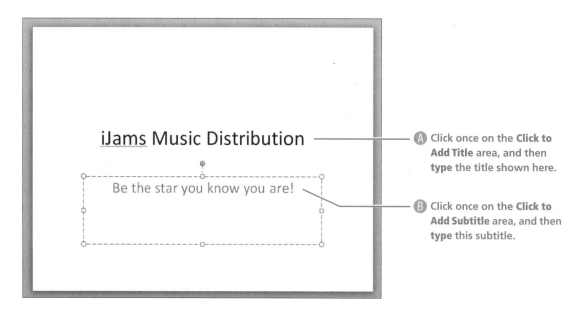

iJams Music Distribution — Ⓐ Click once on the **Click to Add Title** area, and then **type** the title shown here.

Be the star you know you are! — Ⓑ Click once on the **Click to Add Subtitle** area, and then **type** this subtitle.

PowerPoint enters the titles. At this point you have a title slide, but it looks rather plain. This is about to change.

10.2 Using Document Themes

Video Lesson   labyrinthelab.com/videos

You can use PowerPoint's built-in document themes, which provide a ready-made backdrop for your presentations, to easily format all slides in a presentation. When you use a document theme, your presentation automatically includes an attractive color scheme, consistent font style and size, and bulleted lists to synchronize with the design and style of the presentation. Document themes also position placeholders on slides for titles, text, bulleted lists, graphics, and other objects. By using document themes, you can focus on content by simply filling in the blanks as you create the presentation. You access document themes from the Themes group on the Design tab.

Choosing a Theme

There are many document themes included with PowerPoint 2010. Match the theme to the type of presentation you are giving. Keep the design appropriate to the function and the audience.

Finding Additional Themes

New themes are sent to Microsoft daily, so if you just can't find the right one, browse the Microsoft Office Online website for new themes. You can easily browse the site by selecting Design→Themes→More→Search Office Online.

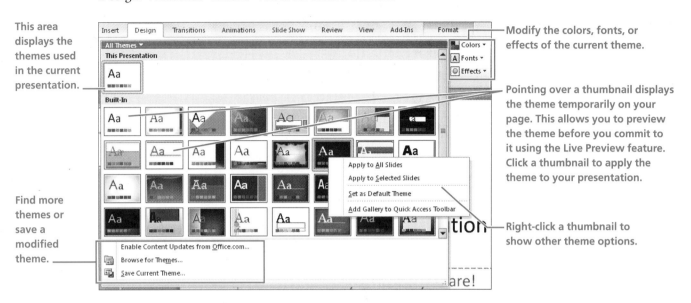

This area displays the themes used in the current presentation.

Find more themes or save a modified theme.

Modify the colors, fonts, or effects of the current theme.

Pointing over a thumbnail displays the theme temporarily on your page. This allows you to preview the theme before you commit to it using the Live Preview feature. Click a thumbnail to apply the theme to your presentation.

Right-click a thumbnail to show other theme options.

Using the PowerPoint Ribbon

The PowerPoint Ribbon is organized into nine default tabs: File, Home, Insert, Design, Transitions, Animations, Slide Show, Review, and View. Like other Office 2010 applications, additional tabs appear when certain elements on a slide are selected. These additional tabs, called contextual tabs, offer commands specific to the selected element; for example, selecting a picture on a slide results in the Picture Tools Format tab being shown. Deselecting the picture returns the Ribbon to its original state with the nine default tabs.

Each tab contains many commands, which are organized in groups. Each group is labeled across the bottom and contains a variety of buttons or button menus.

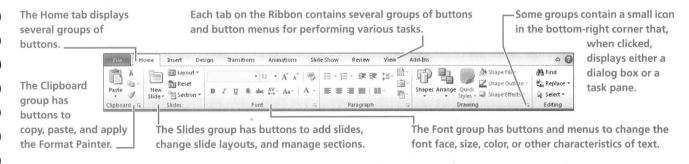

The Home tab displays several groups of buttons.

The Clipboard group has buttons to copy, paste, and apply the Format Painter.

Each tab on the Ribbon contains several groups of buttons and button menus for performing various tasks.

The Slides group has buttons to add slides, change slide layouts, and manage sections.

Some groups contain a small icon in the bottom-right corner that, when clicked, displays either a dialog box or a task pane.

The Font group has buttons and menus to change the font face, size, color, or other characteristics of text.

DEFAULT TABS IN THE POWERPOINT RIBBON

Tab Name	General Tasks
File	Provides access to Backstage view for common tasks such as Save, Open, Close, Print, Options, and Exit.
Home	Perform standard tasks, such as copy/paste, add slides, format text, and find/search/replace.
Insert	Insert graphical elements such as shapes, pictures, clip art, charts, tables, WordArt, and media clips.
Design	Format slides with themes, colors, and backgrounds.
Transitions	Manage slide transitions.
Animations	Animate elements on a slide.
Slide Show	Create and view slide show presentations of all slides or selected slides.
Review	Proof your text with the Spelling and Thesaurus features, translate text to another language, and create comments for reviewers.
View	Change presentation views, show/hide rulers and gridlines, adjust the zoom, change the color mode, or organize multiple document windows.

QUICK REFERENCE   APPLYING A THEME

Task	Procedure
Apply a theme to a presentation	■ Choose Design→Themes from the Ribbon. ■ Choose a theme from the display, or click the More ⬇ button to view additional themes.

DEVELOP YOUR SKILLS 10.2.1
Apply a Document Theme

In this exercise, you will choose a document theme and apply it to the presentation.

1. Follow these steps to choose a theme for the presentation:
   Depending on your monitor resolution, you may see a different number of thumbnails in the Themes group.

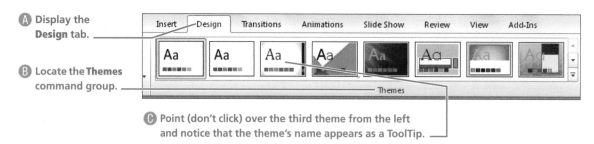

Ⓐ Display the **Design** tab.

Ⓑ Locate the **Themes** command group.

Ⓒ Point (don't click) over the third theme from the left and notice that the theme's name appears as a ToolTip.

PowerPoint displays a Live Preview of the theme on your title slide. This gives you a good idea of the overall design of the theme. Notice that the fonts and locations have changed for the title and subtitle. A different theme can radically redesign your presentation.

2. **Point (don't click)** over several more theme thumbnails.
   You see a Live Preview of each theme on the actual slide. The themes visible on the Ribbon are just a small portion of those available, however.

3. Choose **Design→Themes→More** ⏷ as shown at right.
   PowerPoint displays all of the currently available themes. It also gives options to look for additional themes online or elsewhere on your computer.

4. Follow these steps to choose a theme:

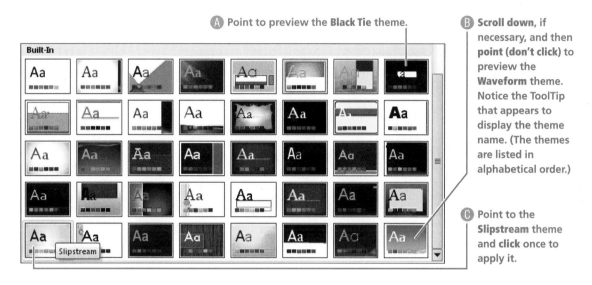

Ⓐ Point to preview the **Black Tie** theme.

Ⓑ **Scroll down**, if necessary, and then **point (don't click)** to preview the **Waveform** theme. Notice the ToolTip that appears to display the theme name. (The themes are listed in alphabetical order.)

Ⓒ Point to the **Slipstream** theme and **click** once to apply it.

PowerPoint applies the theme to your presentation.

10.3 Creating a Basic Presentation

Video Lesson labyrinthelab.com/videos

There is more to creating a presentation than placing one slide after another. Like Carthic Maddix of iJams, you are in the process of creating an image. Choosing the appropriate slide layout, just like choosing the appropriate design, will influence how well your audience understands your message. Use the following guidelines when choosing your slide design and layout:

- **Know your audience:** Will you be speaking to accountants or artists?
- **Know your purpose:** Are you introducing a product or giving a report?
- **Know your expectations:** When the last word of this presentation has been given, how do you want your audience to respond to your facts? Are you looking for approval for a project or customers for a product?

Adding Slides

You can use two methods to add slides to a presentation:

- Choose Home→Slides→New Slide from the Ribbon.
- Right-click a slide on the Slides panel, and then choose New Slide from the pop-up, or context, menu.

PowerPoint always places the new slide after the currently selected slide.

The Slides panel displays thumbnails of your presentation while you work in the Normal view. The Slide Sorter view, like the Slides panel, also displays thumbnails of your slides. This view can be useful when there are more slides than can fit in the Slides panel display.

DEVELOP YOUR SKILLS 10.3.1
Add a New Slide

In this exercise, you will add a new slide to the presentation and then enter content.

1. Follow these steps to add a new slide:

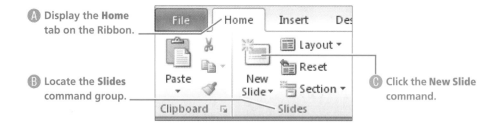

Ⓐ Display the **Home** tab on the Ribbon.

Ⓑ Locate the **Slides** command group.

Ⓒ Click the **New Slide** command.

PowerPoint adds a new slide to the presentation immediately after the title slide.

2. **Click** once in the title placeholder and then type **Our Services** as the title.

3. Click once on the **Click to Add Text** placeholder and then **type** the following list. **Tap** the ⎡Enter⎤ key after each list item except the last one.

- **CD duplication on demand** ⎡Enter⎤
- **Jewel case insert printing** ⎡Enter⎤
- **Full service online sales** ⎡Enter⎤
- **Downloadable MP3 distribution**

PowerPoint adds a bullet in front of each line.

Duplicate a Slide

Sometimes it is more efficient to duplicate a slide and then edit it rather than beginning a new slide from scratch. Slides can be duplicated via the Slides panel.

QUICK REFERENCE	DUPLICATING A SLIDE
Task	**Procedure**
Duplicate a single slide	■ Right-click the slide you wish to duplicate in the Slides panel. ■ Choose Duplicate Slide from the pop-up menu. The new slide is inserted below the original.
Duplicate multiple slides	■ ⎡Ctrl⎤+click or ⎡Shift⎤+click to select the slides you wish to duplicate in the Slides panel. ■ Right-click any of the selected slides and choose Duplicate Slide from the pop-up menu. The new slides are inserted below the selected slides.

Indenting Bulleted Lists

Video Lesson   labyrinthelab.com/videos

When using PowerPoint, you can effortlessly create bulleted lists to outline the thrust of your presentation. The bulleted list layout is an outline of nine levels. A different indentation, and usually a different bullet character, is used for each level. The following illustration shows the Packaging Options slide you will create in the next exercise.

This bulleted list has three levels. Each level uses the same shaped character, but the text and bullet get smaller with each indentation.

Working with Bulleted Lists

When you use a document theme, each paragraph is automatically formatted as a bulleted list. The format includes a bullet style, indentation level, font type, and font size for each bulleted paragraph. This outline for the bulleted list is held within a placeholder or text box. The following Quick Reference table describes the various techniques that can be used with bulleted lists.

Working with List Levels

Indenting a bullet is referred to as *demoting a bullet,* or *increasing the list level.* Typically, a main bullet point has one or more sub-bullets. These sub-bullets, which are smaller than the main bullet, are created by increasing the list level. When a list level is increased, the bullets are indented toward the right. You demote a bullet by choosing the Home→Paragraph→Increase List Level button on the Ribbon. Conversely, decreasing a bullet's indent by moving it more toward the left and increasing the bullet size is referred to as *promoting a bullet*, or *decreasing the list level.* You promote a bullet by choosing the Home→Paragraph→Decrease List Level button on the Ribbon. PowerPoint supports a main bullet and up to eight sub-bullets.

QUICK REFERENCE	WORKING WITH BULLETED LISTS
Task	**Procedure**
Turn bullets on and off	■ Select the desired paragraph(s). ■ Choose Home→Paragraph→Bullets ⬚ from the Ribbon.
Promote bullets by using the Ribbon	■ Select the desired paragraph(s). ■ Choose Home→Paragraph→Decrease List Leve ⬚ from the Ribbon, or use ⌈Shift⌉+⌈Tab⌉.
Demote bullets by using the Ribbon	■ Select the desired paragraph(s). ■ Choose Home→Paragraph→Increase List Level ⬚ from the Ribbon, or tap the ⌈Tab⌉ key.

Create a Bulleted List

In this exercise, you will create a new slide, and then you will enter information into a multilevel bulleted list. The most efficient way to create multilevel bulleted lists is to first type the entire list.

Create the List

1. Choose **Home→Slides→New Slide** ⬚ from the Ribbon.
   PowerPoint creates a new slide after the current slide.

2. **Click** in the title placeholder and type **Packaging Options**.

3. **Click** once in the text placeholder.

4. Type **CD labeling** and tap ⌈Enter⌉.
   PowerPoint formats the new paragraph with the same large bullet. Paragraph formats are carried to new paragraphs when you tap the ⌈Enter⌉ key.

5. **Tap** the ⌈Tab⌉ key.
   PowerPoint indents the line. It also introduces a new, slightly smaller style for the level-2 heading.

6. Type **Full color**.
   PowerPoint formats the line in a smaller font too.

7. **Tap** the [Enter] key.
   PowerPoint maintains the same level-2 heading level for the next line.

8. Type **Laser etching** and **tap** [Enter].

9. While holding down the [Shift] key, **tap** the [Tab] key once.
   PowerPoint promotes the new line back to level 1, which is the level of the first text line on the slide.

Manipulate Heading Levels

You can also adjust the heading level after you have typed a line.

10. **Type** the following lines:
    - **Jewel case**
    - **Back and spine of case**

11. Follow these steps to indent the last bullet:

Ⓐ **Click once** anywhere within the text line to be indented.

Ⓑ Choose **Home→Paragraph→Increase List Level** from the Ribbon.

PowerPoint indents the paragraph and changes the bullet style. Demoting a paragraph makes it subordinate to the preceding paragraph.

12. Click the **Increase List Level** ⊞ button three more times.
    The bullet style changes and the indent increases each time you choose the command. Also, the font size and font style change with each bullet increase. These formats are determined by the Slipstream theme, on which the presentation is based.

13. Click **Home→Paragraph→Decrease List Level** ⊞ from the Ribbon three times until the bullet reaches the second indentation.
    With each promotion, the bullet style changes.

Indent Multiple Bullets

14. **Click** once at the end of the last line and then **tap** [Enter].

15. **Type** the following new lines:
    - **Insert**
    - **Single sheet**
    - **Up to 10 page booklet**

hyphen if adjective before noun

16. Follow these steps to select the last two lines for your next command:

Ⓐ **Point** at the beginning of the text *Single sheet*, taking care that a four-pointed arrow is not visible.

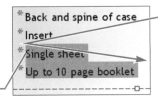

Ⓑ **Drag down** and to the right to select (highlight) the end of the last line, and then release the mouse button.

Ⓒ Ignore a context menu that may be visible for a moment. Take care not to click anywhere else on the slide before you perform the next step.

17. Choose **Home→Paragraph→Increase List Level** from the Ribbon.
PowerPoint indents the two selected lines.

18. **Click** any where outside the border to deselect the text. Your slide should match the following illustration.

Choosing the Slide Layout

Video Lesson   labyrinthelab.com/videos

There are nine slide layouts in PowerPoint 2010, one for any given situation. Slide layouts are named for the type of data they will contain. For example, the Title layout needs only a title and subtitle. The Content layout will hold other information on the slide, so it has a title and a bulleted list for points. Likewise, the Content with Caption layout is divided into three sections: title, text to one side, and an area for clip art or additional text. The slide layout organizes the information you put into the presentation by giving it a place on the slide. Use the command Home→Slides→Layout ▾ to change the layout of your slides. The new layout is applied to all selected slides. Changing layouts is easy. When you click on the new style, the layout is transferred to the selected slide.

Clicking the Layout button from the Slides group on the Home tab allows you to apply a new layout to the selected slide(s).

Change the Slide Layout

In this exercise, you will add a new slide and then change its layout.

1. If necessary, select the **Packaging Options** slide from the Slides panel on the left side of your screen.

2. Choose **Home→Slides→New Slide** from the Ribbon.
   PowerPoint adds another slide to the end of the presentation. Like the previous two slides, this one is set up to display a bulleted list.

3. Follow these steps to choose a new layout for the slide:

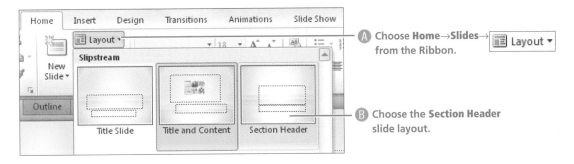

Ⓐ Choose **Home→Slides→** from the Ribbon.

Ⓑ Choose the **Section Header** slide layout.

PowerPoint applies the new layout. Now there are two placeholders for a title and subtext.

4. Enter the following text:
   - **Title:** `Questions?`
   - **Text:** `End of our brief presentation`

Your slide should resemble the following illustration.

Microsoft PowerPoint

Saving the Presentation

Video Lesson   labyrinthelab.com/videos

FROM THE KEYBOARD
Ctrl+S to save

The byword in PowerPoint is to save early and save often. You can use the Save button on the Quick Access toolbar or use the File→Save command. If it's the first time a presentation has been saved, the Save As dialog box will appear because the file will need a name and location on your computer. You can also use the Save As dialog box to make a copy of a presentation by saving it under a new name or to a different location. If the file has already been saved, Power-Point replaces the previous version with the new edited version.

DEVELOP YOUR SKILLS 10.3.4
Save the Presentation

In this exercise, you will save the presentation by giving it a name and a location on your computer.

1. Click the **Save** 💾 button on the Quick Access toolbar, as shown at right.
   PowerPoint displays the Save As dialog box because this presentation has not yet been given a filename.

2. Follow these steps to save the presentation to your file storage location:

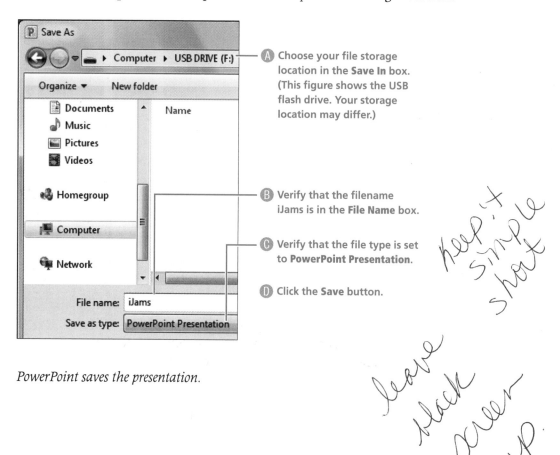

PowerPoint saves the presentation.

Save as Video

PowerPoint 2010 has a new feature that allows you to save your presentation as a video. This is helpful if you want to distribute your presentation to others without requiring them to have PowerPoint or other special software. The video files are saved in the Windows Media Video (.wmv) format and are playable on any Windows computer. When saving as a video, be patient as it takes some time to convert your presentation to the video format.

The status bar at the bottom of the PowerPoint window shows the video conversion progress.

You can cancel the conversion at any time.

 The video version of a presentation can be 15 times larger than the original PowerPoint file. Be aware of the file size before you try to email a video to someone.

QUICK REFERENCE	SAVING A PRESENTATION AS A VIDEO
Task	**Procedure**
Save a presentation as a video	■ Choose File→Save & Send→Create a Video.
	■ Choose the quality setting and whether or not to use slide timings.
	■ Set the number of seconds to display each slide.
	■ Click Create Video, choose a save location, and click Save.
	■ Wait as the video is converted.

10.4 Delivering the Slide Show

Video Lesson   labyrinthelab.com/videos

The slides are created, and the presentation is complete. The first phase of the presentation development is over. The next phase, delivering the presentation, is just beginning. Before you stand before an audience, familiarize yourself with the following tips.

Delivery Tips

It is not only what you say, it is how you say it that makes the difference between an engaging and an unsuccessful presentation. Lead your audience. Help them to focus on the message of your presentation, not on you as the presenter. Use the following *PEER* guidelines to deliver an effective presentation:

■ *Pace:* Maintain a moderate pace. Speaking too fast will exhaust your audience, and speaking too slowly may put them to sleep. Carry your audience with you as you talk.

■ *Emphasis:* Pause for emphasis. As you present, use a brief pause to emphasize your point. The pause you take will give your audience time to absorb the message.

- *Eye contact:* Address your audience. Always face your audience while speaking. A common mistake is to speak while walking or facing the projection screen. Don't waste all of the work you have done in the presentation by losing the interest of your audience now. If you are speaking from a lectern or desk, resist the temptation to lean on it. Stand tall, make eye contact, and look directly at your audience.

- *Relax:* You are enthusiastic and want to convey that tone to the audience. However, when you speak, avoid fast movement, pacing, and rushed talking. Your audience will be drawn to your movements and miss the point. Remember that the audience is listening to you to learn; this material may be old hat to you, but it's new to them. So speak clearly, maintain a steady pace, and stay calm.

Navigating Through a Slide Show

FROM THE KEYBOARD

Spacebar or → to advance a slide

Backspace or ← to back up a slide

You can use the mouse and/or simple keyboard commands to move through a slide show. This is often the easiest way to navigate from one slide to the next.

The Slide Show Toolbar

The Slide Show toolbar is your navigator during the slide show. Notice that the Slide Show toolbar has options to go to the next and previous slides and to end the slide show. The Slide Show toolbar also lets you use a pen tool to draw on the slide and make other enhancements. However, use of this toolbar is unnecessary when you present a simple slide show like this one.

QUICK REFERENCE	USING BASIC SLIDE SHOW NAVIGATION
Task	**Procedure**
Advance a slide	▪ Click once with the mouse, or
	▪ Tap the Spacebar, →, Page Down, or Enter key.
Back up a slide	▪ Tap the Backspace, Page Up, or ← key.
Display the Slide Show toolbar	▪ Move the mouse around on the screen for a moment.

Run the Slide Show

In this exercise, you will navigate through your slide show.

Before You Begin: The iJams presentation should be open in PowerPoint.

1. **Click** once on the first slide in the **Slides** panel as shown at right.
   The Slides panel along the left side of the PowerPoint window is a handy way to navigate to various slides. You will start your presentation by displaying the Title slide.

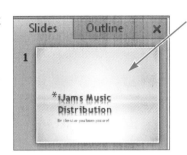

2. Choose **Slide Show→Start Slide Show→ From Beginning** from the Ribbon.
   PowerPoint displays your title slide in full-screen view. All toolbars and other screen objects are hidden from view.

3. Move the **mouse pointer** around the screen for a moment.
   Notice the Slide Show 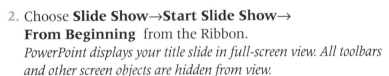 toolbar that appears near the bottom-left corner of the screen when the slides are in full-screen view.

4. Click the **mouse pointer** anywhere on the screen to move to the next slide.

5. **Tap** the [Page Down] key twice and then **tap** [Page Up] twice by using the keys near the main keyboard (not the keys on the numeric keypad).
   PowerPoint displays the next or previous slide each time you tap these keys.

Manipulate the Slide Show Toolbar

6. Click the **Slide Options** button on the Slide Show toolbar.
   Choose **Go to Slide→Packaging Options**.
   In the Go to Slide menu, your entire presentation is outlined by title. Simply choose the slide you want to see.

7. Choose **Go to Slide→iJams Music Distribution**.
   As you can see, there are many ways to navigate slides in an electronic slide show.

End the Slide Show

8. Continue to click anywhere on the screen until the last slide appears (the Questions slide).

9. **Click** once on the last slide.
   The screen turns to a black background, with a small note at the top.

10. **Click** anywhere on the black screen to exit the slide show and return to the main PowerPoint window.

11. Feel free to practice running your slide show again.

12. When you have finished, click the **Save** 🖫 button to save any changes to your presentation.

13. Choose **File→Close** to close the presentation.

10.5 Getting Help

Video Lesson labyrinthelab.com/videos

PowerPoint, like many other software programs, has so many features it is unlikely you will learn and remember everything about it at once. That is where PowerPoint Help comes in. You can use the help system to learn to perform specific tasks or browse general information about a variety of categories.

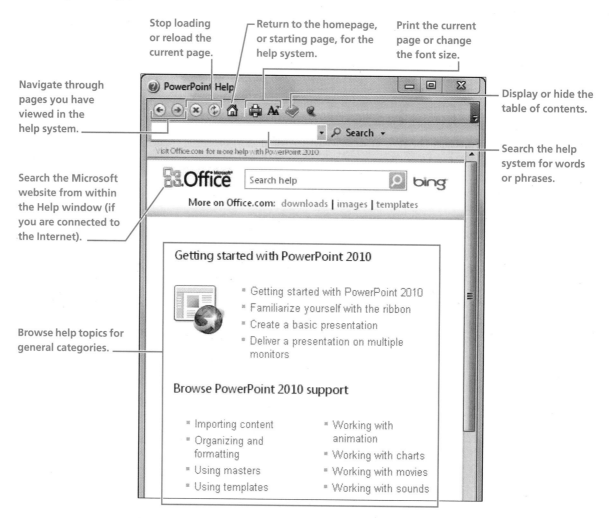

Online and Offline Help

If you are connected to the Internet when you open the PowerPoint Help window, PowerPoint connects to the Microsoft website and displays the most up-to-date help content. If you are not connected to the Internet, offline help topics that were installed when PowerPoint was installed are displayed.

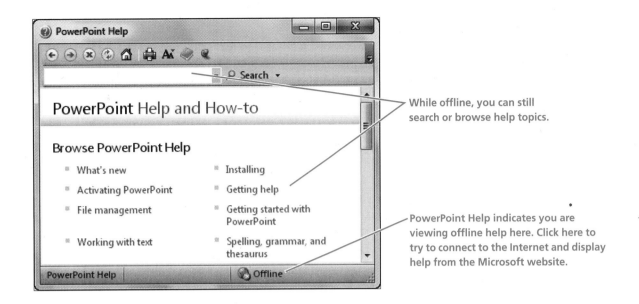

While offline, you can still search or browse help topics.

PowerPoint Help indicates you are viewing offline help here. Click here to try to connect to the Internet and display help from the Microsoft website.

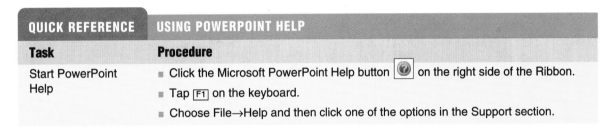

QUICK REFERENCE | **USING POWERPOINT HELP**

Task	Procedure
Start PowerPoint Help	■ Click the Microsoft PowerPoint Help button ⊙ on the right side of the Ribbon.
	■ Tap F1 on the keyboard.
	■ Choose File→Help and then click one of the options in the Support section.

DEVELOP YOUR SKILLS 10.5.1
Use PowerPoint Help

In this exercise, you will use the PowerPoint Help system.

Search for Help

1. Click the **Microsoft PowerPoint Help** ⊙ button on the right side of the Ribbon to display the Help window.

2. Follow these steps to search for help:

Ⓐ Click in the **Search** box and type **font color**.

Ⓑ Tap Enter.

Ⓒ **Click** any of the results to view help about the search topic. Note that your results may differ and your computer may not match the figure.

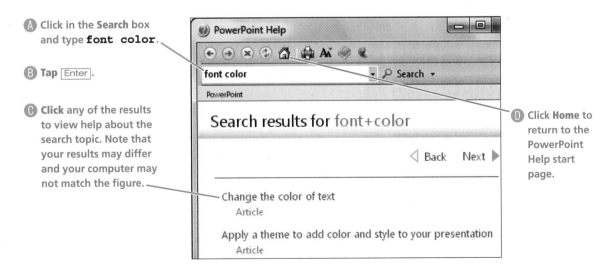

Ⓓ Click **Home** to return to the PowerPoint Help start page.

Use the Table of Contents

3. Follow these steps to browse for help using the table of contents:

Ⓐ Click **Show Table of Contents** to display the Table of Contents pane.

Ⓑ If necessary, scroll down until you see the **Working with Text** topic.

Ⓒ Click **Working with Text** to display the help topics for that category. Your screen may differ from the figure.

Ⓓ Click any of the topics to read them.

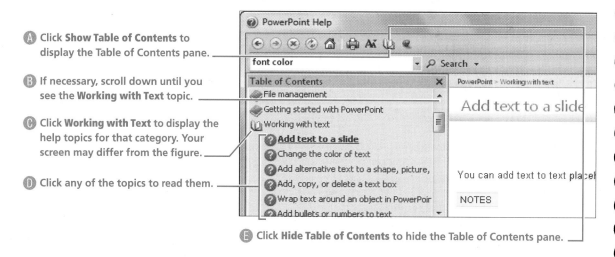

Ⓔ Click **Hide Table of Contents** to hide the Table of Contents pane.

4. **Close** ⬛ the PowerPoint Help window.

5. Choose **File→Exit** to close PowerPoint.

10.6 Concepts Review

Concepts Review   labyrinthelab.com/ob10

To check your knowledge of the key concepts introduced in this lesson, complete the Concepts Review quiz by going to the URL listed above. If your classroom is using Labyrinth eLab, you may complete the Concepts Review quiz from within your eLab course.

Reinforce Your Skills

Create a Presentation

In this exercise, you will create a presentation for the Tropical Getaways travel service. The presentation will be used to sell potential customers a tropical getaway to paradise. The managers of Tropical Getaways will be delivering the presentation to an audience of more than 40 people.

1. **Start** the PowerPoint program.
   A new presentation appears when PowerPoint starts. To gain practice creating a new presentation, you will close that and create a new one.

2. Follow these steps to close the existing presentation:

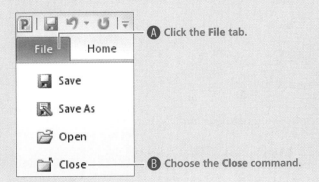

The presentation closes.

3. Choose **File** →**New**.
   The New Presentation window appears.

4. Double-click the **Blank Presentation** choice.
   A new presentation with a single slide is created.

Apply a Document Theme

5. Choose **Design**→**Themes**, and choose the **Civic** theme.
   PowerPoint applies the theme to your presentation.

6. Click in the **Title** placeholder and **type** the title **Tropical Getaways**.

7. Click in the **Subtitle** placeholder and **type** the subtitle **Adventures in Paradise**.
   As you type, the text is converted to uppercase because that is a design element of this particular document theme.

8. **Save** your presentation as **rs-Tropical Getaways** on your file storage location.

Set Up Another Slide

9. Choose **Home→Slides→New Slide**  from the Ribbon.
   A single-column, bulleted list slide is added to the presentation. Notice that the Civic document theme is applied to the new slide.

10. Choose **Home→Slides→** Layout ▾ **→Two Content** from the Ribbon.
    A new two-column layout is applied to the slide.

11. Click in the **Title** placeholder and **type** the title **Most Popular Destinations**.

12. Add the following text to the bulleted list on the left:
    - **Tahiti**
    - **Maui**
    - **Oahu**
    - **Cancun**

13. Add the following text to the bulleted list on the right:
    - **Caribbean**
    - **Fiji**
    - **Singapore**
    - **Australia**

    After you finish typing, your slide should look similar to the following illustration.

14. **Save** your presentation.

Set Up the Remaining Slides

15. Choose **Home→Slides→New Slide** from the Ribbon.
    A third slide is added to the presentation. The new slide has the same Two Content layout as the previous slide.

16. In the **Title** placeholder, enter the phrase **Complete Packages**.

17. In the first bullet of the left bulleted list, enter the phrase **Packages Include** and tap ⎡Enter⎤.

18. Choose **Home→Paragraph→Increase List Level** from the Ribbon.
    The bullet is indented and a new bullet character is applied by the design template.

19. Add the following text to the bulleted list on the left:
    - **Airfare**
    - **Lodging**
    - **Rental car**
    - **Activities**

20. In the first bullet of the bulleted list on the right, enter the phrase **Low Prices** and **tap** Enter.

21. Choose **Home→Paragraph→Increase List Level** from the Ribbon.
    The bullet is indented, and a new bullet character is applied by the design template.

22. Add the following text to the bulleted list on the right:
    - **3 days from $599**
    - **5 days from $799**
    - **7 days from $999**

    After you finish typing, your slide should look similar to the following illustration.

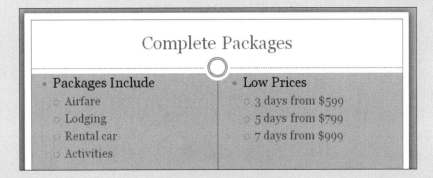

23. Choose **Home→Slides→New Slide** to add a fourth slide to your presentation.

24. Choose **Home→Slides→** Layout ▾ **→Title and Content** to change the slide layout to the Title and Content layout.

25. Enter the title **Travel Now and Save!**

26. **Type** the following bullet points in the text box:
    - **Package 1**
    - **5 days in Oahu**
    - **$429 per person**
    - **Package 2**
    - **7 days in Tahiti**
    - **$1,299 per person**

27. Select the *5 days in Oahu* and *$429 per person* paragraphs and **increase** their list level.

28. Select the *7 days in Tahiti* and *$1,299 per person* paragraphs and **increase** their list level.
After you finish typing, your slide should look similar to the following illustration.

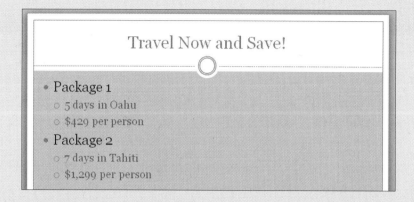

29. Choose **Home→Slides→New Slide** to add the final slide to the presentation.

30. Type **Tropical Getaways** for the title.

31. Type the following in the text box:

- **Angelica Escobedo**
- **(310) 544-8870**

32. Click the **dashed border** around the text box so it turns solid, and choose **Home→Paragraph→Bullets** to remove the bullets.
The bullets are removed from all paragraphs in the text box.

33. Select **Home→Paragraph→Center** ☰ from the Ribbon to center the text on the slide.
After you finish typing, your slide should look similar to the following illustration.

34. Save 🖫 the presentation.
Leave the presentation open if you will continue to the next exercise.

Deliver a Slide Show

In this exercise, you will practice delivering the Tropical Getaways presentation.

Before You Begin: The rs-Tropical Getaways presentation created in Reinforce Your Skills 10.1 should be open in PowerPoint.

1. Select the first slide from the **Slides** panel on the left side of your screen.

2. Choose **Slide Show→Start Slide Show→From Beginning** 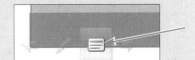 from the Ribbon.
   The Title slide will occupy your whole screen as the slide show starts.

3. Walk through the presentation by **clicking** each slide until the presentation is ended.

4. **Click** once more to return to the PowerPoint program window.

5. Choose **Slide Show→Start Slide Show→From Beginning** from the Ribbon to start the slide show again.

6. After the slide show begins, **position** the mouse pointer at the bottom-left corner of the screen to display the **Slide Show** toolbar.

7. Click the **Slide Options** button as shown at right on the Slide Show toolbar.

8. Choose **Go to Slide→Travel Now and Save!**
   Notice that the Go to Slide drop-down menu displays the title of each slide in your presentation.

9. Use the **Slide Options** button on the Slide Show toolbar to end the slide show by choosing **End Show**.

10. **Save** and **close** the presentation, and then **close** the PowerPoint program window.

Apply Your Skills

Create a Presentation

In this exercise, you will create a presentation for Classic Cars. Classic Cars is an organization devoted to tracking, categorizing, and preserving classic automobiles. The presentation will be given to members of the Classic Cars organization at the annual Classic Cars convention.

1. **Start** PowerPoint.
   A new presentation is started for you automatically.

2. Apply the **Horizon** design document theme, as shown in the following illustration.

3. Add the following text to the **Title** slide:
   - **Title:** Classic Cars
   - **Subtitle:** 2010 Convention Highlights

4. Add a second slide with the following text:

Title	Seminar Topics
Bulleted paragraphs	■ Restoration Techniques
	■ Preservation Techniques
	■ Locating Vehicles
	■ Success Stories
	■ Winning Competitions

5. Add a third slide with the following text:

Title	Collections on Display
Bulleted paragraphs	■ **James McGee – 1950s Corvettes**
	■ **Beth Zelinko – Classic Fords**
	■ **Ricardo Campos – Thunderbirds**
	■ **Ava Peters – Corvairs**

6. Add a fourth slide and change its layout to a **Two Content** layout. Add the following text:

Title	Door Prizes
Left bulleted paragraphs	■ **Car care items**
	■ **Gift certificates**
	■ **Floor mats**
	■ **Waxes and polishes**
	■ **Magazines**
Right bulleted paragraphs	■ **Entertainment**
	■ **Las Vegas vacation**
	■ **Sporting events**
	■ **Movie tickets**
	■ **Dinners**

7. Select all but the first bullet in the **left** text box and increase the list level.

8. Select all but the first bullet in the **right** text box and increase the list level.
   After you finish, the slide should appear similar to the following illustration.

9. Add a final slide to the presentation and apply the **Title and Content** layout.
   - ■ **Title: The 2010 Convention**
   - ■ **Text: Enjoy the Ride…**

10. **Save** the presentation as **as-Classic Cars** to your file storage location.

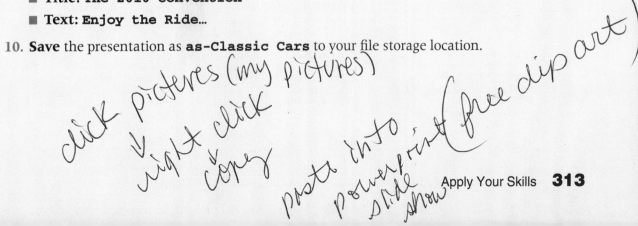

Critical Thinking & Work-Readiness Skills

In the course of working through the following Microsoft Office-based Critical Thinking exercises, you will also be utilizing various work-readiness skills, some of which are listed next to each exercise. Go to labyrinthelab.com/workreadiness *to learn more about the work-readiness skills.*

10.1 Create a Basic Presentation

WORK-READINESS SKILLS APPLIED

- Thinking creatively
- Making decisions
- Reasoning

Carthic decides on three points to make in his iJams conference presentation: 1) Why he founded iJams (a need for a focused website, his industry experience, encouragement from well known musicians); 2) How iJams is different (only covers independent bands, has expert editors, features exclusive downloads); and 3) The special trade show offer (download five songs free by using the code). Open PowerPoint and create a new blank presentation. Use the New Slide command to create one slide for each of the three main points, condensing supporting points to short phrases or single words in a bulleted list. Insert a title slide. Save your presentation as **ct-iJams Points** to your Lesson 10 folder.

10.2 Format a Presentation

WORK-READINESS SKILLS APPLIED

- Thinking creatively
- Interpreting and communicating information
- Speaking

Open ct-iJams Points, if necessary, and use the Save As command to save it with the new name **ct-Formatted**. Experiment with slide layouts, document themes, and indenting bulleted lists. Save the three "best" (in your opinion) solutions as separate files: **ct-Formatted1**, **ct-Formatted2**, and **ct-Formatted3**. View them as slide shows with a group. Discuss which solution is most effective and why. If working alone, type your responses in a Word document named **ct-Questions** saved to your Lesson 10 folder.

10.3 Change and Practice a Presentation

WORK-READINESS SKILLS APPLIED

- Reasoning
- Thinking creatively
- Participating as a member of a team

Open ct-Formatted from the previous exercise. Add a slide with an endorsement that's just come in from a famous musician. Mike Smith of the Rolling Beetles says, "iJams is awesome! I use it almost every day. Congratulations, Carthic!" Place the new slide in what you consider an appropriate place. Be prepared to explain why you put the slide where you did. Now view the presentation as a slide show. Practice the presentation with a group in class, and get feedback, especially on how the slide-to-slide transitions are affected by the addition of a slide. Save the file and close PowerPoint.

Designing the Presentation

LEARNING OBJECTIVES

After studying this lesson, you will be able to:

- Copy and move text
- Use Outline view to create, move, and delete slides and edit text
- Create a presentation from a Microsoft Word outline
- Format and align text and adjust character spacing and line spacing
- Use the Slide Sorter view to rearrange the order of slides
- Use the new Sections feature to manage multiple slides
- Print a presentation

In this lesson, you will build on the fundamental design of the iJams presentation. You will establish a consistent style throughout the presentation and format and organize the text. You will add slides to your presentation from the Outline panel and manipulate your completed presentation by using the Slide Sorter view and Sections. You will also create a presentation from a Microsoft Word outline. Lastly, working with the printing function of PowerPoint 2010, you will examine page setup, print preview, print setup, and the output formats options.

Student Resources   labyrinthelab.com/ob10

Designing a Presentation

Now that the initial slides of the iJams presentation are complete, Carthic Maddix is wondering how he can polish the presentation for the JamWorks trade show. Carthic confers with his administrative assistant, Aurelia, who will be formatting the presentation for him. In turning over the presentation to Aurelia, Carthic asks her to make sure that the style is consistent throughout the presentation. He also wants her to check that the slides are in a logical sequence so the presentation is clear. Carthic knows that Aurelia is an expert in PowerPoint. He is confident in her ability to make the presentation shine.

* Audio CDs
* Downloadable MP3s
* T-shirts
* Baseball caps
* Stickers

* Pencils
* Key chains
* Posters
* Mugs
* Mouse pads

*Products and Promotional Items

Sample of slide formatted with a layout Microsoft calls the Two Content layout

11.1 Working with Slides

Video Lesson labyrinthelab.com/videos

As your presentation progresses and you insert additional slides, you may want to change the layout or the order of your slides. For example, some slides may require two columns of bulleted text while others require only one. PowerPoint makes it easy to change the order of slides using the Slide Sorter view.

Copying Text and Objects

FROM THE KEYBOARD

Ctrl+X to cut
Ctrl+C to copy
Ctrl+V to paste

You can move and copy text and objects by using drag and drop or the Cut, Copy, and Paste commands. It is usually most efficient to use drag and drop if you are moving or copying text or objects within a slide or to another slide that is visible on the screen. Drag and drop is also effective for rearranging slides. Cut, Copy, and Paste are most efficient when moving or copying to a location not visible on the current screen.

QUICK REFERENCE	MOVING AND COPYING TEXT AND OBJECTS
Task	**Procedure**
Drag and drop	■ Select the desired text or click an object, such as a placeholder box.
	■ Drag to move the text or object to the desired location. Press the Ctrl key while dragging if you wish to copy.
Right-drag and drop	■ Select the desired text or click an object, such as a placeholder box.
	■ Use the right mouse button to drag the text or object to the desired location.
	■ Release the mouse button at the desired location and choose Move, Copy, or Cancel from the context menu.
Cut, copy, and paste	■ Select the desired text or click an object, such as a placeholder box.
	■ Click the Cut button or use Ctrl+X to cut the item. Click the Copy button or use Ctrl+C to copy the item.
	■ Navigate to the desired slide and click at the location where you want to paste.
	■ Click the Paste button or use Ctrl+V to paste the item.

Add a New Slide to a Presentation

In this exercise, you will add a new slide to a presentation, enter a bulleted list, and change the layout of the slide. You can always change the layout for a slide after the slide has been created.

1. **Start** PowerPoint.

2. **Open** the iJams Design presentation from the Lesson 11 folder in your file storage location.

Add a Slide

3. Select the **Our Services** slide from the Slides panel on the left side of your screen. *The Our Services slide appears. New slides are placed after the selected slide.*

4. Choose **Home→Slides→New Slide** from the Ribbon.

5. **Click** in the Title placeholder and type **Products and Promotional Items**.

6. **Click** in the bulleted list placeholder and **type** the following bulleted list:

   - **Audio CDs**
   - **Downloadable MP3s**
   - **T-shirts**
   - **Baseball caps**
   - **Stickers**
   - **Pencils**
   - **Key chains**
   - **Posters**
   - **Mugs**
   - **Mouse pads**

   When you begin typing Posters, PowerPoint will reformat all of the bullets with a smaller font size so that all the bullets can fit into the box. As you type the last bullet point, Mouse pads, the font gets even smaller. Because a long list of bullets can be overwhelming, limit the number of bullets to three to six on a slide. If there is more information, consider breaking the list into two columns. In the next two steps, you will use this technique by choosing a different layout for the slide.

7. Follow these steps to change the slide layout:

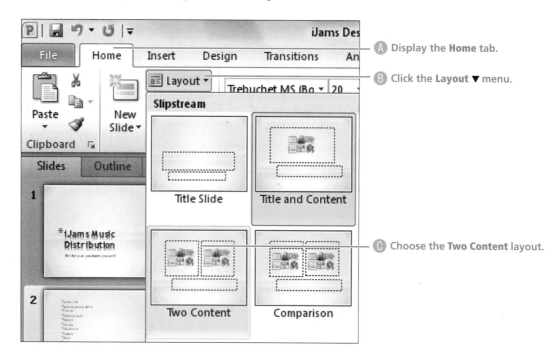

Ⓐ Display the **Home** tab.

Ⓑ Click the **Layout ▼** menu.

Ⓒ Choose the **Two Content** layout.

PowerPoint applies the Two Content layout to the current slide.

8. Follow these steps to move the last five bullets to the second box:

Ⓐ **Select** the last five bulleted paragraphs by dragging the mouse pointer over the text, and then **release** the mouse button.

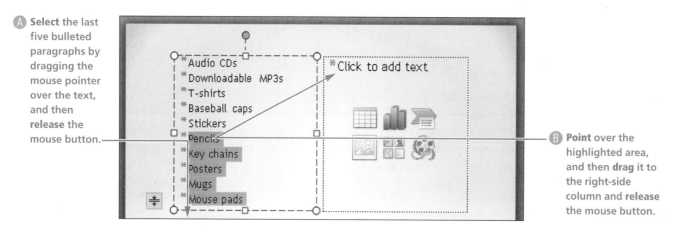

Ⓑ **Point** over the highlighted area, and then **drag** it to the right-side column and **release** the mouse button.

This command moves the last five bulleted paragraphs into the right-side content area.

9. Click the **Save** 🖫 button to save the changes to your presentation.

11.2 Working with Outlines

Video Lesson labyrinthelab.com/videos

Although you have been working primarily in the slide to add or format text, the Outline panel is an alternative way to add, remove, and move text. The Outline panel is a useful interface to organize or structure your presentation.

Using the Outline Panel

The Outline panel helps you to edit and reorganize your slides. The Outline panel is available on the left side of your screen if you are in Normal view. You can type directly in the Outline panel to add or edit text on a slide. You can also select text from the Outline panel and format it with the standard formatting commands on the Ribbon. Any changes made in the Outline panel are immediately reflected in the actual slide.

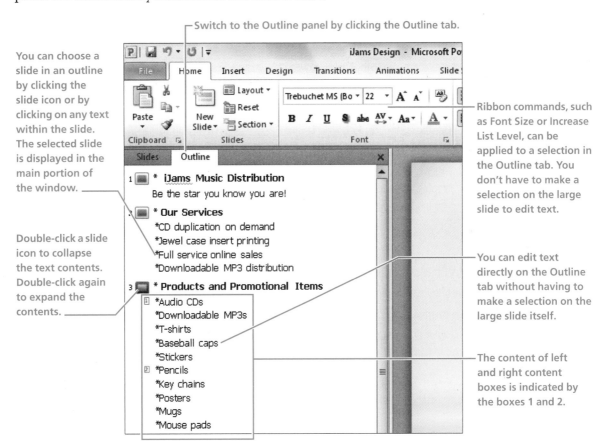

Switch to the Outline panel by clicking the Outline tab.

You can choose a slide in an outline by clicking the slide icon or by clicking on any text within the slide. The selected slide is displayed in the main portion of the window.

Double-click a slide icon to collapse the text contents. Double-click again to expand the contents.

Ribbon commands, such as Font Size or Increase List Level, can be applied to a selection in the Outline tab. You don't have to make a selection on the large slide to edit text.

You can edit text directly on the Outline tab without having to make a selection on the large slide itself.

The content of left and right content boxes is indicated by the boxes 1 and 2.

Task	Procedure
Select text in an outline	Drag over the desired text in the Outline panel.
Select an entire slide	Click the slide icon in the Outline panel.
Expand or collapse a slide	Double-click the slide icon in the Outline panel.
Add a new slide	Place the mouse pointer in the last group of bulleted paragraphs on a slide and press Ctrl+Enter.
Delete a slide	Right-click any text within a slide in the Outline panel, and then choose Delete Slide from the context menu.

DEVELOP YOUR SKILLS 11.2.1
Add a Slide in the Outline Panel

In this exercise, you will work with the Outline panel to add and move slides.

1. Follow these steps to select a slide while in the Outline panel:

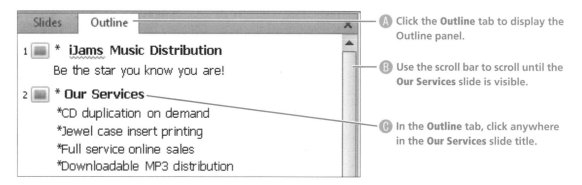

A Click the **Outline** tab to display the Outline panel.

B Use the scroll bar to scroll until the **Our Services** slide is visible.

C In the **Outline** tab, click anywhere in the **Our Services** slide title.

2. **Press** Ctrl + Enter.
   The cursor moves to the next box in the slide.

3. **Press** Ctrl + Enter.
   PowerPoint creates a new slide below the selected slide.

4. Follow these steps to add text to the new slide while in the Outline panel:

Ⓐ Type **Current Artists** directly in the Outline tab. As you type this title in the Outline tab, the text also appears in the large slide in the main portion of your window. ——

Ⓑ **Press** Ctrl+Enter to move to the bulleted paragraph box.

Ⓒ **Type** the three bulleted paragraphs shown here, tapping Enter after each paragraph.

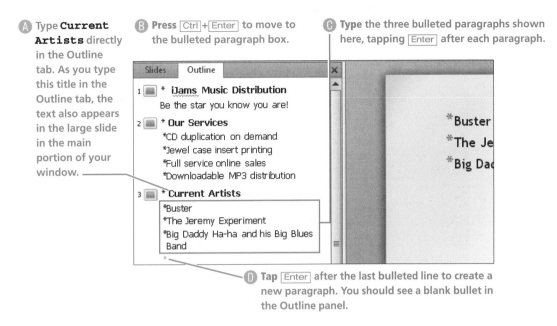

Ⓓ **Tap** Enter after the last bulleted line to create a new paragraph. You should see a blank bullet in the Outline panel.

PowerPoint adds a new slide to the presentation whenever the mouse pointer is positioned within the last box on a slide and the Ctrl+Enter *keystroke combination is issued.*

At this point, you should have a new bulleted paragraph visible in the outline below the Big Daddy Ha-ha paragraph.

Add Two New Slides

5. Follow these steps to promote a paragraph to make a new slide:

   ■ Make sure the **insertion point** is on the blank bulleted paragraph in the outline as shown at right.

   ■ Choose **Home→Paragraph→Decrease List Level** from the Ribbon.

   PowerPoint promotes the bulleted paragraph to create a new slide.

6. Type **New Artist Specials** and tap Enter.
   Notice that tapping Enter *created a new slide. You must use the* Ctrl+Enter *keystroke combination to add a bulleted paragraph after a title slide. However, you will fix this by demoting the new slide in the next step.*

7. Choose **Home→Paragraph→Increase List Level** ⊞ button from the Ribbon.
   The new slide created when you tapped Enter *in step 6 has been converted to a bullet under the New Artist Specials title.*

8. Complete the new slide in the outline as shown, **tapping** Enter after each paragraph (including the last paragraph).

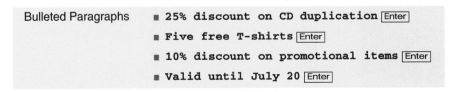

Bulleted Paragraphs	■ **25% discount on CD duplication** Enter
	■ **Five free T-shirts** Enter
	■ **10% discount on promotional items** Enter
	■ **Valid until July 20** Enter

9. Choose **Home→Paragraph→Decrease List Level** 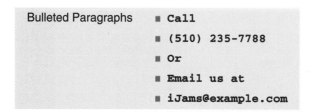 from the Ribbon to promote the new paragraph that follows the Valid Until July 20 paragraph and convert it into a new slide.

10. Type **Contact Us**, and then use ⌈Ctrl⌉+⌈Enter⌉ to create a bullet below the title you just typed.

11. Taking care **not** to tap ⌈Enter⌉ after the last bullet in this slide, complete the new slide as shown.

Bulleted Paragraphs
- **Call**
- **(510) 235-7788**
- **Or**
- **Email us at**
- **iJams@example.com**

You will format this slide in a later activity.

Collapsing and Expanding Slides

Video Lesson labyrinthelab.com/videos

As the Outline panel grows, it can be difficult to manage your slides when all the bulleted text is showing. PowerPoint lets you collapse slides so that only the title is visible. This makes it easier to manage your slides because more slides will be visible in the Outline panel.

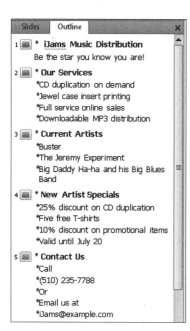 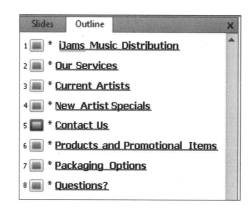

The same presentation in Outline view with all slides expanded and all slides collapsed

Use the Context Menu on the Outline Panel

In this exercise, you will use the context menu from the Outline panel.

1. Follow these steps to explore the Outline panel:

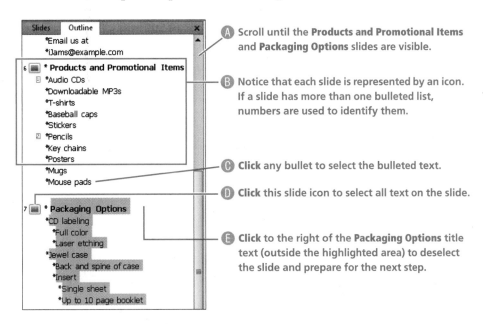

(A) Scroll until the **Products and Promotional Items** and **Packaging Options** slides are visible.

(B) Notice that each slide is represented by an icon. If a slide has more than one bulleted list, numbers are used to identify them.

(C) **Click** any bullet to select the bulleted text.

(D) **Click** this slide icon to select all text on the slide.

(E) **Click** to the right of the **Packaging Options** title text (outside the highlighted area) to deselect the slide and prepare for the next step.

2. **Double-click** the slide icon ▣ to the left of the Products and Promotional Items title.
   The bulleted paragraphs beneath the title are collapsed and hidden.

3. **Double-click** the slide icon ▣ to the left of the Products and Promotional Items title again.
   The bulleted paragraphs beneath the title are expanded and are once again visible.

4. **Right-click** anywhere in the Outline panel and choose **Collapse→Collapse All** from the context menu.
   All bulleted paragraphs are collapsed and hidden. Only the slide titles remain visible.

5. **Right-click** anywhere in the Outline panel and choose **Expand→Expand All** from the context menu.
   All bulleted paragraphs are expanded and are once again visible.

Microsoft PowerPoint

Move a Slide

The easiest way to move a slide in an outline is to first collapse all slides. Then you can click on the desired slide title and drag it to its new position.

6. **Right-click** anywhere in the Outline panel and choose **Collapse→Collapse All**.

7. If necessary, **scroll up** until all slide icons and titles are visible in the outline.

8. Follow these steps to move a slide:

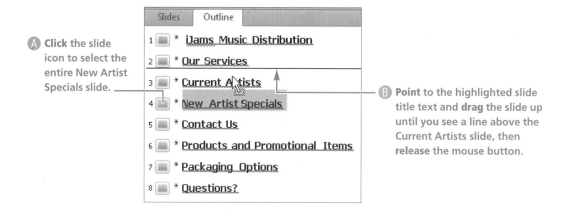

The New Artists Specials slide appears above the Current Artists slide.

9. Using this same method, move the Packaging Options slide to the second position, just below the Title slide.

Deleting Slides

Video Lesson   labyrinthelab.com/videos

You can delete a slide in an outline by clicking the slide icon to select the entire slide and then tapping the Delete key. Likewise, slides can be deleted in Normal and Slide Sorter views by choosing the desired slide(s) and tapping Delete. If you inadvertently delete a slide, you can use the Undo button on the Quick Access toolbar to undo the latest action and restore the deleted slide. If you later decide that you want to keep the change, click the Redo button on the Quick Access toolbar to go back to the previous action.

DEVELOP YOUR SKILLS 11.2.3
Delete a Slide from the Outline

In this exercise, you will delete a slide by using the Outline tab.

1. **Right-click** anywhere in the Outline panel and choose **Expand→Expand All**.

2. **Click** the Current Artists slide icon ▣ (not the title text) to select the entire slide.

3. **Tap** the Delete key on the keyboard to delete the slide.
   A faded bullet may appear at the end of the previous slide. This is PowerPoint readying itself for additional text. The ghost bullet will not display on the slide itself.

4. Using this same method, **delete** the Questions slide.

5. **Save** your presentation and then choose **File→Close** to close it.

11.3 Working with Word Integration

Video Lesson   labyrinthelab.com/videos

Microsoft Word is an excellent word processing program that integrates with PowerPoint. Outlines created in Word can easily be converted to a PowerPoint presentation.

Creating a Presentation Outline in Word

Word's powerful outlining tool makes setting up and modifying outlines easy. You can create an outline in Word and import it to PowerPoint. To use Word outlines in PowerPoint, you must apply the appropriate styles to the paragraphs in the Word document prior to importing the outline. PowerPoint converts the Word outline by using these rules:

- All Level 1 paragraphs translate to Titles in a PowerPoint slide.
- All Level 2 paragraphs translate to Level 1 Body Bullets in a PowerPoint slide.
- All Level 3 paragraphs translate to Level 2 Body Bullets in a PowerPoint slide.

Once a Word outline is imported into PowerPoint, you can promote or demote the bullets, apply layouts and a design template, and make other enhancements.

This Word outline...

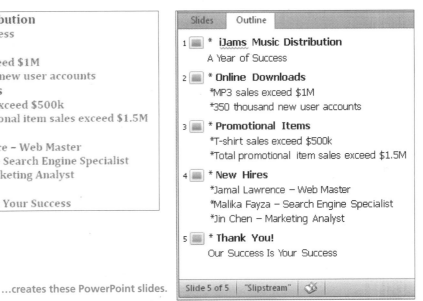

...creates these PowerPoint slides.

Create a Presentation and Import a Word Outline

In this exercise, you will start a new iJams presentation, create an outline in Word, and modify the resulting presentation.

Create an Outline in Word

1. **Start** Word and a blank document will be displayed.
   In the next few steps, you will type and apply Word styles to paragraphs.

2. With the blank document open, choose **View→Document Views→Outline** from the Ribbon to switch to Outline view.

3. Type `iJams Music Distribution` [Enter].

4. **Type** [Tab] `A Year of Success` [Enter].
   Typing [Tab] *increases the list level and creates a Level 2 style.*

5. **Type** [Shift]+[Tab] `Online Downloads` [Enter].
   Typing [Shift]+[Tab] *decreases the list level and returns the text to a Level 1 style.*

6. **Type** the following to create Level 2 style text that will be converted in PowerPoint to text bullets:

   [Tab] `MP3 sales exceed $1M` [Enter]

   `350 thousand new user accounts` [Enter]

   [Shift]+[Tab]

   Pressing [Shift]+[Tab] *returns you to a Level 1 style and you are ready to continue typing the rest of the outline.*

7. Continue **typing** the outline as follows:

   `Promotional Items` [Enter]

   [Tab] `T-shirt sales exceed $500k` [Enter]

   `Total promotional item sales exceed $1.5M` [Enter]

   [Shift]+[Tab] `New Hires` [Enter]

   [Tab] `Jamal Lawrence - Web Master` [Enter]

   `Malika Fayza - Search Engine Specialist` [Enter]

   `Jin Chen - Marketing Analyst` [Enter]

   [Shift]+[Tab] `Thank You!` [Enter]

   [Tab] `Our Success Is Your Success`

   Your outline should match the following figure.

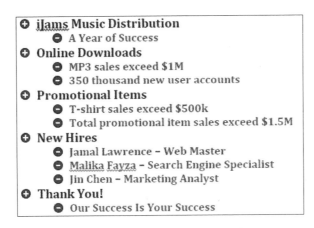

8. Choose **File→Save As** and save the outline to the Lesson 11 folder as **iJams 2010**.

9. Choose **File→Exit** to close the outline and Word.
   Word closes and PowerPoint is visible.

Import the Outline

10. If necessary, **restore** PowerPoint from the Taskbar or start it if it is not running.

11. Choose **File→New** and double-click the **Blank Presentation** icon to create a new blank presentation.

12. Choose **Design→Themes→More→** ▾ **→Apothecary** from the Ribbon to apply a document theme.

13. Choose **Home→Slides→New Slide** ▾ **menu→Slides From Outline** from the Ribbon.

14. Use the **Insert Outline** dialog box to navigate to the Lesson 11 folder.

15. **Choose** the iJams 2010 outline and click the **Insert** button.
    PowerPoint will take a moment to import the outline. Note that the first slide is blank because Power-Point inserted the slides from the outline after the existing blank title slide.

16. Display the **Outline** tab on the Slides panel and examine the PowerPoint outline.
    Observe that each Level 1 paragraph from the outline has become a slide title and each Level 2 paragraph has become a bulleted paragraph under the appropriate title.

17. Display the **Slides** tab to view the slide thumbnails.

18. **Choose** the first slide (the blank slide) and **tap** ⌴Delete⌴ to remove it.
    The blank slide is deleted and the iJams Music Distribution slide becomes selected.

Change a Layout and Apply a Design Template

19. Choose **Home→Slides→Layout** ▾**menu→Title Slide** from the Ribbon.
    The layout of the selected slide changes.

20. Select the final slide, Thank You, and choose **Home→Slides→Layout** ▾**menu→Section Header** from the Ribbon.

21. Choose the first slide, iJams Music Distribution.

22. Each slide is formatted with blue text because Word formatted the heading styles as blue. With the first slide selected, choose **Home→Slides→Reset**.
The text formatting is removed and returns to the default setting for the current document theme.

23. Select the second slide, **press** ⌷Shift⌷, select the last slide, and **release** ⌷Shift⌷.
Slides 2–5 become selected.

24. Choose **Home→Slides→Reset** to reformat the text on the selected slides with the document theme formatting.

25. Choose **File→Save As** and save the presentation as **iJams 2010** in the Lesson 11 folder.

11.4 Formatting Your Presentation

Video Lesson   labyrinthelab.com/videos

PowerPoint 2010 makes it so easy to create a presentation that the slides you create may not need any additional formatting. After all, the placeholders arrange the text, the bullets are automatic, and the color scheme is preformatted. However, in most cases, you will want to fine-tune your presentation. Formatting your presentation will make a good presentation even better.

Formatting Text

FROM THE KEYBOARD
Ctrl+B for bold
Ctrl+U for underline
Ctrl+I for italic

Formatting text is a common step in the development of a presentation. For instance, when reviewing a slide, you might decide that the text could be emphasized by changing the color of the font. If you had the time, you could change the font color of each piece of text on the slide individually by using the Font group on the Home tab of the Ribbon. However, a more efficient way to change the font color is to first select the placeholder and then apply the change of color. By selecting the placeholder, all text within the placeholder is changed in one swoop. The following illustration describes the buttons on the Home tab's Font group that assist you in formatting text.

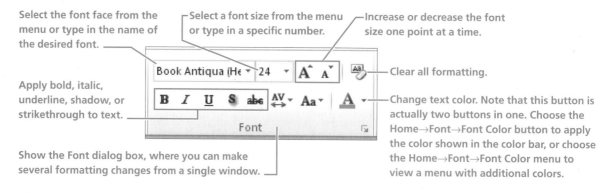

Select the font face from the menu or type in the name of the desired font.

Select a font size from the menu or type in a specific number.

Increase or decrease the font size one point at a time.

Clear all formatting.

Apply bold, italic, underline, shadow, or strikethrough to text.

Change text color. Note that this button is actually two buttons in one. Choose the Home→Font→Font Color button to apply the color shown in the color bar, or choose the Home→Font→Font Color menu to view a menu with additional colors.

Show the Font dialog box, where you can make several formatting changes from a single window.

Setting Character Spacing

Character spacing refers to the horizontal space between characters. PowerPoint lets you adjust this spacing to give your text some breathing room. If none of the preset options fit your needs, you can enter a numerical value to specify he exact amount of spacing. In the professional world of print, this is referred to as *tracking* or *kerning*. After selecting the characters you wish to space, choose the Home→ Font→Character Spacing button from the Ribbon to set your character spacing.

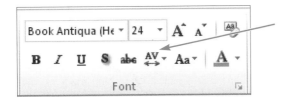

• MP3 sales exceed $1M
• 350 thousand new user accounts

• M P 3 s a l e s e x c e e d $ 1 M
• 3 5 0 t h o u s a n d n e w u s e r a c c o u n t s

The same slide with no character spacing (left) and a large amount of character spacing applied (right)

Setting the Text Case

You can change the case of your text by selecting the text on your slide and choosing Home→ Font→Change Case from the Ribbon.

The following table illustrates the different options available with the Change Case button.

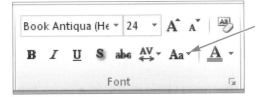

QUICK REFERENCE	SETTING THE TEXT CASE
Menu Option	**How It Affects Text**
Sentence Case	Your text will look like this.
Lowercase	your text will look like this.
Uppercase	YOUR TEXT WILL LOOK LIKE THIS.
Capitalize Each Word	Your Text Will Look Like This.
Toggle Case	Your text case will be toggled. Wherever you typed an uppercase letter, it will become lowercase. Wherever you typed a lowercase letter, it will become uppercase. *Example:* If you type `Your Text Will Look Like This`, Toggle Case will change it to `yOUR tEXT wILL lOOK lIKE tHIS`.

Format Text

In this exercise, you will change the formatting of the fonts in the Title and Subtitle slides.

Format the Subtitle

1. Follow these steps to display the Slides panel and display the title slide:

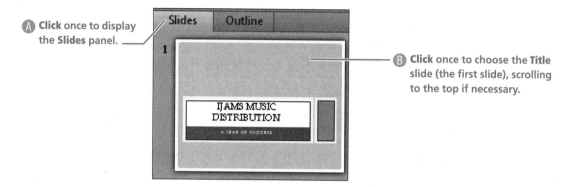

A. **Click** once to display the **Slides** panel.

B. **Click** once to choose the **Title** slide (the first slide), scrolling to the top if necessary.

2. Follow these steps to select the subtitle placeholder box:

A. **Click** anywhere on the text to position the cursor inside the handles for this text box. There will be a dashed line to indicate the border of the text box.

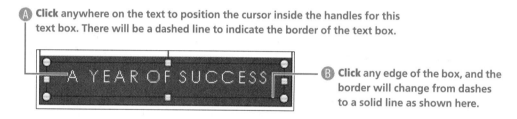

B. **Click** any edge of the box, and the border will change from dashes to a solid line as shown here.

The solid line indicates that the text box is selected. Any formatting change you make now will affect all text within the box.

Notice also that the Home→Font→Font Size **18** ▾ *box on the Ribbon is currently set to 18. The Apothecary theme applied this font size to the subtitle.*

3. Choose **Home→Font→Decrease Font Size** $\boxed{A^{^\vee}}$ from the Ribbon to reduce the font size to 16.

4. Choose **Home→Font→Bold** $\boxed{B}$ from the Ribbon.
   PowerPoint makes the text bold.

5. Choose **Home→Font→Shadow** $\boxed{S}$ from the Ribbon.
   The text stands out from the page a bit more because there is now a slight drop-shadow effect.

6. **Click** on the text of the title, iJams Music Distribution, and then **click** once on the dashed line border to select the Title text box.
The title was formatted as uppercase by the Apothecary theme. The border changes to a solid line to indicate it is selected.

7. Choose **Home→Font→Change Case→Capitalize Each Word** from the Ribbon.
The case is changed, but Ijams needs to be fixed.

8. **Double-click** the word *Ijams*, type **iJams**, and **tap** [Spacebar] to fix the case.

9. **Click** the dashed border around the title again to select the title box.

10. Choose **Home→Font→Font Size ▾** from the Ribbon and point to several different font sizes.
Notice how Live Preview displays the slide title size changes as you point to different settings on the Font Size menu.

11. Set the font size to **72**.
The text is now too large and no longer fits nicely on the background.

12. **Click** on the 72 in the **Home→Font→Font Size** menu. Type **44** and **tap** [Enter].
PowerPoint reduces the size of the text to 44. You can select a font size from the menu or type in your own value.

Setting Line Spacing

Video Lesson labyrinthelab.com/videos

Sometimes, instead of changing the font size or adding many hard returns, you need to only increase or decrease the spacing between lines to have the proper effect. *Line spacing* determines the amount of space between lines of text.

This setting is useful if text appears cramped and you wish to open up some breathing room between lines. Choose Home→Paragraph→Line Spacing to make your adjustments.

The same slide before and after applying Line Spacing

Adjust the Line Spacing

In this exercise, you will adjust the paragraph spacing to increase the amount of space between the bullets.

1. Display the **New Hires** slide on the Slides tab.

2. **Click** in any of the names to display a dashed border.

3. **Click** the dashed border to select the entire text box.

4. Choose **Home→Paragraph→Line Spacing** ⬍≡ **→2.0** from the Ribbon to increase the spacing.
   PowerPoint redistributes the bulleted text vertically on the slide with more spacing between items.

5. **Save** 🖫 and **close** your presentation.

Setting Paragraph Alignment

Video Lesson   labyrinthelab.com/videos

In time, you will be able to "eye" a presentation and notice if the paragraph alignment is not balanced. You can select one or more paragraphs and then click an alignment button on the Ribbon to make the change. Use the following buttons from the Home→Paragraph group on the Ribbon to realign paragraphs.

QUICK REFERENCE		WORKING WITH PARAGRAPH ALIGNMENT
Purpose	**Button**	**Example**
Left-align	≣	This text has been left aligned. Notice how the left column is in a straight line, but the right column appears jagged.
Center-align	≣	This text has been center aligned. Notice how the text is balanced and centered.
Right-align	≣	This text has been right aligned. Notice how the right column is in a straight line.
Justify	≣	This text has been justify aligned. Notice how the text is spaced to maintain straight lines on the left and right.

Format the Contact Us Slide

In this exercise, you will reformat the Contact Us slide.

Format the Contact Us Slide

1. **Open** the iJams Contact presentation from your Lesson 11 folder.

2. If necessary, **display** the Slides panel.

3. If necessary, **scroll down** and then **select** Slide 5, Contact Us.

4. **Click** in the bulleted list and then **click** a border of the text box.

5. Choose **Home→Paragraph→Bullets** ⬛ from the Ribbon to remove bullets from the paragraphs.

6. Choose **Home→Paragraph→Center** ☰ to center the paragraphs within the text box.

7. Drag to select the entire telephone number.
   A faded formatting box appears. Pointing your mouse at it will cause it to become more visible. You may format the selected text from this formatting box, but we will use the Ribbon as in the next steps.

8. Choose **Home→Font→Font Size ▾** and increase the size to 32.

9. Using the same method, **increase** the size of the last line (the email address) to 32.

10. **Save** 💾 your presentation.

11.5 Using the Format Painter

Microsoft PowerPoint

Video Lesson	labyrinthelab.com/videos

🖌 Common to all Office programs, the Format Painter is a great tool that simplifies the formatting process. The Format Painter copies all text formats including the typeface, size, color, and attributes such as bold, italic, and underline. It also copies formatting applied to shapes or clip art. The Format Painter helps you easily maintain a standardized, uniform look in your presentation.

Loading the Format Painter

The key to using the Format Painter successfully is understanding when it is loaded. After formatting has been copied with the Format Painter, its Ribbon icon appears pressed in. This pressed-in icon indicates that the Format painter is loaded and ready to use.

 Format Painter unloaded (no formatting to paste)

 Format Painter loaded and ready to paste formatting

QUICK REFERENCE	COPYING FORMATS WITH THE FORMAT PAINTER
Task	**Procedure**
Copy formats with the Format Painter	■ Select the object (text, picture, drawn line, etc.) with the format you wish to copy. ■ Choose Home→Clipboard→Format Painter 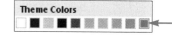 from the Ribbon. ■ Select the object at the new location to which you wish to copy formatting.
Use the Format Painter repeatedly	■ Select the object with formatting to be copied. ■ Double-click Home→Clipboard→Format Painter on the Ribbon. ■ Click with the Format Painter on all objects to which you wish the formatting copied. (The Format Painter will remain active until you switch it off.) ■ Click once on the Format Painter to switch it off again, or tap the Esc key.

While using Format Painter, the mouse pointer changes from an arrow ⬧ to a brush ⬥.

Copy Formatting with the Format Painter

In this exercise, you will copy and paste text formatting with the Format Painter.

Copy Text Formatting

1. Select the fourth slide, **New Artist Specials**.

2. **Double-click** *free* in the second bullet to select it.

3. Choose **Home→Font→Font Size→32** from the Ribbon.

4. Choose **Home→Font→Text Shadow** [S] from the Ribbon.

5. Choose **Home→Font→Font Color ▾→Theme Colors→Red Accent 6** from the Ribbon.

6. Choose **Home→Clipboard→Format Painter** from the Ribbon.
   The Format Painter icon is pressed in and is now loaded.

7. **Click** once on *July* in the last bullet.
   The formatting is copied to the word July, *and the Format Painter icon on the Ribbon becomes unloaded.*

8. Choose **Home→Clipboard→Format Painter** from the Ribbon.
   The Format Painter has been reloaded with the formatting from the word July because that is where the insertion point is.

9. **Click** once on *20* in the last bullet.
   The formatting is copied to 20 and the Format Painter on the Ribbon becomes unloaded.

10. Select the third slide, **Our Services**.

11. **Drag** across *on demand* in the first bullet to select it.

12. Choose **Home→Font→Bold** $\boxed{\text{B}}$ from the Ribbon.

13. Choose **Home→Font→Italic** $\boxed{I}$ from the Ribbon.

14. Choose **Home→Font→Font Color ▼→Theme Colors→Red Accent 6** from the Ribbon.

15. Double-click **Home→Clipboard→Format Painter** 🖌 on the Ribbon.
    Double-clicking the Format Painter will keep it loaded until you turn it off.

16. **Click** on the word *online* in the third bullet.
    The formatting is copied to online, *and the Format Painter remains loaded.*

17. **Click** on the word *sales* in the third bullet.

18. **Click** on the words *MP3* and *distribution* in the last bullet.

19. Choose **Home→Clipboard→Format Painter** 🖌 from the Ribbon.
    The Format Painter has been unloaded.

20. **Save** 💾 your presentation.

11.6 Using the Slide Sorter

Video Lesson labyrinthelab.com/videos

Up until now, you've been working in the Normal view, which is good for manipulating a handful of slides. However, as your presentation grows to more slides than are visible in the Normal view, you will want to explore the function of the Slide Sorter view.

Rearranging Slides

PowerPoint's Slide Sorter view is used to rearrange slides. In the Slide Sorter view, each slide is a thumbnail image so the entire presentation is visible at a glance. As your presentation grows, often the order of the slides needs to be changed to create a logical concept flow. Using the Drag and Drop method in the Slide Sorter view, you can quickly reorganize your slides by moving them to the correct spot.

Use the Slide Sorter View

In this exercise, you will practice using the Slide Sorter view.

1. Choose **View→Presentation Views→Slide Sorter** ⊞ from the Ribbon.

2. Follow these steps to move a slide:

Ⓐ If necessary, use the Zoom slider in the bottom-right corner of your PowerPoint window to change the zoom percentage until all six slides are shown. Don't be concerned if your slides have a different arrangement than shown in the illustration.

Ⓑ **Drag** the Our Services slide to the left of the Packaging Options slide, and a large vertical bar will indicate the eventual position of the slide. Don't be concerned if your slides are on different rows or columns than shown here. Pay attention to the slide numbers, not the position on the grid.

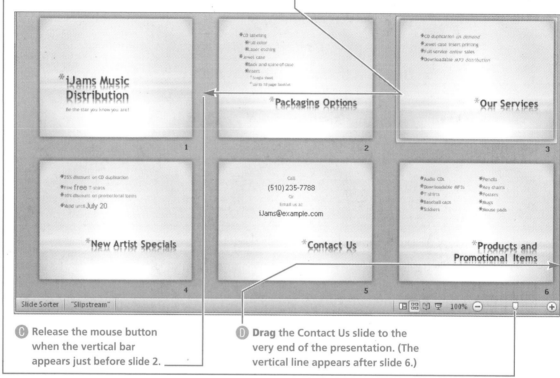

Ⓒ Release the mouse button when the vertical bar appears just before slide 2.

Ⓓ **Drag** the Contact Us slide to the very end of the presentation. (The vertical line appears after slide 6.)

3. Choose **Views→Presentation Views→Normal** from the Ribbon to return to Normal view.

4. **Save** and **close** the presentation.

11.7 Organizing with Sections

Video Lesson labyrinthelab.com/videos

Using the Slide Sorter with individual slides works well for small presentations. For presentations containing many slides, PowerPoint 2010's new Sections feature helps you keep them organized.

Creating Sections

Sections are always created before the selected slide and include all following slides. This often results in a section containing more slides than intended. The fix is to simply create another section after the intended last slide

QUICK REFERENCE	USING SECTIONS
Task	**Procedure**
Create a section	▪ Select the first slide from the Slides panel for the section.
	▪ Choose Home→Slides→Section→Add Section. A new section is started and includes all subsequent slides.
	▪ Select the slide after the last slide in the section and choose Home→Slides→Section→Add Section. Section breaks are always created above the selected slide.
Name a section	▪ Right-click the section's title bar and choose Rename Section.
	▪ Type the new name for the section and click Rename.
Move a section	▪ Drag a section's title bar above or below another section title bar.
Collapse or expand a section	▪ Double-click the section's title bar.
Remove a section	▪ Right-click the section's title bar and choose Remove Section to remove the section but leave the slides, or choose Remove Section & Slides to delete the section and its slides.

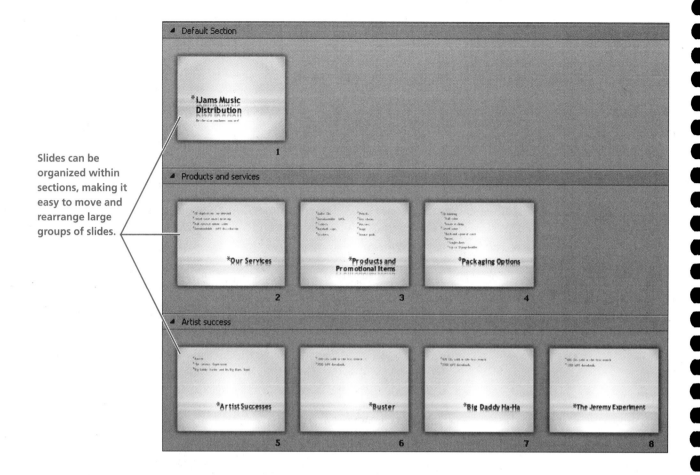

Slides can be organized within sections, making it easy to move and rearrange large groups of slides.

Create Sections

In this exercise, you will create sections.

1. **Open** the iJams Sections presentation from your Lesson 11 folder.
   With so many slides, it may be easier to work in Slide Sorter view.

2. Choose **View→Presentation Views→Slide Sorter** from the Ribbon.

3. Select slide 2, **Artist Successes**, and then choose **Home→Slides→Section→Add Section**.
   A new section named Untitled Section is created before the selected slide. Every slide below it is included in the section.

4. **Right-click** the section title bar and choose **Rename Section**, as in the figure to the right.

   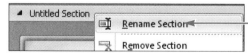

5. Type **Artist success** and click **Rename**.
   The section is renamed, but contains slides not intended for this section.

6. Select slide 6, **Our Services**, and then choose **Home→Slides→Section→Add Section**.
   A new section is started before the selected slide.

7. **Right-click** the Untitled Section title bar, choose **Rename Section**, and rename the section to **Products and services**.

8. **Click** the last slide, Contact Us, and **create** a new section before it.

9. **Rename** the final section **Call to action**.

10. **Save** your presentation.

Managing Sections

Video Lesson   labyrinthelab.com/videos

Once sections have been created, they can be dragged and rearranged in either the Slides panel or Slide Sorter view. Individual slides can even be dragged from one section to another. Additionally, sections can be collapsed similar to slide titles in Outline view. Collapsed sections hide the slides, making it easy to drag and reorder the sections. However, the collapsed sections only hide slides when editing. The collapsed slides will display as normal when running the slide show.

When collapsed, the section title bar indicates how many slides exist in that section.

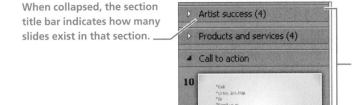

Collapsing sections reduces clutter in the Slides panel.

DEVELOP YOUR SKILLS 11.7.2
Manage Sections

In this exercise, you will rearrange slides by using sections.

1. With the presentation still open in Slide Sorter view, **scroll** until you can see the Artist Success section title bar, if necessary.

2. **Double-click** the Artist Success section title bar to collapse it.

3. **Double-click** the Products and Services section title bar to collapse it.

4. Choose **View→Presentation Views→Normal** to switch to Normal view.
   The selected section does not remain collapsed when you change views.

5. **Double-click** the Products and services section title bar in the Slides panel to collapse it again.

6. Follow these steps to rearrange the sections:

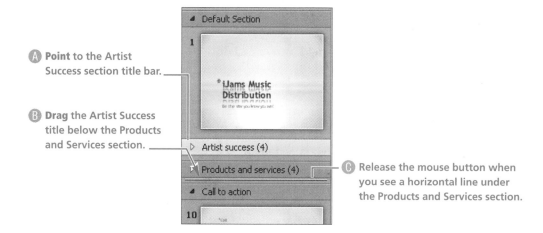

A **Point** to the Artist Success section title bar.

B **Drag** the Artist Success title below the Products and Services section.

C Release the mouse button when you see a horizontal line under the Products and Services section.

7. Choose **View→Presentation Views→Slide Sorter**.

8. **Double-click** the Products and Services section title bar to expand it.

9. **Click** anywhere in the gray area outside the slide thumbnails to deselect any slides.

10. **Scroll down**, if necessary, until you see the entire Call to Action section with the Contact Us slide.

11. Use the **Zoom slider** at the bottom-right corner of the PowerPoint window, if necessary, to make the view smaller. You should see all slides in both the Products and Services and Call to Action sections.

12. **Drag** the last slide of the Products and Services section (New Artist Specials) to the left of the Contact Us slide to move it to the Call to Action section. The Call to Action section should resemble the following figure.

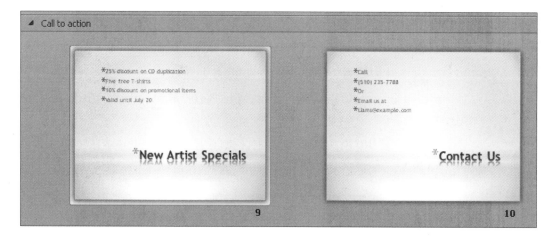

13. **Save** your presentation.

11.8 Printing Your Presentation

Video Lesson labyrinthelab.com/videos

Ninety percent of the time, you will be viewing or projecting the presentations you create from a PC or notebook computer. However, there may be times when a hard copy of the presentation is needed. In this lesson, you will simply explore the options of printing a presentation. In future lessons, you will apply this knowledge to printing handout slides and speaker notes as well.

Knowing What You Can Print

PowerPoint can create the following types of printouts:

■ Slides: Prints each slide of a presentation on a separate page

■ Handouts: Prints one or more slides per page, leaving room for attendees to jot notes during the presentation

■ Speaker Notes: Prints each slide on a separate page, with any speaker notes you created for the slide below

■ Outline: Prints a text outline of each slide, similar to what is seen in the Outline panel

An example of a handout with three slides per page

Microsoft PowerPoint

Previewing a Printout

FROM THE KEYBOARD

Ctrl+P to display the Print tab in Backstage view

The Print window lets you see how each slide will be printed. You can then refine the appearance before printing. The following illustration describes the options available from the Print window.

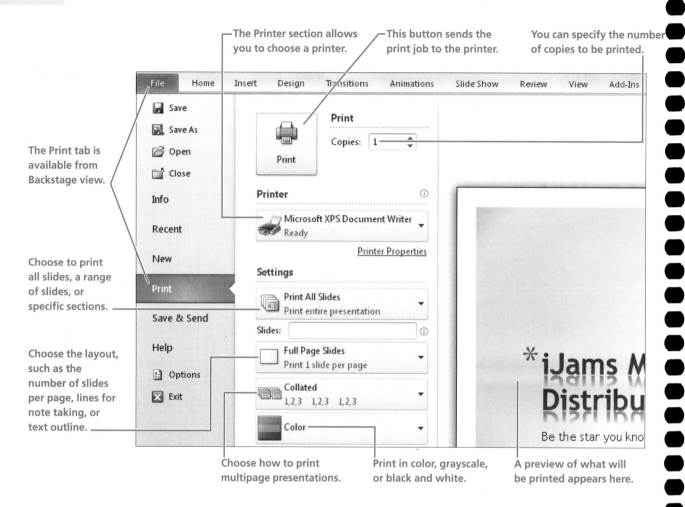

The Printer section allows you to choose a printer.

This button sends the print job to the printer.

You can specify the number of copies to be printed.

The Print tab is available from Backstage view.

Choose to print all slides, a range of slides, or specific sections.

Choose the layout, such as the number of slides per page, lines for note taking, or text outline.

Choose how to print multipage presentations.

Print in color, grayscale, or black and white.

A preview of what will be printed appears here.

Preview a Printout

In this exercise, you will use Backstage view to preview a printout.

1. Choose **File→Print**.

2. Follow these steps to examine the print options:

Ⓐ Notice all ten slides in the presentation are set to be printed. Use the **left arrow** to return to the first slide. You can also use the scrollbar to navigate among slides.

Ⓑ Adjust the **Zoom** level so the whole slide fits in the preview.

Ⓒ Change this option to **Sections→ Products and Services** and note that only the three slides in that section are set to print.

Ⓓ Change this option to **Handouts→ 3 Slides** to preview the text outline. Changing this option to anything other than Full Page Slides causes the Orientation option to appear between the Collated and Color options.

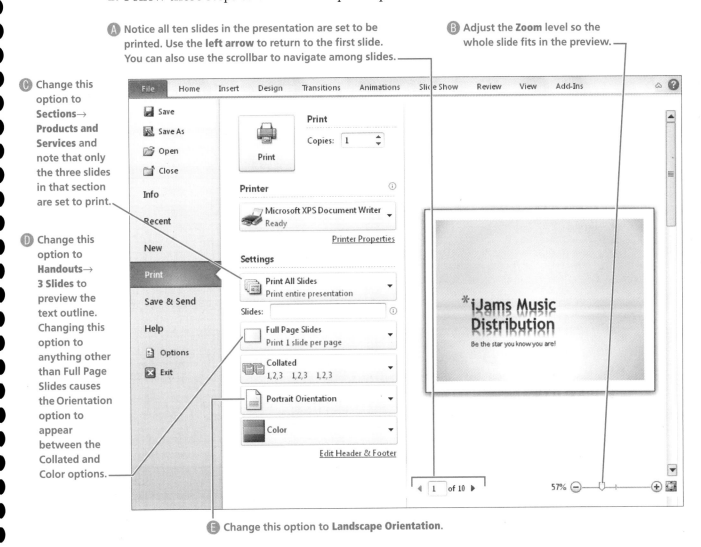

Ⓔ Change this option to **Landscape Orientation**.

3. Choose the **Home** tab from the Ribbon to exit Backstage view without printing.

Microsoft PowerPoint

Using Page Setup and Output Formats

Video Lesson   labyrinthelab.com/videos

If you need to print the presentation itself or transparencies for overhead projection, use the Page Setup dialog box. The Page Setup dialog box can be displayed by choosing Design→Page Setup→Page Setup from the Ribbon. Examine the Page Setup options, along with the different types of output formats you can use by studying the Page Setup dialog box that follows:

PowerPoint provides a variety of output formats in the Slides Sized For menu. Available sizes include overhead transparencies, letter paper, banner, and other various sizes.

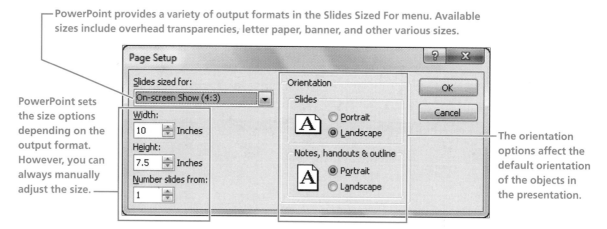

PowerPoint sets the size options depending on the output format. However, you can always manually adjust the size.

The orientation options affect the default orientation of the objects in the presentation.

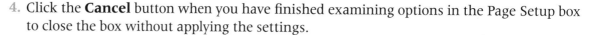

DEVELOP YOUR SKILLS 11.8.2
Explore the Page Setup Box

In this exercise, you will learn about the options provided in the Page Setup dialog box.

1. Choose **Design→Page Setup→Page Setup** as shown at right to display the Page Setup dialog box.

2. Click the **Slides Sized For** list and examine the various output formats.

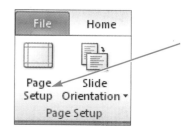

3. Examine the **Orientation** section of the Page Setup dialog box.
   Notice that there are separate settings for printing slides and printing notes and handout pages.

4. Click the **Cancel** button when you have finished examining options in the Page Setup box to close the box without applying the settings.

5. Choose **File→Close** from the Ribbon to close the presentation. Choose **Don't Save** if asked to save your changes.

Using the Print Shortcut

If you have customized your Quick Access toolbar to display the Quick Print [icon] icon, you may find it tempting to just click the Quick Print button. However, before this becomes a habit, know that a click of this button sends the entire presentation to the current printer, whether or not you want to make adjustments. If you are working with a document theme that has a colored background, the printing process will not only be painstakingly slow, but may also waste your toner or ink!

11.9 Concepts Review

| Concepts Review | labyrinthelab.com/ob10 |

To check your knowledge of the key concepts introduced in this lesson, complete the Concepts Review quiz by going to the URL listed above. If your classroom is using Labyrinth eLab, you may complete the Concepts Review quiz from within your eLab course.

Reinforce Your Skills

Practice Formatting

In this exercise, you will format some slides in the Tropical Getaways presentation.

1. Format the Presentation

2. **Open** the rs-Tropical Getaways Design presentation from the Lesson 11 folder.

3. Choose **View→Presentation Views→Normal** from the Ribbon and **select** the title slide from the Slides panel.

4. Click the **Title** box, and then **click** again on the edge of the box to select it.

5. Choose **Home→Font→Increase Font Size** from the Ribbon once to increase the font size.

6. Choose **Home→Font→Bold** to make the title bold.

Change Paragraph Alignment

7. **Display** the Travel Now And Save! slide on the Slides panel.

8. Choose **Home→Slides→New Slide** to add a new slide after Travel Now And Save!

9. Type **Travel Categories** for the title.

10. **Type** the following as bulleted paragraphs:
    - **Adventure**
    - **Leisure**
    - **Family**
    - **Singles**

11. Select the **bulleted text box** by clicking on the border.

12. Choose the **Home→Paragraph→Bullets** button from the Ribbon to remove the bullets from all paragraphs.

13. Choose the **Home→Paragraph→Center** button from the Ribbon to center the text on the slide.

14. Choose **Home→Paragraph→Line Spacing→2.0** to increase the vertical spacing between the bullets.
    After you finish, the slide should appear like the following illustration.

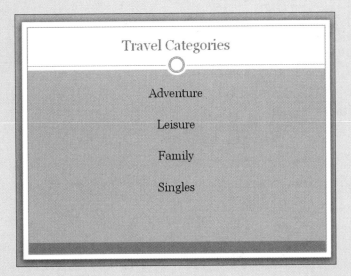

15. **Save** the presentation and continue with the next exercise.

Rearrange Sections

In this exercise, you will create and rearrange sections.

Before you begin: The rs-Tropical Getaways Design presentation in the Lesson 11 folder should be open.

1. Choose **View→Presentation Views→Slide Sorter** from the Ribbon.

2. Select the **Complete Packages** slide.

3. Choose **Home→Slides→Section→Add Section**.

4. **Right-click** the Untitled Section title bar and **choose** Rename Section.

5. Type **Prices** and click Rename.

6. Select the **Travel Categories** slide and choose **Home→Slides→Section→Add Section**.

7. **Right-click** the Untitled Section title bar and **choose** Rename Section.

8. Type **Locations** and **click** Rename.

9. **Select** the Contact Us slide and create a section named **Contact**.

10. **Right-click** the Contact section and **choose** Collapse All.

11. **Drag** the Locations section above the Prices section. Your screen should resemble the following figure.

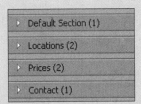

12. **Right-click** any of the sections and choose Expand All.

13. Choose **View→Presentation Views→Normal** from the Ribbon.

14. **Save** your presentation.

Apply Your Skills

Reformat a Presentation

In this exercise, you will add a slide to the Classic Cars Design presentation and change the format.

1. **Open** the as-Classic Cars Design presentation from your Lesson 11 folder.

2. **Add** a new slide after the title slide and **type** the following text:

Title	`Agenda for 2010 Convention`
Bulleted Paragraphs	■ `Locating a Classic Car over the Internet` ■ `Negotiating the Price` ■ `Resources for Restoring` ■ `The 10 Most Popular Road Trips` ■ `Displaying Your Classic Car` ■ `Joining a Classic Car Club` ■ `Insuring your Classic Car` ■ `Leadership Elections`

3. Apply the **Two Content** layout to the slide.

4. Move the last four bullets into the **right column**.

5. Increase the **line spacing** of both bulleted lists to **1.5**.

6. Apply a **font size** of **22** to both bulleted lists.
   Your slide should look similar to the following illustration:

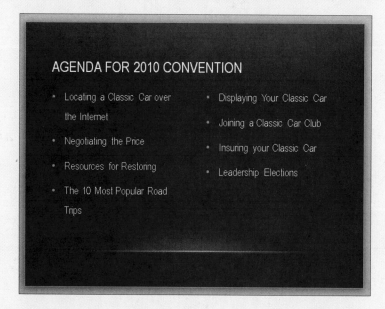

7. **Save** your presentation.

Critical Thinking & Work-Readiness Skills

In the course of working through the following Microsoft Office-based Critical Thinking exercises, you will also be utilizing various work-readiness skills, some of which are listed next to each exercise. Go to labyrinthelab.com/workreadiness *to learn more about the work-readiness skills.*

11.1 Use the Outline Panel and Repurpose a Presentation

Aurelia, the administrative assistant, has been tasked by Carthic to take the presentation he used at JamWorks and polish it into a general presentation he and others can give to any group interested in learning what iJams is all about. Open ct-JamWorks from your Lesson 11 folder and, using the Outline Panel, identify and delete any slides that were only appropriate for the JamWorks conference. Use the Outline panel to add any additional slides you think are necessary. Save the presentation as **ct-JamWorks Revised** to your Lesson 11 folder.

WORK-READINESS SKILLS APPLIED

- Reading
- Reasoning
- Organizing and maintaining information

11.2 Format a Presentation

Start with the ct-JamWorks Revised presentation you created in the previous exercise and save it to your Lesson 11 folder with the new name **ct-JamWorks Formatted**. View it as a slide show and ask yourself if the slides are easy to read and in the best order. Change the document theme, adjust the text layout, rearrange the order of slides, and make any other changes you feel are necessary. Use the Format Painter to quickly duplicate formatting changes. Save your changes.

WORK-READINESS SKILLS APPLIED

- Thinking
- Organizing and maintaining information
- Seeing things in the mind's eye

11.3 Print a Presentation

Presenters often like to review their presentations in print (though some are happy to review and comment in digital format). Carthic likes to edit on paper, so Aurelia wants to give the new general presentation to him in a form he feels comfortable with. Open the ct_JamWorks Formatted presentation, if necessary. Use various tools to check for a final time that the content is as you wish it. Use the Print Preview feature as you test various print options. Then, print the slides, deciding which view would be best and easiest for Carthic's review. Type and print a brief Word memo to accompany the printed slides.

WORK-READINESS SKILLS APPLIED

- Serving clients/customers
- Reasoning
- Writing

U N I T

5

Access 2010

I n this unit, you will explore Access, a powerful database application. You will begin by creating a new database, identifying features of the Access environment, creating a new database table, and adding records to the table. You will build the database by adding forms and reports and additional tables. You will continue to add records to a table using forms, preview and print data, and save a database as a new file.

Microsoft Access

Exploring Access 2010

LEARNING OBJECTIVES

After studying this lesson, you will be able to:

- Define database and key terms associated with databases
- Identify objects contained in modern databases and explain how they are used
- Launch Access 2010 and identify elements of the application window
- Create a new blank database and database table
- Use the Navigation Pane and enter data into a table
- Save and close database objects
- Preview and print datasheets
- Close a database and exit Access 2010

Have you ever wondered how service agents who take your order over the telephone know what questions to ask about the products you order...or how sportscasters come up with little-known facts about teams and players in a flash? In most cases, these service agents and sportscasters have access to a powerful database from which they obtain the information.

In this lesson, you will explore elements of the Microsoft Access 2010 application window, create a new database, and identify features of the database window. As you explore the tools available in Access 2010, you will begin building the new database.

Student Resources labyrinthelab.com/ob10

Updating Raritan Clinic East

Raritan Clinic East is an incorporated medical practice staffed by the finest clinical diagnosticians in the Pediatric fields of General Medicine, Cardiology, Orthopedics, Pediatric, Emergency Medicine, and Neonatology. The practice serves a patient community ranging in ages from newborn to 18 years.

Raritan Clinic East

Pediatric Diagnostic Specialists

Recently, Raritan Clinic East has moved to a new facility located on a wooded six-acre site in the center of Raritan's vast medical professional complex. The 21,000-square-foot state-of-the-art facility was completed in 2009.

James Elliott has recently accepted a position in the human resources department with Raritan Clinic East. He has been tasked with reviewing the current records management system. From this review, he will be able to determine how best to organize data in new databases created using Access 2010. Then he will create a new database in which to store the data so that information can be located and retrieved more efficiently.

The table created to hold employee data

A printout of data from the new database table

12.1 Defining Access Databases

Video Lesson   labyrinthelab.com/videos

If you have ever used a phone book or a catalog, retrieved a note card from a card file, or pulled a file from a file cabinet, you have used a database. If you have ever used an index or a table of contents in a book, you have also used a database—just a different type of database. Each of these items consists of individual pieces of *data* that, when combined, make up a *database*.

What Is a Database?

A *database* is a collection of related data stored together in one electronic file. Historically, individuals and businesses have used databases to store vast amounts of data in an organized fashion to facilitate quick and easy retrieval of facts, figures, and information. Prior to the computer age, database records were stored on index cards, on columnar tablets, and in file folders stored in file cabinets. While these data storage methods are still around today, computer-based databases have reduced the storage requirements of data and have improved the efficiency of data retrieval. As a result, reports from sportscasters, historians, politicians, stock sales, unemployment records, and many other details can be reported with amazing accuracy—and very quickly.

12.2 Exploring the Access Environment

Video Lesson   labyrinthelab.com/videos

When you launch Access 2010, one of the first things you will notice is that, unlike other Microsoft Office applications, Access displays the Backstage view rather than a new blank file. From the Backstage view, you can create a new database or open an existing one.

Launching Access 2010

The basic procedures for launching Access 2010 are the same as those procedures used to launch other Microsoft Office applications. After you launch Access, you are prompted to take action to create or open a database. These procedures may vary somewhat, depending on the version of Windows installed on your computer as well as whether Access has been used on the computer or not.

DEVELOP YOUR SKILLS 12.2.1
Launch Access 2010

In this exercise, you will launch Access 2010 from the Start menu.

1. From the Desktop, click the **Start** button.

2. Choose **All Programs**.

3. Click the **Microsoft Office** folder.

4. Choose **Microsoft Access 2010**.

In future lessons, a Start menu command like this will be written as: Choose All Programs→ Microsoft Office→Microsoft Office Access 2010.

After you launch Access for the first time, the program may appear on the Start menu. You can launch Access directly from the Start menu rather than displaying the menus from the All Programs list.

12.3 Identifying Elements of the Access Window

Video Lesson   labyrinthelab.com/videos

Access, unlike other Microsoft Office applications, displays the Backstage view each time you launch it. From this screen, you can choose to create a new database, open an existing database, open a sample database, or create a new database based on a template.

Using Database Templates

Access 2010 comes with a variety of built-in database templates that you can use as the basis for your new database. In Access, templates create fully designed databases so that all you have to do is enter data. Templates are available for creating the most common types of databases. Databases created using templates are often sufficient to meet the needs of most individuals and some small businesses and organizations. A database created with a template can also be used as a foundation from which a more sophisticated database can be developed.

Creating a Blank Database

An electronic database file serves as a shell that holds all the tools, data, and various database objects that help users enter and organize data and obtain meaningful information from that data. As a result, you must save the empty database shell and give it a name as you create it. After you create a new database, Access automatically creates a blank table named Table1. An Access database is composed of various objects including tables, queries, forms, and reports. Each object type can be created from scratch using a Design View for the particular type of object. Access also provides wizards to help you set up individual objects. You will use both of these techniques as you develop the databases throughout this unit.

Designing a Database

The first step in designing any database is to determine the type of information you will need to keep in your database. Examples of data include the name, address, telephone number, and email address of customers or contacts. Once the needed information has been determined, you can design the database to accommodate it. A database structure can be changed, but modifications to the structure should be kept at a minimum to prevent unwanted loss of data. Sometimes changing the structure can corrupt or delete data that has already been entered. This is why it is important to begin with a good design.

Create a Blank Database

In this exercise, you will create a new blank database named Raritan Clinic East.

1. Launch **Access 2010** and follow these steps to create and name the new database:

Ⓐ Click the **Blank Database** icon in the Available Templates section of the Access window. ⎯

Ⓑ Click the **File Name** text box and type **Raritan Clinic East**.

Ⓒ Click the **folder** button to open the File New Database dialog box.

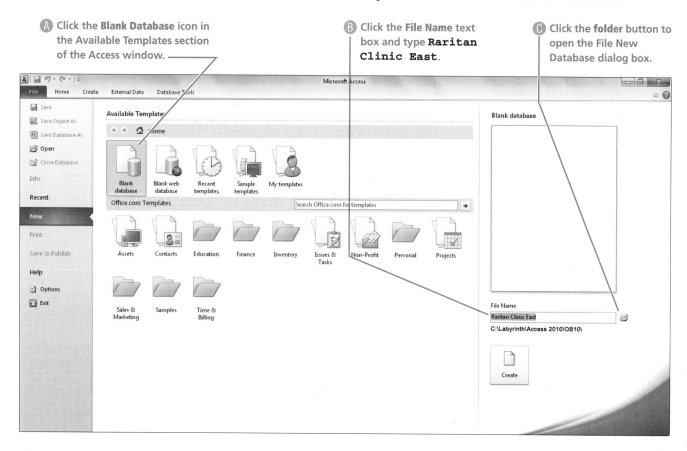

2. Navigate to the Lesson 12 folder or the folder in which you want to store your files and click **OK**.

3. Click the **Create** button.
   Access creates the new database, shows the database name in the application title bar, and displays a blank table named Table1 in the Access window.

12.4 Identifying Features of the Database Window

Video Lesson labyrinthelab.com/videos

Now that you have created the database file, take a moment to study the layout of the window and compare the visual elements of the window with the features you have seen in other Microsoft Office applications.

Tabs on the Ribbon display Access tools.

The title bar shows the database name and the file format for the version of Access you are using.

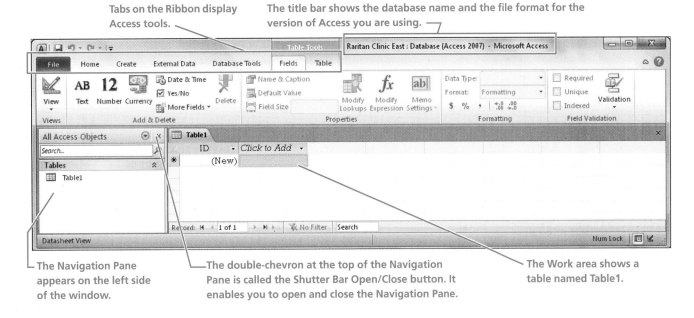

The Navigation Pane appears on the left side of the window.

The double-chevron at the top of the Navigation Pane is called the Shutter Bar Open/Close button. It enables you to open and close the Navigation Pane.

The Work area shows a table named Table1.

Using the Navigation Pane

If you have used Microsoft Office Excel, you know that navigating within a worksheet or workbook is different from navigating within paragraphs of a document. Navigating within an Access database is also different from navigating in a document. As you begin working with the database, some basic procedures for using the Navigation Pane will enable you to navigate the file more efficiently.

A list of tables contained in the database is displayed.

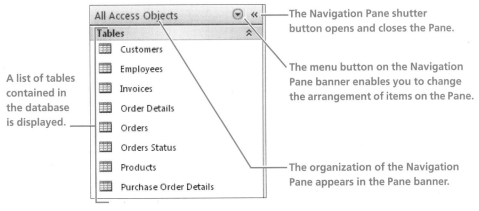

The Navigation Pane shutter button opens and closes the Pane.

The menu button on the Navigation Pane banner enables you to change the arrangement of items on the Pane.

The organization of the Navigation Pane appears in the Pane banner.

NOTE

For new databases, a Search bar also appears on the Navigation Pane, just below the Pane banner.

Identifying Object Types

The current database holds only one table. As a result, the Navigation Pane displays only that table. When you have a fully developed database, the Navigation Pane will display all database contents grouped by type of *object*. In Access, an object is an item contained in a database that is designed to serve a specific purpose in the database. The most common object types and their functions in the database are identified in the following table.

ACCESS DATABASE OBJECT TYPES	
Object	**Description**
Tables	The basic objects in a database that contain the data used in all other database objects. Tables hold the data and are also used as input objects because you can use the tables to add data to a database.
Forms	Objects used to display and input data in a layout that is more aesthetically pleasing than table layout while safeguarding other records and improving data integrity.
Reports	Objects in Access databases that process table data and present the data as meaningful information. Reports are output objects.
Queries	Objects used to retrieve data contained in tables on the basis of specific criteria and conditions.

Objects on the Navigation Pane are grouped according to object type. You can expand and collapse each object list to view each object type. You can also select an object from the Navigation Pane banner to display only one object type.

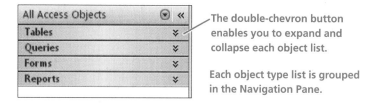

The double-chevron button enables you to expand and collapse each object list.

Each object type list is grouped in the Navigation Pane.

A down-pointing double-chevron indicates that the object list is collapsed and can be expanded; an up-pointing double-chevron indicates that the object list is expanded and can be collapsed.

12.5 Creating Tables in Datasheet View

Video Lesson labyrinthelab.com/videos

As you have already learned, all data stored in a database is stored in tables. As a result, Access creates a table for each new database you create, identifies the object using a generic table number (Table1), and creates one field named ID. Access also displays the Table Tools Fields and Table Ribbons so that the tools you need as you build the first table are available. When a database object is active, Access automatically places new Ribbon tabs at the right end of the Tab bar to make accessing appropriate tools more efficient.

Table Tools are distributed on two tabs.

Before you begin building your first table, there are some terms and rules you need to know about tables.

Working with Tables

A database table is the basic object of any database because tables store all of the raw data placed into the database. All other objects in a database are based on data stored in tables. In most databases, you will find a number of tables, each of which holds data related in some way to data in other tables in the database.

Three key terms are used in relation to the data stored in Access databases:

- **Field**—The basic unit of database tables that holds one piece of data, such as first name, last name, street address, ZIP code, date of birth, and so forth. Each field is displayed by a table column.
- **Record**—A collection of all fields related to one item, such as all fields of data for each person or company, all items placed on an order, and personnel information for each employee. Each record appears on a table row.
- **File**—A collection of all related records stored together, such as all employee records found in a table, all customers, all suppliers, and so forth. Each field and record contained in a database table along with forms, reports, and queries used to input data and retrieve meaningful information make up a database file.

Tables are most commonly displayed in the Datasheet View that presents data from multiple records in the column/row layout shown in Table1. As you review the following sample table and work with tables, you will see how these elements fit together.

Microsoft Access

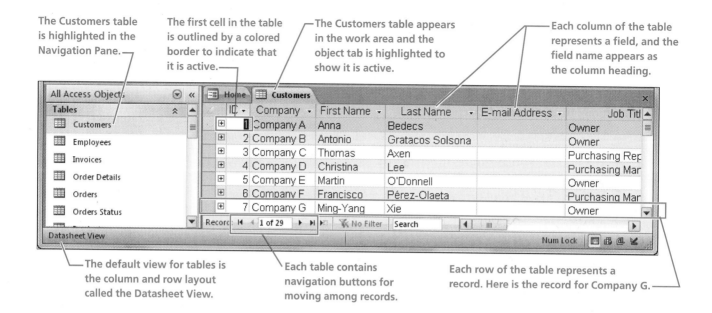

The Customers table is highlighted in the Navigation Pane.

The first cell in the table is outlined by a colored border to indicate that it is active.

The Customers table appears in the work area and the object tab is highlighted to show it is active.

Each column of the table represents a field, and the field name appears as the column heading.

The default view for tables is the column and row layout called the Datasheet View.

Each table contains navigation buttons for moving among records.

Each row of the table represents a record. Here is the record for Company G.

Identifying Table Guidelines

If you are acquainted with the Microsoft Word table feature or Microsoft Excel worksheets, you will find using the Access datasheet familiar. Because tables hold the field names and data used in other database objects, tables must be created first in Access databases.

Each table in the Raritan Clinic East database will contain fields that focus on specific data—patients, supplies, employees, etc. As you build the tables for the database, consider these guidelines:

■ Each table should have a *primary key* field that contains unique data—data that will not be the same for any two database records. Social Security Numbers make a good example of unique data because no two people have the same number; however, most organizations have avoided using Social Security Numbers for security reasons. As a result, most organizations use some type of coded ID such as employee number, patient number, or item number as primary keys.

■ As you have discovered in the database you just created, Access creates the first field (ID) for you when you create a new database. It uses this field as a primary key field designed to hold unique data. To ensure that the data is unique, Access will assign sequential numeric values to each record you enter. You can leave the field as Access presents it or change the ID field to a different field name, depending on how your table is set up.

■ The field identified as the primary key field must contain data—it cannot be empty. When Access creates the primary key field, it automatically sets the key field to automatically number the records. This ensures that each record has a unique number.

■ Planning database tables to share data before you add them to the database reduces the amount of time spent editing and restructuring the tables.

■ Tables have at least one field in common with another database table so that you can tie together information between any two tables to create reports and other database objects. These common fields are sometimes referred to as *foreign keys*. In an Employees table, the EmployeeNumber might tie it to the Customers table and serve as a foreign key.

Identifying Field Data Types

As you access each column in a new table datasheet, Access displays a drop-down list that enables you to identify the type of data you plan to place in the field. When you think about the data you plan to enter for a field, it's easy to see the different types of data—text, currency, dates, and so forth. By defining the type of data each field will contain, Access formats the data to some degree, and reduces the amount of formatting you must apply as you enter the data. A description of data types available for data in Access 2010 databases appears in the following table:

QUICK REFERENCE	IDENTIFYING ACCESS DATA TYPES
Data Type	**Description**
Text	The default data type that contains up to 255 characters consisting of any combination of alphabetic and numeric characters—such as names, addresses, and phone numbers—that will not be used to perform calculations.
Memo	Text entries that contain between 1 and 63,999 characters.
Number	Numeric data to be used in mathematical calculations.
Date & Time	Fields that hold date and time values.
Currency	Numeric values representing dollars and cents or fields in which you want to prevent rounding off during calculations.
AutoNumber	A field for which Access assigns a unique, sequential, or random number as records are added to a table. AutoNumber data cannot be modified or deleted.
Yes/No	Single-character entries in a Yes/No format that are used to enter data that can be only one of two possible values, such as true/false, yes/no, or on/off.
Hyperlink	Links to web pages or other documents that you access by clicking the link.
Attachment	A data type that identifies any type of file—such as a document, an image, and so forth—that will be included in the database as an attachment.
Lookup & Relationship	A field that displays values from another table or from a list of values on the basis of *criteria*—conditions you set so that you can select the value you want to enter.
Calculated Field	A field created by combining values in other fields within the table.

Saving Tables

Each object you create in a database must be saved. As you save the database objects, you assign an appropriate name to the object. An appropriate name for each table, then, should help identify the data it holds. After you save the table, Access displays the name you give the table in the Navigation Pane.

Microsoft Access

Create and Save a Table Using a Datasheet

In this exercise, you will create a table to hold Raritan Clinic East employee data.

1. Choose **Create→Tables→Table**.

2. **Double-click** the ID field column heading to select the text and type **EmployeeNumber**.

3. **Press** Tab and then follow these steps to add a field name for column 2:

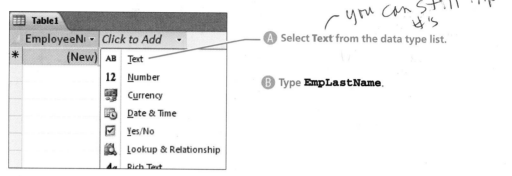

you can still input #'s

Ⓐ Select **Text** from the data type list.

Ⓑ Type **EmpLastName**.

Notice the underlined mnemonic character identified for each data type. As you enter access each column heading and prepare to set the data type, you can use the mnemonic character (such as T for Text) to select the data type and then type the field name.

Field names/column headings truncate because the columns are narrow.

4. **Press** Tab and repeat the procedures outlined in **step 2** to enter the following text fields in the order indicated by the letters:

   a. EmpFirstName   b. EmpStreet
   c. EmpCity   d. EmpState
   e. EmpZIP   f. EmpTelephone

5. Repeat the procedures outlined in **step 2** to add the following three date fields to the datasheet, ensuring that Date & Time is the data type.

   a. EmpDateHired   b. EmpTermDate
   c. EmpDOB

6. Follow these steps to save the table using a new table name:

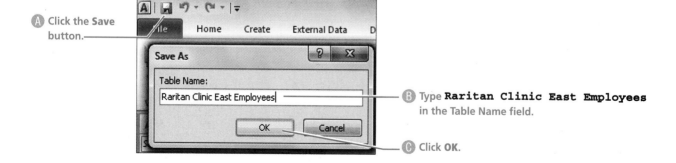

Ⓐ Click the **Save** button.

Ⓑ Type **Raritan Clinic East Employees** in the Table Name field.

Ⓒ Click **OK**.

Navigating Tables and Entering Data

Video Lesson labyrinthelab.com/videos

Now that the table is complete and saved as the first object in the database, you are ready to enter data into the table fields. Because of the column and row layout of the datasheet, moving from field to field within the datasheet is similar to moving among columns and rows of a Word table or cells in an Excel worksheet:

- Press `Tab` or `Enter` to move to the next field.
- Press `Shift`+`Tab` to move to the previous field.
- Click a field to make it active.

As you access each field, you simply type the data required for the record. When you complete the data in the last field, pressing `Tab` or `Enter` takes you to the first field in the next record. Access saves each record as you complete it, so each new record becomes part of the database table when you move to the next record.

Study the following figure to identify key features of the datasheet as you enter data.

Record/row selector buttons appear on the left side of the datasheet. These buttons enable you to select a record.

As you enter data for a record, a pencil appears in the record/row selector button for the record you are typing.

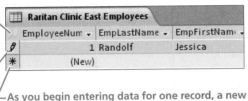

As you begin entering data for one record, a new record appears, and an asterisk (*) displays in the record/row selector.

Working with Tabs and Closing Database Objects

As you have already learned, when you create a new database, Access creates a blank table and displays the table in the work area of the database screen. The tab that appears at the top left of the table displays the table name—Table1—until you save the table. Then the name you assign the table appears on the tab.

As you work with Access and build a database, the number of tables and other objects will grow, so you might have numerous objects open at the same time. When multiple objects are open, Access displays as much of each object as will fit within the work area, and all objects are layered, one on top of the other. The tabs make moving from one object to another more efficient.

At the far right side of the table datasheet window, you will notice the table Close button.

Each open object in this database is identified by a tab.

The Close button at the far right of each tabbed object is the object Close button.

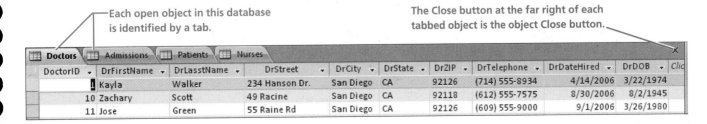

Enter Data into a Table Datasheet

In this exercise, you will enter data for two records into the Raritan Clinic East table of the Raritan Clinic East database.

1. Follow these steps to enter data into the first two fields of the first record in the table:

Ⓐ **Click** the first row of the EmpLastName field.

Ⓑ Type **Allen** and then **press** [Tab].

Ⓒ Type **Jessica**.

Use tap only - no entter (handwritten annotation)

2. Continue **pressing** [Tab] to work through the record fields and enter the following values for the first record in the table:

EmpStreet	EmpCity	EmpState	EmpZIP	EmpTelephone	EmpDateHired	EmpDateTerm	EmpDOB
986 Kilsdonk Ct.	San Diego	CA	98109	6195553902	6/12/2006		11/09/1980

3. **Press** [Tab] to create a new record, add your name in the **EmpLastName** and **EmpFirst-Name** fields, and then complete the second record by entering the following data to complete the record:

EmpStreet	EmpCity	EmpState	EmpZIP	EmpTelephone	EmpDateHired	EmpDateTerm	EmpDOB
23 Ida Way	San Diego	CA	92126	6195551470	8/14/2001		11/15/1947

4. **Press** [Tab] or [Enter] after entering data into the last field to ensure that the record is complete.

12.6 Previewing and Printing Data

Video Lesson   labyrinthelab.com/videos

After entering data into a table datasheet, there may be times when you want to print raw data contained in a table datasheet. Access provides tools for printing all of these objects.

Setting Up Data to Print

When you print from a table datasheet, Access prints the data that actually appears in the datasheet when you issue the print command. You can hide columns to prevent them from printing, change the page layout settings to print the datasheet in landscape layout, and change the margins to fit a datasheet on a single sheet of paper as you can when you print documents or spreadsheets.

Checking Data Accuracy

Ensuring the accuracy of data entered into databases is very important to obtaining meaningful information from the database. In addition, customers and other business contacts are troubled when they see their names misspelled and careless data entry errors. Be sure to check your data for accuracy after it has been entered. One way to check data accuracy is to print the contents of your tables. Proofreading a hard copy (paper printout) is often a good way to spot errors.

Examining the Preview Window

Previewing data before you print helps determine adjustments that need to be made to ensure that the datasheet prints on the page as you want it to. You can view multiple pages in print preview to see how columns line up, what columns appear on separate pages, and so forth, so that you can make the necessary adjustments to the datasheet.

Because the layout of database objects differs, options available in the Print dialog box vary depending on what you are printing. However, the basic procedures used to preview and print database objects are the same and are similar to the procedures used to print files in other applications. When you preview an object, the Print Preview tools appear on the Ribbon. These tools are used to change the layout of the page on which you print.

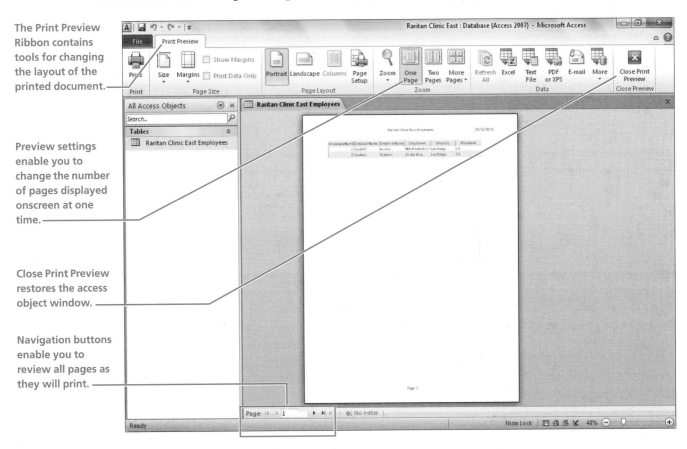

The Print Preview Ribbon contains tools for changing the layout of the printed document.

Preview settings enable you to change the number of pages displayed onscreen at one time.

Close Print Preview restores the access object window.

Navigation buttons enable you to review all pages as they will print.

Preview and Print Data

In this exercise, you will preview and print a database table. The Raritan Clinic East table should be open in Access.

1. Choose **File→Print→Print Preview**.

2. Follow these steps to view pages that will print:

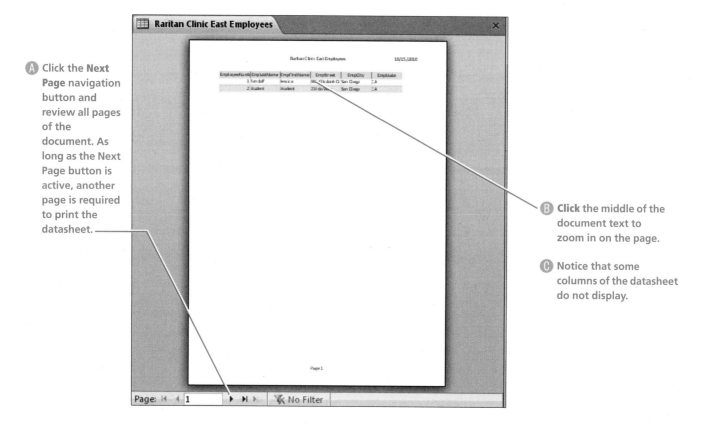

Ⓐ Click the **Next Page** navigation button and review all pages of the document. As long as the Next Page button is active, another page is required to print the datasheet.

Ⓑ **Click** the middle of the document text to zoom in on the page.

Ⓒ Notice that some columns of the datasheet do not display.

3. Follow these steps to display multiple pages in the preview window:

Ⓐ Click the **Two Pages** button to display two pages of the printout together onscreen.

Ⓑ **Click** the text on page 2 of the document to zoom in on it.

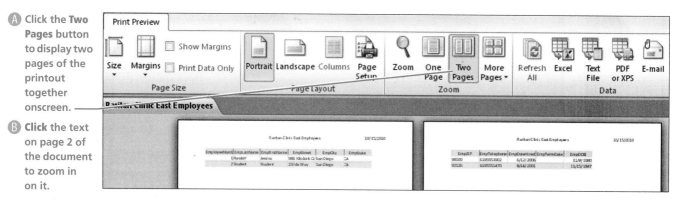

The appearance of buttons and features on the Ribbon varies depending on screen resolution and size as well as the size of the application window.

4. Choose **Print Preview→Page Layout→Landscape** 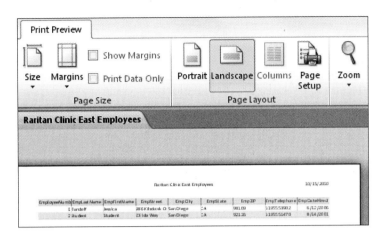 on the Ribbon to display more of the datasheet on one page.

Landscape layout displays more columns together on a sheet.

5. Choose **Print Preview→Print→Print** 🖨 on the Ribbon to open the Print dialog box.

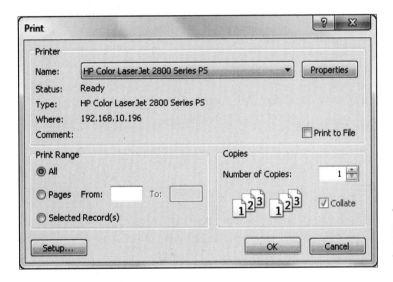

The Print dialog box you see may be different from the one shown here because of the difference in the printer that is active.

6. **Select** options in the Print dialog box to print only **page 1** of the datasheet pages; then, either **print** or click **Cancel**.

7. **Close** ✕ the table. Choose **No** when prompted to save changes.

8. **Close** the Navigation Pane.

12.7 Closing a Database and Exiting Access

Video Lesson   labyrinthelab.com/videos

After all objects in a database are closed, you can close the database and exit Access. The procedures used to perform these tasks are the same as those used to close files and exit other Microsoft Office applications. Use these techniques to close a database and exit Access:

- Choose the File tab and select Close Database to close the database.
- Press ⌐Alt¬+⌐F4¬ from the keyboard to exit Access.
- Click the File tab and select Exit.
- Click the Access 2010 application window Close ⊠ button.

Because Access databases contain numerous objects, it is always a good idea to close each database properly before exiting Access. This ensures that all objects in the database are put away carefully.

DEVELOP YOUR SKILLS 12.7.1
Close a Database and Exit Access

In this exercise, you will close the Raritan Clinic East database and exit Access.

1. Choose **File→Close** Database.
2. Click the Access 2010 application window **Close** ⊠ button.

This lesson provided you with an overview of the basic features and elements related to Access 2010 databases and the basic procedures for creating a database. This sets the foundation for your study of Access. As you progress through your study of Access you will learn more about each element and feature.

12.8 Concepts Review

Concepts Review   labyrinthelab.com/ob10

To check your knowledge of the key concepts introduced in this lesson, complete the Concepts Review quiz by going to the URL listed above. If your classroom is using Labyrinth eLab, you may complete the Concepts Review quiz from within your eLab course.

Reinforce Your Skills

Create a New Database with a Table

First Perk is a coffee shop that is getting ready to open in your town. Before opening, they would like to have a database in place that will enable them to track sales, supplies, menu items, etc. In this exercise, you will create the First Perk database and the first table.

1. Launch **Access** and click the **Blank Database** icon.

2. Type **rs-First Perk** in the File Name text box and click the **Browse** folder to select a folder in which to save the database.

3. Choose **Create** to create the database.

4. Change the ID field name to **ItemNumber**, and then **enter** the following field names into the **Table1** column headings, selecting the data type shown for each field:

Field Name	Data Type
ItemName	Text
Price	Currency

5. **Save** the table using the table name **Menu Items**.

6. Add the following records to the **Menu Items** table:

Item Name	Price
Cappuccino	2
Latte	3

7. **Print** a copy of the datasheet and then **close** the database.

Create a Database Using a Template

In this exercise, you will create a new database using the Tasks template.

1. Launch **Access**, if it is closed, and choose **File→New→Sample Templates**.
   Access displays a list of sample databases in the Backstage view.

2. Follow these steps to select the database type and save the new database:

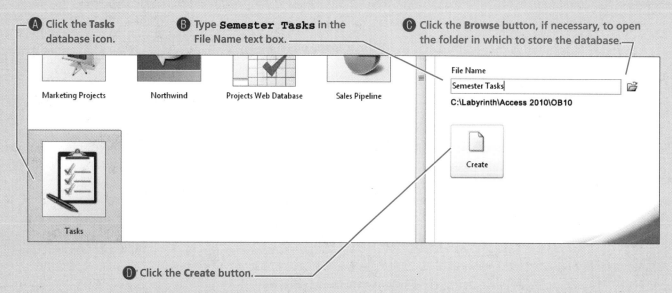

Ⓐ Click the **Tasks** database icon.

Ⓑ Type **Semester Tasks** in the File Name text box.

Ⓒ Click the **Browse** button, if necessary, to open the folder in which to store the database.

Marketing Projects   Northwind   Projects Web Database   Sales Pipeline

Tasks

File Name
Semester Tasks
C:\Labyrinth\Access 2010\OB10

Create

Ⓓ Click the **Create** button.

Access downloads the template, saves it using the filename you assigned, and then opens the database.

Review Database Objects

3. **Enable content**, if necessary, **open** the Navigation Pane, and then change the display in the Navigation Pane to display objects by **Object Type**.

4. **Open** each table, form, query, and report and review the arrangement of data in each object.

5. **Close** the database.

Apply Your Skills

Create a Tech Company Database

Databases have proven to be valuable data storage devices for department stores and other retail businesses because they can store data about employees as well as about suppliers, customers, and orders. In this exercise, you will create a database containing one table for the PriceCo company.

1. Create a **new** blank database named **PriceCo** and store the database with your student files.

2. **Add** the following fields to the table datasheet:

Field Name	Data Type
FirstName	Text
LastName	Text
Street	Text
City	Text
State	Text
ZIP	Text
Telephone	Text
District	Text

3. **Save** the table using the table name **Customers**.
   Leave the database open for the next exercise.

Enter Data and Print Datasheet Data

The Customers table is now ready for data. In this exercise, you will enter data into the Customers table and print a copy of the data.

1. **Enter** the following records into the Customers table in the PriceCo database:

FirstName	LastName	Street	City	State	ZIP	Telephone
Ryan	Manford	12 E. MacArthur	Sacramento	CA	97609	916-555-7523
Earl	Kelly	77 Kingfisher	Salinas	CA	98123	831-555-1368
Jacob	Jones	4323 NW 63rd	Rogers	AR	72757	501-555-5050

2. **Preview** the datasheet and then **print** a copy of the data.

3. **Close** the database.

Critical Thinking & Work-Readiness Skills

In the course of working through the following Microsoft Office-based Critical Thinking exercises, you will also be utilizing various work-readiness skills, some of which are listed next to each exercise. Go to labyrinthelab.com/ workreadiness to learn more about the work-readiness skills.

12.1 Create a New Database

WORK-READINESS SKILLS APPLIED

- Organizing and maintaining information
- Thinking creatively
- Knowing how to learn

Raritan Clinic East is exploring expanding the number of items they currently recycle. To determine if there are additional ways they can recycle, the clinic administrators have asked James Elliott to do some research about recycling in the community. To help James, go online and determine whether your state has information about recycling in the state. Create a new database named **ct-Recycling in [Your State]** that contains one table. The table should include fields for recycling locations throughout the state and a contact name for the person in charge of the recycling facility. Enter data for at least three sites/companies listed online. Finally, add a record containing your school as the site/company and your name as the contact. Print a copy of your table datasheet.

12.2 Outline a Database

WORK-READINESS SKILLS APPLIED

- Solving problems
- Organizing and maintaining information
- Improving or designing systems

Service Guild at Raritan Clinic East is a nonprofit organization created to raise money to help adults with disabilities receive proper medical care. They have successfully raised more than $60,000 annually through sponsoring a home tour in the city. They would like a database that will enable them to track membership, donations from businesses, ticket sales, etc. You can help them plan their database by identifying fields and tables that should be included in the database. On a clean sheet of paper, identify sample fields that you would place in the database.

12.3 Use Online Forums Related to Access

WORK-READINESS SKILLS APPLIED

- Knowing how to learn
- Applying technology to a task
- Acquiring and evaluating information

James Elliott has found that he needs more information about Access. He has asked you to review online forums to see what those who use Access regularly are discussing. Locate several online forums that cover issues related to Access 2010 and identify the five most frequently discussed topics on each forum. Use these discussion items to create a new database named **ct-Access 2010 Forum Topics** that contains a table in which you can store the topics you have identified, along with the names of the forums you reviewed and the web address of the forum.

Building a Database

LEARNING OBJECTIVES

After studying this lesson, you will be able to:
- Open an existing database
- Create a database table using Design View
- Create a form
- Create a report

Whether you are creating a new database or working with an existing database, building the database by creating database objects is often required. Successful projects normally start with a list of tasks to accomplish, an outline of the order in which to complete these tasks, and a projected final product. You can apply these same concepts to building a database. Start with a list of data (fields) to include in the database, and then group the fields into objects—tables, forms, reports—required for the database. After these lists are complete, you can sit down at the computer and begin building the database. In this lesson, you will expand the design of a database for Raritan Clinic East, a pediatric diagnostic and treatment clinic. You will add a new table, a form, and a report to the database.

Student Resources   labyrinthelab.com/ob10

Designing and Building a Database

Dr. Edward Jackson is the chief operating officer of the Raritan Clinic East, a medical practice staffed by clinical diagnosticians in the Pediatric fields of General Medicine, Cardiology, and Orthopedics, Pediatric Emergency Medicine, and Neonatology. The clinic has recently moved to a new location that has state-of-the-art diagnostic equipment and an updated computer system. It is currently in the process of designing and modernizing its database to make it more efficient to use. Dr. Jackson has asked you to work with consultants to design a basic database that can grow with the clinic as the business expands. After reviewing the needs of the clinic and the existing database, you will add a table, a form, and a report to the database. You will then be able to test these objects by adding data to the database table.

Raritan Clinic East

Pediatric Diagnostic Specialists

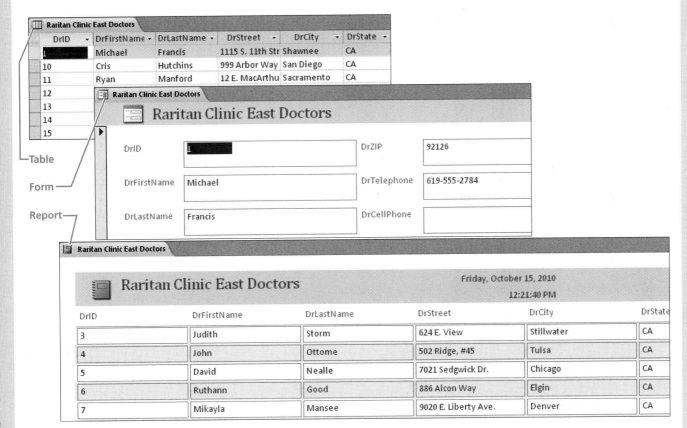

The Raritan Clinic East database will contain a table, a form, and a report. Notice that the icons representing each different object identify the object type.

13.1 Designing a Database

Video Lesson   labyrinthelab.com/videos

Creating a database that contains well-organized database objects requires careful planning. Taking the time to sketch out the elements that are required for the database will reduce the amount of time you spend modifying and editing the database design as you start using it.

Planning a Database Design

The mechanics of sitting down at the computer and creating a database are straightforward and reasonably easy—planning the database is often more time consuming. Before sitting down at the computer, answer the following questions about the database you are creating:

- What information do you want to be able to obtain from the database? This information identifies the reports you will add to the database. Reports provide great insight into the fields you need to include in the database tables.

- What data elements (fields) do you need to include in the database to be able to obtain the information?

- What types of data will you enter into each field: dates, numeric values, amounts of money, text, etc.?

- What fields of data relate to the same basic item and could be grouped together? These form the tables.

- How do the groups of data relate to one another? These are the fields that connect the tables to one another.

- What is the most efficient way to get data into the database tables? The answers to this question help you identify the forms required.

- What questions will you need the database to be able to answer? Answers here will identify the queries you need.

13.2 Opening a Database

Video Lesson   labyrinthelab.com/videos

The procedures for opening an existing file in Access 2010 are basically the same as those found in other Microsoft Office applications. You can choose one of the following procedures:

- Choose File→New and select the file from the list of recently used databases on the File menu in Backstage view.

- Choose File→Open to display the Open dialog box, navigate to the folder containing the file, and open it.

- Choose File→Recent to display a list of databases in Backstage view.

Enabling Macros Controlling Database Security

Many database files contain *macros*—programming codes that automate common tasks. Because Access 2010 is highly security-conscious, settings that may be active within Access prevent these macros from running without your "permission." The files you use throughout this book have been checked before posting on the website and scanned for viruses, so it's okay to open them and enable database content. If security settings in Access 2010 on your system are set above "low," a message bar appears just below the Ribbon onscreen when you open files. Its presence notifies you of disabled content and provides instructions on how to proceed. When you click the *Enable Content* button, all features of the database operate as intended.

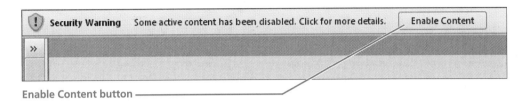

Enable Content button

Setting Trusted Sites

Another way to ensure that the databases you use throughout your study of Access 2010 operate as intended without having to enable the content each time you open the database is to add the folder in which you are storing your files to the Trusted Sites list. Setting the folder as a trusted site instructs Access that the folder and all databases contained in the folder and subfolders are safe, so Access automatically enables content.

DEVELOP YOUR SKILLS 13.2.1

Open a Database, Enable Content, and Set Trusted Site

In this exercise, you will open an existing database, enable the content for the database, and add the folder containing your student data files to the Trusted Sites list.

Open a Database

1. Launch **Access 2010** and choose **File→Open**.

2. Follow these steps to open the Raritan Clinic East database:

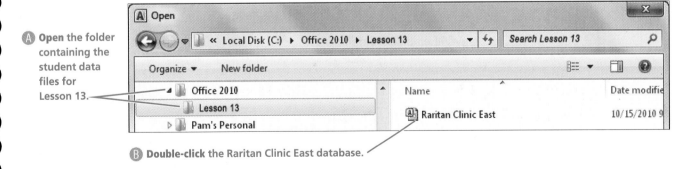

Ⓐ **Open** the folder containing the student data files for Lesson 13.

Ⓑ **Double-click** the Raritan Clinic East database.

Enable Content

3. Click the **Enable Content** button on the Security Warning bar just below the Ribbon.

Set Trusted Site

4. Choose **File→Options** to open the Access Options dialog box.

5. Follow these steps to open the trust center settings:

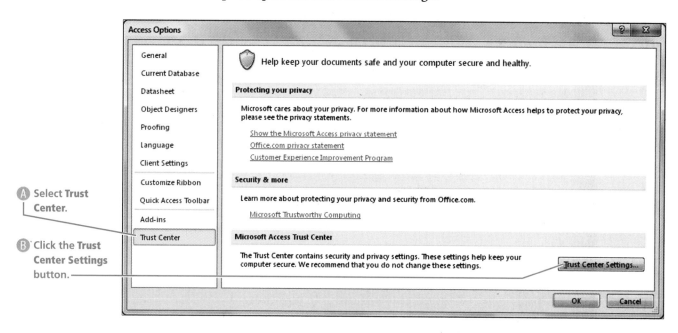

Ⓐ Select **Trust Center**.

Ⓑ Click the **Trust Center Settings** button.

6. Follow these steps to add a new folder to the Trust Center:

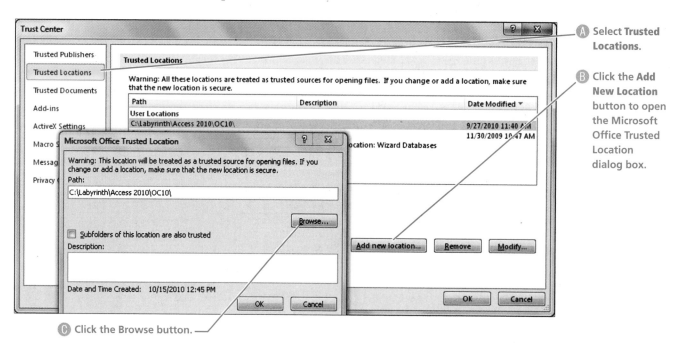

Ⓐ Select **Trusted Locations**.

Ⓑ Click the **Add New Location** button to open the Microsoft Office Trusted Location dialog box.

Ⓒ Click the Browse button.

7. Navigate to the folder containing your student data files, **select** the folder, and click **OK**.

8. Click **OK** to close the Microsoft Office Trusted Location dialog box.

9. Click **OK** to close the Trust Center dialog box.

10. Click **OK** to close the Access Options dialog box.

13.3 Saving a Database as a New File

Video Lesson   labyrinthelab.com/videos

As you work with data in database objects, Access saves the data when you move to a new or different record. As a result, you will want to preserve the original student data file as a new database so that the original is available for reuse, if needed. Creating a new database file helps to prevent unwanted loss of data. Access automatically saves each database record as you enter it and also prompts you to save each object as you modify or change it in any way. As a result, the data stored in a database saves regularly as you work. Existing files often make good files on which to create new files.

Using the Save As Command

You can use the File→Save Database As command to save an existing database as a new database using a different filename just as you would with any other Microsoft Office application. Saving a database as a new file is not only a good way to quickly create a new database for a different purpose, but it is also a good way to create a backup of your data to protect it. Because many databases contain numerous objects, the File menu also displays a Save Object As command for saving each of the database objects as new objects within the existing database. Review the Backstage view of the Save As commands to identify how saving a database as a new file is different from saving other types of files as new files.

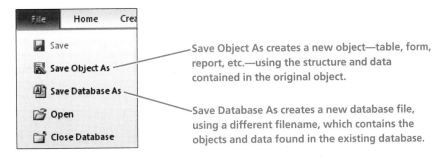

Save Object As creates a new object—table, form, report, etc.—using the structure and data contained in the original object.

Save Database As creates a new database file, using a different filename, which contains the objects and data found in the existing database.

Backstage view of the File menu.

DEVELOP YOUR SKILLS 13.3.1
Save a Database as a New File

In this exercise, you will save the Raritan Clinic East database as a new database file. The Raritan Clinic East database should be open.

1. Choose **File→Save Database As** to open the Save As dialog box.

2. Navigate to the folder in which you ware storing your student data files and **open** the folder.

3. Type **Raritan Clinic East Employees** in the File Name text box and click **Save**.

Opening Existing Database Objects

Each database object is listed on the Navigation Pane, which groups objects by type. The Raritan Clinic East database contains only one object—a table that lists the doctors who practice at the clinic. Access provides a number of different techniques for opening database objects:

- Double-click the object in the Navigation Pane.
- Right-click the object in the Navigation Pane and choose Open.
- Drag the object name from the Navigation Pane to the Work Area of the Access window.

Opening and reviewing the data contained in a database object is a great way to identify key features of a database.

DEVELOP YOUR SKILLS 13.3.2
Open a Database Table

In this exercise, you will open a table in the Raritan Clinic East Employees database. The Raritan Clinic East Employees database should be open.

1. Click the **Shutter Bar Open/Close Button** ⟩⟩ on the Navigation Pane.
   The Navigation Pane opens with the Tables group collapsed.
2. Click the Tables group **Expand** ⌄ button
3. **Double-click** the Raritan Clinic East Doctors table to open it.
4. Review the data contained in the database table.

DrID	DrFirstName	DrLastName	DrStreet	DrCity	DrState	DrZIP	DrTelephone	DrCellPhone	DrDateHired	DrDateTerm	DrDOB
1	Michael	Francis	1115 S. 11th Street	Shawnee	CA	92126	619-555-2784		10/1/2006		
10	Cris	Hutchins	999 Arbor Way	San Diego	CA	92898	619-555-1001		10/23/2006		
11	Ryan	Manford	12 E. MacArthur	Sacramento	CA	92609	619-555-7523		10/22/2006		
12	Earl	Kelly	77 Kingfisher	Salinas	CA	92123	619-555-1368		10/25/2006		
13	Jacob	Jones	4323 NW 63rd	Rogers	CA	92757	619-555-5050		11/11/2006		

Ⓐ Notice that the DrID field numbers the doctors sequentially.

Ⓑ Not all fields contain data. Only key fields require data for each record.

Navigating Records in a Table Datasheet

Video Lesson labyrinthelab.com/videos

Tables display many records onscreen at a time. As the number of records in a table grows, however, some records will appear offscreen. Access provides a set of record navigation tools at the bottom of the work area when a table is open. Buttons on the record navigator can be used to move among all records in a table.

Navigate Records in a Table Datasheet

In this exercise, you will use the record navigator buttons to access various records in the table datasheet. The Raritan Clinic East Doctors should be open in the Raritan Clinic East Employees database.

1. **Press** Tab to move to the DrFirstName column.

   You can continue to press Tab *to move to the next column (field) until you reach the last column containing data. Pressing* Tab *from the last column of the first row (record) moves the cursor to the first column (field) in the second row (record).*

2. Follow these steps to move among table records using table navigation buttons:

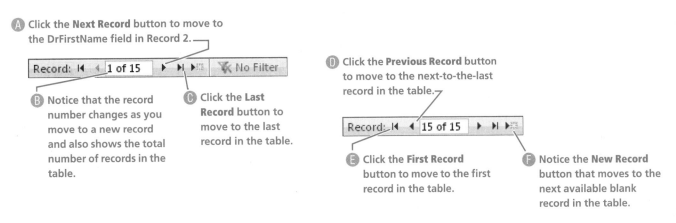

Ⓐ Click the **Next Record** button to move to the DrFirstName field in Record 2.

Ⓑ Notice that the record number changes as you move to a new record and also shows the total number of records in the table.

Ⓒ Click the **Last Record** button to move to the last record in the table.

Ⓓ Click the **Previous Record** button to move to the next-to-the-last record in the table.

Ⓔ Click the **First Record** button to move to the first record in the table.

Ⓕ Notice the **New Record** button that moves to the next available blank record in the table.

3. Click the Raritan Clinic East Doctors table **close** ✕ button to close the table.

13.4 Creating Database Objects

Video Lesson   labyrinthelab.com/videos

As you should already know, all data stored in a database is stored in tables. As a result, Access automatically creates a table when you create a database, identifies the object by type using a generic number (Table1), and creates one field named ID. Access also displays the Table Tools Datasheet tab of the Ribbon so that the tools you need as you enter data into the table are available. Access uses the same object-naming procedure when you create forms, reports, and queries. The name of the object type is sequentially numbered until you save the object using a different object name. Tools for working with each individual object also become available on the Ribbon when you create each object type.

QUICK REFERENCE	CREATING DATABASE OBJECTS
Task	**Procedure**
Create a new database table	▪ Display the Create tab on the Ribbon. ▪ In the Tables command group on the Ribbon, choose Table.
Create a simple form	▪ Choose Create→Forms→Form from the Ribbon.
Create a simple report	▪ Choose Create→Reports→Report from the Ribbon.

Microsoft Access

Creating and Using Forms

Forms are database objects that display table data onscreen one record at a time. Forms serve as input objects for entering data into tables. When you create databases that others will use to enter data, forms are useful data entry objects because they present data fields in a more aesthetically pleasing layout—especially for the novice data entry clerk. Forms gather and display table data. No data is stored in a form.

Creating Simple Forms

Forms obtain their data and fields from database tables or queries. As a result, it is necessary to select or open the table that contains the fields you want to include on the form. Because queries also use fields stored in database tables, you can also use a query as the object from which to create a form. When you create a form using the Form button on the Create tab of the Ribbon, Access creates a simple form that lists each field contained in the selected or active table. Depending on the number of fields contained in the table, Access displays the fields in a one- or two-column layout starting at the left side of the form. The fields appear in the order in which they appear in the table. Data entry boxes appear in a column on the right parallel to the field names.

Record selection bar used to select a record displayed in a form.

Table field names.

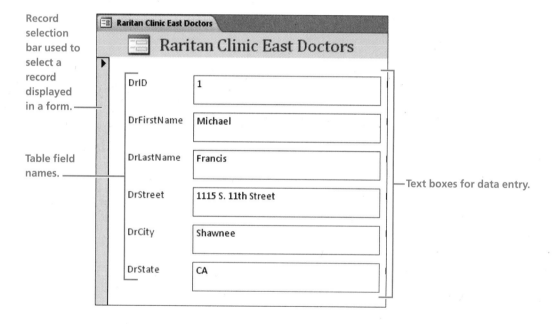

Text boxes for data entry.

Create a Simple Form

In this exercise, you will create a simple form for entering data for the Raritan Clinic East Doctors table. The Raritan Clinic East Employees database should be open with the Raritan Clinic East Doctors table open as well.

1. Follow these steps to create a form for the Raritan Clinic East Doctors table:

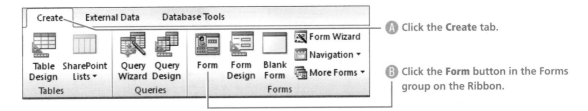

Ⓐ Click the **Create** tab.

Ⓑ Click the **Form** button in the Forms group on the Ribbon.

Access creates the new form, names it using the name of the table from which it gets its data, and displays the Form Layout Tools—Design, Arrange, and Format tabs—on the Ribbon.

2. Follow these steps to save the new form:

Ⓐ **Collapse** the Navigation Pane (optional).

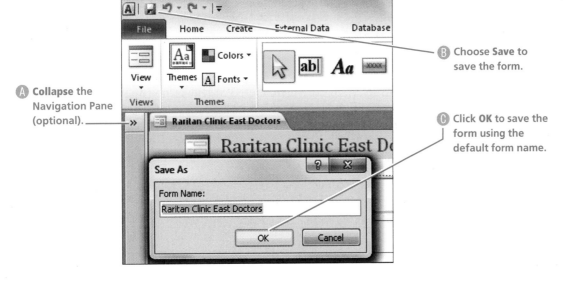

Ⓑ Choose **Save** to save the form.

Ⓒ Click **OK** to save the form using the default form name.

3. **Close** ☒ the form. Choose **Yes** to save any changes if prompted.

4. **Close** ☒ the table.

Entering Data Using Datasheets and Forms

Video Lesson   labyrinthelab.com/videos

Frequently, data entry clerks enter data into only a limited number of table fields. As a result, creating forms that contain only those data entry fields is a valuable tool. The form you created for the Raritan Clinic East Doctors database table contains all the fields included in the Raritan Clinic East Doctors table. You now have two objects in the database to use for entering table data: the table and the form.

After saving and closing forms, Access displays the Home tab of the Ribbon. When a form is open, the View button on the Home tab enables you to switch among the views available for Forms and other objects. Before entering data using the form, you must display the form in Form View. The View button on the Ribbon enables you to change the view of the form you just created so that you can enter data.

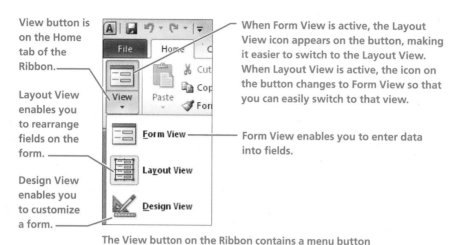

View button is on the Home tab of the Ribbon.

Layout View enables you to rearrange fields on the form.

Design View enables you to customize a form.

When Form View is active, the Layout View icon appears on the button, making it easier to switch to the Layout View. When Layout View is active, the icon on the button changes to Form View so that you can easily switch to that view.

Form View enables you to enter data into fields.

The View button on the Ribbon contains a menu button that displays the views available for the active object.

Using the Record Navigator

Forms display many of the same navigation tools available in tables. The main difference in the display is that records appear onscreen one record at a time. As a result, when you navigate to a specific record, only the data for one item appears. In tables, one record was active as you navigated the table even though multiple records displayed at the same time because of the column and row layout of the tables.

The record navigator appears at the bottom of tables and forms when they are open in the work area. You can use buttons in the record navigator to move to specific records as well as to create a new record.

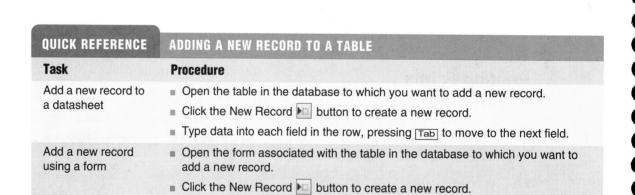

Record: 14 ◄ 15 of 15 ► ►I ►* —— New Record button

QUICK REFERENCE	ADDING A NEW RECORD TO A TABLE
Task	**Procedure**
Add a new record to a datasheet	■ Open the table in the database to which you want to add a new record. ■ Click the New Record ►* button to create a new record. ■ Type data into each field in the row, pressing Tab to move to the next field.
Add a new record using a form	■ Open the form associated with the table in the database to which you want to add a new record. ■ Click the New Record ►* button to create a new record. ■ Type data into each field in the form, pressing Tab to move to the next field.

Add Records to a Table

In this exercise, you will add records to the Raritan Clinic East Doctors table using a form.

1. Open the **Raritan Clinic East Doctors** form.

2. Choose **Home→Views→View** menu and select **Form View**.

3. Click the **New Record** button in the Record Navigator area of the status bar.

Record: ⏮ ◀ 15 of 15 ▶ ⏭ ▶▦ ——— New Record button

4. Click the **DrFirstName** field to make it active and follow these steps to enter the values in each form field:

 Depending on the settings that are active on your computer, the field arrangement may be different from the one shown here. Be sure to note the field name that is active before typing the data.

Ⓐ Type **Clara** into the DrFirstName text box.

Ⓑ Press Enter or Tab to move to the next field and **type** the data shown here.

Ⓒ Continue pressing Enter or Tab to complete the field data in the first column.

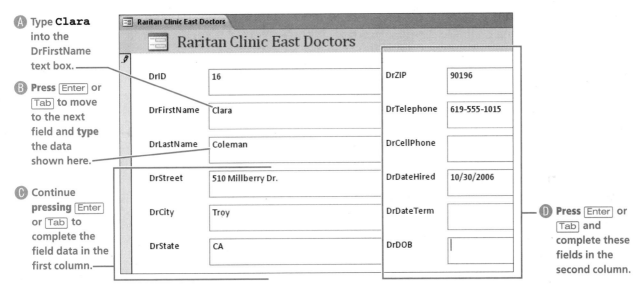

Raritan Clinic East Doctors

DrID	16	DrZIP	90196
DrFirstName	Clara	DrTelephone	619-555-1015
DrLastName	Coleman	DrCellPhone	
DrStreet	510 Millberry Dr.	DrDateHired	10/30/2006
DrCity	Troy	DrDateTerm	
DrState	CA	DrDOB	

Ⓓ Press Enter or Tab and complete these fields in the second column.

5. **Close** ☒ the table, **saving** changes if prompted.

Printing Forms

You can print the form for a record directly from the form by choosing File→Print→Print to display the Print dialog box and then setting the Selected Records option in the dialog box. In addition, you can print forms for all records by displaying the Print dialog box and selecting the All option from the dialog box.

This technique can be useful if you have a large number of fields in a table that print across multiple pages. A form often fits on a single page. On the other hand, printing forms for all records in a table may require a lot of paper. Therefore, selecting the records you want to print before issuing the Print command and then selecting the Selected Records option takes less time and uses far less paper than printing all records.

Creating and Generating Reports

Video Lesson   labyrinthelab.com/videos

While forms are objects used to input data into database tables, reports are database objects used to sort, summarize, and output table data as useful information. Access contains numerous tools designed to help you create new reports. These tools are grouped together on the Create tab in the Report section of the Ribbon, as shown.

Creates a simple report using table fields

Creates a report "from scratch" using Access Report Design tools

Additional tools for creating reports using the Report Wizard, formatted as labels, and starting with a blank report

As you discovered when you created new forms earlier in this lesson, these tools create reports from the most simple to a more complex report that groups and sorts data. In this lesson, the focus will be on a simple report. After you create a report, the Report Layout Tools—Design, Arrange, Format, and Page Setup—tabs appear on the Ribbon.

Creating a Simple Report

Access contains a Report command that, like the Form tool, helps you create a simple report that lists data from a database table or query. Reports you generate using the Report command contain no data summarization or "frills"—they simply report the data contained in the table, but they report it in a more attractive layout when printed than found by printing the table datasheet.

Identifying Report Views

As you discovered with forms, reports have multiple views that are used to edit the report layout, preview data, or print the report. After you create a report, Access displays the report in Layout View. To view the report as it will print, the report should be displayed in Report view. The Views button appears at the left end of the Ribbon when the Home tab is active to make switching among views more efficient. Report views and their uses are described in the following table.

REPORT VIEWS AND THEIR USES	
Report View	**Description**
Report view	Displays the report onscreen with data displayed.
Print Preview	Displays the report as it will print.
Layout view	Displays a sample of the data in an editable layout that enables you to size and position fields so that all data displays appropriately.
Design view	Displays the report on a palette with field names and placeholders so that you can move and position fields.

Previewing and Printing Reports

The report can be previewed using the File→Print→Print Preview command on the Ribbon or by switching the report view to Print Preview. The Print Preview window functions the same way with reports as it does with other objects. The File→Print→Print command opens the Print dialog box and allows you to set options to print an entire report, the current report page, or selected report pages.

DEVELOP YOUR SKILLS 13.4.3
Create a Simple Report

In this exercise, you create a simple report. The Raritan Clinic East Employees database should be open.

1. Follow these steps to create a new report based on data contained in the selected table:

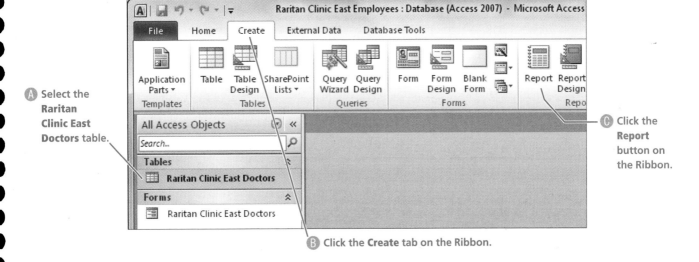

Ⓐ Select the **Raritan Clinic East Doctors** table.

Ⓒ Click the **Report** button on the Ribbon.

Ⓑ Click the **Create** tab on the Ribbon.

2. Choose **Home→Views→View** menu and select **Report View**.

3. Click the **Save** 🖫 button to open the Save As dialog box.

4. Ensure that Raritan Clinic East Doctors appears as the Report Name and then click **OK** to save the report.

5. **Close** ☒ the report.

13.5 Creating Tables Using Design View

Video Lesson   labyrinthelab.com/videos

Creating tables using the datasheet to enter field names, set data types, and enter data is a quick and easy way to start building a database. Access makes this even easier by creating a blank table each time you create a new database. You have most likely found with other Microsoft Office applications that there are a number of different ways to create new files. Because Access databases contain a variety of different database objects, Access offers a variety of procedures for creating database objects. Another way to create database tables is by using Design View.

Displaying and Using Table Design View

When the Design View is active, Access displays the Design tools on the Ribbon. When you switch views during table creation, Access prompts you to save the table if you have not yet done so. Using the Design View to create a new table enables you to type field names, select data types, and enter a description for each field in a table-like layout.

Design graphics appear on the View button to make it easy to switch to Design view.

Data types can be applied to fields added to the datasheet using the Data Type drop-down list.

Tools available on the Ribbon when the Datasheet view is active

When the Design View is active, a datasheet graphic appears on the View button to switch back to Datasheet view.

Tools available on the Ribbon when Design view is active

Entering Field Names in Design View

In old-school databases, field names could contain only alphabetic and numeric characters with no spaces, punctuation, or extraneous symbols, and could only be up to eight characters in length. As a result, field names were abbreviated so dramatically that it was often a challenge to determine exactly what data the field would contain. In modern databases, field names can contain all spaces and symbols, except slashes (\ /), wildcard characters (* and ?), and periods. Access also has a list of reserved words that are set aside for other uses and that cannot be used as field names. You might want to take the time to review this list.

Because some mainframe systems require the old-school format for naming fields, many database designers still use abbreviated field names with no spaces, punctuation, or symbols. The tables and other objects you create in the Raritan Clinic East Employees database are new-world format to make them easier for you to identify.

Setting Field Properties

As you define each field in a database table, Access sets properties for the field that control the number of characters the field can contain as well as the format of the data and the type characters that are valid for the field data. You can accept the default properties Access sets or modify the properties. Properties available depend on the data type selected for the field.

Identifying a Primary Key

Each table in a database should have a *primary key* field that contains unique data—data that will not be the same for any two database records. Most organizations use some type of coded ID, such as customer ID or serial number, as primary keys. Each time you create a new table Access creates an ID field and marks the field as the primary key field. You can rename the field, remove the primary key designation from the field and assign it to another field, or leave the field as Access created it. To ensure that the data contained in the field is unique, Access will assign sequential numeric data to each record you enter.

Requiring Data in Key Fields

The field identified as the primary key field must contain data—it cannot be empty. When Access creates the primary key field, it sets the key field to automatically number the records. This ensures that each record has a unique number. Businesses create a coding system for customers, accounts, and other types of data and rely on this data to be the key field.

The Primary Key button on the Design→Tools tab of the Ribbon enables you to assign a primary key to any field containing unique data.

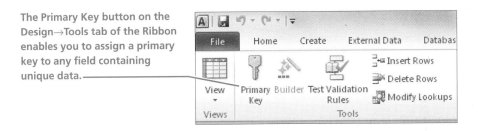

Create a Database Table Using Design View

In this exercise, you will create a new table in the Raritan Clinic East Employees database using Table Design View. The Raritan Clinic East Employees database should be open.

1. Choose **Create→Tables→Table** on the Ribbon to create the new table and then follow these steps to save the table and switch to Design View:

Ⓐ Choose **Fields→ Views→View→ Design View** to display the Save As dialog box.

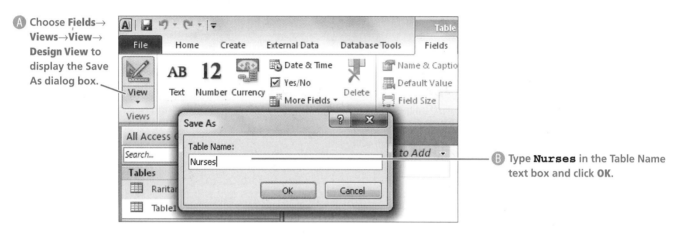

Ⓑ Type **Nurses** in the Table Name text box and click **OK**.

Access displays the Nurses table in Table Design View. Notice that the ID field is identified as the Primary Key field because the Primary Key button is highlighted to show that it is active. A key icon appears beside the field name in the Field Name list.

2. Follow these steps to create the first table field:

Ⓐ Click the **ID Field Name**, type **NurseID** in the first row of the Field Name column, and **press** Tab.

Ⓑ Click the **Data Type** list button and select Text.

Ⓒ **Press** Tab and type **Month and year of hire date and last four digits of SS#--8 digits**.

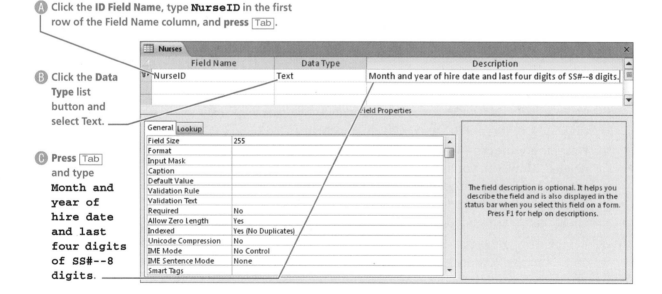

3. **Press** Tab and repeat the procedures outlined in **step 2** to enter the following additional fields and field information:

Field Name	Data Type	Description
NrFirstName	Text	
NrLastName	Text	
NrStreet	Text	
NrCity	Text	
NrState	Text	
NrZIP	Text	
NrTelephone	Text	
NrHireDate	Date/Time	Date of first working day
NrTermDate	Date/Time	Date of last working day
NrDOB	Date/Time	

4. **Save** 🖫 the table and **close** ☒ it.

13.6 Managing Database Objects

Video Lesson labyrinthelab.com/videos

Occasionally, as you work with databases that contain numerous objects, you will find yourself having to manage the objects by performing routine tasks. The most frequently used tasks include each of the following.

■ **Copying Objects**—You can copy tables, forms, reports, and other types of objects and paste them into the same database, to a different database, and to other applications. Copying an object to the same database can be useful if you intend to modify the object. By making a copy, you not only have a backup of the object in case the original is damaged, but you can also use a copy of an existing object such as a table and modify the table to create a new table required for the database.

■ **Deleting Objects**—Objects in a database can also be deleted when they are no longer needed. However, you must be careful when deleting objects because they will be permanently deleted from the database. The Undo feature will not restore the deleted object. Deleting objects can be useful, especially when the object created using a wizard fails to appear as you intended.

■ **Renaming Objects**—Sometimes you will need to rename an object because it was given a default name that does not adequately describe what the object represents or contains. For instance, if you fail to give a table a name, it will be called Table1 by default.

Microsoft Access

QUICK REFERENCE	MANAGING DATABASE OBJECTS
Task	**Procedure**
Copy an object	▪ Select the object to be copied.
	▪ Choose Home→Clipboard→Copy from the Ribbon.
	▪ Choose Home→Clipboard→Paste from the Ribbon.
	▪ Rename the pasted object and specify its paste options.
Delete an object	▪ Select the object to be deleted.
	▪ Choose Home→Records→Delete from the Ribbon.
	▪ Choose Yes to confirm the deletion.
Rename an object	▪ Make sure that neither the object nor any other object which makes use of its data in the case of tables is open. (The object should not be active.)
	▪ Right-click the object in the Navigation Pane and choose Rename from the context menu.

DEVELOP YOUR SKILLS 13.6.1
Manage Database Objects

In this exercise, you will manage objects in the Raritan Clinic East Employees database.

Before You Begin: The Raritan Clinic East Employees database should be open.

1. **Right-click** the Raritan Clinic East Doctors table in the Navigation Pane and choose **Copy**.

2. **Right-click** a blank area of the Navigation Pane and choose **Paste**.
   Access displays the Paste Table As dialog box and assigns the default name of the new table.

3. Click **OK** to save the table using the default name.

4. **Right-click** the Copy of Raritan Clinic East Doctors table and choose **Rename**.
   The table name is selected for text replacement.

5. Type **General Employees** as the new table name and then **press** [Enter].

6. **Right-click** the General Employees table in the Navigation Pane and choose **Delete**.
   Access displays a confirmation message advising you that the action cannot be reversed.

7. Click **Yes** to close the message.

13.7 Concepts Review

Concepts Review	labyrinthelab.com/ob10

To check your knowledge of the key concepts introduced in this lesson, complete the Concepts Review quiz by going to the URL listed above. If your classroom is using Labyrinth eLab, you may complete the Concepts Review quiz from within your eLab course.

Reinforce Your Skills

Create a Table Using Design View

First Perk has worked diligently to implement some of the database features recommended by their consulting team. In this exercise, you will help them build additional objects in their database.

1. Launch **Access** and **open** the rs-First Perk Objects database from the Lesson 13 folder.

2. **Save** the database using the filename **rs-First Perk Objects Rev**.

3. Choose **Create→Tables→Table** on the Ribbon to create a new table.

4. Choose **Datasheet→Views→View** on the Ribbon to switch to Design View.

5. Type **Coffee Types** in the Table Name text box and click **OK** to save the table.

6. Select **ID** in the first field and type **Category Number** to replace ID.

7. **Press** Tab, **click** the Data Type list button, and select **Text**.

8. **Press** Tab and **type** the following in the Description column:
   Single Letter representing category type C, D, F; 1-digit Strength; 2-digit Origin; 2-digit Number.

9. Complete the following list of fields, data types, and descriptions for the table:

Field Name	Data Type	Description
Coffee Name	Text	
Category Type	Text	Caffeinated, Decaffeinated, Free Trade.
Strength	Text	Regular, Espresso, Flavored, Special, Light.
Country of Origin	Text	
Description	Text	

10. **Save** changes to the table and **close** it.

Create a Form and a Report

The First Perk database is taking shape. In this exercise, you will add a form and a report to the database.

1. Launch **Access** and **open** the rs-First Perk Rev database if it is closed.

2. Select the **Menu Items** table and choose **Create→Forms→Form** on the Ribbon to create a form for the table.

3. **Save** the form using the form name **Menu Items**.

4. Select the **Menu Items** table again and choose **Create→Reports→Report** on the Ribbon.

5. **Save** the report using the report name **Menu Items**.

6. **Close** the form and report.

Create Copies of Tables

The First Perk database currently contains two tables. To protect those tables, in this exercise, you will create copies of each table to serve as backups of the main tables.

1. Launch **Access** and **open** the rs-First Perk Rev database if it is closed.

2. **Right-click** the Menu Items table and choose **Copy**.

3. **Right-click** a blank area of the Navigation Pane and choose **Paste**.

4. Type **Menu Items Backup** as the new table name and click **OK**.

5. Repeat the procedures outlined in steps **2–4** to create a table named **Coffee Types Backup** for the Coffee Types table.

6. **Close** the Navigation Pane, **close** the database, and **exit** Access.

Apply Your Skills

APPLY YOUR SKILLS 13.1

Create a New Database Using a Template

Several of the sample templates available in Access are designed to store data related to education such as Students and Faculty, class lists, and so forth. In this exercise, you will use the Education templates to create a new database designed to store student data and enter data into the database using a form.

1. Launch **Access** and display the **sample templates**.

2. Create a **new** database using the Students template, name the database **as-NSW Students** and **save** the file in the folder in which you are storing your student files.

3. **Close** the Student List form that opens when you create the database, **enable content**, and then **open** the Navigation Pane.

4. Review the tables Access created. Answer the following questions:

   ■ What tables are you surprised to see separated from larger, more complex, tables?

   ■ What fields of data are included in database tables that you would have forgotten to include if you had created the database?

   ■ What forms and reports are shown in the database that might also be included in other databases?

5. **Add** your name and other data (real or fictional) to the **Student List** form in the database.

6. **Close** the form and the database.

APPLY YOUR SKILLS 13.2

Create Objects

The VonHamburg Tomb database currently contains numerous tables. In this exercise, you will create forms and reports for each of these tables.

1. **Open** the as-VonHamburg Tomb OE database and save the database using the filename **as-Tomb Objects**.

2. **Open** and examine each table.

3. **Create** a form for each table except the Selling Format table, **saving** the form using the table name.

4. **Create** a report for the Records table.

5. **Print** a copy of the Records report.

6. **Close** all open objects, **close** the database, and **exit** Access.

Critical Thinking & Work-Readiness Skills

In the course of working through the following Microsoft Office-based Critical Thinking exercises, you will also be utilizing various work-readiness skills, some of which are listed next to each exercise. Go to labyrinthelab.com/workreadiness *to learn more about the work-readiness skills.*

13.1 Locate a Template and Build a Database

WORK-READINESS SKILLS APPLIED

- Serving clients/customers
- Applying technology to a task
- Participating as a member of a team

Customer service representatives in the accounting department at Raritan Clinic East have asked James Elliott to create a database for logging customer calls. To help James, search the web for two database templates designed for customer service use and follow onscreen instructions for downloading. Then, create a new database using each template and review the tables, forms, and reports. Save the databases in your Lesson 13 folder as **ct-Customer Service1** and **ct-Customer Service2**. If working in a group, discuss similarities and differences among the templates as well as which template, in general, would best help customer service reps log customer calls. If working alone, type your response in a Word document named **ct-Questions** saved to your Lesson 13 folder.

13.2 Copy Tables from One Database to Another

WORK-READINESS SKILLS APPLIED

- Improving or designing systems
- Reasoning
- Making decisions

Service Guild at Raritan Clinic East would like to include information about donations from businesses and ticket sales for the home tour in the ct-Service Guild Membership database (Lesson 13 folder). Open ct-Charitable Contributions from your Lesson 13 folder. Review the tables, forms, and reports and copy two of the tables. Then close the ct-Charitable Contributions database and open the ct-Service Guild Membership database. Save the database as **ct-Service Guild Revised** and paste the copied tables into it. Create and name simple forms and reports for the new tables. (NOTE: Exiting Access will cause Access to drop the copied tables. Exit the database properly.)

13.3 Create a Database with Excel Data

WORK-READINESS SKILLS APPLIED

- Acquiring and evaluating information
- Thinking creatively
- Using computers to process information

Raritan Clinic East, to encourage the use of local natural resources, is designing floral arrangements in the gift shop using native, natural wildflowers to help build a Green Scene. Open the database named ct-Flowers in [Your State] OE in your Lesson 13 folder and save the database as a new database using the same name but substituting your state for [Your State]. Then, search the Internet (or contact a local plant nursery) to learn what flowers in the table would grow well in your state. Add a State field to the Flowers table, formatting it as a Yes/No field. Check at least five flowers you know will grow well in your state. Print copies of the table, form, and report.

Glossary of Terms

32-bit operating system
An operating system that processes data in 32-bit (character) chunks; can only recognize a maximum of 3 GB of RAM

64-bit operating system
An operating system that processes data in 64-bit (character) chunks; often require special drivers for hardware and can recognize more than 3 GB of RAM

Adjacent
Arrangement of cells, objects, or files that are next to each other; often may be selected as a group by using Shift; also known as contiguous

Aggregate functions
Used to perform specific calculations, such as finding the minimum, maximum, and average values, and counting the number of entries in a datasheet; use these functions in queries, forms, and reports to aid in reporting database data

Alias
Name assigned to expressions designed to perform the same calculation

Alignment
Horizontal placement of text relative to the left and right margins of a cell or a page, where text is left-, right-, or center-aligned; or, vertical placement of text relative to the top and bottom margins of a cell or page, where text is top-, middle-, or bottom-aligned

Antivirus program
Software designed to stop computer viruses from infecting files on the computer

Application program
Software designed to help you get work done

Ascending
Sort order that arranges information alphabetically from A to Z, numerically from smallest to largest, and chronologically from first to last

AutoComplete
Feature that offers to complete a cell or text entry when you type the first few characters

AutoCorrect
Predefined text used for automatically correcting common spelling and capitalization errors; can be customized with user-defined entries

AutoFill
Feature that extends a series, copies data, or copies a formula into adjacent cells

AutoNumber
A field for which Access assigns a unique, sequential, or random number as records are added to a table

Backstage view
Contains common commands such as Open, Save, and Print; available via the File tab

Block style
A letter style that aligns all parts of the letter at the left margin

Byte
Single character of data; composed of 8 bits in a specific order

Cable modem
Device designed to send and receive digital data over television cable system wiring

Cells
Rectangles that make up an Excel worksheet; the intersection of a column and row in a table

Character spacing
Horizontal space between text characters

Character style
A style used to format a single word or selected group of words with text format such as font, bold, font size, etc.; no paragraph formatting is included

Clipboard
Task pane that lets you collect multiple items and paste them in a document; holds up to 24 entries

Color scheme
Each document theme has twelve colors that are applied to text, backgrounds, hyperlinks, and so forth

Column
The vertical arrangement of cells in a table or the text in a document separated from other text by a space known as a gutter

Context menu
Menu that appears when you right-click; also known as a pop-up menu

Contextual tab
Ribbon tab that appears only when a certain object is selected

Currency
Numeric values representing dollars and cents for fields in which you want to prevent rounding off during calculations

Data dictionary
Planning document that lists database objects, fields for each object, and object relationships for documenting a database

Data type
Field descriptors that identify the type of data that will be stored in the field

Database
Collection of related data stored in one electronic file

Datasheet
Column and row format for displaying table data and query results

Date & Time
Fields that hold data and time values

Default
A setting that a computer program assumes you will use unless you specify a different setting

Default values
Field property used to automatically enter data into a field

Demote bullet
A demoted bullet is indented the right; increases the list level

Demote text
Increase the indentation for a paragraph so it appears farther away from the left margin and, if numbered, reduces the numbering level to the next lower level

Descending
Sort order that arranges information alphabetically from Z to A, numerically from highest to lowest, or chronologically from most recent

Dialog box launcher
Appears in some Ribbon groups; opens a dialog box or task pane that contains commands related to the group

Document theme
Preset design consisting of color scheme, text formatting, and placeholder positions

Dots per inch (DPI)
Measure of the sharpness of a printer's output; the higher the dots per inch, the sharper the print will appear on the page

Drag and drop
Method for copying and moving text or objects a short distance

Driver
A small piece of software that tells the operating system how to work with a specific piece of hardware

Field
Basic unit of database tables; holds one specific piece of data

File
Group of computer data with a common purpose

File format
A technique for storing information in a computer file; varies by application

File tab
Expands to a menu containing commands to open, save, and print files; includes commands to prepare and distribute documents

File type
A way of identifying the file format of a file; Windows determines a file's type by its filename extension (docx, xlsx, pptx, etc.)

Filename extension
The three or four characters at the end of a filename; Windows is set by default to hide these extensions

Find and Replace
Feature that finds a word, phrase, or formatting that you specify and, optionally, replaces it with another word, phrase, or formatting

Firewall
Software and hardware designed to prevent attacks on a computer from an external operator

Folder
An electronic location to store a group of files with some related purpose

Form
Database object built from fields contained in tables that are positioned in a layout so that each table record (or row) appears in the form window one record at a time

Form fields
Text boxes, checkboxes, and other controls added to forms to limit or control the data entered in the form

Form field properties
Characteristics associated with a form field that are used to restrict the length, type, and format of data entered in the form field

Format Painter
A tool that allows you to copy formats

Formatting marks
Special characters that Word uses to control the look and layout of documents; also referred to as nonprinting characters; the marks are visible when the Show/Hide button is turned on

Formula Bar
In Excel, the area above the worksheet in which you view, type, and edit cell entries

Function
Predefined formula that performs calculations on table cells

Gigabyte
Approximately one billion bytes of data

Gigahertz (Ghz)
One billion pulses of electricity in an electrical circuit in a single second

Graphical User Interface (GUI)
Group of graphic screen elements that make software programs easier to use; eliminates the need to memorize command languages

Group
Collection of records that has at least one data element in common

Gutter
The space between two columns of text in a multicolumn layout

Hardware
Physical components of a computer system

Indent
Offsets text from the left or right margin

Input mask
Field property used to control the format of field data

Intranet
Internal computer network in a company or organization in which users may access shared files and resources, such as printers

Justify
Text alignment where character spacing is automatically adjusted differently for each line in the paragraph so the left and right sides of the paragraph form straight lines

Kilobyte (KB)
Approximately one thousand bytes of data

Library
A new component of the Windows file storage hierarchy; a library can contain folders and files from more than one storage drive

Line break
A forced new line within a paragraph that keeps the new line as part of the paragraph

Line spacing
Vertical space between lines of text

List style
A style applied to text to convert the text to a list

Live Preview
When pointing at formatting commands on the Ribbon, Live Preview displays how the format would appear on selected text and objects without actually applying the format

Malware
A generic term for malicious software viruses that can damage a computer system

Manual page break

A forced page break created by pressing Ctrl+Enter or the Insert→ Pages→Page Break command

Marquee

Animated, dashed line that surrounds selected cells in Excel during an operation, such as a cut or a copy

Megabyte

Approximately one million bytes of data

Memo

In Access, text entries that contain between 1 and 63,999 characters

Merge cells

Combine the contents of two or more table cells to create a single table cell

Microprocessor

One single silicon chip containing the complete circuitry of a computer

Mini toolbar

Contains frequently used formatting commands; appears when you select cells or text, or when you right-click on cells or text

Modem

Device that lets a computer communicate digital data to other computers over a non-digital communication line

Modified block style

A letter style that aligns the date and signature lines at the center of the page and all other lines at the left margin; the first line of paragraphs may be indented

Multi-core

A processor with the circuitry for multiple computers built into a single chip

Multitasking

Running more than one program at the same time, switching between them as necessary

Native file format

The file format an application program normally saves your work with, unless you specify a different file format

Native resolution

The highest resolution setting a flat panel monitor can display; monitors normally display sharpest at their native resolution

Navigation Pane

Narrow bar that displays down the left side of the application window

Nonadjacent

Arrangement of cells, objects, or files that are not next to each other; often may be selected as a group by using Ctrl; also known as noncontiguous

Nonbreaking space

A space inserted between two or more words to keep the words together on the same line

Normal style

A paragraph style that, by default, sets the font (Calibri), point size (11 pt), alignment (left), and other standards for all new documents

Number

Numeric data to be used in mathematical calculations

Open source

Software that does not contain proprietary code, but instead allows everyone access to its code

Outline pane

Located on the left side of the Power-Point screen; displays the text content of each slide

Page orientation

The direction that text appears on a page: Portrait (vertical) or Landscape (horizontal)

Paragraph style

A style used to format a paragraph or selected group of paragraphs; both paragraph formatting (alignment, spacing, etc.) and character formatting (font, font size, enhancements, etc.) can be included in paragraph styles

PEMDAS

Standard order for performing mathematical operations: Parentheses, Exponentials, Multiplication/Division, Addition/Subtraction

Peripherals

Hardware components outside the system unit

Pixel

A single dot of light on a computer monitor

Port

A place (usually at the back of the computer) to plug in a cable

Print Preview

Feature that allows you to see how a document will look when it is printed

Projection display

Hardware device used to project the computer screen on a wall for viewing by large audiences

Promote bullet

Promoted bullets are outdented to the left; decreases the list level

Promote text

Reduce the indentation of text so that it appears closer to the left margin and, if numbered, elevates the text to the next higher number level

Property Sheet

Panel that appears down the right side of a design window and provides access to properties such as the field format (general number, currency, etc.), font format, alignment, etc.

Quick Access toolbar

Graphical User Interface (GUI) that contains buttons for frequently used commands; can be customized according to your preference

Quick Styles

Styles that appear in the Styles group of the Home tab on the Ribbon

RAM (Random Access Memory)

A computer chip designed to temporarily store data to be processed

Range

Multiple cells in adjacent rows, columns, or both rows and columns

Record

Collection of all fields related to one person, place, thing, or topic in a database

Redundant fields

Fields that appear in multiple tables in a database

Relational database management system (RDMS)

Database management system specifically designed to utilize the relational database model where each object in a database relates to other objects in the database

Report
Object in Access databases that processes table data, sorts, and summarizes the data, and presents the data as meaningful information

Resolution
Measure of the sharpness of a computer monitor display or a printout

Ribbon
Contains commands that help you perform tasks; organized in tabs that relate to a particular type of activity and groups that contain related commands

Router
A network device that helps you hook up four or more computers into a local area network (LAN)

Row
The horizontal group of cells in a table

Scanner
Device that turns photographs and other images into computer files; all-in-one printers have a scanner built in

Sections
Groupings of slides treated as a single object, making it easy to change the order of large blocks of slides

Select text
Highlight text by dragging it with the mouse pointer or other techniques; used in preparation for certain tasks, such as formatting or copying text

Show/Hide
Displays nonprinting characters such as tabs and paragraph marks onscreen for easy access

Shutter Bar Open/Close button
Button at the top of the Navigation Pane in Access; displays a double-chevron used to open/close the Navigation Pane

Slide layout
Preset layout of placeholder boxes on a slide

Slide Show toolbar
Contains navigation controls, drawing tools, and options to be used during a slide show presentation; located in the bottom-left corner of a slide during a slide show

Slide transition
Animation that occurs when navigating from one slide to the next during a slide show

Slides Pane
Located on the left side of the PowerPoint screen; displays thumbnails of each slide

SmartTags
Context-sensitive option buttons that appear on menus to provide easy access to commonly used tasks

Software
Logical component of a computer system; composed of digital code stored in the form of files; some software exists as programs to help you get work done; also stores work

Solid state drive
A new generation of file storage drive that stores data on memory chips rather than the revolving platters of traditional hard drives; also called SSDs

Sort
Arrangement of data in alphabetic or numeric order; can be in ascending (low to high) or descending (high to low) order

Speaker notes
Notes that can be added to slides, then printed, to aid the presenter; not displayed during a slide show

Split cells
Create two or more table cells from a single table cell

Split View
Divide the window for the active document in horizontally so two different parts of the document can be viewed onscreen at the same time

Style
Group of formats that allow you to quickly apply multiple formats at once; also known as Quick Styles

Syntax
The basic rules for constructing formulas, specifically those containing functions

System unit
Main box that contains the primary components of the computer

Tab
Area on the Ribbon that contains groups of commands; also, a code that sets a specific amount of space between two text elements

Table
Basic object in a database that contains the data used in all other database objects

Table style
A style applied to cells, rows, or columns of a table to ensure consistency among tables in a document

Tab stops
Preset stops along the horizontal ruler at every half inch, to control and align text; custom tab stops can be placed anywhere on the ruler

Template
In Access, ready-to-use database that contains all the tables, queries, forms, reports, and design elements need to perform a specific task

Terabyte
One trillion bytes of data

Text
In Access, the default data type that contains up to 255 characters consisting of any combination of alphabetic and numeric characters (such as names, addresses, and phone numbers) that will not be used to perform calculations

Theme
Set of formatting selections that can be applied to a document; includes colors, graphic elements, and fonts all designed to work well together

Title Bar
Appears across the top of the application window; contains the name of the application and the name of the current document

Toggle
Button or setting that switches on when clicked and switches off when clicked again

Truncate
To store a value in a field but display only the portion of the value that fits within the confines of a column width or control size

USB flash drive
A thumb-sized portable file storage device that stores files on a solid state memory chip

USB hub
A device that allows you to plug in multiple USB devices sharing a single cable back to the computer

USB port
Short for Universal Serial Bus port; a single USB port can connect several devices simultaneously, including keyboards, scanners, modems, cameras, and more

Views
Varying ways you can look at a document; optimized for specific types of work

Virus
Program that invisibly "infects" files and disrupts operation of a computer in some way

Widescreen
A monitor (or laptop screen) that conforms to the popular 16:9 proportion used for HD (high-definition) video

Word Wrap
The automatic moving of text to a new line when it extends beyond the right margin of a paragraph; eliminates the need to tap Enter at the end of lines within a paragraph

Workbook properties
Information about a workbook saved with the workbook contents

Zip archive
A file into which other files are compressed for faster and easier transition

Zoom
Command that allows you to view a document in varying levels of magnification

Index

Index

Notes

Notes

Notes

Notes

Notes

Notes

Notes

Notes

Notes

Notes

Notes